THE KEY

STUDENT STUDY GUIDE

Chemistry 30

THE KEY

THE KEY series of student study guides is specifically designed to assist students in preparing for unit tests, provincial achievement tests, and diploma examinations. Each ***KEY*** includes questions, answers, detailed solutions, and practice tests. The complete solutions show problem-solving methods, explain key concepts, and highlight potential errors.

TABLE OF CORRELATIONS

Castle Rock Research has designed ***THE KEY*** by correlating every question and its solution to Alberta Education's curriculum outcomes. Each unit of review begins with a Table of Correlations that lists the General and Specific Outcomes from the Alberta curriculum along with Related Questions that correspond to the outcomes. Usually the emphasis placed on outcomes, concepts, and skills within each unit varies. Students and teachers can quickly identify the relevant importance of each outcome and concept in the unit as determined by the number of related questions provided in ***THE KEY***.

For grades 3, 6, 9, and 12, the weighting of each unit and concept is determined by analyzing the blueprint for the respective provincial achievement tests and diploma examinations. Based on this analysis, the Related Questions for outcomes and concepts are organized on a proportionate basis. For grades other than 3, 6, 9, and 12, the breakdown of each course is determined by consulting with experienced teachers and by reviewing curriculum guides and textbooks.

The Table of Correlations is a critical component of ***THE KEY***. For students, it offers a visual cue for effectively organizing study time. For teachers, the Table of Correlations indicates the instructional focus for each content strand, serves as a curriculum checklist, and focuses on the outcomes and concepts that are the most important in the unit and the particular course of study. Students become "test wise" by becoming familiar with exam and question formats used most often in provincial examinations.

© 1999–2006 by Castle Rock Research Corp.
All rights reserved. No part of this book covered by the copyright hereon may be reproduced or used in any form or by any means graphic, electronic, or mechanical, including photocopying, recording, taping, or information storage and retrieval systems without the express permission of the publisher.

Some material has been reproduced with the permission from Alberta Education, and any reproduction from this booklet is strictly prohibited, unless authorization is obtained from Alberta Education and the publishers of this document.

Canadian Cataloguing in Publication Data

Rao, Gautam, 1961 –.
THE KEY – Chemistry 30

1. Science – Juvenile Literature. I. Title

Published by:
Castle Rock Research Corp.
2340 Manulife Place
10180 – 101 Street
Edmonton, AB T5J 3S4

5 6 7 FP 07 06 05

Printed in Canada

Publisher
Gautam Rao

Editors
Mun Prasad
Shirley Wacowich

Contributors
Rob Schultz

Print Production
Phil Beauchamp
Alesha Braitenbach
Tory Braybrook
Nishi Chadha
Markus Chan
Marissa Letourneau
Lorraine James
Shawna Kozel
James Kropfreiter
Julie May
David Moret
Suzanne Morin
Jackie Pacheco
Tara Pratt
Abhinav Rastogi
Diana Seguin
Jan Witwicky
Richard Yeomans

Dedicated to the memory of Dr. V. S. Rao

THE KEY—CHEMISTRY 30

THE KEY is a study guide specifically designed to assist students in preparing for unit tests and provincial diploma examinations. It is a compilation of questions and answers from previous diploma examinations complete with detailed solutions for all questions. Questions have been grouped by concepts so students may use the resource throughout the year. Detailed solutions are provided for all questions. The following is an overview of the main sections of ***THE KEY***.

I ***Key Factors Contributing to School Success*** provides students with examples of study and review strategies. Topics include information on learning styles, study schedules, and developing review notes.

II ***Unit Review***, with *Challenger Questions,* includes questions related to the three chemistry units of study. All questions are classified according to the units studied in class and are correlated to the specific concept(s) being tested. In *Unit Review*, questions considered to be more difficult are labeled as *Challenger.* **THE KEY provides detailed solutions for all questions.**

III ***Key Strategies for Success on Exams*** explores topics such as common exam question formats, and strategies for responding, directing words most commonly used, how to begin the exam, and managing test anxiety.

IV ***Diploma Examinations*** contains the diploma examinations that were administered in June 2001 and January 2002. It is **recommended** that students work through these exams carefully to become familiar with the exam format and level of difficulty that students are likely to encounter on their final. **Complete step by step solutions are provided for all questions in this section.**

THE KEY *Study Guides* are available for Biology 30, Chemistry 30, Physics 30, English 30-1, English 30-2, Mathematics 30 (Applied), Mathematics 30 (Pure), Social Studies 30 and Social Studies 33.

For information about any of our resources or services, please call Castle Rock Research Corp at 780.448.9619 or visit our web site at http://www.castlerockresearch.com

At Castle Rock Research we strive to produce a resource that is error free. If you should find an error, please contact us so that future editions can be corrected.

CONTENTS

KEY Factors Contributing to School Success

Unit Review

Answers and Solutions

KEY Strategies for Success on Exams

DIPLOMA EXAMINATIONS

ANSWERS AND SOLUTIONS

APPENDICES

NOTES

KEY FACTORS CONTRIBUTING TO SCHOOL SUCCESS

School Success

NOTES

Not for Reproduction

KEY FACTORS CONTRIBUTING TO SCHOOL SUCCESS

You want to do well in school. There are many factors that contribute to your success. While you may not have control over the number or types of assignments and tests that you need to complete, there are many factors that you can control to improve your academic success in any subject area. The following are examples of these factors.

- **REGULAR CLASS ATTENDANCE** – helps you to master the subject content, identify key concepts, take notes and receive important handouts, ask your teacher questions, clarify information, use school resources, and meet students with whom you can study
- **POSITIVE ATTITUDE AND PERSONAL DISCIPLINE** – helps you to come to classes on time, prepared to work and learn, complete all assignments to the best of your ability, and contribute to a positive learning environment
- **SELF-MOTIVATION AND PERSONAL DISCIPLINE** – helps you to set personal learning goals, take small steps continually moving toward achieving your goals, and to "stick it out when the going gets tough"
- **ACCESSING ASSISTANCE WHEN YOU NEED IT** – helps you to improve or clarify your understanding of the concept or new learning before moving on to the next phase
- **MANAGING YOUR TIME EFFICIENTLY** – helps you to reduce anxiety and focus your study and review efforts on the most important concepts
- **DEVELOPING 'TEST WISENESS'** – helps to increase your confidence in writing exams if you are familiar with the typical exam format, common errors to avoid, and know how the concepts in a subject area are usually tested
- **KNOWING YOUR PERSONAL LEARNING STYLE** – helps you to maximize your learning by using effective study techniques, developing meaningful study notes, and make the most efficient use of your study time

Copyright Protected

KNOW YOUR LEARNING STYLE

You have a unique learning style. Knowing your learning style – how you learn best – can help you to maximize your time in class and during your exam preparation. There are seven common learning styles. Read the following descriptions to see which one most closely describes your learning preferences.

- **LINGUISTIC LEARNER** (sometimes referred to as an auditory learner) – learns best by saying, hearing and seeing words; is good at memorizing things such as dates, places, names and facts
- **LOGICAL/MATHEMATICAL LEARNER** – learns best by categorizing, classifying and working with abstract relationships; is good at mathematics, problem solving and reasoning
- **SPATIAL LEARNER** (sometimes referred to as a visual learner) – learns best by visualizing, seeing, working with pictures; is good at puzzles, imaging things, and reading maps and charts
- **MUSICAL LEARNER** – learns best by hearing, rhythm, melody, and music; is good at remembering tones, rhythms and melodies, picking up sounds
- **BODILY/KINESTHETIC LEARNER** – learns best by touching, moving, and processing knowledge through bodily sensations; is good at physical activities
- **INTERPERSONAL LEARNER** – learns best by sharing, comparing, relating, cooperating; is good at organizing, communicating, leading, and understanding others
- **INTRAPERSONAL LEARNER** – learns best by working alone, individualized projects, and self-paced instruction

(Adapted from http://snow.utoronto.ca/Learn2/mod3/mistyles.html)

Your learning style may not fit "cleanly" into one specific category but may be a combination of two or more styles. Knowing your personal learning style allows you to organize your study notes in a manner that provides you with the most meaning. For example, if you are a spatial or visual learner, you may find mind mapping and webbing are effective ways to organize subject concepts, information, and study notes. If you are a linguistic learner, you may need to write and then "say out loud" the steps in a process, the formula, or actions that lead up to a significant event. If you are a kinesthetic learner you may need to use your finger to trace over a diagram to remember it or to "tap out" the steps in solving a problem or "feel" yourself writing or typing the formula.

Not for Reproduction

SCHEDULING STUDY TIME

Effective time management skills are an essential component to your academic success. The more effectively you manage your time the more likely you are to achieve your goals such as completing all of your assignments on time or finishing all of the questions on a unit test or year-end exam. Developing a study schedule helps to ensure you have adequate time to review the subject content and prepare for the exam.

You should review your class notes regularly to ensure you have a clear understanding of the new material. Reviewing your lessons on a regular basis helps you to learn and remember the ideas and concepts. It also reduces the quantity of material that you must study prior to a unit test or year-end exam. If this practice is not part of your study habits, establishing a study schedule will help you to make the best use of your time. The following are brief descriptions of three types of study schedules.

- **LONG-TERM STUDY SCHEDULE** – begins early in the school year or semester and well in advance of an exam; is the **most effective** manner for improving your understanding and retention of the concepts, and increasing self-confidence; involves regular, nightly review of class notes, handouts and text material
- **SHORT-TERM STUDY SCHEDULE** – begins **five to seven days prior to an exam**; must organize the volume of material to be covered beginning with the most difficult concepts; each study session starts with a brief review of what was studied the day before
- **CRAMMING** – occurs the night before an exam; is the **least effective** form of studying or exam preparation; focuses on memorizing and reviewing critical information such as facts, dates, formulas; do not introduce new material; has the potential to increase exam anxiety by discovering something you do not know

Regardless of the type of study schedule you use, you may want to consider the following to maximize your study time and effort:

- establish a regular time and place for doing your studying
- minimize distractions and interruptions during your study time
- plan a ten minute break for every hour that you study
- organize the material so you begin with the most challenging content first

Copyright Protected

- divide the subject content into smaller manageable "chunks" to review
- develop a marking system for your study notes to identify key and secondary concepts, concepts that you are confident about, those that require additional attention or about which you have questions
- reward yourself for sticking to your schedule and/or completing each review section
- alternate the subjects and type of study activities to maintain your interest and motivation
- make a daily task list with the headings "must do", "should do", and "could do"
- begin each session by quickly reviewing what you studied the day before
- maintain your usual routine of eating, sleeping, and exercising to help you concentrate for extended periods of time

KEY STRATEGIES FOR REVIEWING

Reviewing textbook material, class notes, and handouts should be an ongoing activity and becomes more critical in preparing for exams. You may find some of the following strategies useful in completing your review during your scheduled study time.

READING OR SKIMMING FOR KEY INFORMATION

- Before reading the chapter, preview it by noting headings, charts and graphs, chapter questions.
- Turn each heading and sub-heading into a question before you start to read.
- Read the complete introduction to identify the key information that is addressed in the chapter.
- Read the first sentence of the next paragraph for the main idea.
- Skim the paragraph noting key words, phrases, and information.
- Read the last sentence of the paragraph.
- Repeat the process for each paragraph and section until you have skimmed the entire chapter.
- Read the complete conclusion to summarize each chapter's contents.
- Answer the questions you created.
- Answer the chapter questions.

Not for Reproduction

Creating Study Notes

Mind Mapping or Webbing

- Use the key words, ideas or concepts from your reading or class notes to create a *mind map or web* (a diagram or visual representation of the information). A mind map or web is sometimes referred to as a knowledge map.
- Write the key word, concept, theory or formula in the centre of your page.
- Write and link related facts, ideas, events, and information to the central concept using lines.
- Use colored markers, underlining, or other symbols to emphasize things such as relationships, information of primary and secondary importance.
- The following example of a mind map or web illustrates how this technique can be used to develop an essay.

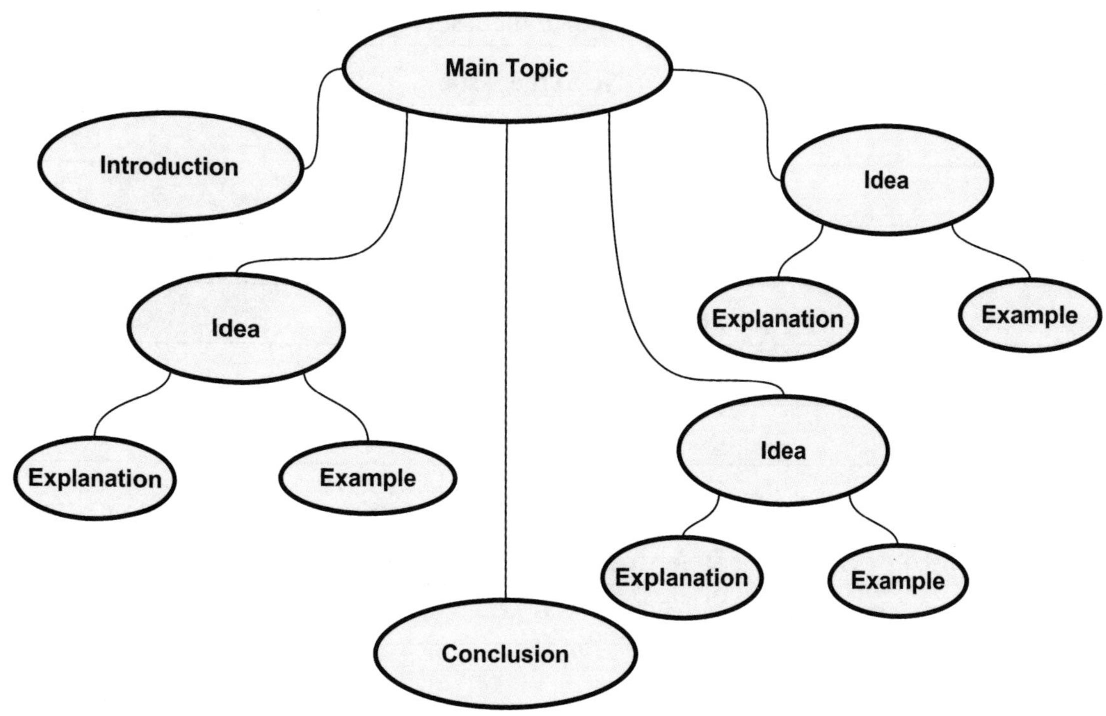

Copyright Protected

Charts

- Use charts to organize your information and relate theories, concepts, definitions, applications and other important details.
- Collect and enter the information in key categories.
- Use the completed chart as a composite picture of the concept or information.

The following is an example of how a chart can be used to help you organize information when exploring an issue in subjects such as Social Studies, the Sciences, or Humanities.

<table>
<tr><th colspan="6">Define Key Words</th></tr>
<tr><td colspan="6">1.</td></tr>
<tr><td colspan="6">2.</td></tr>
<tr><td colspan="6">3.</td></tr>
<tr><th colspan="6">Explore the Issue</th></tr>
<tr><th colspan="2">Yes to the Issue</th><th colspan="2">No to the Issue</th><th colspan="2">Maybe to the Issue</th></tr>
<tr><td colspan="2">1.</td><td colspan="2">1.</td><td colspan="2">1.</td></tr>
<tr><td colspan="2">2.</td><td colspan="2">2.</td><td colspan="2">2.</td></tr>
<tr><td colspan="2">3.</td><td colspan="2">3.</td><td colspan="2">3.</td></tr>
<tr><th colspan="6">Case Studies and Examples</th></tr>
<tr><td colspan="3">1.</td><td colspan="3">1.</td></tr>
<tr><td colspan="3">2.</td><td colspan="3">2.</td></tr>
<tr><td colspan="3">3.</td><td colspan="3">3.</td></tr>
<tr><th colspan="6">Defense of Your Point of View</th></tr>
<tr><td colspan="6">1.</td></tr>
<tr><td colspan="6">2.</td></tr>
<tr><td colspan="6">3.</td></tr>
</table>

Not for Reproduction

Index Cards

- Write a key event, fact, concept, theory, word or question on one side of the index card.
- On the reverse side, write the date, place, important actions and key individuals involved in the event, significance of the fact, salient features of the concept, essence and application of the theory, definition of the word or answer to the question.
- Use the cards to quickly review important information.

International System of Units (SI)

International System of Units (SI)

Base quantity	SI base unit Name	Symbol
length	metre	m
mass	kilogram	kg
time	second	s
amount of substance	mole	mol

Derived Measures

Measures	Unit	Symbol
Volume	cubic metre	m^3

SI Prefixes

Factor	Name	Symbol
10^6	mega	*M*
10^3	kilo	*k*
10^{-2}	centi	*c*
10^{-3}	milli	*m*
10^{-6}	micro	*μ*

Symbols

- Develop your own symbols to use when reviewing your material to identify information you need in preparing for your exam. For example, an exclamation mark (!) may signify something that "must be learned well" because it is a key concept that is likely to appear on unit tests and the year-end exam. A question mark (?) may identify something you are unsure of while a star or asterisk (*) may identify important information for formulating an argument. A check mark (✓) or an (×) can be used to show that you agree or disagree with the statement, sentence or paragraph.

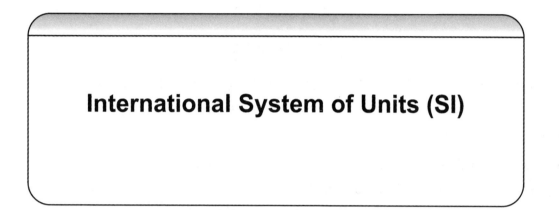

Copyright Protected

Crib Notes

- Develop brief notes that are a critical summary of the essential concepts, dates, events, theories, formulas, supporting facts, or steps in a process that are most likely to be on the exam.
- Use your crib notes as your "last minute" review before you go in to write your exam. You can not take crib notes into an exam.

MEMORIZING

- **ASSOCIATION** relates the new learning to something you already know. For example, in distinguishing between the spelling of 'dessert' and 'desert', you know 'sand' has only one 's' and so should desert.
- **MNEMONIC DEVICES** are sentences you create to remember a list or group of items. For example, the first letters of the words in the sentence "**E**very **G**ood **B**oy **D**eserves **F**udge" helps you to remember the names of the lines on the treble clef staff (E, G, B, D, and F) in music.
- **ACRONYMS** are words formed from the first letters of the words in a group. For example, **HOMES** helps you to remember the names of Canada's five Great Lakes (**H**uron, **O**ntario, **M**ichigan, **E**rie, and **S**uperior).
- **VISUALIZING** requires you to use your mind's eye to "see" the chart, list, map, diagram, or sentence as it exists in your textbook, notes, on the board, computer screen or in the display.

Unit Review

CHEMISTRY 30

Unit Review has been developed to aid students in their study throughout the term. Students can prepare for unit exams while gaining exposure to previous diploma exam questions. This section of ***THE KEY*** is a compilation of questions from the diploma exams that were administered in 2000 (January and June) and 2001 (January). All questions have been organized by content strand to correspond to the units in Chemistry 30. Students will find questions for *Chemical Energetics*, *Reduction-Oxidation*, and *Acids and Bases*.

A Table of Correlations at the beginning of each unit lists the curriculum outcomes and the *multiple choice*, *numerical-response* and *written response* questions that specifically test those concepts. To help students understand the curriculum, ***THE KEY*** provides explanations of the ***KEY*** concepts for each unit. After each explanation, students are directed to questions from previous diploma exams that are related to the underlying concepts. Sample unit tests are included at the end of each unit. The unit tests include the relevant questions from diploma exams administered in 1999 (January and June).

***THE KEY* contains detailed solutions for all questions**. Solutions show the processes and/or ideas used in arriving at the correct answers and may help students gain a better understanding of the concepts that are being tested.

In *Unit Review*, certain questions have been categorized as *Challenger Questions*. Challenger Questions represent the more difficult questions that a student is likely to face, as illustrated in the following example.

CHALLENGER QUESTION	**Difficulty: 30.5**

Numerical Response

16. The volume of 0.160 mol/L $K_2Cr_2O_{7(aq)}$ required to completely react with 10.0 mL of acidic 0.881 mol/L $H_2O_{2(aq)}$ is ____________ mL.
(Record your answer to **three digits**)

The *Difficulty* rating is based on the percentage of students that answered the question correctly when it appeared on the Diploma Exam. In the example, only 30.5% of students answered it correctly (Source: Alberta Education Examiner's Reports). *Challenger Questions* for Chemistry 30 include those with less than a 60% achievement rate, as indicated by *Difficulty*.

CHEMICAL ENERGETICS

Table of Correlations		
Topic	**Outcomes**	**Related Questions**
1. Energy introduction	a. Definition: Energy can be defined as the ability to do work, to generate heat or to create electricity. b. Work can be defined as a force exerted on an object over some distance. Work = force × distance Unit of measurement of work or energy = Nm or Joule (J)	
2. First Law of Thermodynamics	a. Definition: energy cannot be created or destroyed; energy can only be transferred. b. Sources of energy i. exogenous ii. endogenous c. Transference of energy i. heat gained system and mathematical sign ii. heat lost system and mathematical sign d. Signs of transference of energy i. increase in movement or change in temperature ii. change of bonding structure and no increase of temperature e. Types of energies and definition of temperature i. temperature definition ii. kinetic energy iii. potential energy f. Energy diagrams i. E_k diagram ii. E_p diagram	1, 2, 4, 6, 18, 21, 27, 29, 30, 31
3. Energy equations and definition	i. kinetic energy equation($\Delta Q = mc\Delta t$) ii. potential energy equation ($\Delta H = nH$) iii. definition of c and H iv. phase change graph and calculation	5, 16, 19, NR6, NR11, WR1
4. Explanation of energy	Explanation of types of changes and corresponding energies i. intramolecular bond and names of processes ii. intermolecular bond iii. nuclear bond iv. chemical equations to represent the types of changes v. relative magnitude	7, 8, 17, 22, NR7, 25, 26, 28
5. Calorimetry and calculations	a. Calorimetric labs i. ice lab ii. metal lab iii. dissociation lab iv. neutralization lab b. Lab procedures	3, 10, 12, 15, 37
6. Chemical change	a. Exothermic and endothermic equations with ΔH factors b. Energy equations and graphic representation c. Relative stability of chemicals	11, NR1, NR4, 20, 23, 32, 33, NR8, 39
7. Hess's Law and Hess's Equation	a. Names of equation and ΔH factors (formation, combustion, and other reactions) b. Formation method c. Data table information d. Hess's equation e. Predicting ΔH using heat of formation f. Heats of carbon compounds	NR2, 13, NR3, NR5, 34, 35,NR9, 36, NR10
8. Multistep energy calculation		38
9. Combination with other units		
10. Environmental concerns and other applications	a. Heat released to environment b. Acid rain c. Engine production of CO_2 and NO_2	9, 14, 24

Not for Reproduction

CHEMICAL ENERGETICS

1. Energy Introduction

a. Definition: Energy can be defined as the ability to do work, to generate heat or to create electricity.

b. Work can be defined as a force exerted on an object over some distance.

Work = force × distance

Unit of measurement of work or energy = Nm or Joule (J)

All chemical and physical transformations involve energy changes. Energy is often defined as the capacity to do work or to produce change. Enthalpy is a measurement of changes in heat energy as a result of a process occurring at a constant pressure.

Formally, it is:

H = internal energy + pressure × volume

2. First Law of Thermodynamics

a. Definition: energy cannot be created or destroyed. Energy can only be transferred.

b. Origin of energy

i. energy origin

ii. sources of energy and equations

c. Transference of energy

i. heat gained system and mathematical sign

ii. heat lost system and mathematical sign

d. Signs of transference of energy

i. increase in movement or change in temperature

ii. change of bonding structure and no increase of temperature

e. Types of energies and definition of temperature

i. temperature definition

ii. kinetic energy

iii. potential energy

f. Energy diagrams

i. E_k *diagram*

ii. E_p *diagram*

a. The First Law of Thermodynamics can be described in the following ways.

i. The total energy of the universe is constant.

ii. Although energy may take many forms that are interconvertible, it can neither be created nor destroyed.

b. The sources of energy on Earth are essentially twofold.

i. Exogenous: The sun is the source of the radiant energy that drives the biosphere (photosynthesis, weather, etc.) and it provides the energy stored in fossil fuels.

ii. Endogenous: Heat energy released by radioactive decay within Earth contributes energy to the atmosphere (volcanic activity) and the biosphere (mid-ocean rifts).

c. Energy Transfer

From a thermodynamic point of view, the universe has two components—the **system** and its **surroundings.**

The system, for want of a better description, is that part of the universe of interest to us. For example, it could be an ionic compound dissolving, a lump of ice melting, an acid–base neutralization reaction or a lump of metal cooling down.

The surroundings are the rest of the universe outside the system. In a styrofoam cup calorimeter, the water constitutes the surroundings—that part of the calorimeter most affected by the change in the system.

Only two types of energy transfer are relevant to Chemistry 30:

i. Endothermic process – heat energy is gained by the system

ii. Exothermic process – heat energy is lost by the system.

Empirically, the energy change in the surroundings is used to gauge the energy change of a system. This is represented diagrammatically as shown below.

(The arrows represent the flow of heat energy.)

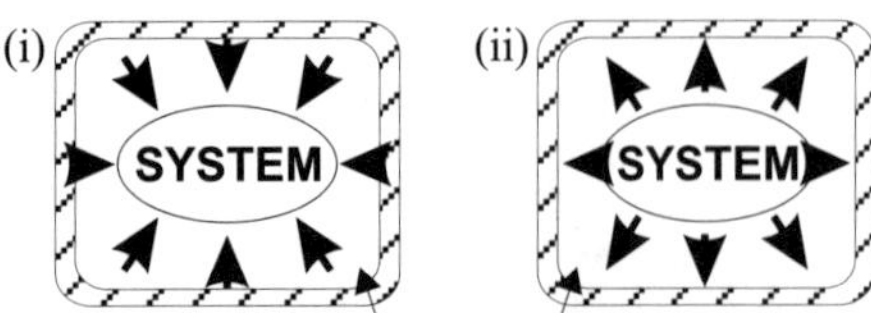

SURROUNDINGS

In situation i, the energy change of the system is, by convention, given a positive sign: $\Delta E_{SYSTEM} > 0$.

In situation ii, the energy change of the system is, by convention, given a negative sign: $\Delta E_{SYSTEM} < 0$.

d. Evidence of Energy Transfer

i. If a sample of matter experiences a change in temperature, it has lost or gained energy (kinetic energy — see below). For example, a lump of metal is warmed up but does not melt.

ii. If a sample of matter undergoes a change of phase or a change in its structure that involves the making and/or breaking of bonds, it has lost or gained energy (potential energy — see below).

For example, when ice melts, methane burns, or hydrogen nuclei fuse to form helium, energy changes have occurred and, in practice, can be measured.

e. Forms of Energy Relevant to Chemistry and Definition of Temperature

i. The temperature of a sample of matter is a measure of the average kinetic energy of that matter's molecules/ions/atoms/particles.

ii. In mathematical terms, the average kinetic energy of a mole of molecules/atoms/ions is $E_{k\,AVE} = \frac{3}{2}RT$

The kinetic energy, E_k, of matter is stored in the motion of the atoms/molecules/ions within the matter.

In simple terms, we consider this kinetic energy to have three forms:

- rotational kinetic energy—E_k of molecular rotation with no change in position
- vibrational kinetic energy—E_k of rapid back and forth movement of bundled atoms with no change of location
- translational kinetic energy—E_k of gross movement (that is, motion from one point to another)

All of the E_k of particles in a solid is likely vibrational E_k. Greater freedom of movement is available to atoms/molecules/ions in liquid and gas phases. In these phases, the average E_k is, to varying extents, vibrational, rotational, and translational in nature.

iii. Potential energy is usually defined as the energy of an object's position or state. This is not always a helpful definition.

Chemical potential energy is the form of energy stored within the bonds of a substance. Consider the following simple explanation.

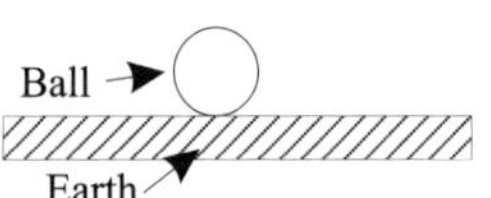

The ball is bonded to Earth by gravitational forces.

Gravitational E_P must be supplied to the ball to break its "bond" with Earth.

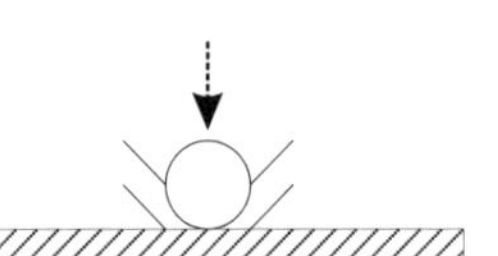

When the ball returns to Earth, its E_P is converted into E_K as it falls, and it does work when it lands.

Clearly, energy must be absorbed to break chemical bonds, and it is released when bonds are formed. ("Energy in to break, energy out to make.")

Not for Reproduction

During phase changes, chemical reactions, or nuclear processes, energy is absorbed and/or released depending on the numbers and strengths of the bonds broken and/or made.

H_2 molecule

H atom

The atoms in H_2 are bonded to each other by electrostatic forces (call it a single bond).

H atom

Chemical E_P must be supplied to break the single bond.

If the atoms reunite and form a single bond, E_P is converted to E_K and work is done on the surroundings

f. Energy Diagrams

i. Heat Curves

The typical heating curve of most substances, from the solid phase through the liquid phase to the gas phase looks like this:

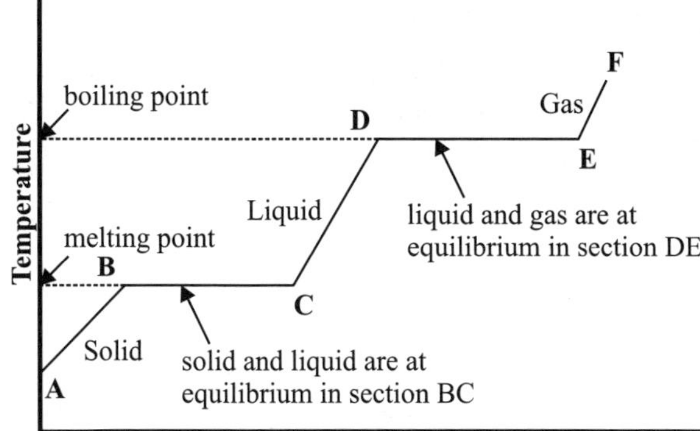

The relative lengths of sections *BC* and *DE* correspond to the relative quantities of energy required to melt/fuse the solid and vaporize the liquid, respectively. Typically, more energy is required, at their respective temperatures, to vaporize a substance in its liquid phase than to melt its solid phase.

The slopes of sections *AB, CD,* and *EF* are determined by the specific heat capacities of the solid, liquid, and vapour phases, respectively. The smaller the specific heat capacity the steeper the slope.

ii. Potential Energy Diagrams

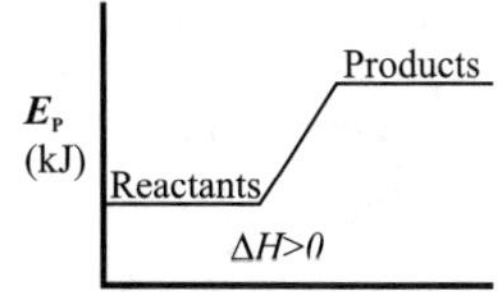

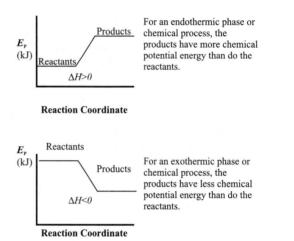

For an endothermic phase or chemical process, the products have more chemical potential energy than do the reactants.

Reaction Coordinate

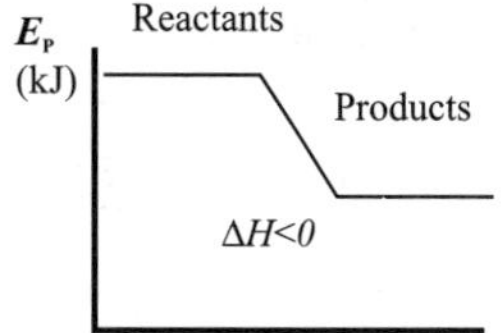

For an exothermic phase or chemical process, the products have less chemical potential energy than do the reactants.

Reaction Coordinate

The E_p graph of a chemical process can also include the activation energy barrier for a reaction—it is usually not drawn to scale. Generally speaking, the reaction with the higher E_a (activation energy) at a given temperature is slower. Remember, E_a is the minimum energy necessary for a reaction collision to have a chance of being successful.

For an exothermic reaction:

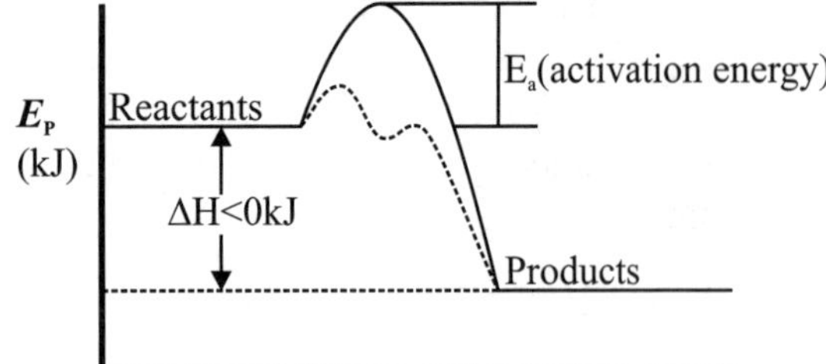

The dotted line represents an alternate reaction pathway available when a catalyst is present. Please note that a catalyst cannot change the net potential energy change of the reaction (ΔH). The net potential energy change of any process is the difference in potential energies of the final and initial states (products and reactants, to you and me).

Related Questions: 1, 2, 4, 6, 18, 21, 27, 29, 30, 31

3. Energy Equations and Definitions

i. kinetic energy equation ($\Delta Q = mc\Delta t$)

ii. potential energy equation ($\Delta H = nH$)

iii. definition of c and H

iv. phase change graph and calculation

i. ΔE_k

Any substance that is warmed or cooled undergoes a change in kinetic energy only. The quantity, q, of energy lost or gained is given by the equation:

$q = mc\Delta t$

where

m = the substance mass (g or kg)

c = the specific heat capacity of the substance $\left(\frac{\text{J}}{\text{g}\times°\text{C}} \text{ or } \frac{\text{kJ}}{\text{g}\times°\text{C}}\right)$

Δt = the absolute value of the temperature change of the substance ($°\text{C}$ or K)

The specific heat capacity of a substance is the quantity of energy required to raise the temperature of a unit mass of that substance by one degree Celsius. A substance capable of absorbing a large quantity of heat energy with a small increase in temperature is said to have a high heat capacity (that is, a high capacity to absorb heat) e.g., $H_2O_{(l)}$ or $H_{2(g)}$.

ii. ΔE_p

Any process in which bonds are made and/or broken undergoes a change in potential energy or enthalpy, ΔH. The appropriate equation for calculating potential energy changes is:

$\Delta H_{process} = nH_{process}$

$\Delta H_{process}$ = the potential energy change of the process (units of kJ)

n = the number of moles of substance changed or produced

$H_{process}$ = the energy required to change or produce one mole of substance. This is called the molar heat, or the molar enthalpy, of the process (units of kJ/mol).

For example: the molar heat enthalpy of combustion of methane to give gaseous products is −802.3kJ/mol; the molar heat/enthalpy of fusion of ice is +6.03kJ/mol.

Using the appropriate heat curves and the formulae, $q = mc\Delta t$ and $\Delta H = nH$ makes it possible to solve a wide variety of common thermodynamic problems involving physical changes only.

Related Questions: 5, 16, 19, NR6, NR11

Not for Reproduction

4. Explanation of Energy

explanation of types of changes and corresponding energies

i. intramolecular bond and names of processes

ii. intermolecular bond

iii. nuclear bond

iv. chemical equation to represent the types of changes

v. relative magnitude

Process/Symbol	What's Happening	Energy
Temperature change ΔE_k / q	The atoms of a substance are moving more or less frantically/energetically	$\approx 1\text{kJ}$
Phase Change $\Delta H_{process}$ (fusion, vaporization, condensation, solidification, and sublimation)	In a molecular substance, weak intermolecular bonds are made { $X_{(g)} \rightarrow X_{(l)}$; $X_{(l)} \rightarrow X_{(s)}$; $X_{(g)} \rightarrow X_{(s)}$} or broken { $X_{(s)} \rightarrow X_{(l)}$; $X_{(l)} \rightarrow X_{(g)}$; $X_{(s)} \rightarrow X_{(g)}$}.	$1-10^2\text{kJ}$
Chemical Reaction $\Delta H_{process}$ (formation, combustion, simple decomposition, etc)	Energy is absorbed to break bonds within the reactants and released when bonds are formed in the products (the bonds involved are often intermolecular bonds).	10^2-10^3kJ
Nuclear Reaction $\Delta H_{process}$ (fission, fusion, α-decay, etc)	Very strong bonds between neutrons and protons within nuclei are made/broken (typically, a mass loss occurs such that $E = \Delta mc^2$).	10^6-10^9kJ and up

iv. Chemical equations can be written to describe the four common processes. For example,

$$H_2O_{(s)}(-35°C) \rightarrow H_2O_{(s)}(-5°C)$$

$$H_2O_{(s)} \rightarrow H_2O_{(l)} \qquad \Delta H = +6.03\text{kJ}$$

$$H_2O_{(l)} \rightarrow H_{2(g)} + \tfrac{1}{2}O_{2(g)} \qquad \Delta H = +285.8\text{kJ}$$

$$^2_1\text{H} + ^3_1\text{H} \rightarrow ^4_2\text{He} + ^1_0\text{n} \qquad \Delta\text{H} = -1.7 \times 10^{12}\text{ kJ}$$

(Balancing simple nuclear reaction equations is easy—just make sure that all the mass numbers and atomic numbers on each side of the equation are balanced.)

Related Questions: 7, 8, 17, 22, 25, NR7, 26, 28

5. Calorimetry and calculations

a. calorimetric labs

i. ice lab

ii. metal lab

iii. dissociation lab

iv. neutralization lab

b. lab procedure

a. Students should know that there are essentially three kinds of calorimetry pertinent to Chemistry 30.

i. Styrofoam Cup Calorimetry: a reaction or process occurs in water or dilute aqueous solution in nested styrofoam cups. It is assumed that any energy absorbed or released by the reaction/process either comes from the water or is absorbed by the water and that styrofoam is a perfect insulator.

Copyright Protected

ii. Metal Can Calorimetry:
a reaction/process occurs in water or dilute aqueous solution in a metal can/beaker. The metal can has a non-negligible mass and, unlike styrofoam, is a conductor of heat and not an insulator. The energy absorbed/released by the reaction/process is assumed to have been released/absorbed by the water and the can.

iii. Bomb Calorimetry: a reaction/process occurs within a specially designed cylinder (the bomb) surrounded by well-circulated water. With careful calibration, the temperature change of all the calorimeter components is taken into account when the reaction/process occurs in the bomb.

For a chemical reaction in a styrofoam calorimeter:

$$\Delta E_{\text{p reaction}} = \Delta E_{\text{k calorimeter}}$$

Or $\Delta H_{\text{reaction}} = q_{\text{cal}}$

Or $nH_{\text{reaction}} = (mc\Delta t)_{\text{cal}}$

For a chemical reaction in a metal can calorimeter:

$$\Delta E_{\text{p reaction}} = \Delta E_{\text{k calorimeter}}$$

Or $\Delta H_{\text{reaction}} = q_{\text{cal}}$

$$nH_{\text{reaction}} = (mc\Delta t)_{H_2O} + (mc\Delta t)_{can}$$

For a chemical reaction in a bomb calorimeter

$$\Delta E_{\text{p reaction}} = \Delta E_{\text{k calorimeter}}$$

Or $\Delta H_{\text{reaction}} = q_{\text{cal}}$

$$\text{n}H_{reaction} = C\Delta t$$

C = the heat capacity of the bomb calorimeter(units kJ/°C).

This is the heat energy required to raise the temperature of the calorimeter by one degree Celsius.

b. Laboratory procedures

Student are expected to be able to design, perform, write procedures for, analyze, and evaluate calorimetric determinations of:

- the specific heat capacity of an unknown sample of matter
- the molar enthalpies of fusion, condensation, formation, solution, neutralization, and so on
- the enthalpy changes of commercial products such as heat/cold packs and driveway/road de-icers

Related Questions: 3, 10, 12, 15, 37

6. Chemical Change

a. Exothermic and endothermic equations with ΔH factors

b. Energy equations and graphic representation

c. Relative stability of chemicals

a. An exothermic reaction loses heat to its surrounding — which is another way of saying that heat is a product in this kind of reaction. In an equation, we can write:

$$\text{A} + \text{B} \rightarrow \text{C} + x\text{kJ}$$

Or

$$\text{A} + \text{B} \rightarrow \text{C} \qquad \Delta H = -x\text{kJ}$$

The negative sign does not imply that the energy is negative. It simply means that the system loses energy.

An endothermic reaction absorbs heat from its surroundings. Thus, heat is a reactant in an endothermic reaction. In a chemical equation, this is written as follows:

$$\text{A} + \text{B} + x\text{kJ} \rightarrow \text{C}$$

Or

$$\text{A} + \text{B} \rightarrow \text{C} \qquad \Delta H = +x\text{kJ}$$

The positive sign means that the system gained energy.

Not for Reproduction

b. Graphically, exothermic and endothermic reactions are represented as follows:

Exothermic Reaction **Endothermic Reaction**

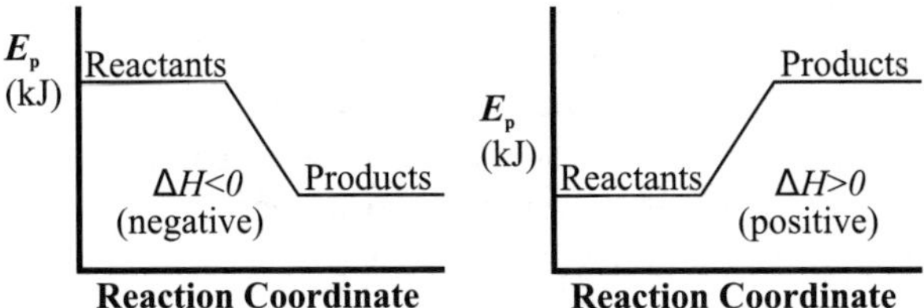

E_p (kJ)
Products
Reactants
$\Delta H>0$ (positive)
Reaction Coordinate

c. Thermodynamic Stability

A compound is more thermodynamically stable than another if it has a more exothermic (more negative) molar enthalpy of formation. For example, $CO_{(g)}(H_f{}^\circ = -110.5\text{ kJ / mol})$ is less thermodynamically stable than $CO_{2(g)}(H_f{}^\circ = -393.5\text{ kJ / mol})$

Related Questions: 11, 20, 23, NR1, NR4, 32, 33, NR8, 39

---

7. Hess's Law and Hess's Equation

a. Names of equation and ΔH factors (formation, combustion, and other reactions)

b. Formation method

c. Data table information

d. Hess's equation

e. Predicting ΔH using heat of formation

f. Heats of carbon compounds

a. Reaction Types

Students must be able to identify chemical equations that describe any phase change, formation, simple decomposition, reduction-oxidation reaction, acid-base neutralization, precipitation, complete combustion, nuclear fusion, nuclear fission, cellular respiration, photosynthesis, or any other relevant reaction.

b. Formation Enthalpies

The energy released or absorbed when one mole of compound is made from its elements in their standard states is called the molar enthalpy of formation of that compound.

For example,

$H^\circ{}_f\,(MgCO_{3(s)}) = -1085.8\text{ kJ / mol}$

means that the reaction

$$Mg_{(s)} + C_{(s)} + \frac{3}{2}O_{2(g)} \rightarrow MgCO_{3(s)}$$

releases 1 085.8 kJ of heat energy per mole of magnesium carbonate formed.

The Chemistry 30 Data Booklet lists the molar enthalpies of formation of many common chemical compounds.

The molar enthalpy of formation of any element in its standard state is, by convention, zero kilojoules per mol.

c. Hess's Law should be memorized: the enthalpy change of a net reaction is the sum of the enthalpies of the reactions combined to make the net reaction.

Consider (1) $A + B \rightarrow C + D \qquad \Delta H = \Delta H_1$

(2) $C + D \rightarrow E + F \qquad \Delta H = \Delta H_2$

Then, the enthalpy change of the reaction

(net) $\quad C + D \rightarrow E + F$

$\Delta H_{net} = \Delta H_1 + \Delta H_2$

Alternatively, Hess's Law exemplifies the principle that regardless of the route from reactants to products, the enthalpy change of a process is the difference in enthalpy between the products and reactants.

d. Hess' Law and the Heat of Formation method

If the tabulated information is available, the enthalpy change of a net reaction is the difference between the total enthalpies of formation of the products and reactants. In equation form, we write:

$$\Delta H^\circ_{net} = \Sigma n H^\circ_f(\text{Products}) - \Sigma n H^\circ_f(\text{Reactants})$$

(Σ means "the sum of")

For example, the enthalpy of combustion of butane is calculated as follows:

$$C_4H_{10(g)} + \tfrac{13}{2}O_{2(g)} \rightarrow 4CO_{2(g)} + 5H_2O_{(g)}$$

$$\Delta H^\circ_f = \begin{pmatrix} 4\text{ mol} \times H^\circ_f(CO_{2(g)}) + \\ 5\text{ mol} \times H^\circ_f(H_2O_{(g)}) \end{pmatrix} - (1\text{ mol} \times H^\circ_f(C_4H_{10(g)}))$$

$$= \begin{pmatrix} 4\text{ mol} \times [-393.5\text{ kJ/mol}] + \\ 5\text{ mol} \times [-241.8\text{ kJ/mol}] \end{pmatrix} - (1\text{ mol} \times [-126.5\text{ kJ/mol}])$$

$$\Delta H^\circ_{net} = -2\,656.5\text{ kJ}$$

The enthalpy of combustion of butane is −2 656.5 kJ. (We could just as easily say the molar enthalpy of combustion of butane to give gaseous products is -2656.5 kJ/mol).

e. Heats of carbon compounds

Much of the energy requirements of modern society are met by burning carbon or carbon compounds (fossil fuels and their derivatives). Generally speaking, the higher the percentage of carbon by mass of a carbon-based fuel, the higher the energy content of that fuel (energy per kilogram).

Related Questions: NR2, 13, NR3, NR5, 34, 35, NR9, 36, NR10

8. Multistep Energy Calculations

Students must be able to amalgamate topics such as Hess' Law, calorimetry, engine/burner efficiency, and energy density to tackle various "real-life" thermodynamic situations. For example: what mass of natural gas (assume 100% methane) must burn in a hot water heater that is 50% efficient in order to warm 125 L of bathwater from 10°C to 40°C?
(The answer is 0.63 kg.)

Related Question: 38

9. Combination Redox and/or Acid–Base and/or Equilibrium and Thermodynamic topics

Students must be able to appreciate that all acid–base, equilibrium, and reduction–oxidation processes can be analyzed from a thermodynamic perspective. For example,

- Diluting or neutralizing acids/bases tend to be exothermic
- Electrolytic cells are comparable to endothermic reactions—that is, they are endoenergetic
- Voltaic cells operate in much the same way as exothermic reactions—they are exoenergetic
- The calculated ΔH of an equilibrium process and Le Châtelier's principle can be used to gauge the effect of heating/cooling that equilibrium

Not for Reproduction

10. Environmental Concerns and Other Applications

a. heat released to environment

b. acid rain

c. engine production of CO_2 and NO_2

a. Heat Pollution

One aspect of our use of fossil fuel combustion to generate electricity is the inefficiency of the power generating process. Considerable quantities of waste heat are released to rivers, lakes, and other bodies of water that, among other things, lower the oxygen concentration of the water—a serious negative impact on the local ecology.

b. Acid Rain

Burning fossil fuels converts the sulfur they contain into $SO_{2(g)}$. Under the conditions of combustion of almost any fuel/air mixture, nitrogen and oxygen combine ultimately to produce $NO_{2(g)}$ in their exhaust gases. Together, $SO_{2(g)}$ and $NO_{2(g)}$, either on their own or in combination with atmospheric moisture, wreak serious environmental damage as acid precipitation.

c. Engine production of CO_2 and NO_2 (The Greenhouse Effect)

Carbon dioxide from complete combustion and volatile organic compounds (VOCs) from incomplete combustion (like methane) trap ever-larger amounts of infrared radiation reflected from Earth's surface. Opinions vary, but anthropogenic (man-made) emissions of $CO_{2(g)}$ and other greenhouse gases are thought to be largely responsible for a steady rise in Earth's mean annual temperature over the last two centuries.

Related Questions: 9, 14, 24

Use the following information to answer the first question.

In most plants, solar energy, water, and carbon dioxide react to form glucose. The reaction is represented by the equation

$$6CO_{2(g)} + 6H_2O_{(l)} + \text{energy} \rightarrow C_6H_{12}O_{6(aq)} + 6O_{2(g)}$$

1. This reaction is an example of

A. respiration

B. photosynthesis

C. redox and neutralization

D. combustion and respiration

Source: January 2000

CHALLENGER QUESTION DIFFICULTY 49.7

2. A stainless steel spoon is used to stir a cup of hot coffee. In this system, the

A. temperature of the coffee will drop because an endothermic phase change occurs

B. gain in kinetic energy of the spoon is dependent only on how fast the coffee is stirred

C. potential energy lost by the coffee is equal to the potential energy gained by the spoon

D. temperature change of the coffee is directly proportional to the mass and specific heat capacity of the spoon

Source: January 2000

Use the following information to answer the next question.

Novacor is a large international company that produces ethene ($C_2H_{4(g)}$) from ethane ($C_2H_{6(g)}$) at its plant in Joffre, Alberta. The essential process in the conversion of ethane to ethene is called cracking, which involves the removal of hydrogen atoms from ethane molecules. The cracking occurs in special alloy pipes at temperatures near 1100°C. The process results in the formation of ethene and other byproducts.

3. When 10.0 g of ethane gas was originally formed from its elements, the decrease in enthalpy was

A. 3.92 kJ **B.** 28.2 kJ

C. 84.7 kJ **D.** 255 kJ

Source: January 2000

4. Liquid ethane, at a pressure of approximately 5 000 kPa and a temperature of –35°C, enters the plant via a pipeline. It passes through a series of heat exchangers and eventually emerges as a gas at 900 kPa and 35°C. This change in the ethane is primarily due to

A. an increase in potential energy and kinetic energy

B. an increase in potential energy only

C. a decrease in density and kinetic energy

D. an increase in density, potential energy, and kinetic energy

Source: January 2000

Use the following information to answer the next question.

Coke (carbon) deposits formed on the inside of the alloy pipes must be periodically removed by a process known as decoking. Passing air and steam through the pipes results in the combustion of the coke according to the equation

$$C_{(s)} + O_{2(g)} \rightarrow CO_{2(g)}$$

5. The decoking process is an oxidation-reduction reaction. The reaction that occurs in the human body in which carbon undergoes the same change in assigned oxidation number as in the decoking process is

A. $6CO_{2(g)} + 6H_2O_{(l)} \rightarrow C_6H_{12}O_{6(aq)} + 6O_{2(g)}$

B. $C_6H_{12}O_{6(aq)} + 6O_{2(g)} \rightarrow 6CO_{2(g)} + 6H_2O_{(l)}$

C. $C_2H_5OH_{(l)} \rightarrow C_2H_4O_{(l)} + H_{2(g)}$

D. $C_2H_5OH_{(l)} \rightarrow C_2H_{4(g)} + H_2O_{(l)}$

Source: January 2000

Not for Reproduction

6. One of the byproducts of the cracking process used at Novacor is ethyne ($C_2H_{2(g)}$). In the presence of a palladium catalyst, the ethyne forms ethene and ethane. This reaction is represented by the **unbalanced** equation

$$C_2H_{2(g)} + H_{2(g)} \rightarrow C_2H_{4(g)} + C_2H_{6(g)} + \text{energy}$$

The energy diagram that represents both the catalyzed (------) and uncatalyzed reactions (——) is

A.

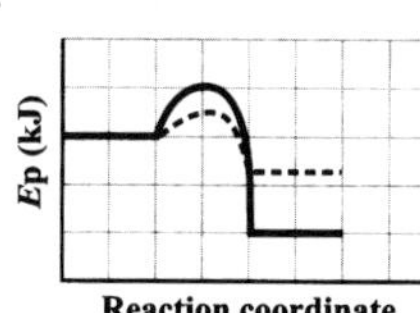

B.

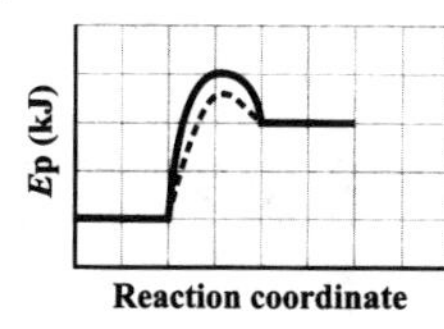

C.

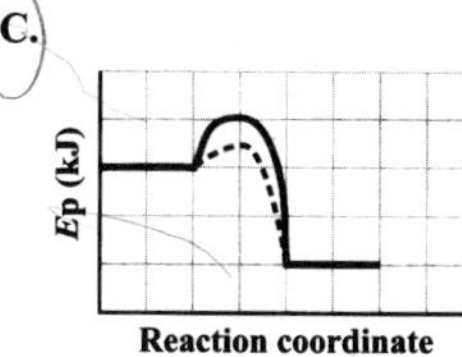

D.

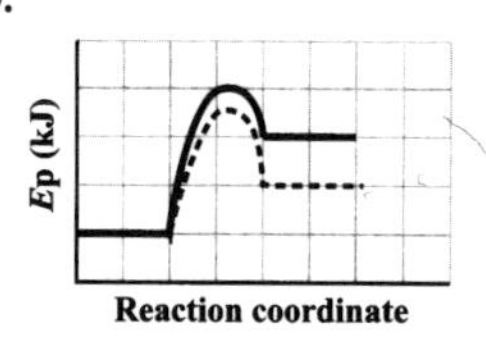

Source: January 2000

7. When energy changes are arranged in **decreasing** order of magnitude, the order is

A. phase, chemical, nuclear fusion

B. nuclear fusion, phase, chemical

C. chemical, nuclear fusion, phase

D. nuclear fusion, chemical, phase

Source: January 2000

8. When hydrogen in the sun is converted into helium, the changes involve primarily

A. intermolecular forces

B. intramolecular forces

C. nuclear forces

D. chemical bonds

Source: January 2000

Use the following information to answer the next question.

Statements Regarding Fossil Fuel Use

I The combustion of these fuels contributes to the greenhouse effect.
II Locating, extracting, and transporting fossil fuels causes environmental damage.
III The energy yield from fossil fuels is low, thus they are poor energy sources.
IV Fossil fuels are a non-renewable resource.

9. The statement about fossil fuel use that is **least** accurate is statement

A. I **B.** II **C.** III **D.** IV

Source: January 2000

Use the following information to answer the next question.

A student made the following four statements about a chemical reaction.

I The reaction is exothermic.
II The reaction has a negative ΔH value.
III The reaction warms up the surroundings.
IV The enthalpy of the products is greater than that of the reactants.

10. Which statement is **not** consistent with the other three?

A. Statement I

B. Statement II

C. Statement III

D. Statement IV

Source: January 2000

Copyright Protected

11. Of the following metallic oxides, the one that would require the greatest energy per mole to decompose into its constituent elements is

A. $SnO_{(s)}$ **B.** $PbO_{(s)}$

C. $Fe_2O_{3(s)}$ **D.** $MnO_{(s)}$

Source: January 2000

CHALLENGER QUESTION **DIFFICULTY 54.1**

Numerical Response

1. The molar enthalpy for the fusion of water is +/– ____ kJ/mol. (Record your **three-digit** answer.)

Source: January 2000

Use the following information to answer the next question.

A student performed a calorimetry experiment and recorded the data below.

Mass of aluminum calorimeter	470.0 g
Mass of calorimeter water	100.0 g
Initial temperature of calorimeter water	23.0°C
Mass of silicon	52.0 g
Initial temperature of silicon	61.6°C
Final temperature of calorimeter, water, and silicon	24.6°C

CHALLENGER QUESTION **DIFFICULTY 57.1**

12. The amount of energy lost by silicon in the experiment is

A. 670 J **B.** 1.35 kJ

C. 2.25 kJ **D.** 3.82 kJ

Source: January 2000

Use the following information to answer the next question.

Ethanol is the alcohol found in beer, wine, and whisky. In the production of ethanol, the starch in barley, grapes, or corn, is reacted to form glucose in the presence of enzymes. During the fermentation process, yeast is added to the glucose. The yeast contains enzymes that act as biological catalysts in the reaction of glucose into ethanol and carbon dioxide. The reaction is represented by the equation

$$C_6H_{12}O_{6(s)} \rightarrow 2CO_{2(g)} + 2C_2H_5OH_{(l)}$$

Numerical Response

2. The molar enthalpy of reaction for the fermentation of glucose is +/– ____ kJ/mol. (Record your **three-digit** answer.)

Source: January 2000

13. In industry, ethanol is produced by a catalyzed reaction between ethene and water. The equation and energy associated with this reaction can be represented as

A. $C_2H_{4(g)} + H_2O_{(l)} \rightarrow C_2H_5OH_{(l)} + 87.6\ kJ$

B. $C_2H_{4(g)} + H_2O_{(l)} + 43.6\ kJ \rightarrow C_2H_5OH_{(l)}$

C. $C_2H_{4(g)} + H_2O_{(l)} \rightarrow C_2H_5OH_{(l)}$ $\Delta H = +87.6\ kJ$

D. $C_2H_{4(g)} + H_2O_{(l)} \rightarrow C_2H_5OH_{(l)}$ $\Delta H = -43.6\ kJ$

Source: January 2000

14. When ethanol is burned in the body, it is

A. reduced in an endothermic reaction

B. oxidized in an endothermic reaction

C. oxidized in an exothermic reaction

D. reduced in an exothermic reaction

Source: January 2000

Not for Reproduction

Use the following information to answer the next question.

The energy from cellular respiration is stored in the form of ATP (adenosine triphosphate) molecules in cells. As energy is required by a cell, it is released from the ATP molecules as they react to form ADP (adenosine diphosphate) molecules. The reaction is represented by the equilibrium equation

$$ATP_{(aq)} \leftrightarrow ADP_{(aq)} + PO_4{}^{3-}{}_{(aq)} + 30.5\ kJ$$

Cells contain large numbers of ADP and ATP molecules.

Numerical Response

3. When you are reading, you use 400 kJ/h of energy. In one hour, the number of moles of ATP reacted to form ADP is ____ mol. (Record your **three-digit** answer.)

Source: January 2000

15. A student mixes 41.8 g of ethanol at 15.8EC with 50.7 g of water at 49.2EC. If the resulting temperature of the solution is 38.4EC, what is the specific heat capacity of the ethanol?

A. 2.43 J/(g•°C)

B. 3.45 J/(g•°C)

C. 4.19 J/(g•°C)

D. 6.51 J/(g•°C)

Source: January 2000

Use the following graph to answer the next question.

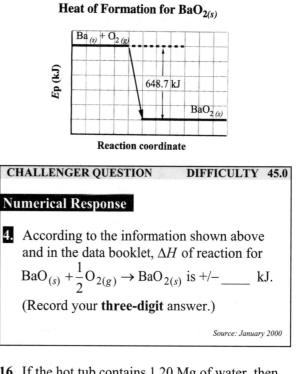

Heat of Formation for $BaO_{2(s)}$

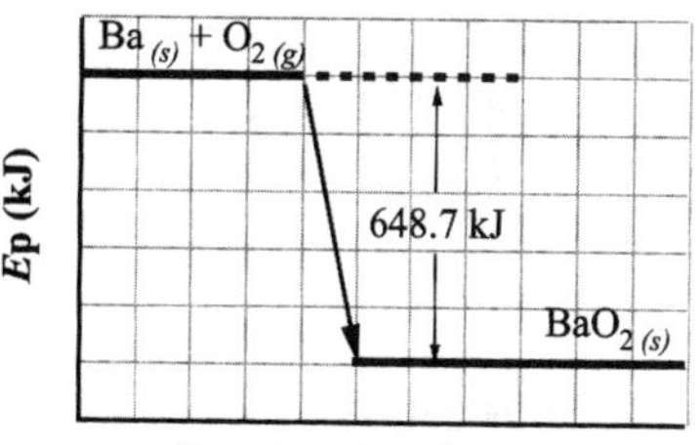

CHALLENGER QUESTION **DIFFICULTY 45.0**

Numerical Response

4. According to the information shown above and in the data booklet, ΔH of reaction for $BaO_{(s)} + \frac{1}{2}O_{2(g)} \rightarrow BaO_{2(s)}$ is +/–____ kJ.
(Record your **three-digit** answer.)

Source: January 2000

16. If the hot tub contains 1.20 Mg of water, then the energy required to warm the water from 12.0°C to 40.0°C is

A. 6.74×10^7 J **B.** 8.99×10^7 J

C. 1.41×10^8 J **D.** 1.60×10^8 J

Source: January 2000

Use the following information to answer the next question.

A basketball player comes out of the shower, still damp, feeling cooler than he did when he entered the locker room. The player feels cooler because the water on his skin is absorbing heat from his body in order to evaporate.

17. The water on the player's skin undergoes an

A. endothermic phase change

B. endothermic chemical change

C. exothermic phase change

D. exothermic chemical change

Source: June 2000

Copyright Protected

18. The human body contains about 70% water by mass. A body temperature close to 37°C is vital to survival. The property of water that allows the body to maintain an almost-constant temperature despite sudden changes in ambient temperature is its high

A. heat of fusion

B. heat of vaporization

C. specific heat capacity

D. enthalpy of formation

Source: June 2000

CHALLENGER QUESTION	DIFFICULTY 51.7

19. When 10.0 g of water evaporates with no change in temperature, the water will

A. release approximately 22.6 kJ of energy

B. release approximately 40.8 kJ of energy

C. absorb approximately 22.6 kJ of energy

D. absorb approximately 40.8 kJ of energy

Source: June 2000

CHALLENGER QUESTION	DIFFICULTY 57.9

Numerical Response

5. In organisms, the reaction of sucrose and oxygen produces carbon dioxide, water, and energy. The energy available may be estimated using the reaction for the combustion of sucrose:

$$C_{12}H_{22}O_{11(aq)} + 12\ O_{2(g)} \rightarrow 12\ CO_{2(g)} + 11\ H_2O_{(l)} + 5\ 640.3\ \text{kJ}$$

The quantity of energy available when 1.00 g of sucrose reacts is________ kJ.
(Record your **three-digit** answer.)

Source: June 2000

Numerical Response

6. Liquid mercury is used in many thermometers because it has a relatively low freezing point and a relatively high boiling point. A particular mercury thermometer contains 3.21 g of mercury. When the thermometer reading changes from 17.3°C to 101.2°C, the mercury has absorbed ____________J of energy.
(Record your **three-digit** answer.)

Source: June 2000

20. When phosphorus, $P_{4(s)}$, is exposed to air, it ignites spontaneously and rapidly releases 2 940 kJ/mol. Which of the following potential energy diagrams best represents this reaction?

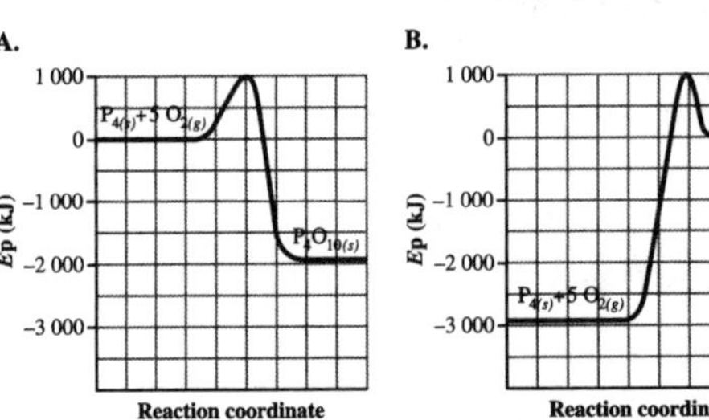

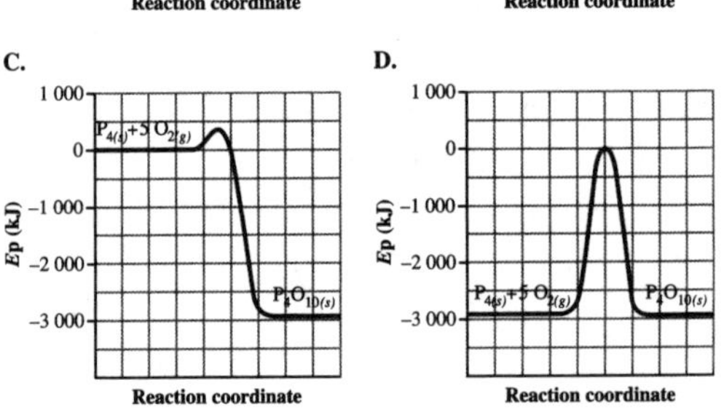

Source: June 2000

CHALLENGER QUESTION	DIFFICULTY 48.3

21. A substance undergoes a change that causes the temperature of its surroundings to increase. The temperature of the substance does not change. This occurs as the

A. substance melts at its freezing point

B. substance condenses at its boiling point

C. kinetic energy of the substance decreases

D. potential energy of the substance increases

Source: June 2000

Not for Reproduction

Use the following information to answer the next question.

Superphénix, a nuclear "breeder" reactor in Lyon, France, was shut down for repair in the late 1980s after a liquid sodium leak. The liquid sodium was used as a coolant in the reactor.

22. The equation representing a nuclear change in a breeder reactor is

A. $U_{(s)} + 3\ F_{2(g)} \rightarrow UF_{6(s)}$

B. ${}^{238}_{92}U + {}^{1}_{0}n \rightarrow {}^{239}_{94}Pu + 2{}^{0}_{-1}e$

C. $Na_{(s)} \rightarrow Na_{(l)}$

D. $NaNO_{3(s)} \rightarrow Na^{+}{}_{(aq)} + NO_3^{-}{}_{(aq)}$

Source: June 2000

Use the following information to answer the next question.

Reaction Equations

1 $6\ C_{(s)} + 6\ H_{2(g)} + 3\ O_{2(g)} \rightarrow C_6H_{12}O_{6(s)}$

2 ${}^{1}_{1}H + {}^{2}_{1}H \rightarrow {}^{3}_{2}He$

3 $6\ CO_{2(g)} + 6\ H_2O_{(g)} \rightarrow C_6H_{12}O_{6(aq)} + 6\ O_{2(g)}$

4 ${}^{235}_{92}U + {}^{1}_{0}n \rightarrow {}^{137}_{52}Te + {}^{97}_{40}Zr + 2{}^{1}_{0}n$

Numerical Response

7. Identify the equation, as numbered above, that represents each of the reaction types listed below.

Nuclear fusion _________

Nuclear fission _________

Photosynthesis _________

Formation _________

Source: June 2000

Use the following information to answer the next two questions.

Fuel cells used to power electric vehicles are high-efficiency voltaic cells that consume conventional fuels under conditions of controlled combustion. The half-reactions that occur in a propane–oxygen fuel cell are

$O_{2(g)} + 4H^{+}{}_{(aq)} + 4e^{-} \rightarrow 2H_2O_{(l)}$

$C_3H_{8(g)} + 6H_2O_{(l)} \rightarrow 3CO_{2(g)} + 20H^{+}{}_{(aq)} + 20e^{-}$

23. The substance in the propane-oxygen fuel cell that has a standard heat of formation of zero is

A. $O_{2(g)}$

B. $CO_{2(g)}$

C. $H_2O_{(l)}$

D. $C_3H_{8(g)}$

Source: June 2000

24. Many scientists believe that the most significant problem caused by $CO_{2(g)}$ emissions is

A. metal corrosion

B. the biomagnification of toxins

C. the destruction of the ozone layer

D. its contribution to the greenhouse effect

Source: June 2000

Copyright Protected

Use the following information to answer the next question.

Methanoic (formic) acid is the irritant secreted during an ant bite. The irritation is partially due to the ionization of methanoic acid. The equilibrium equation for the ionization can be represented as

$$HCOOH_{(aq)} + H_2O_{(l)} \rightleftharpoons H_3O^+{}_{(aq)} + HCOO^-{}_{(aq)}$$

25. Which of the substances in the equation above could function as an amphiprotic species?

A. $H_2O_{(l)}$ and $H_3O^+{}_{(aq)}$

B. $H_2O_{(l)}$

C. $H_3O^+{}_{(aq)}$ and $HCOO^-{}_{(aq)}$

D. $H_2O_{(l)}$, $H_3O^+{}_{(aq)}$, and $HCOO^-{}_{(aq)}$

Source: June 2000

26. Which of the following processes requires the **least** energy per mole?

A. Helium forming hydrogen

B. Ice at 0°C forming liquid water

C. Liquid water at 100°C forming steam

D. Water forming hydrogen and oxygen gas

Source: January 2001

27. Which of the following processes is always endothermic?

A. Neutralization

B. Photosynthesis

C. Oxidation

D. Reduction

Source: January 2001

28. Nuclear reactions involve greater enthalpy changes than chemical reactions because

A. nuclear forces are stronger than chemical bonds

B. nuclear explosions are more energetic than chemical explosions

C. nuclear reactions involve different elements than chemical reactions

D. nuclear reactions involve elements with larger atomic numbers than chemical reactions

Source: January 2001

Not for Reproduction

Use the following information to answer the next question.

Sketch of a Heating Curve for the Distillation of Liquid Air

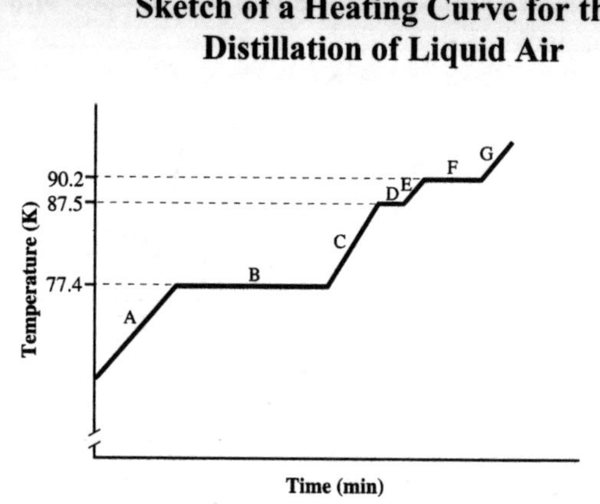

Through careful distillation, the three main components of liquid air can be separated. Their respective boiling points are:
nitrogen 77.4 K argon 87.5 K
oxygen 90.2 K

29. Which of the following statements about the above graph is true?

A. Sections A, C, E, and G represent changes in potential energy.

B. Sections A, C, and E represent the vaporization of each component of liquid air.

C. Sections B, D, and F represent the vaporization of each component of liquid air.

D. Section B represents melting, section D represents vaporization, and section F represents sublimation.

Source: January 2001

Use the following information to answer the next question.

One theory to explain firewalking, the ability to walk barefoot across red-hot coals unscathed, is based on the insulating quality of steam formed between the coals and the underside of the firewalker's perspiring feet.

CHALLENGER QUESTION **DIFFICULTY 50.6**

30. According to this theory, water molecules in perspiration gain

A. vibrational energy as they warm up and translational energy as they vaporize

B. vibrational energy and rotational energy as they warm up and translational energy as they vaporize

C. potential energy as they warm up and vibrational, rotational, and translational energy as they vaporize

D. vibrational, rotational, and translational energy as they warm up and potential energy as they vaporize

Source: January 2001

Copyright Protected

Use the following information to answer the next two questions.

Commercially available "cold packs" and "hot packs" contain an inner pouch of a solid ionic compound within an outer pouch containing water. When the inner pouch is broken, the solid dissolves in the water of the outer pouch. When ammonium nitrate dissolves, the water temperature decreases; whereas, when calcium chloride dissolves, the water temperature increases.

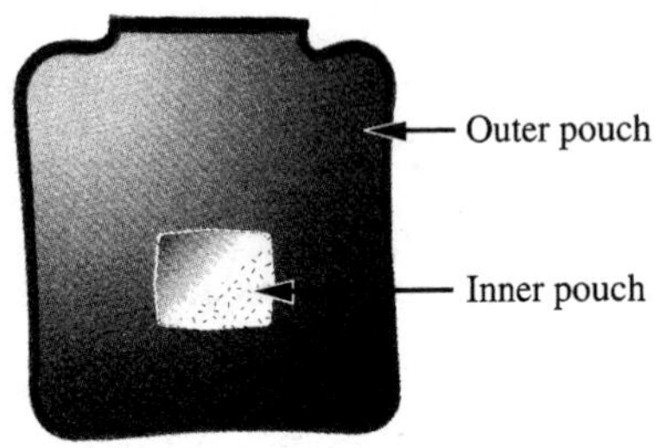

31. Based on this information, a student determined that a hot pack could contain

A. calcium chloride, which undergoes an exothermic dissolving process

B. calcium chloride, which undergoes an endothermic dissolving process

C. ammonium nitrate, which undergoes an exothermic dissolving process

D. ammonium nitrate, which undergoes an endothermic dissolving process

Source: January 2001

CHALLENGER QUESTION DIFFICULTY 57.6

32. Which of the following diagrams represents the heat of solution for either a cold pack or a hot pack?

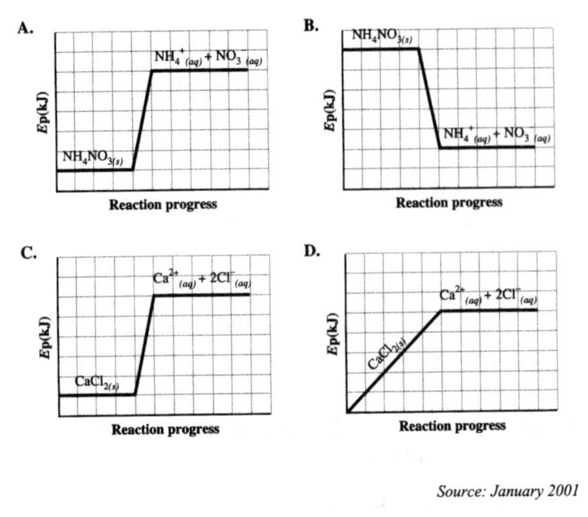

Source: January 2001

Use the following information to answer the next question.

A student comparing cellular respiration and hydrocarbon combustion reactions made the following statements.

I In both reactions, C–H bonds break and C=O bonds form.
II Combustion is exothermic, and cellular respiration is endothermic.
III Both reactions are examples of redox reactions.

CHALLENGER QUESTION DIFFICULTY 46.4

33. The student's correct statements were

A. I and II

B. I and III

C. II and III

D. I, II, and III

Source: January 2001

Not for Reproduction

Use the following information to answer the next question.

Standard Heats of Formation

Substance	ΔH_f° (kJ / mol)
X	–22.5
Y	+78.3
Z	–54.8

Given: X + 3 Y ° 2 Z + 2 W

$\Delta H = -562.0$ kJ

CHALLENGER QUESTION **DIFFICULTY 59.4**

34. The standard molar heat of formation of substance W is

A. +442.0 kJ/mol

B. –120.0 kJ/mol

C. –240.0 kJ/mol

D. –451.4 kJ/mol

Source: January 2001

Use the following information to answer the next question.

Ethanol, $C_2H_5OH_{(l)}$, is a very versatile compound that has applications in the fuel, chemical, and pharmaceutical industries. Some properties of ethanol can be studied in the lab by applying thermodynamic principles.

A student assembled the apparatus shown below in order to determine the molar heat of combustion of ethanol.

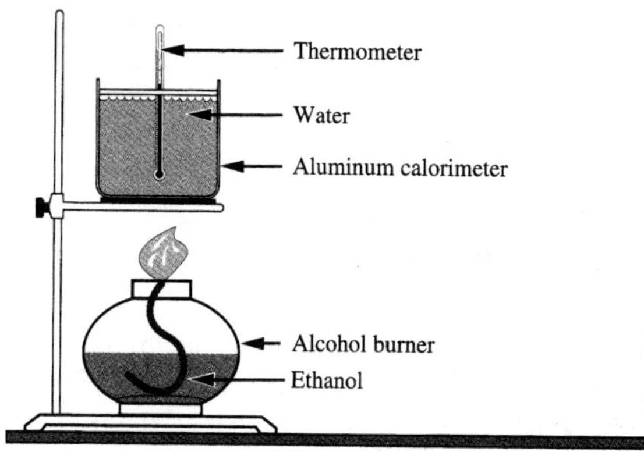

35. The balanced equation and the appropriate enthalpy change for the combustion of ethanol are

A. $C_2H_5OH_{(l)} + 3O_{2(g)} \rightarrow 2CO_{2(g)} + 3H_2O_{(g)}$ $\Delta H = +1235.3$ kJ

B. $C_2H_5OH_{(l)} + O_{2(g)} \rightarrow CO_{2(g)} + 3H_2O_{(l)}$ $\Delta H = -1235.3$ kJ

C. $C_2H_5OH_{(l)} + 3O_{2(g)} \rightarrow 2CO_{2(g)} + 3H_2O_{(g)}$ $\Delta H = -1235.3$ kJ

D. $C_2H_5OH_{(l)} \rightarrow C_{(s)} + 3H_{2(g)} + \frac{1}{2}O_{2(g)}$ $\Delta H = +1235.3$ kJ

Source: January 2001

Copyright Protected

Use the following information to answer the next question.

Calorimetric Data

1 maximum temperature change of water
2 mass of aluminum calorimeter
3 mass of aluminum calorimeter and water
4 initial temperature of aluminum calorimeter
5 maximum temperature change of ethanol
6 mass change of ethanol

Numerical Response

8. The data required to determine the molar heat of combustion for ethanol, listed in numerical order, are _______, _______, _______, and _______.

Source: January 2001

Numerical Response

9. In an experiment, a student heated 500 g of water from 25.0°C to 91.0°C using 0.133 mol of ethanol. If it is assumed that all the heat energy was absorbed by the calorimeter water, the experimental molar enthalpy of combustion for ethanol was +/– _______ MJ/mol.
(Record your **three-digit** answer.)

Source: January 2001

36. The thermochemical equation that represents the molar enthalpy of formation for ethanol is

A. $C_2H_5OH_{(l)} + 277.1\text{ kJ} \rightarrow 2\,C_{(s)} + 3\,H_{2(g)} + \frac{1}{2}O_{2(g)}$

B. $C_2H_5OH_{(l)} + 3\,O_{2(g)} \rightarrow 2\,CO_{2(g)} + 3\,H_2O_{(g)} + 1235.3\text{ kJ}$

C. $2\,C_{(s)} + 3\,H_{2(g)} + \frac{1}{2}O_{2(g)} \rightarrow C_2H_5OH_{(l)} + 277.1\text{ kJ}$

D. $C_2H_5OH_{(l)} + H_2O_{(l)} \rightarrow C_2H_5O^-{}_{(aq)} + H_3O^+{}_{(aq)}$ $K = 1.3 \times 10^{-16}$

Source: January 2001

Use the following information to answer the next question.

Commercial drain cleaners typically contain sodium hydroxide and aluminum. When the solid cleaner is poured down the drain and water is added, the reaction that occurs is represented by the equation

$$2\,NaOH_{(s)} + 2\,Al_{(s)} + 2\,H_2O_{(l)} \rightarrow 2\,NaAlO_{2(aq)} + 3\,H_{2(g)}$$

$\Delta H = -850.0\text{ kJ}$

Numerical Response

10. In the production of 4.00 mol of $NaAlO_{2(aq)}$, the heat released is ________ MJ.
(Record your **three-digit** answer.)

Source: January 2001

Not for Reproduction

CHALLENGER QUESTION **DIFFICULTY 52.3**

37. In a chemistry experiment, 12 g of $(NH_4)_2SO_{4(s)}$ was dissolved in 120 mL of water in a simple calorimeter. A temperature change from 20.2°C to 17.8°C was observed. The experimental molar enthalpy of solution for ammonium sulphate was

A. −13 kJ/mol

B. −1.2 kJ/mol

C. +1.2 kJ/mol

D. +13 kJ/mol

Source: January 2001

CHALLENGER QUESTION **DIFFICULTY 42.6**

38. How much heat is produced when 1.00 g of butane in a disposable lighter is completely burned to form gaseous carbon dioxide and water vapour?

A. 45.7 kJ **B.** 124.7 kJ

C. 2 656.5 kJ **D.** 5 313.0 kJ

Source: January 2001

Numerical Response

11. Canadian five-cent coins (nickels) minted prior to 1982 were made of pure nickel; therefore, they exhibit a type of magnetism called ferromagnetism. If these nickels are heated to 375°C, they will lose their ferromagnetic properties. The energy required to heat a 2.03 g nickel from 25.0°C to 375°C, in scientific notation, is _____ $\times 10^2$ J.
(Record your **three-digit** answer.)

Source: January 2001

Use the following information to answer the next question.

At the Banff Wastewater Treatment plant, bacteria are used to treat organic "sludge" $(CH_2O)_{n(s)}$ in a process called autothermal thermophilic aerobic digestion (ATAD). The digestion of the sludge can be represented by the equation

$$(CH_2O)_{n(s)} + n\,O_{2(g)} \xrightarrow{\text{bacteria}} n\,CO_{2(g)} + n\,H_2O_{(l)} + \text{energy}$$

39. The ATAD process is

A. a reduction

B. exothermic

C. endothermic

D. an acid–base reaction

Source: January 2001

Copyright Protected

Written Response 15%

Use the following information to answer the next question.

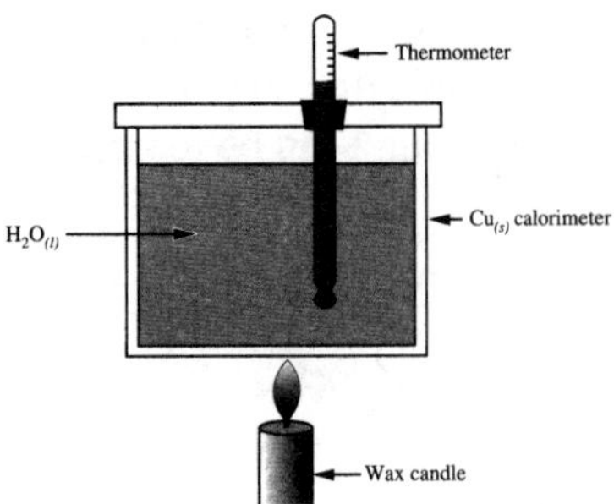

The above apparatus was used to determine experimentally the molar enthalpy of the combustion of candle wax, $C_{25}H_{52(s)}$.

1 **a)** List all the measurements that must be taken in order to determine the molar enthalpy of combustion.

b) Write a mathematical equation that uses the data collected and that will allow you to determine the molar heat of combustion. Label each of the mathematical variables used in the equation.

c) Suggest two improvements to the experimental design.

Source: June 2000

Not for Reproduction

UNIT TEST 1 – CHEMICAL ENERGETICS

Use the following information to answer the first question.

Many Alberta industries burn methane to provide the energy they require. The combustion of methane can be represented by the equation

$CH_{4(g)} + 2O_{2(g)} \rightarrow CO_{2(g)} + 2H_2O_{(g)}$

1. As combustion proceeds, there is a significant decrease in the molecules'

A. translational motion

B. rotational motion

C. vibrational motion

D. potential energy

Use the following information to answer the next question.

Heating Diagram for 2.00 mol of Water

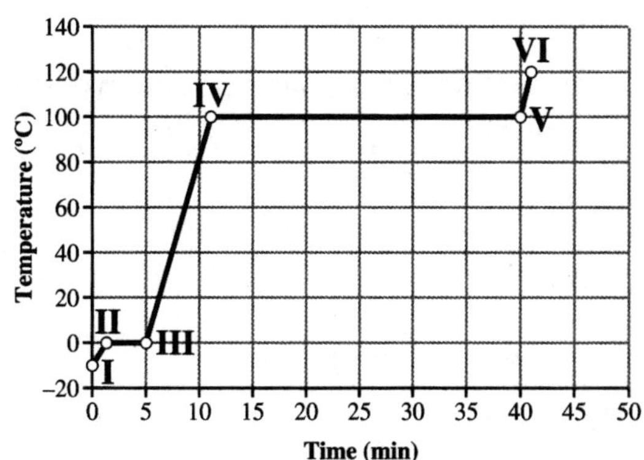

2. The region on the diagram where liquid water is undergoing a change primarily in kinetic energy is between

A. II and III

B. III and IV

C. IV and V

D. V and VI

3. When a 25.0 g sample of a metal is heated from 20.0°C to 50.0° C, 178 J of energy is absorbed from the surroundings. The specific heat capacity of the metal is

A. 7.12 J/g •°C

B. 0.356 J/g •°C

C. 0.237 J/g •°C

D. 0.142 J/g •°C

Use the following information to answer the next question.

Heating of 11.2 g of an Unknown Compound

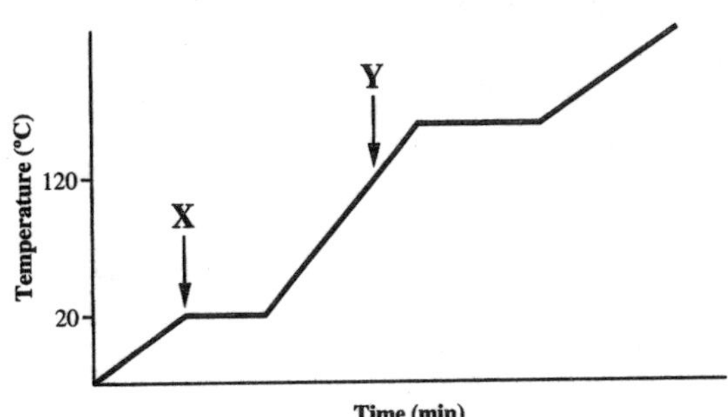

Characteristic Properties

1 Melting point
2 Boiling point
3 Specific heat capacity of liquid
4 Molar heat of fusion
5 Molar heat of vaporization

4. In order to calculate the amount of energy required to heat the unknown compound from point X to point Y, the characteristic properties listed above that must be known in addition to the information given in the graph are properties

A. 1 and 4

B. 2 and 5

C. 3 and 4

D. 3 and 5

Copyright Protected

5. Which of the following changes would release the largest amount of energy per mole?

A. $H_2O_{(g)} \rightarrow H_2O_{(s)}$

B. $^{222}_{86}Rn \rightarrow ^{218}_{84}Po + ^{4}_{2}He$

C. $C_{12}H_{22}O_{11(s)} + 12O_{2(g)} \rightarrow 12CO_{2(g)} + 11H_2O_{(g)}$

D. $C_2H_{2(g)} + \frac{5}{2}O_{2(g)} \rightarrow 2CO_{2(g)} + H_2O_{(g)}$

Numerical Response

1. The molar enthalpy for the vaporization of water is ________ kJ/mol. (Record your **three-digit** answer.)

Use the following key to answer next question.

Types of Bonds
1 Intermolecular
2 Intramolecular
3 Intranuclear

Numerical Response

2. Identify the type of bond, as numbered above, that is primarily involved in each change listed below.

Dry ice sublimes ________

Hydrogen atoms fuse into helium ________

Gasoline burns in an automobile engine ________

Water vapour condenses ________

6. Radiant energy from the sun is stored by plants. This energy is released when plant material undergoes a

A. phase change

B. nuclear change

C. chemical change

D. formation reaction

Use the following equations to answer the next question.

I $H_{2(g)} + \frac{1}{2}O_{2(g)} \rightarrow H_2O_{(g)} \quad \Delta H = -241.8\ \text{kJ}$

II $\frac{1}{2}N_{2(g)} + \frac{1}{2}O_{2(g)} + 90.2\ \text{kJ} \rightarrow NO_{(g)}$

III $C_{(s)} + \frac{1}{2}O_{2(g)} \rightarrow CO_{(g)} + 110.5\ \text{kJ}$

IV $\frac{1}{2}H_{2(g)} + \frac{1}{2}I_{2(s)} \rightarrow HI_{(g)} \quad \Delta H = +26.5\ \text{kJ}$

7. Which of these equations represent exothermic reactions?

A. I and II

B. I and III

C. II and IV

D. III and IV

Use the following information to answer the next question.

Cold packs are used to treat sprains and bruises. A chemical commonly used in cold packs is ammonium nitrate, $NH_4NO_{3(s)}$, which can produce a cooling effect.

A student designed a calorimetry experiment to determine the energy change for the dissolving of ammonium nitrate and recorded the following results:

heat capacity of calorimeter and water:	228 J/°C
initial temperature of water	21.6°C
final temperature of water	16.4°C
mass of ammonium nitrate	0.250 g

Numerical Response

3. The amount of energy involved in this change is _________ kJ.
(Record your **three-digit** answer.)

Use the following information to answer the next question.

The calorimeter shown in this diagram can be used to determine the specific heat capacity of copper. The calorimeter was at room temperature before the heated copper sample was added.

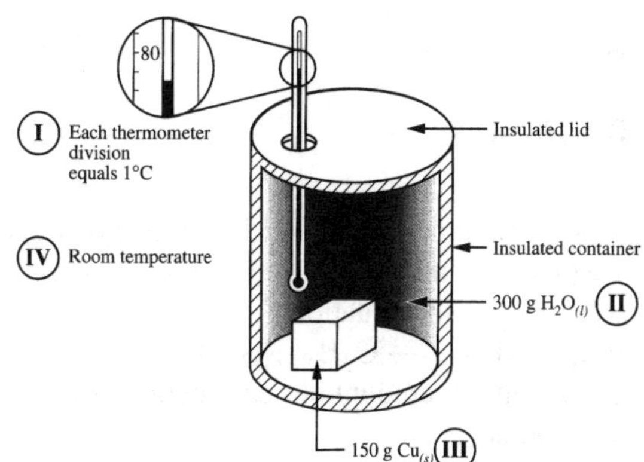

8. Two variables that could have been manipulated in this calorimetry experiment are

A. I and III

B. I and IV

C. II and III

D. II and IV

Numerical Response

4. A 24.6 g sample of molten copper at its melting point is lowered into a calorimeter containing 200 g of water. As soon as solidification is complete, the sample is quickly removed. The temperature of the water in the calorimeter rises from 11.23°C to 17.34°C. In this experiment, the molar heat of solidification for copper is – _____ kJ/mol.
(Record your **three-digit** answer.)

Copyright Protected

9. The molar heat of solution for $NaOH_{(s)}$ is –44.6 kJ/mol. If 25.0 g of $NaOH_{(s)}$ is dissolved in water in a calorimeter, the heat released inside the calorimeter is

A. 27.9 kJ

B. 71.4 kJ

C. 1.12 MJ

D. 1.78 MJ

10. When 24.0 g of carbon and 10.0 g of hydrogen are placed in a bomb calorimeter and reacted according to the equation $3C_{(s)} + 4H_{2(g)} \rightarrow C_3H_{8(g)} + 103.8\text{ kJ}$, the maximum amount of heat liberated by this reaction is

A. 69.1 kJ

B. 128 kJ

C. 257 kJ

D. 619 kJ

Use the following information to answer the next question.

$$Al_4C_{3(s)} + 12H_2O_{(l)} \rightarrow 4\,Al(OH)_{3(s)} + 3CH_{4(g)}$$

$$\Delta H = -1\ 763.0\text{ kJ}$$

11. If this equation is rewritten to show the production of one mole of $CH_{4(g)}$ and the energy is expressed as a term in the equation, then the energy will be

A. 587.7 kJ on the reactant side

B. 1 763.0 kJ on the reactant side

C. 587.7 kJ on the product side

D. 1 763.0 kJ on the product side

Use the following information to answer the next question.

Cold packs are used to treat sprains and bruises. A chemical commonly used in cold packs is ammonium nitrate, $NH_4NO_{3(s)}$, which can produce a cooling effect.

12. The change that occurs in this cold pack is an

A. endothermic change, which results in an increase in temperature

B. exothermic change, which results in an increase in temperature

C. endothermic change, which results in a decrease in temperature

D. exothermic change, which results in a decrease in temperature

Use the following information to answer the next question.

Bricks are produced by mixing clay and water. This mixture is then shaped into "green bricks." The green bricks are carefully heated in a kiln to transform the clay into brick. The bricks then undergo a controlled cooling before being packaged. One of the intermediate reactions in the transformation of clay into brick is

$$3\,Al_4O_6 \bullet Si_3O_{6(s)} \rightarrow (Al_2O_3)_6(SiO_2)_{4(s)} + 5SiO_{2(s)} + 190.4\text{ kJ}$$

13. In the kiln, this reaction would

A. produce energy, reducing the amount of fuel required

B. produce energy, increasing the amount of fuel required

C. absorb energy, increasing the amount of fuel required

D. absorb energy, reducing the amount of fuel required

Not for Reproduction

14. The reason that dynamite releases a great amount of heat energy when it explodes is that the

A. products have more potential energy than the reactants in this endothermic reaction

B. reactants have more potential energy than the products in this endothermic reaction

C. products have more potential energy than the reactants in this exothermic reaction

D. reactants have more potential energy than the products in this exothermic reaction

Use the following diagram to answer the next question.

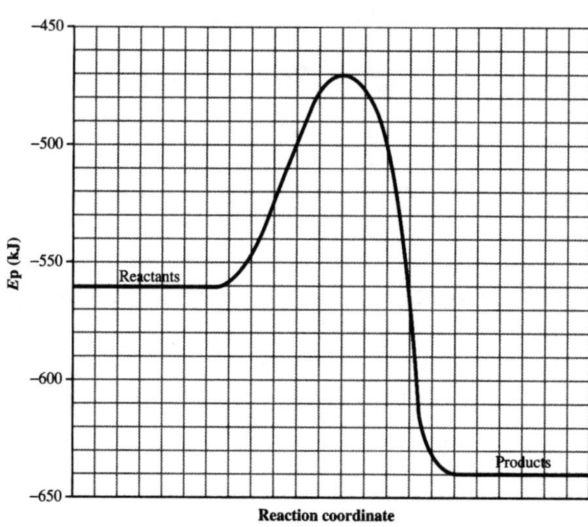

15. The potential energy change for this reaction is

A. +170 kJ

B. +90 kJ

C. –80 kJ

D. –170 kJ

Use the following information to answer the next question.

Cold packs are used to treat sprains and bruises. A chemical commonly used in cold packs is ammonium nitrate, $NH_4NO_{3(s)}$, which can produce a cooling effect.

A student designed a calorimetry experiment to determine the energy change for the dissolving of ammonium nitrate and recorded the following results:

heat capacity of calorimeter and water	228 J/°C
initial temperature of water	21.6°C
final temperature of water	16.4°C
mass of ammonium nitrate	0.250 g

16. The calculated energy change represents the enthalpy of

A. solution

B. combustion

C. neutralization

D. formation

Use the following information to answer the next question.

The reaction X → W can proceed directly or through a series of steps, as shown.

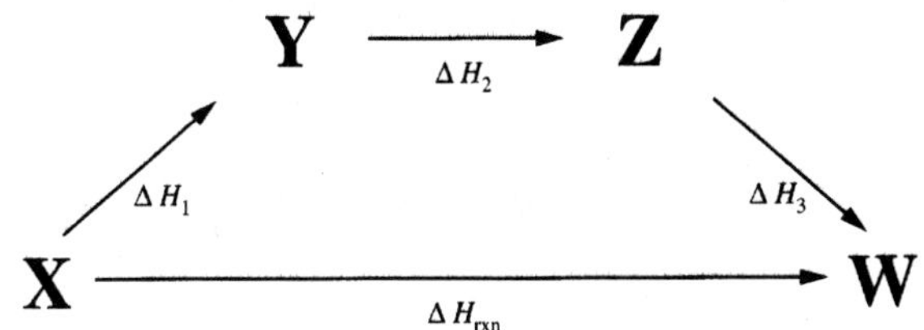

17. This diagram illustrates

A. the Law of Conservation of Mass

B. an exothermic reaction

C. an endothermic reaction

D. Hess's Law

Copyright Protected

Use the following information to answer the next question

One component of acid rain can be formed in the atmosphere by the reaction

$SO_{3(g)} + H_2O_{(l)} \rightarrow H_2SO_{4(aq)} + 227.8\text{ kJ}.$

18. The molar heat of formation of $H_2SO_{4(aq)}$ in the atmosphere, under standard conditions, is

A. –453.7 kJ/mol

B. –586.7 kJ/mol

C. –814.0 kJ/mol

D. –909.3 kJ/mol

Use the following reactions to answer the next question.

Glucose Reactions

I $C_6H_{12}O_{6(aq)} + 6O_{2(g)} \rightarrow 6H_2O_{(l)} + 6CO_{2(g)}$

II $C_6H_{12}O_{6(s)} + 6O_{2(g)} \rightarrow 6H_2O_{(g)} + 6CO_{2(g)}$

19. Which of the following statements describes the reactions above?

A. Carbon is reduced in both reactions.

B. Both reactions are endothermic.

C. Reaction **I** could be classified as cellular respiration and reaction **II** could be classified as combustion.

D. The state of the water produced makes no difference when the heat of reaction is calculated.

20. A property that is **not** consistent with the behaviour of water is that water is able to

A. act both as an acid and a base in proton transfer reactions

B. absorb 241.8 kJ when one mole of water vapour is formed from its elements

C. act as an oxidizing agent or reducing agent in electrolytic cells

D. react with acids to produce hydronium ions

21. In the reaction $2Sn_{(s)} + O_{2(g)} \rightarrow 2SnO_{(s)}$, tin is

A. reduced and the reaction is exothermic

B. reduced and the reaction is endothermic

C. oxidized and the reaction is endothermic

D. oxidized and the reaction is exothermic

Use the following information to answer the next question

One component of acid rain can be formed in the atmosphere by the reaction

$SO_{3(g)} + H_2O_{(l)} \rightarrow H_2SO_{4(aq)} + 227.8\text{ kJ}$

22. As $SO_{3(g)}$ dissolves, acid rain

A. increases in pH and decreases in temperature

B. increases in pH and increases in temperature

C. decreases in pH and increases in temperature

D. decreases in pH and decreases in temperature

Not for Reproduction

23. "The use of fossil fuels as an industrial energy source contributes to global warming." The perspective of this statement is

A. scientific

B. political

C. economic

D. ecological

Written Response

1. The combustion of sugar in a bomb calorimeter is similar to the oxidation of sugar in the body. A student ate three sugar cubes, with masses of 6.84 g, 6.75 g, and 6.79g.

a) Calculate the overall molar enthalpy of oxidation of sugar, $C_{12}H_{22}O_{11(s)}$, in the body.

b) Using these three sugar cubes as representative of regular-sized cubes, determine the amount of energy released by an average-sized cube.

c) Draw and label a potential energy diagram representing the molar enthalpy of oxidation of sugar in the body.

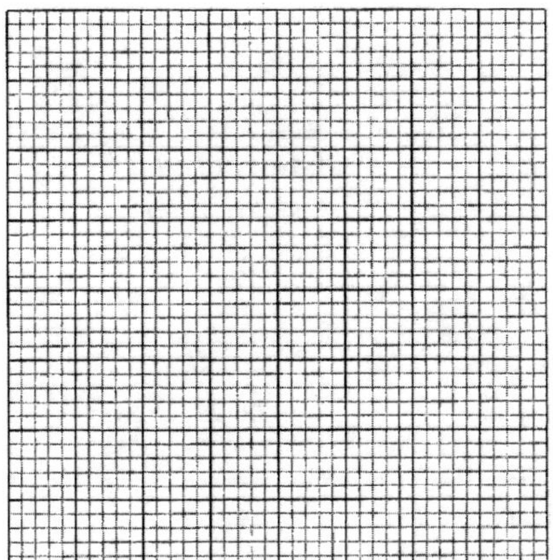

Use the following information to answer the next question.

The Uranium-235 isotope is used as a fuel in some nuclear power plants. This isotope is used to enrich natural uranium ore. Prior to the enrichment process, the uranium ore, $UO_{2(s)}$, is converted to $UF_{6(s)}$. This conversion is represented by the following sequential equations.

Equation I

$UO_{2(s)} + 4HF_{(g)} \rightarrow UF_{4(s)} + 2H_2O_{(g)}$

Equation II

$UF_{4(s)} + F_{2(g)} \rightarrow UF_{6(s)}$

2. **a)** Use molar heats of formation to calculate the amount of heat energy involved in producing 2.00 Mg of $UF_{6(s)}$ from natural uranium ore, $UO_{2(s)}$.

Molar Heats of Formation

Substance	ΔH_f° (KJ/mol)
$UO_{2(s)}$	–1 129.7
$UF_{4(s)}$	–1 914.0
$UF_{6(s)}$	–2 112.9

b) Evaluate the use of nuclear energy for the generation of electricity. Include two reasons for and two reasons against the use of nuclear energy.

REDUCTION–OXIDATION

Table of Correlations		
Topic	**Outcomes**	**Related Questions**
1. Electrochemistry introduction	a. What is electrochemistry? b. What is an electrochemical equation?	
2. Spontaneity	a. What is a spontaneous reaction? Methods of determining spontaneity b. basic definitions: oxidation and reduction, oxidized and reduced, oxidizing agent and reducing agent c. ability to select oxidizing agent (OA) and reducing agent (RA) from given equation d. information from data table (dual OA & RA, generalizations)	6, 11, 17, 18 NR9, 39
3. Predicting redox reactions	a. listing major species (table 5.2 page 118 Nelson) b. identifying strongest OA and strongest RA from equation c. copying half-reactions from data table d. net ionic equations e. observations of redox reactions	NR1, 12, 15, NR6, 25 34, WR2
4. Oxidation number	a. identifying oxidation state in chemical species b. balancing equation in acidic medium c. balancing equation in basic medium	4, 7, 13, NR5, 19, 20, 26, 32, 33
5. Solution stoichiometry	a. stoichiometry b. redox titration (lab 2: acidified permanganate and dichromate solution)	NR3, NR4
6. Application	a. electrochemical cells (anode, cathode, etc.) b. oxidation potentials and reduction potentials: standard potential and conditions c. electrolytic cells i. competing for reaction with enough voltage in an actual electrolysis d. molten cells i. bauxite electrolysis e. commercial cells	1, 2, 5, 8, NR2, 14, 21, 23, 24, NR8, 28, WR1, 36, 37, 38, 40, 41, 42, NR11, NR12, WR2
7. Faraday's Law and electrical energy	a. predicting mass, time, or electric current b. electrical energy	16, NR7, 30, NR10, WR2
8. Cathodic and anodic protection	a. sacrificial anode b. impressed current	9, 10, 35
9. Combining with other units	a. heat energy and electrical energy b. acid–base reaction and electrochemical reactions c. safety concerns	3, 22, 27, 29, 31

Copyright Protected

REDUCTION–OXIDATION

1. Electrochemistry introduction

a. What is electrochemistry?

b. What is an electrochemical equation?

a. What is electrochemistry?

Countless chemical reactions (e.g. formation, simple decomposition, single replacement, complete combustion, to name a few) involve the transfer of electrons between the reactants. The study of these types of reactions (some of which occur in cells and batteries) is called electrochemistry.

b. What is an electrochemical equation?

Reduction and oxidation half-reactions, which include electrons as reactants and products, respectively, are prime examples of electrochemical equations. Any reaction in which there are changes in oxidation states/numbers in going from reactants to products is a reduction oxidation reaction.

2. Spontaneity

a. What is a spontaneous reaction? Methods of determining spontaneity

b. basic definitions: oxidation & reduction, oxidized & reduced, oxidizing agent & reducing agent

c. ability to select oxidizing agent (OA) and reducing agent (RA) from given equation

d. information from data table (dual OA & RA, generalizations)

a. What is a spontaneous reaction?

In simple terms, a spontaneous reaction occurs without the continuous addition of energy. **This does not mean that a spontaneous reaction occurs quickly**, only that it proceeds without external help. An electrochemical reaction will likely proceed spontaneously if the reduction potential of the strongest oxidizing agent is greater than the reduction potential of the strongest reducing agent.

b. Some defnitions

- Oxidation is the loss of electrons.
- Reduction is the gain of electrons.
- A chemical entity that oxidizes another entity (an oxidizing agent) is itself reduced in the process (oxidizing agents are reduced).
- A chemical entity that reduces another entity (a reducing agent) is itself oxidized in the process (reducing agents are oxidized).

c. Selecting the oxidizing agent (OA) or reducing agent (RA) in a chemical equation.

The OA is the reactant that, over the course of the reaction, ends up with a lower oxidation number or lower ion charge, or that is bound to less oxygen (if it is present).

The RA is the reactant that, over the course of the reaction, ends up with a higher oxidation number or higher ion charge, or that is bound to more oxygen (if it is present).

d. Selecting OAs and RAs from Empirical Data

Students must be able to design, perform, and analyze activity series data to construct a simple reduction half-reaction table. From the differing reactivities of select OAs and RAs, it is possible to construct a reduction half-reaction table given that, for a spontaneous reaction, the OA lies above the RA in the reduction half-reaction table to be constructed.

Related Questions: 6, 11, 17, 18, NR9, 39

3. Predicting and Balancing Redox Reactions from Tabulated Half-Reactions

a. listing major species (table 5.2 page 118 Nelson)

b. identifying SOA & SRA from equation

c. copying half-reactions from data table

d. net - ionic equations

e. observations of redox reactions

Not for Reproduction

a. The Species List

Students must be able to list all the chemical entities present in a reaction mixture and label them as OAs (on the left side of a reduction half-reaction table) or RAs (on the right side of a reduction half-reaction table). Care must be taken in labelling those entities that act in combination as OAs (for example, $MnO^-_{(aq)}$ and $H^+_{(aq)}$; $PbO_{2(s)}$, $SO_4{}^{2-}{}_{(aq)}$, and $H^+_{(aq)}$) or as RAs (for example, $H_{2(g)}$ and $OH^-_{(aq)}$; $H_2SO_{3(aq)}$ and $H_2O_{(l)}$).

b. Identifying the SOA and SRA

The strongest OA (SOA) in a reaction mixture is the entity in a species list that lies highest on the left side of a reduction half-reaction table.

The strongest RA (SRA) in a reaction mixture is the entity in a species list that is lowest on the right side of a reduction half-reaction table.

c. Tabulated Half-Reactions

The reduction half-reaction of the SOA proceeds as shown in the reduction half-reaction table. The oxidation half-reaction of the SRA is the reverse of the reduction reaction shown in the table.

d. The Reduction-Oxidation

A balanced net reduction-oxidation is made by combining multiples of the oxidation and the reduction half-reactions such that the number of electrons lost/gained is the same.

Related Questions: NR1, 12, 15, NR6, 25, 34, WR2

4. Balancing Skeletal Oxidation–Reduction Equations

a. identifying oxidation state in chemical species

b. balancing equation in acidic medium

c. balancing equation in basic medium

a. Oxidation Numbers (ONs)

Students must know how to assign the ON of an atom in any ionic compound, molecule, or polyatomic ion by using simple algebra and the common ONs of O, H, halogens, elements and monotonic ions. For example, what are the ONs of all the atoms in lead (II) chromate, $PbCrO_{4(s)}$? Answer: $PbCro_{4(s)}$ is Pb^{2+} and $CrO_4{}^{2-}$ $ON_{Pb} = +2$.

In $CrO_4{}^{2-}$, $ON_0 = -2(common)$ and thus $ON_{Cr} - 8 = -2$, so $ON_{Cr} = +6$.

b. i. Balancing Reduction–Oxidation Equations with ONs (Acid Solution)

The numeric increase in ON of a reactant atom is the number of e^- lost by that atom in the SRA. The numeric decrease in ON of a reactant atom is the number of e^- gained by that atom in the SOA.

Once the stoichiometric ratio of the SOA/SRA is adjusted to make e^- lost = e^- gained, $H_2O_{(l)}$ and $H^+_{(aq)}$ are added as necessary to balance the oxidation–reduction equation.

For example, balance the following equation in acidic solution, using oxidation numbers:

$$Cl^-{}_{(aq)} + VO_4{}^{-3}{}_{(aq)} + I^-{}_{(aq)} \rightarrow ICl_{(aq)} + VO^{2+}{}_{(aq)}$$

$$-\overset{-1}{Cl^-}{}_{(aq)} + \overset{+5}{V}O_4{}^{3-}{}_{(aq)} + \overset{-1}{I^-}{}_{(aq)} \rightarrow \overset{+1}{I}\overset{-1}{Cl}_{(aq)} + \overset{+4}{V}O^{2+}{}_{(aq)}$$

$$-\overset{-1}{Cl^-}{}_{(aq)} + \underset{gain\,1e^-/VO_4^{3-}}{\overset{+5}{V}O_4{}^{3-}{}_{(aq)}} + I^-{}_{(aq)} \rightarrow \overset{+1}{I}\overset{-1}{Cl}_{(aq)} + \overset{+4}{V}O^{2+}{}_{(aq)}$$

$$-\overset{-1}{Cl^-}{}_{(aq)} + \underset{gain\,1e^-/VO_4^{3-}}{\overset{+5}{V}O_4{}^{3-}{}_{(aq)}} + \underset{loss\,2e^-/I^-}{I^-{}_{(aq)}} \rightarrow \overset{+1}{I}\overset{-1}{Cl}_{(aq)} + \overset{+4}{V}O^{2+}{}_{(aq)}$$

$$-\overset{-1}{Cl^-}{}_{(aq)} + \underset{\substack{gain\,1e^-/VO_4^{3-}\\ \times 2}}{\overset{+5}{V}O_4^{3-}{}_{(aq)}} + \underset{\substack{loss\,2e^-/I^-\\ \times 1}}{I^-{}_{(aq)}} \rightarrow \overset{+1}{I}\overset{-1}{Cl}_{(aq)} + \overset{+4}{V}O^{2+}{}_{(aq)}$$

$$-Cl^-{}_{(aq)} + 2VO_4{}^{-3}{}_{(aq)} + I^-{}_{(aq)} \rightarrow ICl_{(aq)} + 2VO^{2+}{}_{(aq)}$$

$$-Cl^-{}_{(aq)} + 2VO^{3-}{}_{(aq)} + I^-{}_{(aq)} + 12H^+{}_{(aq)} \rightarrow$$

$$ICl_{(aq)} + 2VO^{2+}{}_{(aq)} + 6H_2O_{(l)}$$

Copyright Protected

ii. Balancing Reduction–Oxidation Equations by Making Half-Reactions (Acid Solution)

The obvious halves of a skeletal reaction are balanced separately for the core atoms using whole numbers: O is balanced with $H_2O_{(l)}$, H is balanced with $H^+_{(aq)}$, and charges are balanced with e^-.

The net equation comes from recombining whole multiples of the balanced half-reactions such that e^- lost = e^- gained.

For example, balance the following in acidic solution by making half-reactions:

$$CH_3CH_2NO_{2(aq)} + Ti^{3+}{}_{(aq)} \rightarrow CH_3CH_2NH_{2(aq)} + Ti^{4+}{}_{(aq)}$$

$$— \begin{Bmatrix} Ti^{3+}{}_{(aq)} \times Ti^{4+}{}_{(aq)} \\ CH_3CH_2NO_{2(aq)} \times CH_3CH_2NH_{2(aq)} \end{Bmatrix}$$

$$— \begin{Bmatrix} Ti^{3+}{}_{(aq)} \rightarrow Ti^{4+}{}_{(aq)} \\ CH_3CH_2NO_{2(aq)} \rightarrow \\ CH_3CH_2NH_{2(aq)} + 2H_2O_{(l)} \end{Bmatrix}$$

$$— \begin{Bmatrix} Ti^{3+}{}_{(aq)} \rightarrow Ti^{4+}{}_{(aq)} \\ CH_3CH_2NO_{2(aq)} + 6H^+{}_{(aq)} \rightarrow \\ CH_3CH_2NH_{2(aq)} + 2H_2O_{(l)} \end{Bmatrix}$$

$$— \begin{Bmatrix} Ti^{3+}{}_{(aq)} \rightarrow \\ CH_3CH_2NO_{2(aq)} + 6H^+{}_{(aq)} + 6e^- \rightarrow \end{Bmatrix}$$

$$\begin{matrix} Ti^{4+}{}_{(aq)} + e^- \\ CH_3CH_2NH_{2(aq)} + 2H_2O_{(l)} \end{matrix} \Bigg\}$$

$$— 6Ti^{3+}{}_{(aq)} + CH_3CH_2NO_{2(aq)} + 6H^+{}_{(aq)} \rightarrow 6Ti^{4+}{}_{(aq)} + CH_3CH_2NH_{2(aq)} + 2H_2O_{(l)}$$

c. Balancing Reduction–Oxidation Equations in Basic Solution

Typically, we balance the reduction-oxidation reaction in acid solution and then add sufficient $OH^-{}_{(aq)}$ to both sides of the equation to remove all the $H^+{}_{(aq)}$ on the reactant or product side. For example, the unbalanced equation

$$MnO_4{}^-{}_{(aq)} + CH_3OH \rightarrow MnO_4{}^{2-}{}_{(aq)} + CO_3{}^{2-}{}_{(aq)}$$

balanced in acid solution gives

$$6MnO_4{}^-{}_{(aq)} + CH_3OH_{(aq)} + 2H_2O_{(l)} \rightarrow 6MnO_4{}^{2-}{}_{(aq)} + CO_3{}^{2-}{}_{(aq)} + 8H^+{}_{(aq)}$$

and balanced in basic solution gives

$$6MnO_4{}^-{}_{(aq)} + CH_3OH_{(aq)} + 8OH^-{}_{(aq)} \rightarrow 6MnO_4{}^{2-}{}_{(aq)} + CO_3{}^{2-}{}_{(aq)} + 6H_2O_{(l)}$$

Related Questions: 4, 7, 13, NR5, 19, 20, 26, 32, 33

Not for Reproduction

5. Solution Stoichiometry

a. stoichiometry

b. redox titration (lab 2: acidified permanganate and dichromate solution)

a. Solution Stoichiometry

Students must be able to construct a balanced reduction-oxidation reaction equation and use it to calculate reactant/product quantities such as mass, solution volume, solution concentration, and gas volume. (For example, what is the concentration of a 10.0 mL sample of $H_2O_{2(aq)}$ that requires 13.2 mL of 8.00 mmol/L $KMnO_{4(aq)}$ for complete reaction under acidic conditions?

The balanced equation is (table methods):

$$2MnO_4{}^-{}_{(aq)} + 6H^+{}_{(aq)} + 5H_2O_{2(aq)} \rightarrow$$
$$2Mn^{2+}{}_{(aq)} + 5O_{2(g)} + 8H_2O_{(l)}$$

$$n_{MnO_4^-} = 13.2\text{ mL} \times 0.00800\frac{\text{mol}}{\text{L}} = 0.106\text{ mmol}$$

$$n_{H_2O_2} = \frac{5}{2} n_{MnO_4^-}$$
$$= \frac{5}{2} \times 0.106\text{ mmol} = 0.264\text{ mmol}$$

$$[H_2O_{(aq)}] = \frac{0.264\text{ mmol}}{10.0\text{ mL}}$$
$$= 0.0264\frac{\text{mol}}{\text{L}}\left(\text{or } 26.4\frac{\text{mmol}}{\text{L}}\right)$$

b. Titration Analysis

Students must be able to design, perform, write procedures for, analyze, and evaluate redox titration analyses of oxidizing and reducing agents. It is important to know that reagents like permanganate and dichromate, in the appropriate concentrations, are self-indicating at the endpoint of the reaction. Indicators are used in many reduction–oxidation titrations. They tend to be suitable oxidizing or reducing agents that change colour dramatically when they react with one drop of excess titrant (the reagent in the burette).

Related Questions: NR3, NR4

6. Electrochemical Cells

a. electrochemical cells (anode, cathode etc)

b. oxidation potentials and reduction potentials: standard potential & conditions

c. electrolytic cells

i. competing for reaction with enough voltage in an actual electrolysis

d. molten cells

i. bauxite electrolysis

e. commercial cells

a. *i. Cells in general*

All cells contain two solid electrodes separated by an electrically conducting medium—the electrolyte. The electrodes may be any solid conductive material, while the electrolyte can be an aqueous solution, a paste, or, in some new applications, a solid (ceramic or polymer).

The anode is the electrode at which oxidation occurs, while the cathode is the electrode at which reduction occurs. In the external electrical circuit, electrons flow from the anode to the cathode. Under the influence of the electric field across the electrolyte, anions migrate to the anode through the electrolyte and cations migrate to the cathode.

ii. Voltaic Cells

These cells host spontaneous reactions that convert chemical energy into electrical energy. The standard net potential (E°_{net}) of such cells is positive.

A porous barrier between the two electrodes, within the cell, prevents unnecessary side reactions.

iii. Electrolytic Cells

Non-spontaneous reaction is driven in these cells by an applied potential that is the same or bigger than the magnitude of the negative net cell potential of the cell. A porous barrier between the two electrodes, within the cell, may be employed to prevent reaction of the cell products but it is not always necessary.

Copyright Protected

b. The Standard Cell Potential E°_{net}

- The standard potential of a cell is given by $E^{\circ}_{net} = E^{\circ}_{RC} - E^{\circ}_{RA}$
- E°_{net} = net cell potential under standard conditions
- E°_{RC} = the cathode reduction potential under standard conditions
- E°_{RA} = the anode reduction potential under standard conditions
- If any two of E°_{net}, E°_{RC}, or E°_{RA} are known, the third may be calculated by simple substitution. Using tabulated reduction potentials, it is possible to calculate the E°_{net} of almost any reduction oxidation reaction.

Standard conditions are present when all the solid and gaseous cell components are in their standard states at 25°C and 100 kPa, and all aqueous solutions are 1.0 mol/L. The electrode reduction potentials are measured relative to the standard hydrogen electrode (S.H.E., $Pt_{(s)} / H_{2(g)}, H^{+}_{(aq)}$ $E^{\circ}_{R} = 0.00$ V).

c. Electrolytic Cells

These cells are employed to prepare many elements/compounds on a large scale. For example, the Chlor-Alkali cell is used to produce $Cl_{2(aq)}$, $H_{2(g)}$, and $NaOH_{(aq)}$ from the electrolysis of $NaCl_{(aq)}$.

The Downs Cell is used to produce alkali metals (for example, $Na_{(s)}$) from the electrolysis of molten salts.

The Hall-Heroult cell is used to produce $Al_{(l)}$ from the electrolysis of $Al_{(2)}O_{3(s)}$ dissolved in molten $Na_3AlF_{6(l)}$ (cryolete).

Electrolysis is used to produce ultrapure $Cu_{(s)}$ from $CuSO_{4(aq)}$.

Electroplating of many objects with $Sn_{(s)}$, $Ni_{(s)}$, and $Cr_{(s)}$ is accomplished in electrolytic cells containing the appropriate electrolyte.

Electrolysis of brine solution is a new means of chlorinating some swimming pools; it is called salt water chlorination.

d. Commercial Voltaic Cells

Most commercial cells do not operate with standard solutions. Students must be able to identify the anode/cathode half-reactions and/or the anode/cathode materials in any simple commercial cell. Rechargeable batteries/cells (or secondary cells) are voltaic and electrolytic cells (voltaic when they produce energy and electrolytic when they are recharged). Fuel cells are voltaic cells that operate with a continuous supply of oxidizing and reducing agents (for example, the oxygen/hydrogen fuel cell).

Related Questions: 1, 2, 5, 8, NR2, 14, 21, 23, 24, NR8, 28, WR1, 36, 37, 38, 40, 41, 42, NR11, NR12, WR2

7. Faraday's Law and Electrical Energy

a. predicting mass, time, or electric current

b. electrical energy

Cell Factors

The number of moles of electrons transferred in any cell is directly proportional to the cell current I (in amperes or Coulombs/second) and the duration of cell operation t (in seconds) such that $n_{e^-} = \frac{It}{F}$, where F is the charge carried by one mole of electrons, 9.65×10^4 Coulombs/mol.

Not for Reproduction

With the appropriate half-reaction, it is possible to calculate the mass of reactants/products involved during cell operation. (e.g., What mass of chromium from a Cr(III) aqueous solution could be plated on a car bumper in a time of 5.00 minutes with a current of 4 500 ampere?

$$Cr^{3+}_{(aq)} + 3e^- \rightarrow Cr_{(s)}$$

$$n_{e^-} = \frac{4\ 500\ \text{C/s} \times (5.00 \times 60)\text{s}}{9.65 \times 10^4\ \text{C/mol}} = 14.0\ \text{mol}$$

$$n_{\text{Cr}} = \frac{1}{3} n_{e^-} = \frac{1}{3} \times 14.0\ \text{mol} = 4.66\ \text{mol}$$

$$m_{\text{Cr}} = 4.66\ \text{mol} \times 52.00 \frac{\text{g}}{\text{mol}} = 242\ \text{g}$$

Some 242 g of $Cr_{(s)}$ would plate onto the bumper.

Related Questions: 16, NR7, 30, NR10, WR2

8. Cathodic and Anode Protection and Rust Prevention

a. sacrificial anode

b. impressed current

When exposed to the principle oxidizing agents in the environment ($O_{2(g)}$ and $H_2O_{(l)}$, $O_{2(g)}$ and $H^+_{(aq)}$), some parts of large iron objects become anodic. If iron is anodic, it corrodes, and rust is the product of this corrosion. Three methods are employed to combat rust and corrosion:

a. Coatings

Iron is coated in grease, oil, paint, or other metals to prevent the attack of environmental oxidizing agents. Many metals that successfully protect iron, either as a coating or, in some cases, when alloyed with iron, do so by forming tough/durable oxide coats that protect against all further environmental attack, if left intact. This process is called *passivation*.

b. Sacrificial Anodes

$Zn_{(s)}$ or $Mg_{(s)}$ blocks, when attached directly to large iron structures, become preferentially oxidized, and in doing so, direct e^- into the $Fe_{(s)}$, thereby making it cathodic and less likely to corrode.

c. Impressed Currents

Buried iron pipelines are made cathodic by directing electric currents into them at various points along their length. Once again, iron that is cathodic is less likely to corrode. The anode of a car battery is grounded to the bodywork to provide this kind of protection.

Related Questions: 9, 10, 35

9. Combination Redox / Acid-Base / Equilibrium / Thermodynamics topics

a. Heat energy and electrical energy

b. Acid–base reaction and electrochemical reactions

c. Safety concerns

a. Thermodynamics

From an energetics perspective, voltaic cells are akin to exothermic reactions, while electrolytic cells are much like endothermic reactions. Many redox reactions release heat in aqueous solution (for example, $Cu_{(s)} + Zn(NO_3)_{2(aq)}$ or $Mg_{(s)} + HCl_{(aq)}$).

b. Acid–base Topics

Many reduction–oxidation reactions are possible only in the presence of excess acid or base. Therefore, increases/decreases in pH often accompany many complex reduction oxidation reactions.

Equilibrium

The operating voltaic cell contains a reduction–oxidation reaction that is very far from equilibrium. Energy is released as the cell approaches equilibrium, which is met when the cell potential falls to zero volts.

Copyright Protected

c. Safety Concerns

Oxidation–reduction reactions can occur in various situations that pose a threat to public safety. For example,

- when metal foil/cutlery touch dental fillings
- when different metals are in contact in a metal structure
- when iron structures are inadequately protected from environmental oxidizing agents

Related Questions: 3, 22, 27, 29, 31

Use the following information to answer the next two questions.

Novacor is a large international company that produces ethene ($C_2H_{4(g)}$) from ethane ($C_2H_{6(g)}$) at its plant in Joffre, Alberta. The essential process in the conversion of ethane to ethene is called cracking, which involves the removal of hydrogen atoms from ethane molecules. The cracking occurs in special alloy pipes at temperatures near 1 100°C. The process results in the formation of ethene and other byproducts.

Novacor obtains caustic soda solution from a company that electrolyzes brine ($NaCl_{(aq)}$).

CHALLENGER QUESTION **DIFFICULTY 36.2**

1. The primary reaction that occurs at the anode during the electrolysis of $NaCl_{(aq)}$ is

A. $2H_2O_{(l)} + 2e^- \rightarrow H_{2(g)} + 2OH^-_{(aq)}$

B. $Na^+_{(aq)} + e^- \rightarrow Na_{(s)}$

C. $2Cl^-_{(aq)} \rightarrow Cl_{2(g)} + 2e^-$

D. $2H_2O_{(l)} \rightarrow 4\ H^+_{(aq)} + O_{2(g)} + 4e^-$

Source: January 2000

Use your recorded answer from ***Multiple Choice 1*** *to answer* ***Multiple Choice 2.***

CHALLENGER QUESTION **DIFFICULTY 55.7**

2. A small sample of the anode product is tested. The predicted test result is that

A. a glowing splint will reignite

B. red litmus paper will turn white

C. red litmus paper will turn blue

D. the product will react vigorously with water

Source: January 2000

Use the following information to answer the next question.

A breathalyzer contains a reference ampoule and a test ampoule, each containing acidified potassium dichromate solution. As alcohol in a person's breath is exhaled into the breathalyzer, the test ampoule solution changes colour. This reaction is represented by the **unbalanced** equation

$$Cr_2O_7{}^{2-}{}_{(aq)} + C_2H_5OH_{(l)} + H^+_{(aq)} \rightarrow Cr^{3+}_{(aq)} + H_2O_{(l)} + CH_3COOH_{(aq)}$$

CHALLENGER QUESTION **DIFFICULTY 46.1**

3. When alcohol reacts in the test ampoule, the pH of the solution

A. remains the same

B. decreases as $H^+_{(aq)}$ is consumed

C. increases as $H^+_{(aq)}$ is consumed

D. decreases as $CH_3COOH_{(aq)}$ is produced

Source: January 2000

Not for Reproduction

Use the following information to answer the next question.

Ethanol reacts with acidified permanganate ion, as represented by the equation

$$5C_2H_5OH_{(l)} + 4MnO_4^-{}_{(aq)} + 12H^+{}_{(aq)} \rightarrow 5CH_3COOH_{(aq)} + 4Mn^{2+}{}_{(aq)} + 11H_2O_{(l)}$$

4. In this reaction, the oxidation number for the oxidizing agent changes from

A. +7 to +2 **B.** +28 to +8

C. +2 to 0 **D.** +10 to 0

Source: January 2000

5. In a voltaic cell, there is a conversion of

A. chemical energy to electrical energy in a spontaneous change

B. chemical energy to electrical energy in a non-spontaneous change

C. electrical energy to chemical energy in a spontaneous change

D. electrical energy to chemical energy in a non-spontaneous change

Source: January 2000

6. Which of the following reducing agents is the strongest?

A. $I^-{}_{(aq)}$

B. $Br_{2(l)}$

C. $H_2O_{(l)}$

D. $Al_{(s)}$

Source: January 2000

Use the following equations to answer the next question.

1 $Fe^{2+}{}_{(aq)} + Cr^{3+}{}_{(aq)} \rightarrow Fe^{3+}{}_{(aq)} + Cr^{2+}{}_{(aq)}$

2 $NH_{3(aq)} + H_2O_{(l)} \rightarrow NH_4^+{}_{(aq)} + OH^-{}_{(aq)}$

3 $2NH_{3(g)} + \frac{7}{2}O_{2(g)} \rightarrow 2NO_{2(g)} + 3H_2O_{(g)}$

4 $Mg^{2+}{}_{(aq)} + 2\ OH^-{}_{(aq)} \rightarrow Mg(OH)_{2(s)}$

5 $Sn^{2+}{}_{(aq)} + 2NO_3^-{}_{(aq)} + 4H^+{}_{(aq)} \rightarrow Sn^{4+}{}_{(aq)} + 2NO_{2(g)} + 2H_2O$

6 $PbSO_{4(s)} + SO_3^{2-}{}_{(aq)} + 2OH^-{}_{(aq)} \rightarrow H_2O_{(l)} + Pb_{(s)} + 2SO_4^{2-}{}_{(aq)}$

CHALLENGER QUESTION **DIFFICULTY 23.7**

Numerical Response

1. The equations that represent oxidation-reduction reactions, listed in any order, are ____ , ____ , ____ , and ____ .

Source: January 2000

7. The oxidation number of Mo in $CaMoO_{4(s)}$ is

A. +2

B. +4

C. +6

D. −2

Source: January 2000

Copyright Protected

Use the following information to answer the next three questions.

Corrosion of iron costs the public millions of dollars annually. The corrosion process can be simply represented by two half-reactions:

$$Fe_{(s)} \rightarrow Fe^{2+}{}_{(aq)} + 2e^{-}$$

$$O_{2(g)} + 2H_2O_{(l)} + 4e^{-} \rightarrow 4OH^{-}{}_{(aq)}$$

The $\Phi\varepsilon(OH)_{2(\sigma)}$ that forms is further oxidized by $O_{2(\gamma)}$ in the presence of water to form rust, a mixture of hydrated oxides that is represented by the general formula $Fe_2O_3 \times H_2O_{(\sigma)}$. One region on the iron surface acts as the anode, and another region, where the wet iron is exposed to oxygen, acts as the cathode.

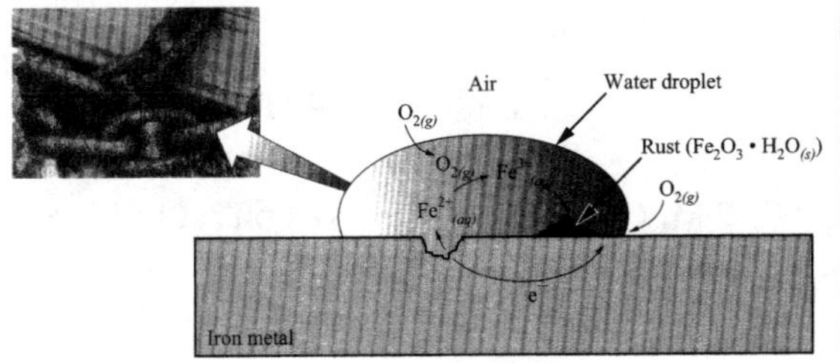

—from John McMurry and Robert C. Fay, 1995

8. Under standard conditions, the net voltage for the oxidation–reduction reaction that results in the formation of $Fe(OH)_{2(s)}$ is

A. −0.85 V

B. +0.85 V

C. −1.30 V

D. +1.30 V

Source: January 2000

9. Iron is often alloyed with zinc to minimize corrosion. The zinc in the alloy acts as the

A. anode and is oxidized

B. anode and is reduced

C. cathode and is oxidized

D. cathode and is reduced

Source: January 2000

10. Salt spread on highways during the winter months increases the rate of rust formation on cars because the salt

A. reacts with the rust to form iron salts

B. reacts with the iron salts to form iron

C. increases the conductivity of the electrolyte solution

D. decreases the conductivity of the electrolyte solution

Source: January 2000

Numerical Response

2. Under standard conditions, hydrogen gas reacts with $Au^{3+}{}_{(aq)}$ ions to produce $Au_{(s)}$. The net cell potential for the reaction is +/–____ V. (Record your **three-digit** answer.)

Source: January 2000

Not for Reproduction

Use the following information to answer the next question.

The reactions below involve hypothetical metals and metallic ions.

Reaction	Observation
$Z^{3+}{}_{(aq)} + X_{(s)}$	no evidence of reaction
$X^{2+}{}_{(aq)} + D_{(s)}$	evidence of reaction
$D^{+}{}_{(aq)} + A_{(s)}$	evidence of reaction
$Z^{3+}{}_{(aq)} + D_{(s)}$	no evidence of reaction
$A^{2+}{}_{(aq)} + Z_{(s)}$	no evidence of reaction

11. The order of oxidizing agents, from strongest to weakest, is

A. $X^{2+}{}_{(aq)}, Z^{3+}{}_{(aq)}, A^{2+}{}_{(aq)}, D^{+}{}_{(aq)}$

B. $A^{2+}{}_{(aq)}, Z^{3+}{}_{(aq)}, D^{+}{}_{(aq)}, X^{2+}{}_{(aq)}$

C. $Z^{3+}{}_{(aq)}, X^{2+}{}_{(aq)}, A^{2+}{}_{(aq)}, D^{+}{}_{(aq)}$

D. $X^{2+}{}_{(aq)}, D^{+}{}_{(aq)}, Z^{3+}{}_{(aq)}, A^{2+}{}_{(aq)}$

Source: January 2000

Use the following information to answer the next three questions.

Titration of 20.0 mL Samples of Acidified $H_2O_{2(l)}$ with 0.15 mol/L $KMnO_{4(aq)}$

Trial	I	II	III	IV
Final buret volume (mL)	18.3	34.6	17.4	33.8
Initial buret volume (mL)	0.4	18.3	0.9	17.4
Colour at endpoint	purple	pink	pink	pink

12. The balanced equation for the titration is

A. $2\,MnO_4{}^-{}_{(aq)} + 16H^+{}_{(aq)} + 5\,H_2O_{2(l)} \rightarrow 2\,Mn^{2+}{}_{(aq)} + 8\,H_2O_{(l)} + 5O_{2(g)}$

B. $2\,MnO_4{}^-{}_{(aq)} + 6\,H^+{}_{(aq)} + 5\,H_2O_{2(l)} \rightarrow 2\,Mn^{2+}{}_{(aq)} + 4\,H_2O_{(l)} + O_{2(g)}$

C. $2\,MnO_4{}^-{}_{(aq)} + 6\,H^+{}_{(aq)} + 5\,H_2O_{2(l)} \rightarrow 2\,Mn^{2+}{}_{(aq)} + 3\,H_2O_{(l)} + 5O_{2(g)}$

D. $2\,MnO_4{}^-{}_{(aq)} + 6\,H^+{}_{(aq)} + 5\,H_2O_{2(l)} \rightarrow 2\,Mn^{2+}{}_{(aq)} + 8\,H_2O_{(l)} + 5O_{2(g)}$

Source: January 2000

Numerical Response

3. The volume of potassium permanganate that should be used in subsequent calculations is ____ mL.
(Record your **three-digit** answer.)

Source: January 2000

Copyright Protected

*Use your recorded answer from **Numerical Response 3** to answer **Numerical Response 4**.**

CHALLENGER QUESTION DIFFICULTY 54.5

Numerical Response

4. The hydrogen peroxide concentration is ____ mol/L.
(Record your **three-digit** answer.)

Source: January 2000

13. A redox reaction in which carbon is reduced is

A. $6\ H_2O_{(l)} + 6\ CO_{2(g)} \rightarrow C_6H_{12}O_{6(aq)} + 6\ O_{2(g)}$

B. $HCO_3^-{}_{(aq)} + H_3O^+{}_{(aq)} \rightarrow H_2CO_{3(aq)} + H_2O_{(g)}$

C. $CH_{4(g)} + 2\ O_{2(g)} \rightarrow CO_{2(g)} + 2\ H_2O_{(g)}$

D. $C_6H_{12}O_{6(aq)} + 6O_{2(g)} \rightarrow 6\ CO_{2(g)} + 6H_2O_{(l)}$

Source: June 2000

Use the following information to answer the next question.

Superphénix, a nuclear "breeder" reactor in Lyon, France, was shutdown for repair in the late 1980s after a liquid sodium leak. The liquid sodium was used as a coolant in the reactor.

CHALLENGER QUESTION DIFFICULTY 57.1

14. The liquid sodium used in the reactor can be produced by the electrolysis of molten $NaCl_{(l)}$. During this electrolysis,

A. sodium ions are reduced at the anode

B. oxygen gas is produced at the cathode

C. chloride ions migrate toward the anode

D. the pH around the cathode increases

Source: June 2000

Numerical Response

5. When the redox reaction

$$\_H_2O_{(l)} + \_NO_2^-{}_{(aq)} + \_Al_{(s)} \rightarrow \_NH_{3(g)} + \_AlO_2^-{}_{(aq)} + \_H^+{}_{(aq)}$$

is balanced using lowest whole number coefficients, the coefficient of

$H_2O_{(l)}$ is ______ $NO_2^-{}_{(aq)}$ is ________

$Al_{(s)}$ is ______ $H^+{}_{(aq)}$ is ________

Source: June 2000

Use the following information to answer the next three questions.

Leaching technology is used in the mining and refining of copper core. In the first step of the leaching process, sulphuric acid flows through a copper ore deposit. Under ideal conditions, the copper metal in the ore reacts with the concentrated sulphuric acid to form copper(II) ions. The resulting copper(II) slurry is transferred to an electrolytic cell where pure copper is produced. (Assume that the sulphuric acid completely ionizes to hydrogen ions and sulphate ions.)

15. A non-spontaneous reaction may occur if the concentrations are manipulated. The balanced net ionic equation for the reaction of copper metal with sulphuric acid under these ideal conditions is

A. $Cu_{(s)} + SO_4^{2-}{}_{(aq)} + 4H^+{}_{(aq)} \rightarrow Cu^{2+}{}_{(aq)} + H_2SO_{3(aq)} + H_2O_{(l)}$

B. $Cu^{2+}{}_{(aq)} + H_2S_{(aq)} \rightarrow Cu_{(s)} + 2H^+{}_{(aq)} + S_{(s)}$

C. $Cu_{(s)} + H_2S_{(aq)} \rightarrow Cu^{2+}{}_{(aq)} + H_{2(g)} + S^{2-}{}_{(aq)}$

D. $Cu_{(s)} + 2H^+{}_{(aq)} \rightarrow Cu^{2+}{}_{(aq)} + H_{2(g)}$

Source: June 2000

Not for Reproduction

CHALLENGER QUESTION **DIFFICULTY 49.8**

16. What mass of pure copper is produced from the electrolysis of excess copper(II) ions over a 24.0 h period when the cell is operated at 100 A?

A. 2.84 kg **B.** 5.69 kg

C. 11.4 kg **D.** 549 kg

Source: June 2000

17. The net ionic equation for the conversion of copper(II) oxide in copper ore is
$CuO_{(s)} + 2H^{+}{}_{(aq)} \rightarrow Cu^{2+}{}_{(aq)} + H_2O_{(l)}$
The copper in the copper(II) oxide is

A. reduced

B. oxidized

C. the oxidizing agent

D. neither oxidized nor reduced

Source: June 2000

Use the following information to answer the next two questions.

In order to "hide" gold during the Second World War, Nobel Prize winner Neils Bohr "dissolved" the gold, stored it in a solution, and recovered it at the end of the war.

One way to "dissolve" gold is to react it with *Aqua-Regia*, a mixture of nitric and hydrochloric acids. The unbalanced equation for this reaction is

$$Au_{(s)} + HNO_{3(aq)} + HCl_{(aq)} \rightarrow HAuCl_{4(aq)} + H_2O_{(l)} + NO_{2(g)}$$

18. The atom that undergoes reduction in this reaction is

A. Au **B.** H

C. N **D.** Cl

Source: June 2000

CHALLENGER QUESTION **DIFFICULTY 57.8**

19. When this equation is balanced using lowest whole number coefficients, the coefficient for nitric acid is

A. 2 **B.** 3

C. 4 **D.** 5

Source: June 2000

Copyright Protected

Use the following information to answer the next question.

ICCP (Impressed Current Cathodic Protection) is a corrosion prevention technique that is used to protect buried metal structures. A low-voltage current (electron flow) is applied to the buried metal structure such that only reduction reactions can occur at its surface.

Numerical Response

6. The ground water surrounding the buried metal structure may contain the following ions.

1	$Pb^{2+}{}_{(aq)}$
2	$Fe^{2+}{}_{(aq)}$
3	$Fe^{3+}{}_{(aq)}$
4	$Cd^{2+}{}_{(aq)}$

The order in which these ions are reduced on the surface of the metal structure is________, ________ ,________ and ________ .

Source: June 2000

20. The chemical reaction in which a single species is both oxidized and reduced is known as disproportionation. An example of this type of reaction is

A. $2NH_{3(aq)} + NaOCl_{(aq)} \rightarrow N_2H_{4(aq)} + NaCl_{(aq)} + H_2O_{(l)}$

B. $Cl_{2(aq)} + H_2O_{(l)} \rightarrow HOCl_{(aq)} + H^+{}_{(aq)} + Cl^-{}_{(aq)}$

C. $2F_{2(g)} + O_{2(g)} \rightarrow 2OF_{2(g)}$

D. $2Na_{(s)} + I_{2(s)} \rightarrow 2NaI_{(s)}$

Source: June 2000

21. In the Hall–Heroult process, aluminum is produced by the electrolysis of molten $Al_2O_{3(l)}$. The half-reactions that occur are:

$$C_{(s)} + 2O^{2-}{}_{(l)} \rightarrow CO_{2(g)} + 4e^-$$
$$Al^{3+}{}_{(l)} + 3e^- \rightarrow Al_{(l)}$$

The mass of $Al_{(l)}$ produced for each 1.00 kg of $C_{(s)}$ consumed is

A. 1.69 kg **B.** 2.45 kg

C. 3.00 kg **D.** 6.00 kg

Source: June 2000

Use the following information to answer the next question.

The sodium metal in television picture tubes reacts with oxygen that would otherwise oxidize the tungsten and phosphorus found in the tubes. Tungsten and phosphorus are vital to the function of the picture tubes.

Numerical Response

7. The mass of sodium that will react when 0.350 mol of electrons is transferred is ________ g. (Record your **three digit** answer.)

Source: June 2000

Not for Reproduction

Use the following information to answer the next two questions.

When a car is started, the starter motor draws a current from the battery. The battery recharges while the car is running.

22. Before the car is started, the battery's chemical energy is in the form of

A. kinetic energy

B. potential energy

C. vibrational energy

D. translational energy

Source: June 2000

23. A car is started and then left running to recharge the battery. In these two processes, the battery

A. acts as an electrolytic cell only

B. acts as a voltaic cell only

C. first acts as an electrolytic cell, then as a voltaic cell

D. first acts as a voltaic cell, then as an electrolytic cell

Source: June 2000

Use the following information to answer the next question.

A particular voltaic cell is represented by
$Ag_{(s)} / Ag^{+}_{(aq)} // Cr_2O_7^{2-}{}_{(aq)}, Cr^{3+}_{(aq)}, H^{+}_{(aq)} / C_{(s)}$

24. The net ionic equation for this voltaic cell is

A. $6Ag_{(s)} + Cr_2O_7^{2-}{}_{(aq)} + 14H^{+}_{(aq)} \rightarrow 6Ag^{+}_{(aq)} + 2Cr^{3+}_{(aq)} + 7H_2O_{(l)}$

B. $6Ag^{+}_{(aq)} + Cr_2O_7^{2-}{}_{(aq)} + 14H^{+}_{(aq)} \rightarrow 6Ag_{(s)} + 2Cr^{3+}_{(aq)} + 7H_2O_{(l)}$

C. $Ag^{+}_{(aq)} + Cr_2O_7^{2-}{}_{(aq)} + 14H^{+}_{(aq)} \rightarrow Ag_{(s)} + 2Cr^{3+}_{(aq)} + 7H_2O_{(l)}$

D. $Ag_{(s)} + Cr_2O_7^{2-}{}_{(aq)} + 14H^{+}_{(aq)} \rightarrow Ag^{+}_{(aq)} + 2Cr^{3+}_{(aq)} + 7H_2O_{(l)}$

Source: June 2000

Use the following information to answer the next question.

An Electrochemical Cell

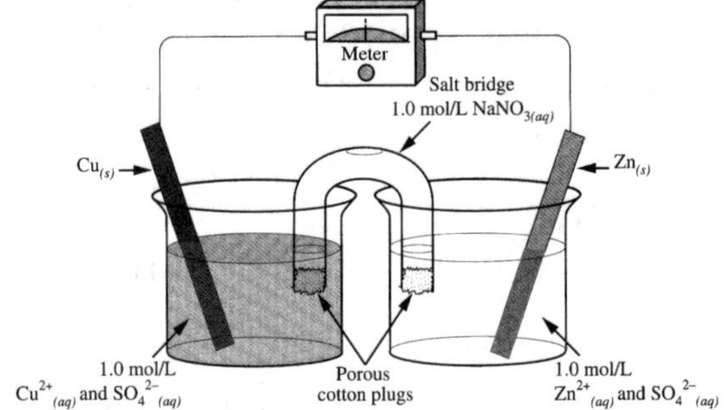

Numerical Response

8. A student attempted to replicate a traditional Daniell Cell by setting up the electrochemical cell shown above. Under standard conditions, the electrical potential of the cell should be +/– ________ V.
(Record your **three-digit** answer.)

Source: June 2000

Use the following information to answer the next two questions.

Voltaic cells are used as portable sources of electrical energy. One common cell is the rechargeable nickel-cadmium cell.

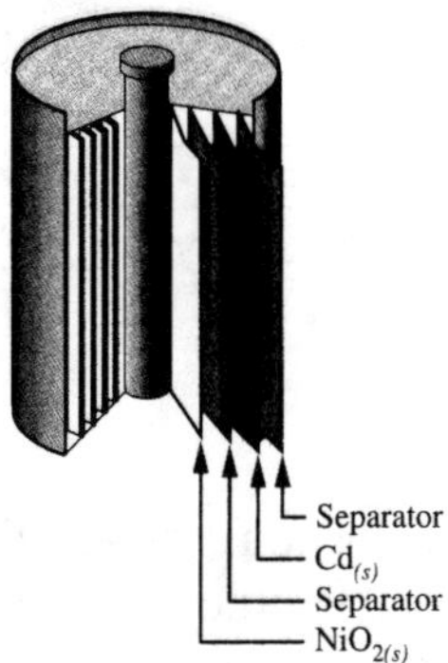

The equation representing the discharge of this cell is

$$NiO_{2(s)} + Cd_{(s)} + 2H_2O_{(l)} \rightarrow Cd(OH)_{2(s)} + Ni(OH)_{2(s)}$$

25. The oxidation half-reaction for the discharge of this cell is

A. $Cd_{(s)} + 2\ OH^-_{(aq)} \rightarrow Cd(OH)_{2(s)} + 2\ e^-$

B. $NiO_{2(s)} + 2\ H_2O_{(l)} + 2\ e^- \rightarrow Ni(OH)_{2(s)} + 2\ OH^-_{(aq)}$

C. $NiO_{2(s)} + 2H_2O_{(l)} \rightarrow Ni(OH)_{2(s)} + 2OH^-_{(aq)} + 2e^-$

D. $Cd_{(s)} + 2\ OH^-_{(aq)} + 2\ e^- \rightarrow Cd(OH)_{2(s)}$

Source: June 2000

CHALLENGER QUESTION **DIFFICULTY 55.1**

26. In this system, the strongest oxidizing agent is

A. $NiO_{2(s)}$

B. $Cd_{(s)}$

C. $Cd(OH)_{2(s)}$

D. $H_2O_{(l)}$

Source: June 2000

Not for Reproduction

Use the following information to answer the next two questions.

Voltaic Cell

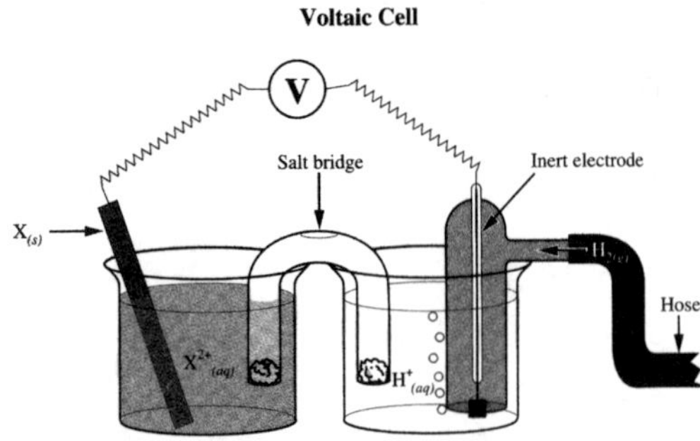

In this apparatus, the anions in the solution move from the hydrogen half-cell solution into the salt bridge and migrate toward the $X_{(s)}$ electrodes.

CHALLENGER QUESTION **DIFFICULTY 32.5**

27. As this cell operates, electrons flow from

A. $X_{(s)}$ to the inert electrode and the pH in the hydrogen half-cell increases

B. $X_{(s)}$ to the inert electrode and the pH in the hydrogen half-cell decreases

C. the inert electrode to $X_{(s)}$ and the pH in the hydrogen half-cell increases

D. the inert electrode to $X_{(s)}$ and the pH in the hydrogen half-cell decreases

Source: June 2000

28. If the voltmeter reads +0.45 V under standard conditions, then $X_{(s)}$ is most likely

A. $Ni_{(s)}$

B. $Fe_{(s)}$

C. $Zn_{(s)}$

D. $Mg_{(s)}$

Source: June 2000

Use the following information to answer the next three questions.

Fuel cells used to power electric vehicles are high-efficiency voltaic cells that consume conventional fuels under conditions of controlled combustion. The half-reactions that occur in a propane-oxygen fuel cell are

$$O_{2(g)} + 4H^+_{(aq)} + 4e^- \rightarrow 2H_2O_{(l)}$$

$$C_3H_{8(g)} + 6H_2O_{(l)} \rightarrow 3CO_{2(g)} + 20H^+_{(aq)} + 20e^-$$

29. The balanced net equation and the predicted energy released per mole of propane consumed for this fuel cell are, respectively,

A. $C_3H_{8(g)} + 5O_{2(g)} \rightarrow 3\ CO_{2(g)} + 4H_2O_{(l)}$ $\Delta H = -2.219.9$ kJ

B. $C_3H_{8(g)} + 5O_{2(g)} \rightarrow 3CO_{2(g)} + 4H_2O_{(l)}$ $\Delta H = -103.8$ kJ

C. $C_3H_{8(g)} + 5O_{2(g)} \rightarrow 3CO_{2(g)} + 4H_2O_{(l)}$ $\Delta H = -2.043.9$ kJ

D. $C_3H_{8(g)} + O_{2(g)} + 4H_2O_{(l)} \rightarrow 3CO_{2(g)} + 16H^+_{(aq)} + 16e^-$ $\Delta H = +66.5$ kJ

Source: June 2000

Use the following information to answer the next question.

During the operation of a propane-oxygen fuel cell, 15.7 g of gas are consumed at the anode.

30. The number of moles of gas consumed is

A. 9.981 mol

B. 0.693 mol

C. 0.491 mol

D. 0.356 mol

Source: June 2000

Copyright Protected

31. The combustion of propane and cellular respiration are similar processes. The reactions that occur in both processes are

A. exothermic, and carbon is reduced

B. exothermic, and carbon is oxidized

C. endothermic, and carbon is reduced

D. endothermic, and carbon is oxidized

Source: June 2000

Use the following information to answer the next question.

Commercial drain cleaners typically contain sodium hydroxide and aluminum. When the solid cleaner is poured down the drain and water is added, the reaction that occurs is represented by the equation

$$2\,NaOH_{(s)} + 2\,Al_{(s)} + 2\,H_2O_{(l)} \rightarrow 2\,NaAlO_{2(aq)} + 3\,H_{2(g)}$$

$$\Delta H = -850.0\text{ kJ}$$

32. In this reaction, the oxidation number of aluminum changes from

A. 0 to +1

B. 0 to +3

C. +2 to +6

D. +3 to +6

Source: January 2001

Use the following information to answer the next question.

At the Banff Wastewater Treatment plant, bacteria are used to treat organic "sludge" $(CH_2O)_{n(s)}$ in a process called autothermal thermophilic aerobic digestion (ATAD). The digestion of the sludge can be represented by the equation

$$(CH_2O)_{n(s)} + n\,O_{2(g)} \xrightarrow{\text{bacteria}} n\,CO_{2(g)} + n\,H_2O_{(l)} + \text{energy}$$

33. During the digestion process, the carbon in the sludge is

A. reduced

B. oxidized

C. amphoteric

D. precipitated

Source: January 2001

Use the following information to answer the next question.

$$U^{3+}{}_{(aq)} + La_{(s)} \rightarrow La^{3+}{}_{(aq)} + U_{(s)}$$
$$Y^{3+}{}_{(aq)} + U_{(s)} \rightarrow \text{no reaction}$$
$$Y^{3+}{}_{(aq)} + La_{(s)} \rightarrow La^{3+}{}_{(aq)} + Y_{(s)}$$

34. The oxidizing agents above, listed from strongest to weakest, are

A. $U^{3+}{}_{(aq)}, La^{3+}{}_{(aq)}, Y^{3+}{}_{(aq)}$

B. $U^{3+}{}_{(aq)}, Y^{3+}{}_{(aq)}, La^{3+}{}_{(aq)}$

C. $Y^{3+}{}_{(aq)}, U^{3+}{}_{(aq)}, La^{3+}{}_{(aq)}$

D. $U_{(s)}, Y_{(s)}, La_{(s)}$

Source: January 2001

Not for Reproduction

Use the following information to answer the next question.

An acidic solution of nickel(II) nitrate is poured into a tin container.

Chemical Changes

1 does not react
2 is oxidized
3 is reduced
4 reacts but there is no change in its oxidation number

CHALLENGER QUESTION **DIFFICULTY 31.3**

Numerical Response

9. Match each of the chemical changes listed above with the reaction species given below.

tin ________
nitrate ion ________
nickel(II) ion ________
hydrogen ion ________

Source: January 2001

CHALLENGER QUESTION **DIFFICULTY 37.4**

35. If a block of refined copper were selected to serve as a sacrificial anode and if it were bolted onto the iron hull of a ship, one would expect the

A. iron to oxidize $Cl^-_{(aq)}$

B. copper to oxidize before the iron

C. copper to corrode at a faster rate than the iron

D. copper to remain unchanged and the iron to continue to oxidize

Source: January 2001

Use the following information to answer the next four questions.

A chemistry student constructs the cell shown below.

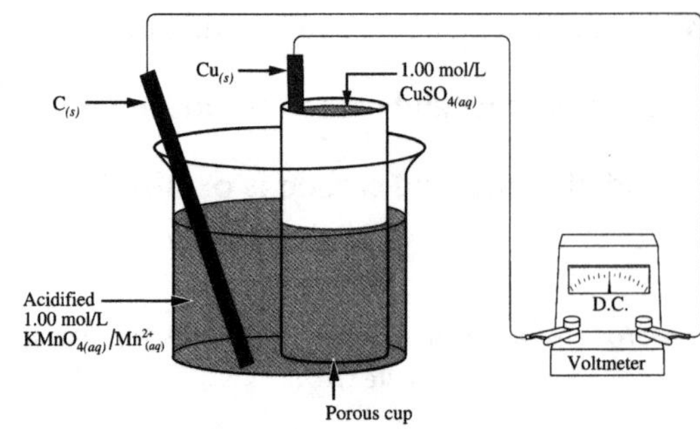

36. The net equation and the predicted voltage for the operating cell are

A. $MnO_4{}^-{}_{(aq)} + 8\,H^+{}_{(aq)} + Cu_{(s)} \rightarrow Mn^{2+}{}_{(aq)} + 4\,H_2O_{(l)} + Cu^{2+}{}_{(aq)}$ $E°_{net} = +1.17\ V$

B. $MnO_4{}^-{}_{(aq)} + 8\,H^+{}_{(aq)} + Cu_{(s)} \rightarrow Mn^{2+}{}_{(aq)} + 4\,H_2O_{(l)} + Cu^{2+}{}_{(aq)}$ $E°_{net} = +1.85\ V$

C. $2\,MnO_4{}^-{}_{(aq)} + 16\,H^+{}_{(aq)} + 5\,Cu_{(s)} \rightarrow 2\,Mn^{2+}{}_{(aq)} + 8\,H_2O_{(l)} + 5\,Cu^{2+}{}_{(aq)}$ $E°_{net} = +1.17\ V$

D. $2\,MnO_4{}^-{}_{(aq)} + 16\,H^+{}_{(aq)} + 5\,Cu_{(s)} \rightarrow 2\,Mn^{2+}{}_{(aq)} + 8\,H_2O_{(l)} + 5\,Cu^{2+}{}_{(aq)}$ $E°_{net} = +\,1.85\ V$

Source: January 2001

Copyright Protected

*Use your recorded answer for **Multiple Choice 36** to answer **Numerical Response 10**.*

CHALLENGER QUESTION **DIFFICULTY 51.6**

Numerical Response

10. During the operation of this cell, if 0.354 mol of $MnO_4^-{}_{(aq)}$ were consumed, then the mass of the copper electrode would decrease by _________ g.
(Record your **three-digit** answer.)

Source: January 2001

37. During the operation of this cell,

A. electrons flow from the copper electrode to the carbon electrode

B. cations migrate toward the copper electrode

C. anions migrate toward the carbon electrode

D. the concentration of sulphate ions decreases

Source: January 2001

CHALLENGER QUESTION **DIFFICULTY 53.0**

38. Which of the following statements does **not** apply to the operation of this cell?

A. The oxidation state of the reducing agent changes from 0 to +2.

B. $MnO_4^-{}_{(aq)}$ is reduced at the carbon cathode.

C. $Cu_{(s)}$ is oxidized at the anode.

D. $MnO_4^-{}_{(aq)}$ loses electrons.

Source: January 2001

Use the following information to answer the next question.

Standard Electrode Potentials

$$VO_2^+{}_{(aq)} + 2\,H^+{}_{(aq)} + e^- \rightarrow VO^{2+}{}_{(aq)} + H_2O_{(l)} \quad E° = +0.999\ V$$

$$VO^{2+}{}_{(aq)} + 2\,H^+{}_{(aq)} + e^- \rightarrow V^{3+}{}_{(aq)} + H_2O_{(l)} \quad E° = +0.340\ V$$

$$VO_2^+{}_{(aq)} + 4\,H^+{}_{(aq)} + 5\,e^- \rightarrow V_{(s)} + 2\,H_2O_{(l)} \quad E° = -0.250\ V$$

$$V^{3+}{}_{(aq)} + e^- \rightarrow V^{2+}{}_{(aq)} \quad E° = -0.255\ V$$

CHALLENGER QUESTION **DIFFICULTY 39.7**

39. Which of the following substances is the strongest reducing agent?

A. $V^{2+}{}_{(aq)}$

B. $V^{3+}{}_{(aq)}$

C. $VO_2^+{}_{(aq)}$

D. $VO^{2+}{}_{(aq)}$

Source: January 2001

Not for Reproduction

Use the following information to answer the next four questions.

Concern about increased air pollution and the increasing use of non-renewable resources has accelerated research into alternatives to the internal combustion engine. One alternative is a battery-powered electric motor. Several "new" efficient batteries are being tested. The diagram below represents one of these batteries.

Aluminum–Air Battery

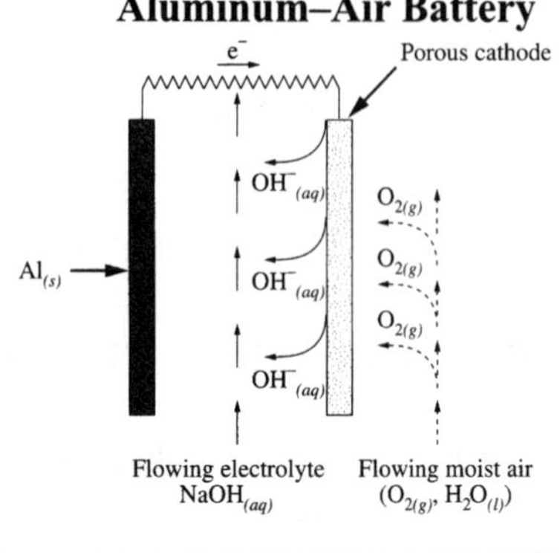

CHALLENGER QUESTION **DIFFICULTY 59.6**

40. In this aluminum–air battery, the $O_{2(g)}$ acts as the

A. reducing agent and gains electrons

B. reducing agent and loses electrons

C. oxidizing agent and gains electrons

D. oxidizing agent and loses electrons

Source: January 2001

41. The reduction half-reaction for this aluminum–air battery is

A. $2\,H_2O_{(l)} + 2\,e^- \rightarrow H_{2(g)} + 2\,OH^-{}_{(aq)}$

B. $Na^+{}_{(aq)} + e^- \rightarrow Na_{(s)}$

C. $O_{2(g)} + 4\,H^+{}_{(aq)} + 4\,e^- \rightarrow 2\,H_2O_{(l)}$

D. $O_{2(g)} + 2\,H_2O_{(l)} + 4\,e^- \rightarrow 4\,OH^-{}_{(aq)}$

Source: January 2001

*Use the answer you selected for **Multiple Choice 41** to answer **Multiple Choice 42**.*

42. The standard voltage produced by this aluminum–air cell is

A. +2.36 V

B. +2.06 V

C. +0.83 V

D. −1.05 V

Source: January 2001

*Use your recorded answer for **Multiple Choice 42** to answer **Numerical Response 11**.*

Numerical Response

11. When three aluminum-air cells are connected in series, the net voltage generated by the battery is +/– ______ V.
(Record your **three digit** answer.)

Source: January 2001

Use the following equation to answer the next question.

$$2\,RhCl_6{}^{3-}{}_{(aq)} + 3\,Zn_{(s)} \rightarrow 3\,Zn^{2+}{}_{(aq)} + 2\,Rh_{(s)} + 12\,Cl^-{}_{(aq)} \qquad E^\circ_{net} = +1.20\text{ V}$$

Numerical Response

12. The standard electrode potential for the half-reaction
$RhCl_6{}^{3-}{}_{(aq)} + 3\,e^- \rightarrow Rh_{(s)} + 6\,Cl^-{}_{(aq)}$
is +/– ______ V.
(Record your **three digit** answer.)

Source: January 2001

Copyright Protected

Written Response — 15%

Use the following information to answer the next question.

In the table below, the time, in hours, that each of three cells would operate four particular devices is given. The cost of each cell is also given.

	Type of D Cell		
	Leclanché	Zinc Chloride	Alkaline
Motor Toy	1.0 h	3.0 h	11.0 h
Cassette Player	1.0 h	2.5 h	5.7 h
Flashlight	1.0 h	2.0 h	4.6 h
Pocket Radio	1.0 h	1.8 h	4.1 h
Cost of Cell:	$0.75	$0.95	$2.25

Leclanché Cell ($Zn_{(s)}$ / $MnO_{2(s)}$)

Overall Reaction

$$2\,MnO_{2(s)} + 2\,NH_4Cl_{(aq)} + Zn_{(s)} \rightarrow ZnCl_2 \times 2\,NH_{3(s)} + Mn_2O_3 \times H_2O_{(s)}$$

Operating Temperature Range –5°C to 55°C

Voltage 1.5 V

Zinc Chloride Cell ($Zn_{(s)}$ / $MnO_{2(s)}$)

Overall Reaction

$$8\,MnO_{2(s)} + 4\,Zn_{(s)} + ZnCl_{2(s)} + 9\,H_2O_{(l)} \rightarrow 8\,MnOOH_{(s)} + ZnCl_2 \times 4\,ZnO \times 5\,H_2O_{(s)}$$

Operating Temperature Range –20°C to 55°C

Voltage 1.5 V

Alkaline/Manganese Dioxide Cell ($Zn_{(s)}$ / $MnO_{2(s)}$)

Overall Reaction

$$2\,Zn_{(s)} + 3\,MnO_{2(s)} \rightarrow 2\,ZnO_{(s)} + Mn_3O_{4(s)}$$

Operating Temperature Range –30°C to 55°C

Voltage 1.5 V

1. **a)** Identify the anode common to all of the D cells. Indicate the change in oxidation number for the anode.

b) For how many hours could a Leclanché cell operate at 0.300 A if the limiting reagent was a 10.0 g anode?

c) Which type of D cell battery would you use to operate a portable cassette player outside on a mild winter day when the temperature was –12°C? Justify your choice from two different perspectives.

Source: January 2000

Use the following information to answer the next question.

In some industrial processes, sodium chromate is added to water coolants. When the coolant is drained, the chromate ions can be removed through an electrolysis process that uses an iron anode. The products of the electrolysis are aqueous iron(II) ions and solid chromium(III) hydroxide, a recoverable pollutant. The half-reaction involving the chromate ion is

$$CrO_4{}^{2-}{}_{(aq)} + 4\,H_2O_{(l)} + 3\,e^- \rightarrow Cr(OH)_{3(s)} + 5\,OH^-{}_{(aq)}$$

2. **a)** Provide the half-reactions and a net redox reaction for this electrochemical process.

b) A current of 3.00 A is applied for 48.0 h to a cell containing a 400 g iron anode. What is the final mass of the iron anode?

c) Suggest an alternative anode material that would last longer than iron. Support your answer with relevant calculations and explanations.

Source: January 2001

Copyright Protected

UNIT TEST 2 – REDUCTION-OXIDATION

1. Four metals represented by the symbols R, S, T, and V and their ions combine with each other in the following manner:

$$S^{2+}{}_{(aq)} + 2\,T_{(s)} \rightarrow 2\,T^{+}{}_{(aq)} + S_{(s)}$$

$$R^{3+}{}_{(aq)} + T_{(s)} \rightarrow \text{No Reaction}$$

$$2R^{3+}{}_{(aq)} + 3\,V_{(s)} \rightarrow 3\,V^{2+}{}_{(aq)} + 2R_{(s)}$$

When the oxidizing agents are arranged from strongest to weakest, the order is

A. $S^{2+}{}_{(aq)}$, $T^{+}{}_{(aq)}$, $R^{3+}{}_{(aq)}$, $V^{2+}{}_{(aq)}$

B. $V^{2+}{}_{(aq)}$, $R^{3+}{}_{(aq)}$, $T^{+}{}_{(aq)}$, $S^{2+}{}_{(aq)}$

C. $V_{(s)}$, $R_{(s)}$, $T_{(s)}$, $S_{(s)}$

D. $S_{(s)}$, $T_{(s)}$, $R_{(s)}$, $V_{(s)}$

Use the following information to answer the next three questions.

Restorers of antique cars often refinish chrome-plated parts by electroplating them. The part is attached to one electrode of an electrolytic cell in which the other electrode is lead. The electrolyte is a solution of dichromic acid, $H_2Cr_2O_{7(aq)}$.

2. The plating of chromium metal will take place at the

A. anode where oxidation occurs

B. anode where reduction occurs

C. cathode where oxidation occurs

D. cathode where reduction occurs

3. During the operation of this cell,

A. $Pb_{(s)}$ is reduced

B. $H_2Cr_2O_{7(aq)}$ is oxidized

C. the pH of the solution increases

D. the total energy of the system decreases

4. A metal that will react spontaneously with $Cr^{3+}{}_{(aq)}$ in a chromium-plating solution is

A. aluminum

B. cadmium

C. lead

D. tin

Use the following information to answer the next question.

A farmer noticed a white substance around the scratches on his zinc-coated steel grain bins. His daughter, who had just completed Chemistry 30, correctly told him that the zinc was being oxidized.

5. In the process of being oxidized, the zinc

A. gained electrons to produce more $Zn_{(s)}$

B. lost electrons and became $Zn^{2+}{}_{(aq)}$

C. gained protons to produce $Zn^{2+}{}_{(aq)}$

D. lost protons and became $Zn_{(s)}$

Not for Reproduction

Use the following information to answer the next three questions.

A student dipped 12.50 g strips of four different metals, $Ag_{(s)}$, $Cu_{(s)}$, $Pb_{(s)}$, and $Mg_{(s)}$, into a beaker containing 250 mL of 1.00 mol/L $HCl_{(aq)}$ in order to determine an activity series. One of the metals reacted immediately and vigorously with the acid.

6. The balanced net-ionic equation for the first reaction that occurred is

A. $2Ag_{(s)} + 2H^{+}_{(aq)} \rightarrow H_{2(g)} + 2Ag^{+}_{(aq)}$

B. $Cu_{(s)} + 2H^{+}_{(aq)} \rightarrow H_{2(g)} + Cu^{2+}_{(aq)}$

C. $Pb_{(s)} + 2H^{+}_{(aq)} \rightarrow H_{2(g)} + Pb^{2+}_{(aq)}$

D. $Mg_{(s)} + 2H^{+}_{(aq)} \rightarrow H_{2(g)} + Mg^{2+}_{(aq)}$

Use the answer selected for ***Multiple Choice 6*** *to answer* ***Numerical Response 1.***

Numerical Response

1. The electrical potential for this reaction is +/– __________ V.
(Record your **three-digit** answer.)

Numerical Response

2. The mass of metal that reacted with the hydrochloric acid is _________ g.
(Record your **three-digit** answer.)

7. In a reaction, $Sn^{2+}_{(aq)}$

A. will undergo oxidation when combined with $Pb(NO_3)_{2(s)}$

B. act as a reducing agent when combined with $Ni_{(s)}$

C. always act as an oxidizing agent

D. act as an oxidizing agent when combined with $Cd_{(s)}$

8. When chlorine gas is bubbled through a sodium iodide solution, the solution

A. becomes reddish-brown because iodide ions are oxidized

B. becomes reddish-brown because iodide ions are reduced

C. becomes reddish-brown because chlorine is oxidized

D. stays colourless

Copyright Protected

Use the following information to answer the next question.

Bricks are produced by mixing clay and water. This mixture is then shaped into "green bricks." The green bricks are carefully heated in a kiln to transform the clay into brick. The bricks then undergo a controlled cooling before being packaged. One of the intermediate reactions in the transformation of clay into brick is

$$3\,Al_4O_6 \bullet Si_3O_{6(s)} \rightarrow (Al_2O_3)_6(SiO_2)_{4(s)} + 5\,SiO_{2(s)} + 190.4\text{ kJ}$$

9. This reaction can be classified as

A. a redox reaction

B. a Brønsted–Lowry acid–base reaction

C. a redox reaction and a Brønsted–Lowry acid-base reaction

D. neither a redox reaction nor a Brønsted–Lowry acid–base reaction

Use the following information to answer the next question.

The colour of brick depends upon the type of clay and additives used. The reaction that occurs when clays containing iron(II) persulphide, $FeS_{2(s)}$, are heated in the kiln is

$$4FeS_{2(s)} + 11O_{2(g)} \rightarrow 2Fe_2O_{3(s)} + 8SO_{2(g)}$$

10. In this reaction, the oxidation state of iron

A. changes from 0 to +3

B. changes from +2 to +3

C. changes from +2 to 0

D. does not change

Use the following information to answer the next question.

The following reaction will occur at high temperatures.

$$2Na_{(g)} + Cl_{2(g)} \rightarrow 2NaCl_{(g)} + \text{energy}$$

11. The half-reaction for the reduction that occurs in this reaction is

A. $Na_{(g)} \rightarrow Na^+_{(g)} + e^-$

B. $Na_{(g)} + e^- \rightarrow Na^+_{(g)}$

C. $Cl_{2(g)} + 2e^- \rightarrow 2Cl^-_{(g)}$

D. $Cl_{2(g)} \rightarrow 2Cl^-_{(g)} + 2e^-$

Use the following information to answer the next question.

Restorers of antique cars often refinish chrome-plated parts by electroplating them. The part is attached to one electrode of an electrolytic cell in which the other electrode is lead. The electrolyte is a solution of dichromic acid, $H_2Cr_2O_{7(aq)}$.

When chromium is electroplated onto a car bumper, one of the chemicals put into the electrolytic solution is $CrO_{3(s)}$. This chemical reacts with water as represented by the equation

$$2CrO_{3(s)} + H_2O_{(l)} \rightarrow 2H^+_{(aq)} + Cr_2O_7{}^{2-}_{(aq)}$$

12. A correct statement concerning this reaction is that

A. the chromium undergoes oxidation

B. the resulting solution will have a pH > 7

C. this is a Brønsted–Lowry acid–base reaction

D. the oxidation state of chromium does not change

Not for Reproduction

13. In $HCO_3^-{}_{(aq)}$, carbon has an oxidation state of

A. +4 **B.** +1

C. 0 **D.** –4

14. In the balanced redox reaction equation

$$3Cu_{(s)} + 2NO_3^-{}_{(aq)} + 8H^+{}_{(aq)} \rightarrow 3Cu^{2+}{}_{(aq)} + 2NO_{(g)} + 4H_2O_{(l)},$$

the oxidation number of nitrogen

A. decreases by 3

B. increases by 3

C. increases by 2

D. decreases by 6

Use the following information to answer the next question.

To prevent it from contaminating the air, chlorine gas can be reacted as represented by the **unbalanced** equation

$$Cl_{2(g)} + S_2O_3^{2-}{}_{(aq)} + H_2O_{(l)} \rightarrow SO_4^{2-}{}_{(aq)} + H^+{}_{(aq)} + Cl^-{}_{(aq)}$$

15. The balanced oxidation half-reaction for this change is

A. $H_2O_{(l)} + S_2O_3^{2-}{}_{(aq)} \rightarrow SO_4^{2-}{}_{(aq)} + 4e^- + 2H^+{}_{(aq)}$

B. $Cl_{2(g)} + 2e^- \rightarrow 2Cl^-{}_{(aq)}$

C. $5H_2O_{(l)} + S_2O_3^{2-}{}_{(aq)} \rightarrow 2SO_4^{2-}{}_{(aq)} + 10H^+{}_{(aq)} + 8e^-$

D. $5H_2O_{(l)} + S_2O_3^{2-}{}_{(aq)} + 4e^- \rightarrow 2SO_4^{2-}{}_{(aq)} + 10H^+{}_{(aq)}$

Numerical Response

3. When the equation $V_2O_{5(s)} + Mn_{(s)} \rightarrow VO_{(s)} + MnO_{2(s)}$ is balanced using the lowest whole number coefficients, the coefficient of

$V_2O_{5(s)}$ is ______

$Mn_{(s)}$ is ______

$VO_{(s)}$ is ______

$MnO_{2(s)}$ is ______

Use the following information to answer the next question.

Nitrogen forms a number of oxides. Examples include

$NO_{(g)}$, $NO_{2(g)}$, $N_2O_{(g)}$, and $N_2O_{5(g)}$.

Numerical Response

4. The oxidation number of nitrogen in each compound listed above is, respectively, _____, _____, _____, and _____.

16. In an experiment, a student used 11.33 mL of $H_2O_{2(aq)}$ to titrate a 17.00 mL sample of acidified 8.0×10^{-3} mol/L $KMnO_{4(aq)}$. If $Mn^{2+}{}_{(aq)}$ is one of the products, then the concentration of the $H_2O_2{}_{(aq)}$ is

A. 1.2×10^{-2} mol/L

B. 1.5×10^{-2} mol/L

C. 3.0×10^{-2} mol/L

D. 6.0×10^{-2} mol/L

Copyright Protected

17. "Tin" cans used to store food are made from steel electroplated with a thin layer of tin. The standard electrical potential for the reduction of $Sn^{2+}{}_{(aq)}$ ions for this process is

A. – 0.15 V

B. – 0.14 V

C. +0.14 V

D. +0.15 V

18. In an experiment, a student compares several electrochemical cells. Each cell contains two metal strips in their metallic ion solutions. A voltmeter is connected by a wire between the metal strips, and a salt bridge connects the solutions. The dependent (responding) variable is the

A. voltage

B. concentration of the solution

C. reaction of a metal and a metallic ion

D. metal and metallic ion solution selected

Use the following information to answer the next question.

During the operation of a NiCad battery, the two half-reactions that occur are

I $Cd_{(s)} + 2OH^-{}_{(aq)} \rightarrow Cd(OH)_{2(s)} + 2e^-$ $\quad E° = ?\ V$

II $NiO_{2(s)} + 2H_2O_{(l)} + 2e^- \rightarrow Ni(OH)_{2(s)} + 2OH^-{}_{(aq)}$ $\quad E° = -0.49\ V$

Numerical Response

5. On discharging, the electrical potential of a NiCad battery is +1.40 V. The redcutionpotential for half-reaction I is – ________ V.
(Record your **three-digit** answer.)

Use the following diagram to answer the next question

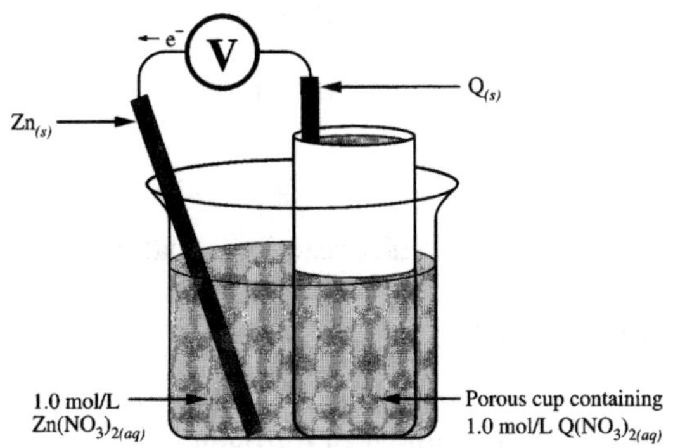

19. Given that the reading on the voltmeter for this cell is +1.74 V, which of the following statements is correct?

A. The reduction potential of $Q^{2+}{}_{(aq)}$ is +2.50 V.

B. $Zn_{(s)}$ is a weaker reducing agent than $Q_{(s)}$.

C. $Q^{2+}{}_{(aq)}$ would react spontaneously with $Cu_{(s)}$.

D. $Q^{2+}{}_{(aq)}$ is a stronger oxidizing agent than $Zn^{2+}{}_{(aq)}$.

20. An electrolytic cell differs from a voltaic cell in that the electrolytic cell

A. is spontaneous

B. consumes electricity

C. has an anode and a cathode

D. has a positive $E°_{net}$ value

Not for Reproduction

Use the following diagram to answer the next question.

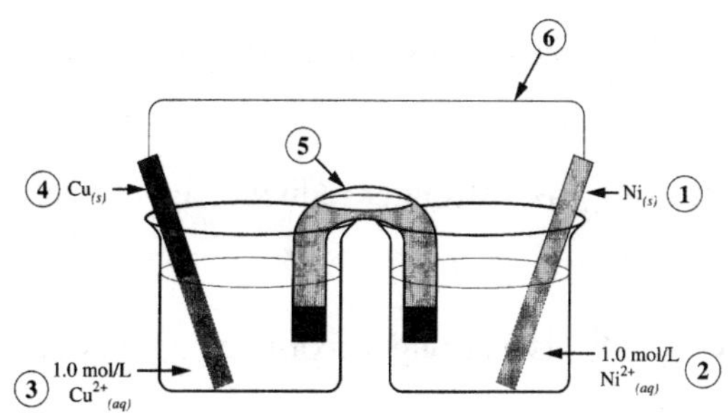

Numerical Response

6. Identify the part of the electrochemical cell, as numbered above, that corresponds to the terms listed below.

Cathode __________

External electron circuit __________

Oxidizing agent __________

Anode __________

21. The voltage of an electrochemical cell is +0.20 V. If one of the half-reactions is the reduction of $Cu^{2+}{}_{(aq)}$, then the other half-reaction that occurs could be

A. $2I^-{}_{(aq)} \rightarrow I_{2(s)} + 2e^-$

B. $S_{(s)} + 2H^+{}_{(aq)} + 2e^- \rightarrow H_2S_{(aq)}$

C. $H_2S_{(aq)} \rightarrow S_{(s)} + 2H^+{}_{(aq)} + 2e^-$

D. $I_{2(s)} + 2e^- \rightarrow 2I^-{}_{(aq)}$

Use the following information to answer the next question.

The following materials are used by Chemistry 30 students in laboratory work.

1 electrodes	**5** thermometer
2 insulated containers	**6** electrolytes
3 pH paper	**7** external circuit
4 porous boundary	**8** buret

Numerical Response

7. The materials necessary to construct an operational voltaic cell are, in numerical order, _____, _____, _____, and _____.

Copyright Protected

Use the following information to answer the next question.

In a laboratory, a student obtained the following results when testing, under standard conditions, reactions between various metals and their corresponding ions.

	$Ga_{(s)}$	$Fe_{(s)}$	$Zn_{(s)}$	$Mg_{(s)}$
$Ga^{3+}_{(aq)}$	–	×	✓	✓
$Fe^{2+}_{(aq)}$	√	–	✓	✓
$Zn^{2+}_{(aq)}$	×	×	–	✓
$Mg^{2+}_{(aq)}$	×	×	×	–

Key

✓ denotes reaction

× denotes no reaction

– denotes no test performed

22. The reduction potential of the $Ga^{3+}_{(aq)}$ could be

A. –0.53 V

B. –1.41 V

C. +1.21 V

D. +1.92 V

23. A net cell potential value that would represent a spontaneous reaction is

A. –1.05 V

B. –0.08 V

C. 0.00 V

D. +0.15 V

24. Electrolysis of $MgCl_{2(aq)}$ will not produce magnesium metal because

A. $Cl^-_{(aq)}$ is a stronger oxidizing agent than $Mg^{2+}_{(aq)}$

B. $H_2O_{(l)}$ is a stronger reducing agent than $Mg^{2+}_{(aq)}$

C. $H_2O_{(l)}$ is a stronger oxidizing agent than $Mg^{2+}_{(aq)}$

D. $Cl^-_{(aq)}$ is a stronger reducing agent than $Mg^{2+}_{(aq)}$

25. If the $Cu^{2+}_{(aq)}/Cu_{(s)}$ reduction half-reaction was assigned a reduction potential value of 0.00 V for an electrode potential table, then the $Ni^{2+}_{(aq)}$ / $Ni_{(s)}$ half-reaction on that table would have a reduction potential value of

A. +0.26 V

B. +0.08 V

C. –0.26 V

D. –0.60 V

Not for Reproduction

Use the following diagram to answer the next question.

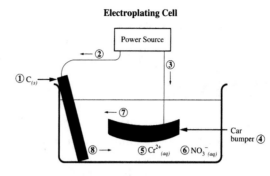

Electrochemical Cell

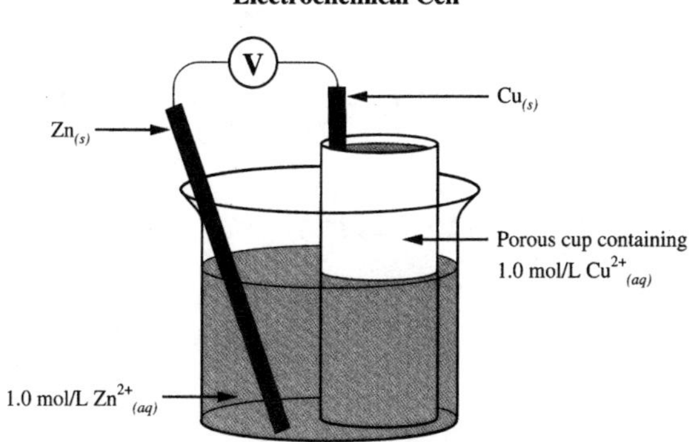

26. For this cell, the potential is

A. +1.10 V

B. +0.42 V

C. –0.42 V

D. –1.10 V

Use the following information to answer the next question.

Chromium plating of objects, such as iron car bumpers, to prevent corrosion actually involves the plating of three different metals in three separate electrolytic cells. The first cell contains a solution of a copper salt, the second a solution of nickel salt, and the third a solution of chromium salt.

27. During the nickel stage of the electroplating process, the nickel(II) ions

A. gain electrons, and metal is deposited on the anode

B. gain electrons, and metal is deposited on the cathode

C. lose electrons, and metal is deposited on the anode

D. lose electrons, and metal is deposited on the cathode

Use the following diagram to answer the next question.

Electroplating Cell

Power Source
②
③
① $C_{(s)}$
⑦
Car bumper ④
⑧
⑤ $Cr^{2+}_{(aq)}$
⑥ $NO_3^{-}{}_{(aq)}$

Numerical Response

8. Use the numbers that identify the parts of the electroplating cell in the diagram above to complete the statements below.

The cathode is identified by _________.

The electron movement is identified by _____.

The cation movement is identified by _______.

The anion is identified by ___________.

28. If the electrochemical cell $Cd_{(s)}$ / $Cd^{2+}{}_{(aq)}$ // $Ag^{+}{}_{(aq)}$ / $Ag_{(s)}$ produces a 6.00 A current for 2.00 h, the mass change of the anode will be a

A. 25.2 g decrease

B. 2.25 g increase

C. 48.3 g decrease

D. 48.3 g increase

Copyright Protected

Use the following information to answer the next two questions.

A chromium electroplating cell needs to operate at a current of 2 000 A to plate 112 g of chromium onto a car bumper.

Numerical Response

9. In order to plate the bumper, the number of moles of chromium(II) ions that must react in the cell is ______ mol.
(Record your **three-digit** answer.)

*Use your recorded answer for **Numerical Response 9** to answer **Numerical Response 10.***

Numerical Response

10. In order to plate the bumper, the cell must operate for ______ min.
(Record your **three-digit** answer.)

29. Sacrificial metals may be used to protect pipelines, septic tanks, and ship propellers. A metal that could be used as a sacrificial anode to protect iron is

A. magnesium

B. tin

C. lead

D. silver

30. In the reaction of sodium metal with water, the reduction half-reaction produces

A. hydroxide ions, which results in a pH greater than 7

B. hydroxide ions, which results in a pH less than 7

C. hydrogen gas, which results in a pH less than 7

D. hydrogen gas, which results in a pH of 7

31. Oxidation–reduction reactions occur in biological systems. A net oxidation–reduction reaction that occurs in the body is

A. $Mg^{2+}{}_{(aq)} + 2OH^{-}{}_{(aq)} \rightarrow Mg(OH)_{2(s)}$

B. $HCO_3{}^{-}{}_{(aq)} + H_3O^{+}{}_{(aq)} \rightarrow H_2CO_{3(aq)} + H_2O_{(l)}$

C. $CH_{4(g)} + 2O_{2(g)} \rightarrow CO_{2(g)} + 2H_2O_{(g)}$

D. $C_6H_{12}O_{6(aq)} + 6O_{2(g)} \rightarrow 6CO_{2(g)} + 6H_2O_{(l)}$

32. In the reaction $2Sn_{(s)} + O_{2(g)} \rightarrow 2SnO_{(s)}$, tin is

A. reduced and the reaction is exothermic

B. reduced and the reaction is endothermic

C. oxidized and the reaction is endothermic

D. oxidized and the reaction is exothermic

Not for Reproduction

Use the following equations to answer the next question.

1 $HSO_3^-{}_{(aq)} + HCO_3^-{}_{(aq)} \rightarrow H_2CO_{3(aq)} + SO_3^{2-}{}_{(aq)}$

2 $C_6H_{12}O_{6(aq)} + 6O_{2(g)} \rightarrow 6CO_{2(g)} + 6H_2O_{(l)}$

3 $Ni^{2+}{}_{(aq)} + Fe_{(s)} \rightarrow Fe^{2+}{}_{(aq)} + Ni_{(s)}$

4 $Co^{2+}{}_{(aq)} + 2Fe^{2+}{}_{(aq)} \rightarrow 2Fe^{3+}{}_{(aq)} + Co_{(s)}$

5 $6CO_{2(g)} + 6H_2O_{(l)} \rightarrow C_6H_{12}O_{6(aq)} + 6O_{2(g)}$

Numerical Response

11. Match the equations, as numbered above, with the corresponding descriptions listed below.

A biological redox reaction carried out in a plant cell but not in an animal cell ______

A biological redox reaction carried out in both animal and plant cells ______

A spontaneous, non-biological redox reaction ______

A non-spontaneous, non-biological redox reaction ______

ACIDS AND BASES

Table of Correlations		
Topic	**Outcomes**	**Related Questions**
1. Defining solutions (empirical and theoretical definitions)	a. Acidic, basic, neutral ionic, and neutral molecular solutions b. Water c. Acidity and basicity of common substances (Data table information)	
2. Theoretical explanations	a. Two theories i. Arrhenius Theory ii. Brønsted–Lowry Theory b. How to explain strong acids vs. weak acids; strong bases vs. weak bases; Differentiating between strength and concentration of common species present in solution c. Comparing the two theories	3, 20, NR7, 29, 33, NR10, 40, 45
3. Simple acids and bases calculations	a. [acid] & [base] b. $[H+_{(aq)}]$ & $[OH_{(aq)}]$ c. pH and pOH	15, 19, NR8, WR1, 35, 38, NR11, NR13
4. Brønsted–Lowry Theory	a. Reaction mechanism (acids are proton donator and bases are proton acceptor) b. Reversibility of reactions 1. Equilibrium reactions: i. theory (conjugate acid and base) ii. methods of describing equilibrium iii. manipulating equilibrium (Le Châtelier's principle) iv. factors influencing equilibrium (catalyst) c. Water equilibrium d. Information from the data table: amphoteric substances e. Quadratic equation to find pH; K_a and K_b description and comparison	4, NR2, 7, 8, 9, 10, 11, NR3, 21, 23, NR5, 24, 27, 30, 32, 34, 44, 46, 47, 48
5. Predicting A - B equation (limitations and deviations)	a. $Al_2(SO_4)_3$ solution: deviation from Brønsted–Lowry theory b. Empirical observations from reactions	6, 12, WR2
6. Titration	a. Polyprotic acid and polybasic species b. Stoichiometry c. Titration graph	NR1, NR4, 22, 25, NR6, 28, NR9, 31, 36, 37, 42, NR12, WR3
7. Indicators		1, 5, 13, 26, 39, 49
8. Buffers		14, 17, 18, 41, 43
9. Combining with other units	a. energy of neutralization	2, 16, 50, 51

Not for Reproduction

ACIDS AND BASES

1. Defining solutions (empirical and theoretical definitions)

a. acidic, basic, neutral ionic, and neutral molecular solutions

b. water

c. acidity and basicity of common substances (Data table information)

1. Empirical Definitions of Aqueous Solutions

a. Acids and bases are operationally defined as follows

Acids	Bases
Turn litmus red	Turn litmus blue
Are electrolytes	Are electrolytes
Neutralize bases	Neutralize acids
Taste sour	Taste bitter
React with $Zn_{(s)}$ and $Mg_{(s)}$	Feel soapy

Neutral ionic solutions, while electrolytes, have no effect on litmus. Solutions of molecular compounds are typically non-electrolytes and have no effect on litmus.

b. Water

From an empirical point of view, water is a neutral nonelectrolyte.

c. Common Substances

Though not a perfect definition, household cleaning agents tend to be basic, foodstuffs tend to be acidic, and cosmetics/ointments and shampoos tend to be close to neutral.

2. Theoretical explanations

a. two theories

i. Arrhenius Theory

ii. Brønsted–Lowry Theory

b. how to explain strong acids vs. weak acids; strong bases vs. weak bases; differentiating between strength and concentration common species present in solution

c. comparing the two theories

2. Theoretical Explanations of Acids/Bases

a. i. Arrhenius Dissociation Theory

Acids dissociate in water to release $H^+_{(aq)}$.

Bases dissociate in water to release $OH^-_{(aq)}$.

ii. Arrhenius Modified Theory

Acids react with water to produce $H_3O^+_{(aq)}$.

Bases react with water to produce $OH^-_{(aq)}$.

iii. Brønsted–Lowry Theory

Acids donate/lose an H^+ in a neutralization.

Bases remove/accept an H^+ in a neutralization.

b. Strength and Concentration

- At any concentration, a strong acid dissociates completely or reacts with water completely to give $H^+_{(aq)}$ or $H_3O^+_{(aq)}$, respectively.
- At most normal concentrations, weak acids dissociate less than 100%, or react incompletely with water to give $H^+_{(aq)}$ or $H_3O^+_{(aq)}$, respectively.
- Strong bases, in water, dissociate completely or react completely with water to produce $OH^-_{(aq)}$.
- Weak bases, in water, react incompletely to produce $OH^-_{(aq)}$.

The strength of an acid/base is unrelated to its concentration. Thus, a dilute/low concentration strong acid can have a higher $[H^+_{(aq)}]$ than a more concentrated weak acid (. . .the pH of 1.0 mol/L $CH_3COOH_{(aq)}$ is 2.37 — about the same as the pH of 4.32 mmol/L $HCl_{(aq)}$; the pH of 2.0 mol/L $NH_{3(aq)}$ is 11.77 — the same as 5.9 mmol/L $NaOH_{(aq)}$)

Copyright Protected

c. A Comparison of the Acid–Base Theories

Students often ask "What theory is the best one?"

The answer is ". . .whichever one works best in the situation." Thus:

- Both Arrhenian Acid–Base theories need $H_2O_{(l)}$ to be present, but its absence is no hindrance to Brønsted–Lowry theory.
- Dissociation theory only works well for H^+ containing acids and strong bases (containing OH^-).
- The Arrhenian theories have excellent explanatory power but weak predictive capability.

Any of the theories can be used for stoichiometric calculation, but Arrhenian theory is easier to use.

Related Questions: 3, 20, NR7, 29, 33, NR10, 40, 45

3. *Simple acids and bases calculations*
   a. *[acid] & [base]*
   b. *[H+$_{(aq)}$] & [OH $_{(aq)}$]*
   c. *pH and pOH*

3. Simple Acid–Base Calculations

a. The reactions of strong acids and bases are quantitative. Thus, simple stoichiometries can be employed to calculate the acid and base concentrations from titration data (see below) or the $[H^+_{(aq)}]$ or $[OH^-_{(aq)}]$ of an acid or base solutions.

b. $[H^+_{(aq)}]$ and $[OH^-_{(aq)}]$ from [acid] or [base]

For all the strong acids (except $H_2SO_{4(aq)}$) below 0.6 mol/L, the $[H^+_{(aq)}]$ = [acid]

For all the group I metal hydroxides and thalium (I) hydroxide $[OH^-_{(aq)}]=[MOH_{(aq)}]$. For barium and strontium hydroxides, $[OH^-_{(aq)}]=\frac{2}{1}\times[M(OH)_{2(aq)}]$.

If the $[H^+_{(aq)}]$ or $[OH^-_{(aq)}]$ of an aqueous solution is known at 25°C, the relationship $[H^+_{(aq)}][OH^-_{(aq)}]=1.0\times10^{-14}\left(\frac{\text{mol}}{\text{L}}\right)^2$ is used to calculate the corresponding $[OH^-_{(aq)}]$ or $[H^+_{(aq)}]$.

Note, the K_a values of strong acids are not used to calculate the pH of their aqueous solutions.

c. pH and pOH

By definition, $pH=-\log[H^+_{(aq)}]$ and $[H^+_{(aq)}]=10^{-pH}$

$pOH=-\log[OH^-_{(aq)}]$ and $[OH^-_{(aq)}]=10^{-pOH}$

$pH+pOH=14.00$ at 25°C,

where $[H^+_{(aq)}]$ and $[OH^-_{(aq)}]$ are in units of mol/L.

pH values range from below 7 to above 7.

Thus, pH values may be negative or above 15.

Example 1: What is the pH of 1.6 mol/L $HCl_{(aq)}$?

$pH=-\log[H^+_{(aq)}]$ but $[H^+_{(aq)}]=[HCl_{(aq)}]$

$pH=-\log(1.6\text{ mol/L})=-0.20$

A 1.6 mol/L $HCl_{(aq)}$ solution has a pH of –0.20.

(The number of decimal places in a pH equals the number of significant digits in the $[H^+_{(aq)}]$. The same rule applies to pOH.)

Not for Reproduction

Example 2: What is the pH of $2.0\,\text{mol/L NaOH}_{(aq)}$?

$\text{pOH} = -\log[\text{OH}^-_{(aq)}]$ but

$[\text{OH}^-_{(aq)}] = [\text{NaOH}_{(aq)}]$

$\text{pOH} = -\log(2.0\,\text{mol/L}) = -0.30$

$\text{pH} = 14.00 - \text{pOH} = 14.00 - (-0.30) = 14.30$

A 2.0 mol/L $\text{NaOH}_{(aq)}$ solution has a pH of 14.30.

Where excess strong acid is added to strong base, or vice versa, the pH of the resulting solution can be determined from the number of moles of excess $\text{H}^+_{(aq)}$ or $\text{OH}^-_{(aq)}$ remaining and the total solution volume.

Example 3: Calculate the solution pH after 75 mL of 0.10 mol/L $\text{NaOH}_{(aq)}$ has been added to 50 mL of 0.10 mol/L $\text{HCl}_{(aq)}$ during a titration investigation.

$$\text{NaOH}_{(aq)} + \text{HCl}_{(aq)} \rightarrow \text{NaCl}_{(aq)} + \text{H}_2\text{O}_{(l)}$$

$\text{NaOH}_{(aq)}$	$\text{HCl}_{(aq)}$
75 mL	50 mL
0.10 mol/L	0.10 mol/L

$$n_{OH^-} = 75\,\text{mL} \times 0.10\frac{\text{mol}}{\text{L}} = 7.5\,\text{mmol}$$

$$n_{H^+} = 50\,\text{mL} \times 0.10\frac{\text{mol}}{\text{L}} = 5.0\,\text{mmol}$$

Clearly, $\text{OH}^-_{(aq)}$ is in excess

$$n_{OH^-\,excess} = 7.5\,\text{mmol} - 5.0\,\text{mmol} = 2.5\,\text{mmol}$$

$$[\text{OH}^-_{(aq)}] = \frac{2.5\,\text{mmol}}{125\,\text{mL}} = 0.020\,\text{mol/L}$$

(total solution volume)

$\text{pOH} = -\log(0.020\,\text{mol/L}) = 1.70$

$\text{pH} = 14.00 - 1.70$ The solution pH will be 12.30.

Related Questions: 15, 19, NR8, 35, 38, NR11, NR13, WR1

4. Brønsted–Lowry theory

- *a. reaction mechanism (acids are proton donator and bases are proton acceptor)*
- *b. reversibility of reactions*
  - *1. Equilibrium reactions:*
    - *i. theory (conjugate acid and base)*
    - *ii. methods of describing equilibrium*
    - *iii. manipulating equilibrium (Le Châtelier's principle)*
    - *iv. factors influencing equilibrium (catalyst)*
  - *2. Water equilibrium*
  - *3. Information from the data table: amphoteric substances*
  - *4. Quadratic equation to find pH; K_a and K_b description and comparison*

4. Equilibria and Acid–Base Theory

a. Acid–base Equilibria

When weak acids and bases react, an equilibrium results. The equilibrium has more products than reactants if the reactant acid lies above the reactant base in a Strengths of Acids and Bases Table. Given a select set of acid–base reactions and their extent of reaction, it is possible to construct a small Strengths of Acids and Bases Table. All Brønsted–Lowry acid–base reactions contain two acid–base conjugate pairs.

b. The Dynamic Equilibrium

i. A dynamic equilibrium occurs in a closed system when a reversible reaction proceeds constantly at the same rate in the forward and reverse directions, such that the macroscopic properties of the system (pH, mass, colour, conductivity, concentrations, pressures, etc.) are constant.

Copyright Protected

ii. Generically, the extent of an equilibrium reaction is described in a variety of ways.

The equilibrium constant and the equilibrium constant expression:

$$aA + bB \text{"} cC + dD \qquad K = \frac{[C]^c[D]^d}{[A]^a[B]^b}$$

where $[A]-[D]=$ the reactant and product concentrations—partial pressures can also be used—and a – d = the reactant and product coefficients.

If $0< K < 1$, there is likely, though not always, more reactant than product present at equilibrium.

If $K \cong 1$, there are often comparable quantities of reactant and product present at equilibrium.

If $K > 1$, there is likely more product than reactant present at equilibrium.

The % reaction may be described as $< 50\%(0< K < 1), > 50\%(K > 1)$, or $100\%(K >> 1)$.

An equilibrium can be said to favour the products (when $K > 1$) or favour the reactants (when $0 < K < 1$).

iii. Le Châtelier's Principle

If stress is applied to a system at equilibrium, the equilibrium will readjust to minimize the effects of that stress.

- An equilibrium shifts to consume added reagents or replace those that are removed.
- An equilibrium will counteract:
  - an increase in total system pressure from a volume decrease by making fewer moles of gas molecules, if it can
  - a decrease in system pressure from a volume increase by making more moles of gas molecules, if it can.
- Added inert gas has no effect on an equilibrium (although it increases the total system pressure, it does not change the partial pressures of the equilibrium components).
- Added catalyst shortens the time it takes for a system to reach equilibrium.
- Only temperature changes can change the value of K for an equilibrium. Adding heat to an equilibrium causes a shift away from that side of the equilibrium containing heat energy. When heat is removed, the equilibrium shifts to the side containing heat energy.

iv. Equilibrium Graphs

In any graph of the concentrations/ pressures of all the components of an equilibrium, the point at which the lines representing each component become parallel and horizontal signifies that equilibrium has been reached.

In a graph of equilibrium concentrations, stresses applied to the equilibrium are easily interpreted.

- Additions/removals of equilibrium components produce sharp ("spiky") changes in the graph.
- Changes in pressure/temperature tend to produce more smooth/curved changes in the graph.
- Added catalyst brings the point of equilibrium closer to the graph's y-axis.

c. Water Equilibrium

The equilibrium constant of the reaction

$H_2O_{(l)} \text{"} H^+_{(aq)} + OH^-_{(aq)}$ (Arrhenius Dissociation) or

$H_2O_{(l)} + H_2O_{(l)} \text{"} H_3O^+_{(aq)} + OH^-_{(aq)}$

(Brønsted–Lowry neutralization) is

$K_w = [H^+_{(aq)}][OH^-_{(aq)}]$ or

$K_w = [H_3O^+_{(aq)}][OH^-_{(aq)}]$,

and it has the value

$$K_w = 1.0 \times 10^{-14} \left(\frac{\text{mol}}{\text{L}}\right)^2 \text{ at } 25°\text{C}.$$

Not for Reproduction

The K_w is called the ion product or ionization constant of water. An increase in the $[H^+_{(aq)}]/[H_3O^+_{(aq)}]$ of an aqueous solution causes a corresponding decrease in the $[OH^-_{(aq)}]$ of the solution (increased $[OH^-_{(aq)}]$ leads to decreased $[H^+_{(aq)}]/[H_3O^+_{(aq)}]$).

d. Amphiprotic Substances ($HX^-_{(aq)}$)

Amphiprotic substances can be proton acceptors (Brønsted–Lowry bases) or proton donators (Brønsted–Lowry acids). Typically, amphiprotics appear on both sides of a "strengths of acids and bases" chart.

Amphiprotic substances in water have a K_a value and a K_b value. Amphiprotics are acids if their $K_a > K_b$ and bases if their $K_b > K_a$.

According to Alberta Education's Chemistry 30 Data Booklet, page 11, an amphiprotic entity is acidic in water if it lies above $HCO_3^-{}_{(aq)}$ on both sides of the table while all those amphiprotics below $HCO_3^-{}_{(aq)}$ are bases in water ($HCO_3^-{}_{(aq)}$ is basic in water).

e. K_a, K_b, pH, and the Quadratic Relation.

For any acid $HA_{(aq)}$, the constant K_a describes the equilibrium:

$$HA_{(aq)} + H_2O_{(l)} \rightleftharpoons H_3O^+_{(aq)} + A^-_{(aq)}$$

where $K_a = \dfrac{[H_3O^+_{(aq)}][A^-_{(aq)}]}{[HA_{(aq)}]}$

K_a is used to calculate the pH of weak acids. Unless the ratio of $[HA_{(aq)}]_{initial}$ to K_a is large (>1000) the quadratic relation ought to be used to solve for $[H_3O^+_{(aq)}]$.

For any weak base $A^-_{(aq)}$, the constant K_b describes the equilibrium:

$$A^-_{(aq)} + H_2O_{(l)} \rightleftharpoons HA_{(aq)} + OH^-_{(aq)}$$

where $K_b = \dfrac{[HA_{(aq)}][OH^-_{(aq)}]}{[A^-_{(aq)}]}$

Unless the ratio of $[A^-_{(aq)}]_{initial}$ to K_b is large (>1000), the quadratic relation ought to be used to solve for $[OH^-_{(aq)}]$.

For the conjugate acid base pair ($HA_{(aq)}$, $A^-_{(aq)}$),

$$K_{a_{HA}} \times K_{b_{A^-}} = K_w$$

e.g., What is the K_b of $HCO_3^-{}_{(aq)}$?

$$K_{bHCO_3^-} = \frac{K_w}{K_{a_{H_2CO_3}}} = \frac{1.0\times10^{-14}}{4.4\times10^{-7}}\text{ mol/L}$$
$$= 2.3\times10^{-8}\text{ mol/L}$$

What is the pH of 0.10 mol/L $NaHCO_{3(aq)}$?

$$HCO_3^-{}_{(aq)} + H_2O_{(l)} \rightleftharpoons H_2CO_{3(aq)} + OH^-_{(aq)}$$

Initially:	0.10 mol/L	—	—	—
Equilibrium:	0.10 $-x$	—	x	x

$$K_b = \frac{x^2}{0.10-x} \cong \frac{x^2}{0.10} \text{ because } \frac{[HCO_3^-{}_{(aq)}]}{K_b} > 1\,000$$

thus

$$x = \sqrt{0.10\times K_b} = 4.8\times10^{-5}\text{ mol/L} = [OH^-_{(aq)}]$$

$$pOH = -\log[OH^-_{(aq)}] = -\log(4.8\times10^{-5}\text{ mol/L})$$
$$= 4.32 \quad\text{and}\quad pH = 14.00 - 4.32 = 9.68$$

(Using the quadratic relation gives the same answer.)

Related Questions: 4, NR2, 7, 8, 9, 10, 11, NR3, 21, 23, NR5, 24, 27, 30, 32, 34, 44, 46, 47, 48

Copyright Protected

5. *Predicting A - B equation (limitations and deviations)*
   a. *$Al_2(SO_4)_3$ solution: deviation from Bronsted–Lowry Theory*
   b. *empirical observations from reactions*

5. Unusual Acids and Bases

a. Metal Ion Hydrolysis

Empirical observations of metal ion salts that might ordinarily be expected to be neutral (e.g. $MCl_{n(aq)}$) reveal that they are, strange though it may seem, rather acidic in some cases. The sources of this acidity are the water molecules that surround the hydrated metal ion, $M(H_2O)_n^{n+}$ (e.g. $Al(H_2O)_{6(aq)}^{3+}$), as follows:

$$M(H_2O)_{n\,(aq)}^{n+} + H_2O_{(l)} \text{''} \; M(OH)(H_2O)_{n-1(aq)}^{(n-1)+} + H_3O^+_{(aq)}$$

$$Al(H_2O)_{6\,(aq)}^{3+} + H_2O_{(l)} \text{''} \; Al(OH)(H_2O)_{5\,(aq)}^{2+} + H_3O^+_{(aq)}$$

The K_a values of many hydrated metal ions range form 5.1×10^{-2} for $Ti^{3+}_{(aq)}$ to 2.5×10^{-11} for $Ni^{2+}_{(aq)}$ — as wide a range of acidity as $HOOCCOOH_{(aq)}$ to $HCO_3^-{}_{(aq)}$.

b. Empirical observations of neutralizations

When an acid is neutralized by a base, the final solution pH typically ends up closer to 7.00.

The conjugate bases of strong acids, except for $H_2SO_{4(aq)}$, are neutral in water. The conjugate bases of weaker acids tend to be stronger conjugate bases. Similarly, the weaker a base is, the stronger is the acidity of its conjugate acid. For example, $HCN_{(aq)}$ is a weaker acid than $HF_{(aq)}$, thus $CN^-_{(aq)}$ is a stronger base than $F^-_{(aq)}$.

Related Questions: 6, 12, WR2

6. *Titration*
   a. *polyprotic acid and polybasic species*
   b. *stoichiometry*
   c. *titration graph*

6. Titration

a. Polyprotic Acids and Bases

When polyprotic acids/bases are titrated with strong base/acid, more than one H^+ is transferred. The number of protons transferred corresponds to the mole ratio of the reactants. For example, every mole of $HOOCCOOH_{(aq)}$ is capable of neutralizing two moles of $NaOH_{(aq)}$. The conjugate base following the removal of an H^+ from a polyprotic acid is amphiprotic (capable of reacting as an acid and a base) and a weaker acid than the acid it originated from. For the mythical polyprotic acid $H_4X_{(aq)}$, in terms of acidity,

$$H_4X_{(aq)} > H_3X^-{}_{(aq)} > H_2X^{2-}{}_{(aq)} > HX^{3-}{}_{(aq)}$$

Similarly for the polyprotic base $X^{4-}{}_{(aq)}$, in terms of basicity,

$$X^{4-}{}_{(aq)} > HX^{3-}{}_{(aq)} > H_2X^{2-}{}_{(aq)} > H_3X^-{}_{(aq)}$$

b. Stoichiometry

The mole ratio of an acid to a base during a neutralization corresponds to the number of equivalence points (quantitative reactions) noted in a pH curve.

For example, two equivalence points are noted when $H_3PO_{4(aq)}$ is neutralized by $NaOH_{(aq)}$ as shown:

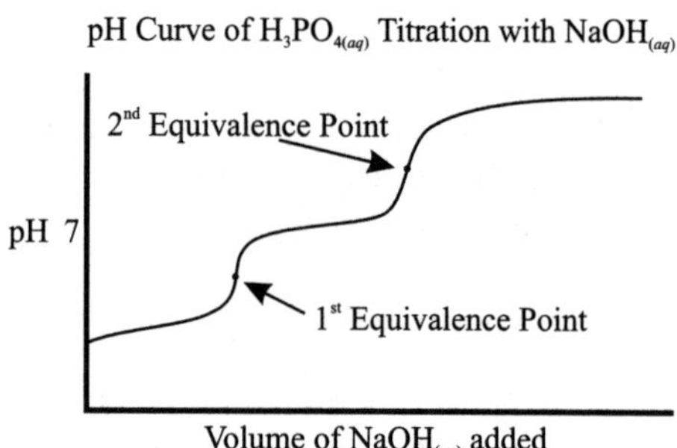

Not for Reproduction

The balanced acid–base reaction is either

$$H_3PO_{4(aq)} + 2OH^-_{(aq)} \rightarrow HPO_4^{2-}{}_{(aq)} + 2H_2O_{(l)}$$

or

$$H_3PO_{4(aq)} + 2NaOH_{(aq)} \rightarrow Na_2HPO_{4(aq)} + 2H_2O_{(l)}$$

c. pH Curves

A graph of solution pH versus the volume of titrant added for the titration of an acid/base with strong base/acid is called a pH curve. In general, when titrant is added to a sample, the pH changes gradually most of the time. When an acid/base is being completely neutralized, the pH changes in a characteristic rapid manner. The point at which each reactant is present in equal amounts (moles) is called the equivalence point. The pH of an equivalence point depends on the acidity/basicity of the conjugate produced.

Weak acids titrated with strong base generally have equivalence point pH values greater than 7. Weak bases titrated with strong acid tend to have equivalence point pH values less than 7.

d. Laboratory procedures

Students are expected to be able to design, perform, write procedures for, analyse, and evaluate laboratory investigations to, among other possibilities,

- differentiate a strong and a weak acid/base
- differentiate a monoprotic from a polyprotic acid/base
- determine the concentration of an acid/base
- determine the effect of a stress on an equilibrium
- follow the course of a neutralization reaction

In addition, students must be able to select/name the appropriate apparatus and chemicals necessary for a laboratory procedure.

Related Questions: NR1, NR4, 22, 25, NR6, 28, NR9, 31, 36, 37, 42, NR12, WR3

7. Indicators

7. Indicators

These are vividly coloured weak conjugate acid–base pairs $HIn_{(aq)}$, $In^-_{(aq)}$, described by the equilibrium

$$HIn_{(aq)} + H_2O_{(l)} \text{”} In^-_{(aq)} + H_3O^+_{(aq)}$$

In general, at some high pH (high $[OH^-_{(aq)}]$), the equilibrium shifts right, and $In^-_{(aq)}$ and its colour predominate; at some low pH (high $[H_3O^+_{(aq)}]$), the equilibrium shifts left, and $HIn_{(aq)}$ and its colour predominate. The precise high and low pH ranges for each indicator are outlined in Alberta Education's Chemistry 30 Data Booklet.

The best choice of indicator for a titration changes colour dramatically once one drop of titrant has been added after an equivalence point. Typically, the pH range of the indicator should overlap the equivalence point pH.

It is important to remember that only a few drops of indicator are present in a sample being titrated. Practically speaking, the indicator "indicates" the chemistry that occurs—it does not participate to any extent.

Related Questions: 1, 5, 13, 26, 39, 49

8. Buffers

8. Buffers

a. Buffer regions are those "flattish" parts of pH curves that occur before and between the equivalence points when weak acids or bases are titrated.

b. What is a buffer?

A buffer is a weak acid–base conjugate pair ($HA_{(aq)}$, $A^-_{(aq)}$) that is capable of maintaining a near constant pH when small amounts of $H_3O^+_{(aq)}$ or $OH^-_{(aq)}$ are added to them. The acid component neutralizes the $OH^-_{(aq)}$ while the base component neutralizes the $H_3O^+_{(aq)}$. Buffer capacity is essentially the concentration of the buffer. If $HA_{(aq)}$ or $A^-_{(aq)}$ is completely neutralized, buffering no longer occurs.

c. Buffer pH

The pH of a buffer solution is easily calculated by substituting the concentration of each buffer component into the K_a Expression for the equilibrium

$$HA_{(aq)} + H_2O_{(l)} \text{"} H_3O^+_{(aq)} + A^-_{(aq)}$$

For example: Estimate the pH of the buffer solution that contains 24 mmol/L $NaHCO_{3(aq)}$ and 12 mmol/L $H_2CO_{3(aq)}$.

$$H_2CO_{3(aq)} + H_2O_{(l)} \text{ ο } HCO_3^-{}_{(aq)} + H_3O^+{}_{(aq)}$$

$$K_a = \frac{[H_3O^+_{(aq)}][HCO_3^-{}_{(aq)}]}{[H_2CO_{3(aq)}]}$$

$$[H_3O^+_{(aq)}] = \frac{K_a[H_2CO_{3(aq)}]}{[HCO_3^-{}_{(aq)}]}$$

$$= \frac{(12\text{ mmol/L})(4.4\times10^{-7}\text{ mol/L})}{24\text{ mmol/L}}$$

$$= 2.2\times10^{-7}\text{ mol/L}$$

$$pH = -\log(2.2\times10^{-7}\text{ mol/L})$$

$$= 6.66$$

Related Questions: 14, 17, 18, 41, 43

9. Combining with other units

a. energy of neutralization

9. Combining with other Units

a. Thermodynamics Unit

Generally speaking, the enthalpies of solution dilution and neutralization of strong acids and bases tend to be exothermic.

Those enthalpies of formation for acid and base solutes in the Chemistry 30 Data Booklet are for the pure solute, not their aqueous solutions.

b. Reduction Oxidation Unit

Acids and bases, particularly strong varieties, are necessary for the reaction of many oxidizing and reducing agents, respectively. During the operation of electrochemical cells, local changes in pH can occur where $H^+_{(aq)}/OH^-_{(aq)}$ are consumed/produced at the electrodes.

Related Questions: 2, 16, 50, 51

Not for Reproduction

Use the following information to answer the first two questions.

Novacor is a large international company that produces ethene ($C_2H_{4(g)}$) from ethane ($C_2H_{6(g)}$) at its plant in Joffre, Alberta. The essential process in the conversion of ethane to ethene is called cracking, which involves the removal of hydrogen atoms from ethane molecules. The cracking occurs in special alloy pipes at temperatures near 1 100°C. The process results in the formation of ethene and other byproducts.
After the ethene is separated from the byproducts of the cracking process, it is washed with a caustic soda solution ($NaOH_{(aq)}$).

Numerical Response

1. A lab technician titrated 10.0 mL of a 2.57 mol/L caustic soda solution with a 0.860 mol/L standardized $HCL_{(aq)}$ solution. The volume of $HCl_{(aq)}$ needed to completely neutralize the caustic soda solution is ____ mL.
(Record your **three-digit** answer.)

Source: January 2000

1. The indicator that would best identify the equivalence point of this titration is

   A. methyl violet

   B. bromocresol green

   C. bromothymol blue

   D. 1, 3, 5-trinitrobenzene

Source: January 2000

Use the following information to answer the next question.

When you drink alcoholic beverages, only 5% of the alcohol is removed through functions such as breathing and sweating. Your liver is responsible for eliminating the other 95%. The alcohol reacts with $NAD^{+}{}_{(aq)}$, a substance present in the liver. The reaction is catalyzed by an enzyme called alcohol dehydrogenase and is represented by the equation

$$C_2H_5OH_{(l)} + NAD^{+}{}_{(aq)} \xrightarrow[\text{dehydrogenase}]{\text{alcohol}}$$

$$CH_3CHO_{(aq)} + NADH_{(aq)} + H^{+}{}_{(aq)} + \text{energy}$$

2. If you had a low level of the biological catalyst, alcohol dehydrogenase,

   A. you would feel hotter than normal

   B. the concentration of $NADH_{(aq)}$ would increase

   C. your blood alcohol level would decrease at a faster rate than normal

   D. your blood alcohol level would remain high for a longer period than normal

Source: January 2000

Copyright Protected

Use the following information to answer the next five questions.

Vinegar, an aqueous solution of acetic acid, is used to preserve and flavour food. Most of the vinegar used for this purpose has an acetic acid concentration of 0.83 mol/L.

3. The vinegar used in food has a

A. $[H_3O^+{}_{(aq)}]$ equal to $[CH_3COO^-{}_{(aq)}]$

B. $[H_3O^+{}_{(aq)}]$ greater than $[CH_3COOH_{(aq)}]$

C. $[CH_3COO^-{}_{(aq)}]$ equal to $[CH_3COOH_{(aq)}]$

D. $[CH_3COO^-{}_{(aq)}]$ greater than $[H_3O^+{}_{(aq)}]$

Source: January 2000

4. The $[H_3O^+{}_{(aq)}]$ of the 0.83 mol/L $CH_3COOH_{(aq)}$ is

A. 8.3×10^{-1} mol/L

B. 3.9×10^{-3} mol/L

C. 1.8×10^{-5} mol/L

D. 1.5×10^{-5} mol/L

Source: January 2000

Use your recorded answer from ***Multiple Choice 4*** *to answer* ***Numerical Response 2.***

Numerical Response

2. The pH of the vinegar is ____ .
(Record your **three-digit** answer.)

Source: January 2000

5. Pickling vinegar has a pH of 2.37. When 3 drops of bromocresol green and 3 drops of phenolphthalein are added to a sample of this vinegar, the resulting colour of the solution is

A. yellow **B.** green

C. blue **D.** purple

Source: January 2000

6. Vinegar ($CH_3COOH_{(aq)}$) and baking soda ($NaHCO_{3(s)}$) are added to recipes to produce baked products with light, fluffy textures. The net ionic equation for the reaction that occurs is

A. $H_3O^+{}_{(aq)} + HCO_3^-{}_{(aq)} \rightarrow CO_{2(g)} + 2\,H_2O_{(l)}$

B. $HCO_3^-{}_{(aq)} + CH_3COO^-{}_{(aq)} \rightarrow CH_3COOH_{(aq)} + CO_3^{2-}{}_{(aq)}$

C. $CH_3COOH_{(aq)} + NaHCO_{3(aq)} \rightarrow NaCH_3COO_{(aq)} + CO_{2(g)} + H_2O_{(l)}$

D. $CH_3COOH_{(aq)} + HCO_3^-{}_{(aq)} \rightarrow CH_3COO^-{}_{(aq)} + CO_{2(g)} + H_2O_{(l)}$

Source: January 2000

Use the following equation to answer the next two questions.

$HNO_{2(aq)} + H_2BO_3^-{}_{(aq)}$ ○ $NO_2^-{}_{(aq)} + H_3BO_{3(aq)}$

7. A conjugate acid–base pair in the reaction is

A. $H_2BO_3^-{}_{(aq)}$ and $NO_2^-{}_{(aq)}$

B. $H_3BO_{3(aq)}$ and $H_2BO_3^-{}_{(aq)}$

C. $HNO_{2(aq)}$ and $H_2BO_3^-{}_{(aq)}$

D. $H_3BO_{3(aq)}$ and $NO_2^-{}_{(aq)}$

Source: January 2000

Not for Reproduction

8. The amphiprotic species in the reaction is

A. $H_2BO_3{}^-{}_{(aq)}$

B. $HNO_{2(aq)}$

C. $NO_2{}^-{}_{(aq)}$

D. $H_3BO_{3(aq)}$

Source: January 2000

Use the following information to answer the next four questions.

Solutions of carbolic acid, commonly known as phenol ($HC_6H_5O_{(aq)}$), are widely used as disinfectants. One such solution has a concentration of 6.44×10^{-2} mol/L and a pH of 5.60. Carbolic acid dissociates in water according to the equation

$$HC_6H_5O_{(aq)} + H_2O_{(l)} \rightleftharpoons C_6H_5O^-{}_{(aq)} + H_3O^+{}_{(aq)}$$

9. The K_a expression for the equation is

A. $K_a = \dfrac{[C_6H_5O^-{}_{(aq)}][H_3O^+{}_{(aq)}]}{[HC_6H_5O_{(aq)}][H_2O_{(l)}]}$

B. $K_a = \dfrac{[HC_6H_5O_{(aq)}][H_2O_{(l)}]}{[C_6H_5O^-{}_{(aq)}][H_3O^+{}_{(aq)}]}$

C. $K_a = \dfrac{[C_6H_5O^-{}_{(aq)}][H_3O^+{}_{(aq)}]}{[HC_6H_5O_{(aq)}]}$

D. $K_a = \dfrac{[HC_6H_5O_{(aq)}]}{[C_6H_5O^-{}_{(aq)}][H_3O^+{}_{(aq)}]}$

Source: January 2000

CHALLENGER QUESTION **DIFFICULTY 48.3**

10. The K_a for this carbolic acid is

A. 6.3×10^{-12} **B.** 9.8×10^{-11}

C. 2.5×10^{-6} **D.** 3.9×10^{-5}

Source: January 2000

11. In the *CRC Handbook of Chemistry and Physics*, the K_a for carbolic acid at 20.0°C is 1.3×10^{-10}. The K_b for $C_6H_5O^-{}_{(aq)}$ is

A. 1.1×10^{-12}

B. 1.1×10^{-5}

C. 7.7×10^{-5}

D. 1.3×10^{-10}

Source: January 2000

*Use your recorded answer from **Multiple Choice 11** to answer **Numerical Response 3**.*

Numerical Response

3. The pOH of 0.10 mol/L $NaC_6H_5O_{(aq)}$ at 20.0°C is ____.
(Record your **three-digit** answer.)

Source: January 2000

Use the following graph to answer the next question.

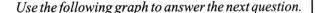

Thermometric Titration of 20.0 mL of 0.20 mol/L $HCl_{(aq)}$ with $NaOH_{(aq)}$

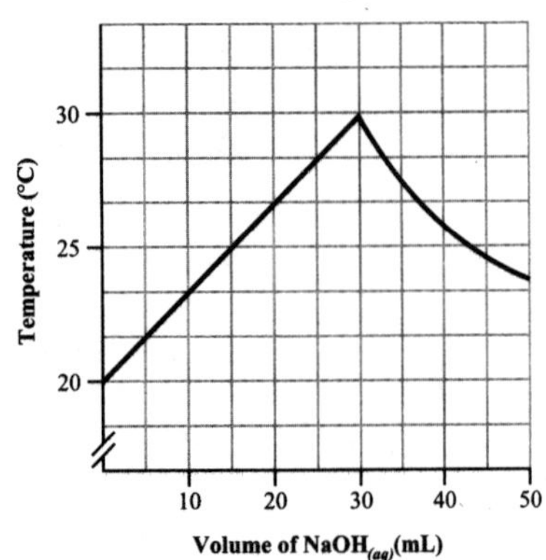

Numerical Response

4. This experiment is an example of a thermometric titration in which a change in temperature occurs as the reagents react. The $[NaOH_{(aq)}]$ for this titration is _______ mol/L. (Record your **three-digit** answer.)

Source: January 2000

Use the following information to answer the next three questions.

Beverages such as carbonated soft drinks contain carbonic acid. In addition, citric acid and phosphoric acid are often added to ensure that the pH is below 4.5. This is considered the "safety zone" for these beverages because below this pH, the risk of microbial contamination is very low.

12. The equation representing the equilibrium of phosphoric acid is

A. $H_3PO_{4(aq)} + H_2O_{(l)}$ ” $H_2PO_4^-{}_{(aq)} + OH^-{}_{(aq)}$

B. $H_3PO_{4(aq)}$ ” $H_3O^+{}_{(aq)} + PO_3^-{}_{(aq)}$

C. $H_3PO_{4(aq)}$ ” $3\,H^+{}_{(aq)} + PO_4^{3-}{}_{(aq)}$

D. $H_3PO_{4(aq)} + H_2O_{(l)}$ ” $H_3O^+{}_{(aq)} + H_2PO_4^-{}_{(aq)}$

Source: January 2000

Use the following information to answer the next question.

A student sketched a titration curve based on data collected during a reaction between 0.050 mol/L $NaOH_{(aq)}$ titrant and a 25.0 mL sample of a soft drink

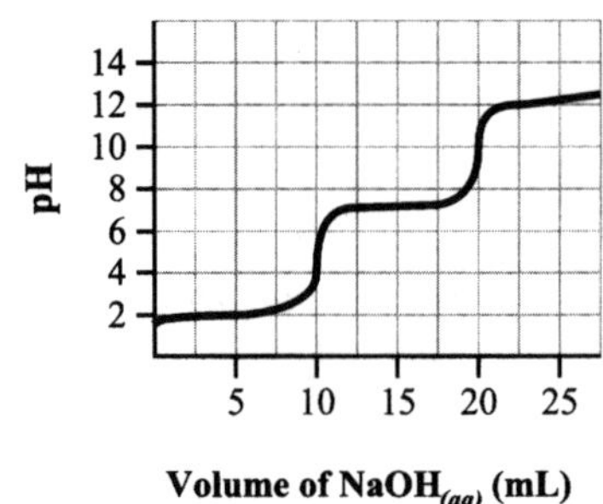

Volume of $NaOH_{(aq)}$ (mL)

13. The most suitable indicator to identify the equivalence point of the second reaction is

A. phenolphthalein

B. bromothymol blue

C. methyl red

D. methyl orange

Source: January 2000

Not for Reproduction

14. A glass of orange juice contains enough hydronium ions to kill you if your blood is not buffered to a pH of about 7.35. One of the several buffer systems that your blood contains is $H_2PO_4{}^-{}_{(aq)} - HPO_4{}^{2-}{}_{(aq)}$. This system initially buffers the addition of hydronium ions from orange juice by the reaction

A. $H_3O^+{}_{(aq)} + H_2PO_4{}^-{}_{(aq)}{}^{\circ}$
$H_3PO_{4(aq)} + H_2O_{(l)}$

B. $H_3O^+{}_{(aq)} + HPO_4{}^{2-}{}_{(aq)}{}^{\circ}$
$H_2PO_4{}^-{}_{(aq)} + H_2O_{(l)}$

C. $2H_3O^+{}_{(aq)} + PO_4{}^{3-}{}_{(aq)}{}^{\circ}$
$H_2PO_4{}^-{}_{(aq)} + H_2O_{(l)}$

D. $2H_3O^+{}_{(aq)} + 2H_2PO_4{}^-{}_{(aq)}{}^{\circ}$
$PO_4{}^{3-}{}_{(aq)} + 2H_2O_{(l)}$

Source: January 2000

Use the following information to answer the next two questions.

Hot tub owners can control disease-causing bacteria and algae by adding solid sodium hypochlorite pellets, $NaClO_{(s)}$, to the water. This results in the formation of $HClO_{(aq)}$, as represented by the equilibrium

$ClO^-{}_{(aq)} + H_2O_{(l)}$ ”$HClO_{(aq)} + OH^-{}_{(aq)}$

Undissociated $HClO_{(aq)}$ effectively kills bacteria and algae. A pH of 7.40 is considered ideal for a hot tub.

15. Ideally, the water in a hot tub has a hydronium ion concentration of

A. 4.0×10^{-8} mol/L and is basic

B. 2.5×10^{-7} mol/L and is basic

C. 4.0×10^{-8} mol/L and is acidic

D. 2.5×10^{-7} mol/L and is acidic

Source: January 2000

16. When using a hot tub, bathers release substances from their bodies into the water that result in an increase in the pH of the water. As the pH increases, there is

A. an increase in $[H_3O^+{}_{(aq)}]$, which results in an equilibrium shift that is more favourable to bacterial growth

B. a decrease in $[H_3O^+{}_{(aq)}]$, which results in an equilibrium shift that is more favourable to bacterial growth

C. an increase in $[H_3O^+{}_{(aq)}]$, which results in an equilibrium shift that is less favourable to bacterial growth

D. a decrease in $[H_3O^+{}_{(aq)}]$, which results in an equilibrium shift that is less favourable to bacterial growth

Source: January 2000

Use the following information to answer the next two questions.

Body chemistry involves a number of chemical systems that are critically dependent on pH, buffering action, and concentration of gas solutes such as $CO_{2(g)}$ and $O_{2(g)}$.

17. The function of chemical buffers in the blood is to

A. control all reactions

B. act as catalysts to increase the rate of reaction

C. withstand the continual addition of acid or base

D. maintain a constant pH when a small amount of acid or base is added

Source: June 2000

18. One of the buffers present in blood is

A. $HSO_3{}^-{}_{(aq)} - H_2SO_{3(aq)}$

B. $HCO_3{}^-{}_{(aq)} - H_2CO_{3(aq)}$

C. $NO_3{}^-{}_{(aq)} - HNO_{3(aq)}$

D. $Cl^-{}_{(aq)} - Hcl_{(aq)}$

Source: June 2000

Use the following information to answer the next question.

Antibiotics formed by different species of the genus of bacteria *Penicillium* are among the most widely prescribed drugs in the world today.

One of these antibiotics is penicillin G (benzylpenicillinic acid), which is represented as $HPn_{(s)}$. This acid is only slightly soluble in water. The saturated aqueous solution is represented by the equilibrium

$$H_2O_{(l)} + HPn_{(s)} \text{"} H_3O^+{}_{(aq)} + Pn^-{}_{(aq)}$$

19. This system is at equilibrium when the rate of formation of $Pn^-{}_{(aq)}$ in the forward reaction is

A. favoured over the rate of the formation of $HPn_{(s)}$ in the reverse reaction

B. slower than the rate of the formation of $HPn_{(s)}$ in the reverse reaction

C. faster than the rate of the formation of $HPn_{(s)}$ in the reverse reaction

D. equal to the rate of the formation of $HPn_{(s)}$ in the reverse reaction

Source: June 2000

Use the following information to answer the next question.

When a car is started, the starter motor draws a current from the battery. The battery recharges while the car is running.

20. An automotive student obtained 500 mL of acid from a car battery. The student poured 50 mL of the acid into beaker I, 100 mL into beaker II, and then conducted several tests. In this investigation, the student determined that

A. both solutions conducted an electric current equally

B. there was a lower $[H_3O^+{}_{(aq)}]$ in beaker I than in beaker II

C. magnesium metal reacted more quickly in beaker I than in beaker II

D. one drop of methyl red produced a deeper red in beaker II than in beaker I

Source: June 2000

Not for Reproduction

Use the following information to answer the next five questions.

Methanoic (formic) acid is the irritant secreted during an ant bite. The irritation is partially due to the ionization of methanoic acid. The equilibrium equation for the ionization can be represented as

$HCOOH_{(aq)} + H_2O_{(l)}$ ” $H_3O^+{}_{(aq)} + HCOO^-{}_{(aq)}$

CHALLENGER QUESTION **DIFFICULTY 40.7**

21. In a comparison of the species present in $HCOOH_{(aq)}$, the

A. $[H_3O^+{}_{(aq)}]$ is greater than $[HCOOH_{(aq)}]$

B. $[H_3O^+{}_{(aq)}]$ is equal to $[HCOOH_{(aq)}]$

C. $[HCOOH_{(aq)}]$ is greater than $[HCOO^-{}_{(aq)}]$

D. $[HCOOH_{(aq)}]$ is equal to $[HCOO^-{}_{(aq)}]$

Source: June 2000

CHALLENGER QUESTION **DIFFICULTY 39.6**

22. When a 0.100 mol/L $HCOOH_{(aq)}$ is titrated with 0.100 mol/L $NaOH_{(aq)}$, an appropriate choice of indicator for this titration is

A. orange IV **B.** cresol red

C. methyl red **D.** indigo carmine

Source: June 2000

CHALLENGER QUESTION **DIFFICULTY 49.1**

23. The $[OH^-{}_{(aq)}]$ in 0.10 mol/L $NaHCOO_{(aq)}$ is

A. 1.3×10^{-2} mol/L

B. 4.2×10^{-3} mol/L

C. 2.4×10^{-6} mol/L

D. 7.5×10^{-6} mol/L

Source: June 2000

*Use your recorded answer from **Multiple Choice 23** to answer **Numerical Response 5**.*

CHALLENGER QUESTION **DIFFICULTY 52.8**

Numerical Response

5. The pH of 0.10 mol/L $NaHCOO_{(aq)}$ is ________ . (Record your **three-digit** answer.)

Source: June 2000

CHALLENGER QUESTION **DIFFICULTY 55.8**

24. Methanoic acid slowly decomposes to form $CO_{(g)}$ and $H_2O_{(l)}$. The rate of reaction is increased if a catalyst is present. Compared with the uncatalyzed reaction, the catalyzed reaction has

A. the same K_{eq}

B. a larger K_{eq}

C. a smaller ΔH

D. a larger ΔH

Source: June 2000

Copyright Protected

Use the following information to answer the next three questions.

Ethanoic acid (vinegar) has a variety of uses. To ensure that production plants meet concentration specifications, technicians monitor the concentration of the acid by titrating samples of the ethanoic acid as it comes off the production line.

Titration of 10.0mL of $\mathbf{CH_3COOH_{(aq)}}$ with 0.20 mol/L $\mathbf{NaOH_{(aq)}}$

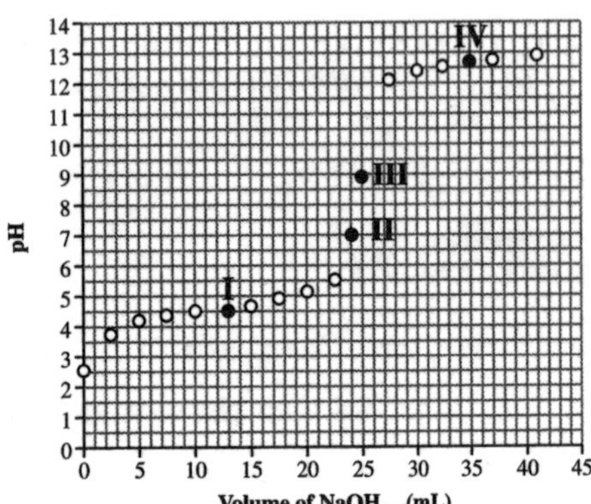

25. On this graph, the equivalence point is indicated by Roman numeral

A. I **B.** II

C. III **D.** IV

Source: June 2000

Use your recorded answer from ***Multiple Choice 25*** *to answer* ***Numerical Response 6.***

CHALLENGER QUESTION	DIFFICULTY 48.7

Numerical Response

6. The concentration of this ethanoic acid sample is________ mol/L.
(Record your **three-digit** answer.)

Source: June 2000

Use your recorded answer from ***Multiple Choice 25*** *to answer* ***Multiple Choice 26.***

26. The best indicator to use for this titration is

A. indigo carmine

B. phenolphthalein

C. bromothymol blue

D. bromocresol green

Source: June 2000

Use the following information to answer the next question.

The equilibrium law expression for an industrial method of producing ethanol is

$$K_{eq} = \frac{[C_2H_5OH_{(g)}]}{[C_2H_{4(g)}][H_2O_{(g)}]}$$

Under certain conditions, the $K_{eq} = 300.0$.
At equilibrium, a 5 000 L reaction vessel contains
115 mol of $C_2H_{4(g)}$ and 110 mol of $H_2O_{(g)}$.

27. Under these conditions, the equilibrium concentration of $C_2H_5OH_{(g)}$ is

A. 1.60×10^{-6} mol/L

B. 0.152 mol/L

C. 75.0 mol/L

D. 5.92×10^{5} mol/L

Source: June 2000

CHALLENGER QUESTION **DIFFICULTY 58.7**

28. To completely react 50 mL of 0.10 mol/L acid, 150 mL of 0.10 mol/L KOH $_{(aq)}$ was required. The number of protons donated by each acid molecule was

A. 1 **B.** 2

C. 3 **D.** 4

Use the following information to answer the next question.

A student was asked to rank the relative strength of the following four acids.

1 Formic acid ($HCOOH_{(aq)}$)

2 Hydrazoic acid ($HN_{3\,(aq)}$)

3 Hypobromous acid ($HOBr_{(aq)}$)

4 Nitrous acid ($HNO_{2(aq)}$)

The student was given the following information.

$HNO_{2(aq)} + HCOO^{-}{}_{(aq)}$ ” $NO_{2}^{-}{}_{(aq)} + HCOOH_{(aq)}$
(Products favoured)

$HN_{3(aq)} + OBr^{-}{}_{(aq)}$ ” $N_{3}^{-}{}_{(aq)} + HOBr_{(aq)}$
(Products favoured)

$HN_{3(aq)} + HCOO^{-}{}_{(aq)}$ ” $N_{3}^{-}{}_{(aq)} + HCOOH_{(aq)}$
(Reactants favoured)

CHALLENGER QUESTION **DIFFICULTY 59.7**

Numerical Response

7. Based on the reaction evidence, the four acids, ranked from strongest to weakest, are ________, ________, ________ and ________.

(Record your **four-digit** answer.)

Source: June 2000

Use the following information to answer the next three questions.

Sodium hydrogen carbonate, $NaHCO_{3(s)}$ (baking soda), is used in baking. When lactic acid, $HC_3H_5O_{3(aq)}$, and baking soda are present, they cause doughs and batters to rise. Lactic acid, a component of buttermilk, has a $K_a = 1.4 \times 10^{-4}$.

CHALLENGER QUESTION **DIFFICULTY 54.5**

29. The net ionic equation that best illustrates the reaction responsible for the dough rising is

A. $H_3O^{+}{}_{(aq)} + HCO_3^{-}{}_{(aq)} \rightarrow CO_{2(g)} + 2H_2O_{(l)}$

B. $HCO_3^{-}{}_{(aq)} + C_3H_5O_3^{-}{}_{(aq)} \rightarrow HC_3H_5O_{3(aq)} + CO_3^{2-}{}_{(aq)}$

C. $NaHCO_{3(aq)} + H_3O^{+}{}_{(aq)} \rightarrow H_2CO_{3(aq)} + H_2O_{(l)} + Na^{+}{}_{(aq)}$

D. $HCO_3^{-}{}_{(aq)} + HC_3H_5O_{3(aq)} \rightarrow H_2O_{(l)} + CO_{2(g)} + C_3H_5O_3^{-}{}_{(aq)}$

Source: June 2000

CHALLENGER QUESTION **DIFFICULTY 58.5**

30. The $[H_3O^{+}{}_{(aq)}]$ in 0.20 mol/L $HC_3H_5O_{3(aq)}$ is

A. 2.8×10^{-3} mol/L

B. 5.3×10^{-3} mol/L

C. 2.6×10^{-2} mol/L

D. 7.0×10^{-4} mol/L

Source: June 2000

Copyright Protected

*Use your recorded answer from **Multiple Choice 30** to answer **Numerical Response 8**.*

Numerical Response

8. The pH of the $HC_3H_5O_{3(aq)}$ is ________.
(Record your **three-digit** answer.)

Source: June 2000

Use the following information to answer the next three questions.

The Stelco Plant in Camrose, Alberta, uses phosphoric acid to remove rust from steel pipes before they are welded. A technician is responsible for ensuring that the proper concentration of phosphoric acid is used. The technician titrated 10.00 mL of the $H_3PO_{4(aq)}$ with 0.125 mol/L $NaOH_{(aq)}$ to the second equivalence point. The technician obtained the following data.

Volume of $NaOH_{(aq)}$ Used

Trial	**1**	**2**	**3**	**4**
Final buret reading (mL)	12.8	24.1	35.5	46.7
Initial buret reading (mL)	0.7	12.8	24.1	35.5

Numerical Response

9. The average volume of sodium hydroxide required to determine the $[H_3PO_{4(aq)}]$ is ________ mL.
(Record your **three-digit** answer.)

Source: June 2000

CHALLENGER QUESTION **DIFFICULTY 29.8**

31. Based on the data gathered at the second equivalence point, the concentration of the phosphoric acid was

A. 47.1 mmol/L **B.** 70.6 mmol/L

C. 141 mmol/L **D.** 283 mmol/L

Source: January 2001

CHALLENGER QUESTION **DIFFICULTY 45.3**

32. In 0.10 mol/L $H_3PO_{4(aq)}$, the species present in highest concentration is

A. $H_3PO_{4(aq)}$

B. $H_2PO_4{}^{-}{}_{(aq)}$

C. $HPO_4{}^{2-}{}_{(aq)}$

D. $H_3O^{+}{}_{(aq)}$

Source: June 2000

CHALLENGER QUESTION **DIFFICULTY 50.3**

33. When ammonium nitrate dissolves in water, the resulting solution will be

A. basic

B. acidic

C. neutral

D. a non-electrolyte

Source: January 2001

Use the following information to answer the next two questions.

At the Banff Wastewater Treatment plant, bacteria are used to treat organic "sludge" $(CH_2O)_{n(s)}$ in a process called autothermal thermophilic aerobic digestion (ATAD). The digestion of the sludge can be represented by the equation $(CH_2O)_{n(s)} + n\,O_{2(g)} \xrightarrow{\text{bacteria}} n\,CO_{2(g)} + n\,H_2O_{(l)}$ + energy

34. At the treatment plant, the enzymes in the bacteria act as

A. buffers

B. reducing agents

C. oxidizing agents

D. biological catalysts

Source: January 2001

35. A 10.0 mL sample of domestic sewage has an effluent pH of 6.80. After this sewage has been treated, the effluent pH is 7.00. The change in hydronium ion concentration is

A. 0.63 mol/L

B. 0.20 mol/L

C. 2.0×10^{-2} mol/L

D. 5.8×10^{-8} mol/L

Source: January 2001

Use the following information to answer the next two questions.

A group of students performed a titration and graphed their results, as shown below.

Acid–Base Titration Curve

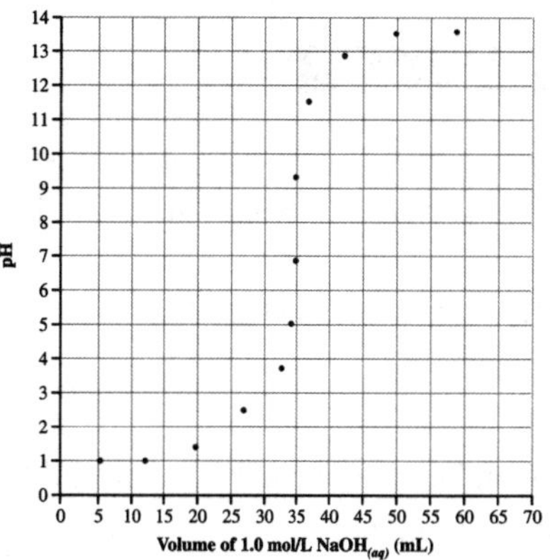

36. For this graph, the pH at the equivalence point is approximately

A. 1

B. 2

C. 7

D. 13

Source: January 2001

37. This titration curve represents the addition of a

A. strong base to a strong acid

B. weak base to a strong acid

C. strong acid to a strong base

D. weak acid to a strong base

Source: January 2001

Copyright Protected

Use the following information to answer the next question.

0.10 mol/L Solutions

1	$NaNO_{2(aq)}$	**3**	$HNO_{3(aq)}$
2	$NaHCO_{3(aq)}$	**4**	$Ba(OH)_{2(aq)}$

Numerical Response

10. When the solutions above are ordered from most basic to least basic, the order is ______, ______, ______ and ______.
(Record your **four-digit** answer.)

Source: January 2001

38. Sour pickles have a pH of about 3.00. The $[OH^-{}_{(aq)}]$ in a typical sour pickle is

A. 1.0×10^{-11} mol/L

B. 3.0×10^{-11} mol/L

C. 1.0×10^{-3} mol/L

D. 3.0×10^{-3} mol/L

Source: January 2001

Numerical Response

11. The concentration of $H_3O^+{}_{(aq)}$ ions in a particular bottle of wine is 3.2×10^{-4} mol/L. The pH of this wine is ____.
(Record your **three-digit** answer.)

Source: January 2001

39. The indicator that would most accurately identify a solution with a pH between 4.00 and 4.30 is

A. thymol blue

B. methyl orange

C. litmus

D. methyl red

Source: January 2001

40. An equilibrium that would favour the products is

A. $NH_4^+{}_{(aq)} + H_2PO_4^-{}_{(aq)}$ ○ $NH_{3(aq)} + H_3PO_{4(aq)}$

B. $HCN_{(aq)} + HS^-{}_{(aq)}$ ○ $CN^-{}_{(aq)} + H_2S_{(aq)}$

C. $HCO_3^-{}_{(aq)} + HBO_3^{2-}{}_{(aq)}$ ○ $H_2BO_3^-{}_{(aq)} + CO_3^{2-}{}_{(aq)}$

D. $HSO_4^-{}_{(aq)} + HSO_3^-{}_{(aq)}$ ○ $H_2SO_{3(aq)} + SO_4^{2-}{}_{(aq)}$

Source: January 2001

41. Which of the following mixtures could act as a buffer solution?

A. $HF_{(aq)}$ and $H_2S_{(aq)}$

B. $NaOH_{(aq)}$ and $HCl_{(aq)}$

C. $Na_2CO_{3(aq)}$ and $NH_{3(aq)}$

D. $NaH_2BO_{3(aq)}$ and $Na_2HBO_{3(aq)}$

Source: January 2001

Not for Reproduction

Use the following information to answer the next question.

During the titration of an unknown base solution with a perchloric acid solution, the following data were collected.

Volume of Acid Added (mL)	pH of Solution
0.0	14.00
20.0	12.63
40.0	12.05
60.0	9.83
70.0	7.56
80.0	6.96
100.0	6.38
120.0	2.20
140.0	1.78

42. The hydronium ion concentration of the original base solution was

A. 1.7×10^{-2} mol/L

B. 7.4×10^{-8} mol/L

C. 1.5×10^{-13} mol/L

D. 1.0×10^{-14} mol/L

Source: January 2001

CHALLENGER QUESTION **DIFFICULTY 57.3**

43. One important buffer that exists in blood is composed of $H_2PO_4{}^-{}_{(aq)}$ and $HPO_4{}^{2-}{}_{(aq)}$. The net ionic equation that represents the reaction of hydrochloric acid with this buffer is

A. $H_3O^+{}_{(aq)} + HPO_4{}^{2-}{}_{(aq)}$ ○ $H_2O_{(l)} + H_2PO_4{}^-{}_{(aq)}$

B. $HCl_{(aq)} + H_2PO_4{}^-{}_{(aq)}$ ○ $Cl^-{}_{(aq)} + H_3PO_{4(aq)}$

C. $H_3O^+{}_{(aq)} + H_2PO_4{}^-{}_{(aq)}$ ○ $H_2O_{(l)} + H_3PO_{4(aq)}$

D. $HCl_{(aq)} + HPO_4{}^{2-}{}_{(aq)}$ ○ $Cl^-{}_{(aq)} + H_2PO_4{}^-{}_{(aq)}$

Source: January 2001

CHALLENGER QUESTION **DIFFICULTY 36.6**

Numerical Response

12. A certain headache relief tablet is composed of monoprotic acetylsalicylic acid ($C_9H_8O_{4(s)}$) and an inert filler. A 4.00 g tablet was crushed and dissolved to make 40.0 mL of solution. The solution was then titrated with 0.900 mol/L $NaOH_{(aq)}$. The volume of $NaOH_{(aq)}$ needed to neutralize the dissolved tablet was 20.1 mL. The experimental value for the mass of $C_9H_8O_{4(s)}$ present in the tablet was ___________ g.
(Record your **three-digit** answer.)

Source: January 2001

Copyright Protected

Use the following information to answer the next three questions.

Coal and natural gas contain trace amounts of sulphur compounds, which when burned, may lead to acid rain pollution.

Reactions Related to Acid Rain

I $2\,H_2S_{(g)} + 3\,O_{2(g)}\ ^\circ 2\,H_2O_{(g)} + 2\,SO_{2(g)}$

II $2\,SO_{2(g)} + O_{2(g)}\ ^\circ 2\,SO_{3(g)}$

III $SO_{2(g)} + H_2O_{(l)}\ ^\circ H_2SO_{3(aq)}$

IV $SO_{3(g)} + H_2O_{(l)}\ ^\circ H_2SO_{4(aq)}$

44. The equilibrium law expression for reaction I is

A. $K_{eq} = \dfrac{[H_2O_{(g)}]^2 + [SO_{2(g)}]^2}{[H_2S_{(g)}]^2 + [O_{2(g)}]^3}$

B. $K_{eq} = \dfrac{[H_2S_{(g)}]^2 + [O_{2(g)}]^3}{[H_2O_{(g)}]^2 + [SO_{2(g)}]^2}$

C. $K_{eq} = \dfrac{[H_2S_{(g)}]^2\,[O_{2(g)}]^3}{[H_2O_{(g)}]^2\,[SO_{2(g)}]^2}$

D. $K_{eq} = \dfrac{[H_2O_{(g)}]^2\,[SO_{2(g)}]^2}{[H_2S_{(g)}]^2\,[O_{2(g)}]^3}$

Source: January 2001

45. The conjugate base of $H_2SO_{3(aq)}$ is

A. $HSO_3{}^-{}_{(aq)}$ **B.** $SO_3{}^{2-}{}_{(aq)}$

C. $OH^-{}_{(aq)}$ **D.** $H_2O_{(l)}$

Source: January 2001

Use the following information to answer the next question.

At 900 K, the equilibrium constant for reaction II is 13.0. The equilibrium concentrations are

$[SO_{2(g)}] = 0.361$ mol/L
$[SO_{3(g)}] = 0.840$ mol/L

46. Given the values above, the calculated equilibrium concentration of $O_{2(g)}$ is

A. 0.179 mol/L **B.** 0.416 mol/L

C. 2.40 mol/L **D.** 5.59 mol/L

Source: January 2001

Use the following information to answer the next question.

Some of the $SO_{2(g)}$ produced from the burning of coal and natural gas can react with $NO_{2(g)}$ in the atmosphere according to the equation

$SO_{2(g)} + NO_{2(g)}\ ^\circ NO_{(g)} + SO_{3(g)}$ $\Delta H = -41.9$ kJ

47. The equilibrium concentration of $SO_{3(g)}$ in the reaction could be increased by

A. raising the temperature

B. adding a catalyst

C. removing $SO_{2(g)}$

D. adding $NO_{2(g)}$

Source: January 2001

Numerical Response

13. If the pH of a sample of rainwater is 3.2, then the pOH is ____________ .
(Record your **three-digit** answer.)

Source: January 2001

Not for Reproduction

CHALLENGER QUESTION **DIFFICULTY 29.7**

48. Which of the following acid solutions has the lowest pH?

A. 300 mL of 1.00×10^{-2} mol/L $H_2S_{(aq)}$

B. 100 mL of 1.00×10^{-4} mol/L $H_2SO_{3(aq)}$

C. 100 mL of 1.00×10^{-3} mol/L $H_2SO_{4(aq)}$

D. 10.0 mL of 1.00×10^{-4} mol/L $H_2SO_{4(aq)}$

Source: January 2001

CHALLENGER QUESTION **DIFFICULTY 41.0**

49. A drop of thymol blue indicator in its blue form added to 10.0 mL of 0.10 mol/L $H_2SO_{4(aq)}$ would become

A. yellow because the indicator would gain one proton

B. yellow because the indicator would lose one proton

C. red because the indicator would gain two protons

D. red because the indicator would lose two protons

Source: January 2001

50. Acid rain is linked to the leaching of heavy metals and their ions in lakes and rivers. Biomagnification of these metals and ions increases levels of disease in fish and wildlife. Based on this information, a decision to reduce sulphur dioxide emissions would be

A. political **B.** scientific

C. technological **D.** environmental

Source: January 2001

51. Another contributor to the acidity of precipitation is $CO_{2(g)}$. Atmospheric $CO_{2(g)}$ levels are **not** increased by

A. photosynthesis

B. combustion of fossil fuels

C. respiration of plants and animals

D. cars equipped with catalytic converters

Source: January 2001

Written Response — 15%

1. Identify a stress that would shift the following equilibrium system to favour the products.

$$2NO_{2(g)} \rightleftharpoons N_2O_{4(g)} + 101.4\ \text{kJ}$$

brown colourless

Your response should include

- an explanation, based on Le Chatelier's Principle, of how the stress would shift this equilibrium
- a procedure that would demonstrate the effect of applying the stress
- a prediction of what evidence there would be that the shift had occurred

Source: January 2000

Copyright Protected

2. Describe a chemical process that might have caused the changes illustrated by the two photos of the same statue.

Photograph taken early 1900s

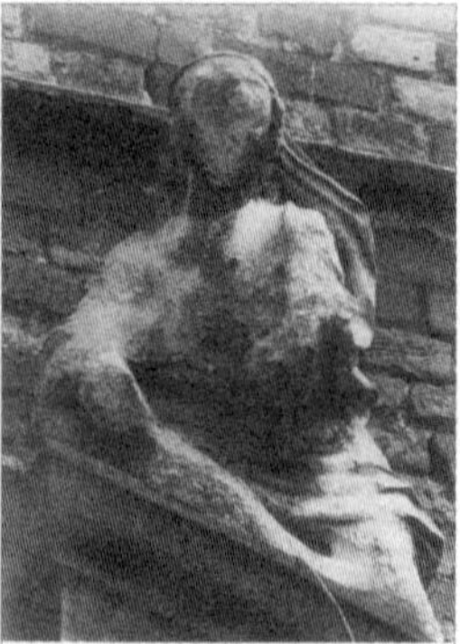
Photograph taken after 1960

—from *The Extraordinary Chemistry of Ordinary Things*

Your response should include

- an explanation of the factors causing the changes
- appropriate chemical reactions
- ways in which society addresses the problem

Source: June 2000

Use the following information to answer the next question.

Representative Antacid	Principal Active Ingredient	Neutralization Reaction
I Alka-Seltzer	Sodium bicarbonate	$NaHCO_{3(s)} + HCl_{(aq)} \rightarrow NaCl_{(aq)} + H_2CO_{3(aq)}$
II Phillips' Milk of Magnesia	Magnesium hydroxide	$Mg(OH)_{2(s)} + 2\ HCl_{(aq)} \rightarrow MgCl_{2(aq)} + 2\ H_2O_{(l)}$
III Rolaids	Dihydroxy–aluminum sodium carbonate	$Al(OH)_2\ NaCO_{3(s)} + 4\ HCl_{(aq)} \rightarrow AlCl_{3(aq)} + NaCl_{(aq)} + 2\ H_2O_{(l)} + H_2CO_{3(aq)}$
IV Tums	Calcium carbonate	$CaCO_{3(s)} + 2\ HCl_{(aq)} \rightarrow CaCl_{2(aq)} + H_2CO_{3(aq)}$
V Di–Gel	Aluminum hydroxide	$Al(OH)_{3(s)} + 3\ HCl_{(aq)} \rightarrow AlCl_{3(aq)} + 3\ H_2O_{(l)}$
	Magnesium carbonate	$MgCO_{3(s)} + 2\ HCl_{(aq)} \rightarrow MgCl_{2(aq)} + H_2CO_{3(aq)}$
	Magnesium hydroxide	$Mg(OH)_{2(s)} + 2\ HCl_{(aq)} \rightarrow MgCl_{2(aq)} + 2\ H_2O_{(l)}$

— from *The Extraordinary Chemistry of Ordinary Things, 1992*

3. Plan an experiment to test the effectiveness of antacids.
Your response should include:

- an experimental design
- a data table for your experimental design
- three factors that should be considered when choosing an antacid

Source: January 2001

Not for Reproduction

UNIT TEST 3 – ACIDS AND BASES

1. Which of the following dilute solutions would likely have a sour taste?

A. $NH_{3(aq)}$

B. $NaOH_{(aq)}$

C. $NaHCO_{3(aq)}$

D. $CH_3COOH_{(aq)}$

2. The pH of bottled lemon juice is best described as

A. greater than 7

B. equal to 7

C. $0 < pH < 7$

D. $7 < pH < 14$

Use the following information to answer the next question.

Two cleaning solutions were accidentally mixed. A strong smell of ammonia alerted a technician to the accident. After checking the labels of the cleaners and discovering that one container held $NH_4Cl_{(aq)}$ and the other $KOH_{(aq)}$, the technician determined that the smell came from the following reaction:

$NH_4{}^{+}{}_{(aq)} + OH^{-}{}_{(aq)}$ ” $NH_{3(aq)} + H_2O_{(l)}$

3. In this equilibrium, the Brønsted–Lowry acids are

A. $NH_{3(aq)}$ and $H_2O_{(l)}$

B. $NH_4{}^{+}{}_{(aq)}$ and $H_2O_{(l)}$

C. $NH_{3(aq)}$ and $OH^{-}{}_{(aq)}$

D. $NH_4{}^{+}{}_{(aq)}$ and $OH^{-}{}_{(aq)}$

4. The conjugate base of $N_2H_5{}^{+}{}_{(aq)}$ is

A. $HOH_{(l)}$

B. $OH^{-}{}_{(aq)}$

C. $N_2H_{4(aq)}$

D. $N_2H_6{}^{2+}{}_{(aq)}$

5. A reaction favouring reactants in which $HCO_3{}^{-}{}_{(aq)}$ acts as an acid is

A. $HCO_3{}^{-}{}_{(aq)} + HBO_3{}^{2-}{}_{(aq)}$ ” $H_2BO_3{}^{-}{}_{(aq)} + CO_3{}^{2-}{}_{(aq)}$

B. $HCO_3{}^{-}{}_{(aq)} + HPO_4{}^{2-}{}_{(aq)}$ ” $H_2PO_4{}^{-}{}_{(aq)} + CO_3{}^{2-}{}_{(aq)}$

C. $HCO_3{}^{-}{}_{(aq)} + CH_3COOH_{(aq)}$ ” $H_2CO_{3(aq)} + CH_3COO^{-}{}_{(aq)}$

D. $HCO_3{}^{-}{}_{(aq)} + HSO_4{}^{-}{}_{(aq)}$ ” $H_2CO_{3(aq)} + SO_4{}^{2-}{}_{(aq)}$

6. When $Na_2CO_{3(s)}$ is added to an unknown solution, bubbles are produced. The unknown solution would be expected to

A. feel slippery

B. have a high pH

C. turn litmus red

D. turn thymolphthalein blue

Copyright Protected

Use the following information to answer the next question.

When 20.0 mL of 0.10 mol/L solutions of $NaHCO_{3(aq)}$, $NaHS_{(aq)}$, $NaOCl_{(aq)}$, and $NaH_2BO_{3(aq)}$ were each reacted with 20.0 mL of 0.10 mol/L $HBrO_{(aq)}$, the following positions of equilibrium were established.

$HCO_3{}^-{}_{(aq)} + HBrO_{(aq)}$ ” favours reactants

$HS^-{}_{(aq)} + HBrO_{(aq)}$ ” favours reactants

$OCl^-{}_{(aq)} + HBrO_{(aq)}$ ” favours reactants

$H_2BO_3{}^-{}_{(aq)} + HBrO_{(aq)}$ ” favours products

7. Based on these positions, the placement of $HBrO_{(aq)}$ on the Relative Strengths of Acids and Bases chart is

A. below boric acid

B. above carbonic acid

C. below hypochlorous acid

D. above hydrosulphuric acid

Use the following equilibrium to answer the next question.

$HSO_4{}^-{}_{(aq)} + HCOO^-{}_{(aq)}$ ” $HCOOH_{(aq)} + SO_4{}^{2-}{}_{(aq)}$

1 2 3 4

Numerical Response

1. Match each acid or base in the forward reaction, as numbered above, with the corresponding term given below.

Acid ______

Conjugate base ______

Base ______

Conjugate acid ______

8. If the following solutions are of equal concentration, then which of them would be the best conductor of an electric current?

A. $CH_3COOH_{(aq)}$

B. $H_2CO_{3(aq)}$

C. $HF_{(aq)}$

D. $HCN_{(aq)}$

Use the following information to answer the next four questions.

Rainwater is acidic because it contains dissolved atmospheric $CO_{2(g)}$ that occurs naturally. It may also contain air pollutants, $NO_{x(g)}$, and $SO_{x(g)}$ from industrial sources.

One component of acid rain can be formed in the atmosphere by the reaction

$$SO_{3(g)} + H_2O_{(l)} \rightarrow H_2SO_{4(aq)} + 227.8\ \text{kJ}$$

9. If each of the following components of acid rain is of equal concentration, then which of them would have the lowest pH?

A. $HNO_{3(aq)}$

B. $HNO_{2(aq)}$

C. $H_2SO_{3(aq)}$

D. $H_2SO_{4(aq)}$

Not for Reproduction

Use the following additional information to answer the next question.

A sample of rainwater is poured into five test tubes. A different indicator is added to each test tube. Four of the observations are recorded in the table below.

Indicator	Colour
methyl red	yellow
Phenol red	yellow
bromocresol green	blue
phenolphthalein	colourless
bromothymol blue	?

10. The pH of the rainwater and the predicted colour of the sample containing bromothymol blue are

A. 6.0 and blue **B.** 7.6 and blue

C. 6.0 and yellow **D.** 7.6 and yellow

11. When rain containing sulphurous acid falls into lakes containing dissolved calcium carbonate, the pH of the lake drops slightly and then remains relatively constant. Which of the following statements best describes a change that occurs in the lake water?

A. Carbonic acid is formed.

B. The calcium sulphite formed neutralizes the sulphurous acid.

C. The carbonate ion decomposes into carbon dioxide and water.

D. The formation of bicarbonate ion, $HCO_3^-{}_{(aq)}$, creates a buffer system with carbonate ion, $CO_3^{2-}{}_{(aq)}$.

Use the following additional information to answer the next question.

12. The molar heat of formation of $H_2SO_{4(aq)}$ in the atmosphere, under standard conditions, is

A. –453.7 kJ/mol **B.** –586.7 kJ/mol

C. –814.0 kJ/mol **D.** –909.3 kJ/mol

13. The main buffer solution of plasma and tissue fluid found in our bodies is $H_2CO_{3(aq)} - HCO_3^-{}_{(aq)}$. When excess hydronium ions enter our blood, the equation that represents the reaction that occurs is

A. $H_3O^+{}_{(aq)} + OH^-{}_{(aq)} \rightarrow 2H_2O_{(l)}$

B. $H_2CO_{3(aq)} + OH^-{}_{(aq)} \rightarrow HCO_3^-{}_{(aq)} + H_2O_{(l)}$

C. $H_2CO_{3(aq)} + H_2O_{(l)} \rightarrow H_3O^+{}_{(aq)} + HCO_3^-{}_{(aq)}$

D. $H_3O^+{}_{(aq)} + HCO_3^-{}_{(aq)} \rightarrow H_2CO_{3(aq)} + H_2O_{(l)}$

14. The $[OH^-{}_{(aq)}]$ of a solution with a pH = 3.45 is

A. 1.9×10^{-14} mol/L

B. 2.8×10^{-11} mol/L

C. 3.6×10^{-4} mol/L

D. 0.54 mol/L

Copyright Protected

Use the following information to answer the next three questions.

Sodium azide, which is found in automobile air bags, reacts readily with acids to form the highly toxic and explosive hydroazoic acid $HN_{3(aq)}$. The K_a for hydroazoic acid is 1.9×10^{-5}.

15. The K_a expression for hydroazoic acid is

A. $K_a = \dfrac{[HN_{3(aq)}]}{[H_3O^+_{(aq)}][N_3{}^-_{(aq)}]}$

B. $K_a = \dfrac{[H_3O^+_{(aq)}][N_3{}^-_{(aq)}]}{[HN_{3(aq)}]}$

C. $K_a = \dfrac{[HN_{3(aq)}]^3}{[H_3O^+_{(aq)}][N_3{}^-_{(aq)}]^3}$

D. $K_a = \dfrac{[H_3O^+_{(aq)}][N_4{}^-_{(aq)}]^3}{[HN_{3(aq)}]^3}$

16. In a solution of hydroazoic acid, the

A. $[HN_{3(aq)}] < [N_3{}^-_{(aq)}]$

B. $[HN_{3(aq)}] > [H_3O^+_{(aq)}]$

C. $[HN_{3(aq)}] > [H_2O_{(l)}]$

D. $[HN_{3(aq)}] = [H_3O^+_{(aq)}]$

Numerical Response

2. The pH of a 0.28 mol/L $HN_{3(aq)}$ solution is ________. (Record your **three-digit** answer.)

Numerical Response

3. The volume of 6.00 mol/L $NaOH_{(aq)}$ required to neutralize 2.20 kg of $HN_{3(l)}$ is ________ L. (Record your **three-digit** answer.)

Numerical Response

4. At a temperature of 300°C and a pressure of 40.5 MPa, 90.0 mol of $H_{2(g)}$ and 80.0 mol of $N_{(2(g)}$ are injected into a reaction vessel. When equilibrium is established, 37.0 mol of $NH_{3(g)}$ are present. The number of moles of $H_{2(g)}$ present in this equilibrium mixture is ______ mol.
(Record your **three-digit** answer.)

Use the following information to answer the next question.

Hydrogen fluoride is produced by reacting hydrogen with fluorine.

$$H_{2(g)} + F_{2(g)} \text{”} 2HF_{(g)} \qquad \Delta H = -542.2 \text{ KJ}$$

17. A stress that would shift the equilibrium toward the products would be to

A. remove $H_{2(g)}$

B. add $HF_{(g)}$

C. decrease the volume of the reaction vessel

D. decrease the temperature of the reaction vessel

18. The K_b of $F^-_{(aq)}$ is

A. 6.6×10^{-4}

B. 1.5×10^{17}

C. 1.5×10^{-11}

D. 1.0×10^{-14}

19. In which of the following reactions does equilibrium favour the products?

A. $HSO_4{}^-_{(aq)} + F^-_{(aq)} \text{”} HF_{(aq)} + SO_4{}^{2-}_{(aq)}$

B. $HF_{(aq)} + H_2O_{(l)} \text{”} H_3O^+_{(aq)} + F^-_{(aq)}$

C. $HF_{(aq)} + SO_4{}^{2-}_{(aq)} \text{”} HSO_4{}^-_{(aq)} + F^-_{(aq)}$

D. $H_3BO_{3(aq)} + F^-_{(aq)} \text{”} HF_{(aq)} + H_2BO_3{}^-_{(aq)}$

Not for Reproduction

20. Which of the following species could act as either an acid or a base?

A. $H_2SeO_{4(aq)}$ **B.** $AsO_4{}^{3-}{}_{(aq)}$

C. $HCOO^-{}_{(aq)}$ **D.** $H_2BO_3{}^-{}_{(aq)}$

21. Chemical systems reach equilibrium when

A. no reaction is occurring

B. the rates of forward and reverse reactions become equal

C. the mass of products equals the mass of reactants

D. the number of moles of products equals the number of moles of reactants

Use the following information to answer the next question.

The equilibrium $2NO_{2(g)}$”$N_2O_{4(g)}$ is established when 0.734 mol of $NO_{2(g)}$ at 25°C is placed in a 2.00 L flask.

22. The initial concentration of the $NO_{2(g)}$ was

A. 0.734 mol/L

B. 0.367 mol/L

C. 0.184 mol/L

D. 1.47 mol/L

Use your recorded answer for ***Multiple Choice 22*** *to answer* ***Numerical Response 5.***

Numerical Response

5. The equilibrium concentration of $N_2O_{4(g)}$ is 0.125 mol/L. The equilibrium constant for the reaction is _______.
(Record your **three-digit** answer.)

23. Most plants grow best in soil with a pH between 6 and 7. Higher or lower pH values prevent them from absorbing essential nutrients. Plants can absorb phosphorus in the form of $H_2PO_4{}^-{}_{(aq)}$. In basic soil, $H_2PO_4{}^-{}_{(aq)}$ could be converted to

A. $P_{4(s)}$ **B.** $PO_4{}^{3-}{}_{(aq)}$

C. $H_3PO_{4(aq)}$ **D.** $HPO_4{}^{2-}{}_{(aq)}$

24. The amphiprotic (amphoteric) species that reacts with bromothymol blue to produce a yellow colour is

A. $NaHSO_{4(aq)}$ **B.** $NaHCO_{3(aq)}$

C. $NaOCl_{(aq)}$ **D.** $H_2O_{(l)}$

Use the following information to answer the next question.

pH of Blood	Effect
7.50	alkalosis (life threatening) ↑
7.35	*healthy individual*
7.20	↓ acidosis (life threatening)

25. Which of the following substances can be added to the blood of a young child with kidney disease in order to control acidosis?

A. $CO_{2(g)}$ **B.** $HCO_3^-{}_{(aq)}$

C. $H_2O_{(l)}$ **D.** $H_2CO_{3(aq)}$

Copyright Protected

Use the following information to answer the next two questions.

A student titrated a 10.0 mL sample of nitric acid with sodium hydroxide solution in the presence of an indicator.

Volume of 5.00 mmol/L $NaOH_{(aq)}$ Used				
Trial	1	2	3	4
Final Buret Reading (mL)	7.99	14.51	21.02	27.53
Initial Buret Reading (mL)	1.00	7.99	14.51	210.2

Numerical Response

6. The average volume of titrant used is ________ mL.
(Record your **three-digit** answer.)

*Use your recorded value from **Numerical Response 6** to answer **Numerical Response 7.***

Numerical Response

7. The concentration of the nitric acid is _______ mmol/L. (Record your **three-digit** answer.)

Use the following information to answer the next question.

Chemical Species

1	$HA^{3-}_{(aq)}$
2	$H_3A^{-}_{(aq)}$
3	$H_2A^{2-}_{(aq)}$
4	$H_4A_{(aq)}$

Numerical Response

8. As a solution of $NaOH_{(aq)}$ is continuously added to the acid $H_4A_{(aq)}$, a sequence of quantitative reactions occurs. The order in which the species listed above would react is _____, _____, _______, and _______.

Use the following information to answer the next question.

A student was asked to determine the concentration of an aqueous $HCl_{(aq)}$ solution by titrating it with 1.13 mol/L $NaOH_{(aq)}$ in the presence of bromothymol blue indicator. Since burets were not available, the student used droppers for each solution and assumed that each drop was of equal volume. It took 26 drops of $NaOH_{(aq)}$ to neutralize 20 drops of the $HCl_{(aq)}$ solution and to reach the bromothymol blue end-point.

Numerical Response

9. The concentration of the $HCl_{(aq)}$ solution was ______ mol/L.
(Record your **three-digit** answer.)

Not for Reproduction

26. A solution was tested and found to have a pOH of 3.2. This solution would most likely

A. be a proton donor

B. react violently with zinc

C. cause thymolphthalein to be blue

D. cause bromocresol green to be yellow

27. As a 1.0 mol/L $HCl_{(aq)}$ solution is added continuously to a 1.0 mol/L $NaOH_{(aq)}$ solution containing thymol blue indicator, the colour changes from

A. blue to green to yellow to orange to red

B. red to orange to yellow to green to blue

C. yellow to orange to red

D. yellow to green to blue

Use the following information to answer the next question.

Titration Plot for 25.0 mL of 0.100 mol/L $NH_{3(aq)}$ with 0.100 mol/L $HCl_{(aq)}$

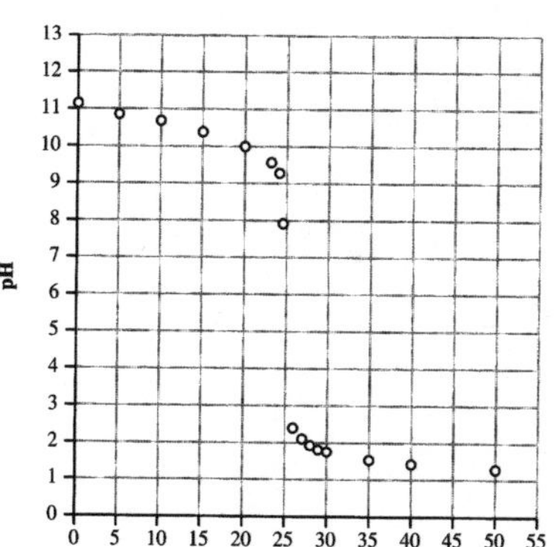

Volume of hydrochloric acid (mL)

28. The most suitable indicator for the titration is

A. phenolphthalein

B. methyl violet

C. chlorophenol red

D. methyl orange

29. A student added sodium hydroxide to a hydrochloric acid solution containing equal amounts of bromothymol blue and phenolphthalein indicator until the solution just turned a definite purple. The most likely pH at this end-point is

A. 10.0

B. 7.0

C. 7.6

D. 8.2

30. Blood maintains a nearly constant pH because it contains

A. sodium ions and chloride ions that keep the pH of the blood at 7

B. hemoglobin that maintains the oxygen levels in the blood

C. catalysts (enzymes) that control the equilibrium in the blood

D. buffers that regulate the hydronium ion concentration in the blood

31. Which of the following equimolar solutions could act as a buffer system?

A. $KH_2PO_{4(aq)} / H_3PO_{4(aq)}$

B. $KCl_{(aq)} / HCl_{(aq)}$

C. $KClO_{4(aq)} / HClO_{4(aq)}$

D. $KNO_{3(aq)} / HNO_{3(aq)}$

Copyright Protected

Written Response

1. An unidentified acid with a concentration of 1.0 mol/L has been given to you to identify. The acid appears in your data booklet on the Relative Strengths of Acids and Bases table. The following test results were recorded:

- Methyl violet is yellow when added to the acid.
- The acid did not form a precipitate when a solution containing $Ag^{+}{}_{(aq)}$ was added to it.
- The solution turned blue and a gas was formed when a strip of copper was added to the acid.

Based on these test results, identify the acid and justify your choice. Your answer should include equations and/or calculations where appropriate.

2. A student predicts that the K_a value of a weak acid may be affected by the temperature of the acid solution. Given an acid of known concentration, design an experiment to test this prediction using commonly available laboratory apparatus. Your response should include

- a procedure
- identification of controlled, manipulated, and responding variables
- indication of the calculations necessary to solve for K_a

ANSWERS AND SOLUTIONS
CHEMICAL ENERGETICS – UNIT REVIEW

1. B	**NR1. 6.03**	**19. C**	**27. B**	**NR9. 1.04**
2. D	**12. B**	**NR5. 16.5**	**28. A**	**36. C**
3. B	**NR2. 68.1**	**NR6. 37.2**	**29. C**	**NR10. 1.70**
4. A	**13. D**	**20. C**	**30. D**	**37. D**
5. B	**14. C**	**21. B**	**31. A**	**38. A**
6. C	**NR3. 13.1**	**22. B**	**32. A**	**NR11. 3.15**
7. D	**15. A**	**NR7. 2, 4, 3, 1**	**33. B**	**39. B**
8. C	**NR4. 95.2**	**23. A**	**34. B**	
9. C	**16. C**	**24. D**	**35. C**	
10. D	**17. A**	**25. B**	**NR8. 1, 2, 3, 6*** **(* any order)**	
11. C	**18. C**	**26. B**		

1. B

The net reaction for the storage of the sun's energy by plants combines $CO_{2(g)}$, $H_2O_{(l)}$ and energy to make $C_6H_{12}O_{6(aq)}$ (a representative carbohydrate) and $O_{2(g)}$.

Cellular respiration is the opposite of photosynthesis. Photosynthesis is a redox reaction (C is reduced and O is oxidized) but not a neutralization reaction as normally defined.

2. D

Only E_k changes occur when a metal spoon is used to stir hot coffee. The temperature change of the coffee that results from its loss in E_k is directly dependent on the gain in E_k of the spoon. The gain in E_k of the spoon (q or $\Delta E_k = mc\Delta t$) is dependent on its mass and specific heat capacity.

Faster stirring (B) will likely make the coffee cool down a little bit quicker and with no E_p changes involved, alternernatives A and C are not correct.

3. B

Proportionately less energy is released when 10g (approx. $\frac{1}{3}$ mol) of ethane is formed from its elements than if one mole is formed: $H°_f\ C_2H_{6(g)} = 84.7\ \text{kJ/mol}$. Thus,

$$\Delta H = nH$$

$$= 10.0\ \text{g} \times \frac{\text{mol}}{30.08\ \text{g}} \times \left(\frac{-84.7\ \text{kJ}}{\text{mol}}\right)$$

$$= -28.2\ \text{kJ}$$

Alternatives C and D are the amounts of energy released by forming one and three mole of ethane, respectively.

Copyright Protected

4. A

When ethane is transformed from a cool liquid into a warmer gas, intermolecular bonds are broken (an absorption / increase in E_p), and the molecules of ethane become hotter (an increase in E_k) and farther apart (a decrease in density).

Alternative B ignores the temperature change. Alternative C has the wrong E_k change and alternative D misrepresents the density change.

5. B

The oxidation number of carbon in the decoking reaction is from 0 (in $C_{(s)}$) to +4 (in $CO_{2(g)}$).

In alternative B, the oxidation number of C in $C_6H_{12}O_{6(aq)}$ is 0, and this becomes +4 in $CO_{2(g)}$.

The net change in the oxidation number of C in alternative A is from +4 to 0; alternative C from –2 to –1; and in alternative D from –2 to –2 (no net change).

6. C

When a reaction is catalyzed, it proceeds via an alternate pathway that has the same net enthalpy change but a lower activation energy. The cracking of ethane is exothermic (that is, the reaction loses energy). Only the diagram in alternative C fits the description.

The processes depicted in alternatives A and D do not have the same enthalpy change, while alternative B is an enthalpy diagram for an endothermic process.

7. D

All the processes listed involve making and/or breaking bonds.

Phase changes involve making or breaking intermolecular bonds.

Chemical changes involve making and breaking intramolecular bonds.

Nuclear changes involve making and breaking intranuclear bonds.

Since the magnitude of the bond energies involved decreases in the order:

intranuclear > intramolecular > intermolecular, the energy changes arranged in order of decreasing magnitude are nuclear fusion, chemical, and phase.

8. C

It is only when nuclei are disrupted that elements can be transformed from one kind to another. This is what happens when hydrogen is converted into helium in the sun. These changes involve primarily nuclear forces. Alternative A refers to phase changes. Alternative B refers to a chemical reaction, and alternative D cannot be right.

9. C

Fossil fuels are exploited largely because they have a high energy yield, thus they are good energy sources.

Statements I, II, and IV are true.

10. D

An exothermic reaction loses heat and energy to its surroundings and has a negative ΔH value because the total formation enthalpies of the products is less than that of the reactions. Clearly, it is statement IV that is inconsistent.

11. C

The molar enthalpy of simple decomposition of a compound (call it $H°_{sd}$) is the exact opposite of its standard molar enthalpy of formation.

Compound	$H°_f\left(\frac{\text{kJ}}{\text{mol}}\right)$	$H°_{sd}\left(\frac{\text{kJ}}{\text{mol}}\right)$
$SnO_{(s)}$	–285.8	+285.8
$PbO_{(s)}$	–219.0	+219.0
$Fe_2O_{3(s)}$	–824.2	+385.2
$MnO_{(s)}$	–385.2	+385.2

It is now obvious why one mole of $Fe_2O_{3(s)}$ would require the greatest input of energy to decompose into its constituent elements.

NR1. 6.03

Fusion of water is the phase change for the process: $H_2O_{(s)} \rightarrow H_2O_{(l)}$. Page 3 of the Chemistry 30 Data Booklet gives this as +6.03kJ/mol.

The fusion referred to here is a physical process, not a nuclear process!

12. B

The ranges of the temperature changes recorded make it obvious that a warm mass of silicon was added to liquid water in an aluminum calorimeter and that no phase changes occurred. In other words, all the energy changes were increases or decreases in E_k. The E_k decrease of the silicon is equal in magnitude to the E_k increase of the surroundings (the water and the aluminum calorimeter). Thus,

$$q_{Si} = m_{Si}c_{Si}\Delta t_{Si}$$

$$= 0.0520\ \text{kg} \times 0.703\frac{\text{kJ}}{\text{kg°C}} \times (61.6 - 24.6)°\text{C}$$

$$= 1.35\ \text{kJ}$$

Or

$$q_{calorimeter} = q_{H_2O} + q_{Al}$$

$$= mc\Delta t + m_{Al}c_{Al}\Delta t_{Al}$$

(note: $\Delta t_{Al} = \Delta t_{H_2O}$**)**

$$= 0.100\ \text{kg} \times 4.19\frac{\text{kJ}}{\text{kg°C}} \times (24.6 - 23.0)°\text{C}$$

$$+ 0.470\ \text{kg} \times 0.900\frac{\text{kJ}}{\text{kg°C}} \times (24.6 - 23.0)°\text{C}$$

$$= 1.35\ \text{kJ}$$

The amount of energy lost by the silicon is 1.35 kJ.

Unlike a styrofoam cup calorimeter, the aluminum calorimeter in this experiment has a non-negligible mass and specific heat capacity. In addition, $Al_{(s)}$ is not a good insulator.

This is why its contribution was considered in computing the answer.

Alternative A gives the amount of energy absorbed by the water alone.

NR2. 68.1

Hess's Law is used to compute an enthalpy change for fermentation.

$$\Delta H^\circ_{net} = \Sigma nH^\circ_f\,(\text{products}) - \Sigma nH^\circ_f\,(\text{reactants})$$

$$= \left(2\,\text{mol} \times \left\{-393.5\frac{\text{kJ}}{\text{mol}}\right\} + 2\,\text{mol} \times \left\{-277.1\frac{\text{kJ}}{\text{mol}}\right\}\right)$$

$$-\left(1\,\text{mol} \times \left\{-1\,273.1\frac{\text{kJ}}{\text{mol}}\right\}\right)$$
$$= -68.1\,\text{kJ}$$

$$H^\circ_{fermentation\ C_6H_{12}O_{6(s)}} = \frac{\Delta H^\circ_{\text{net}}}{n_{C_6H_{12}O_6}}$$

$$= -68.1\frac{\text{kJ}}{\text{mol}}$$

Or, since only one mole of glucose is fermented, the molar enthalpy of fermentation is $-68.1\frac{\text{kJ}}{\text{mol}}$.

13. D

The balanced equation for the reaction is
$C_2H_{4(g)} + H_2O_{(l)} \rightarrow C_2H_5OH_{(l)}$

Hess's Law allows us to compute an enthalpy change.

$$\Delta H^\circ_{net} = \Sigma nH^\circ_f\,(\text{products}) - \Sigma nH^\circ_f\,(\text{reactants})$$

$$= 1\,\text{mol} \times \left\{+52.3\frac{\text{kJ}}{\text{mol}}\right\} + 1\,\text{mol} \times \left\{-285.8\frac{\text{kJ}}{\text{mol}}\right\}$$
$$-\left(1\,\text{mol} \times \left\{-277.1\frac{\text{kJ}}{\text{mol}}\right\}\right)$$

$$= -43.6\,\text{kJ}$$

This is an exothermic change corresponding to alternative D.

Wrong alternatives B and C are the result of subtracting ΣnH°_f (products) from ΣnH°_f (reactants), and in alternative C, $H^\circ_f\,(H_2O_{(g)})$ is used instead of $H^\circ_f\,(H_2O_{(l)})$. Alternative A employs the correct formula but uses $H^\circ_f\,(H_2O_{(g)})$ instead of $H^\circ_f\,(H_2O_{(l)})$.

14. C

When ethanol is metabolized in the body, the net reaction is as follows:

$$C_2H_5OH_{(l)} + 3O_{(g)} \rightarrow 2CO_{2(g)} + 3H_2O_{(l)}$$

The enthalpy change for this reaction, calculated using $\Delta H^\circ_{net} = \Sigma nH^\circ_f\,(\text{products}) - \Sigma nH^\circ_f\,(\text{reactants})$ is -1367.3kJ. Clearly it is an exothermic reaction. The oxidation number of each C in $C_2H_5OH_{(l)}$ increases from -2 to $+4$ as it forms $CO_{2(g)}$. Thus, the ethanol is oxidized. Alternatively, the reaction of most entities with oxygen results in oxidation of that entity.

NR3. 13.1

When one mole of ATP is consumed, the enthalpy change is $-30.5\frac{\text{kJ}}{\text{mol}}$ (H_{rxn} ATP). An enthalpy change of -400 kJ (ΔH_{rxn} ATP) requires

$$n_{\text{ATP}} = \frac{\Delta H_{rxn}}{H_{rxn}} = \frac{-400\text{ kJ}}{-30.5\text{kJ/mol}} = 13.1\text{ mol of ATP}$$

Not for Reproduction

15. A

The loss in E_k of the water, given that the energy from chemical reaction/ process is negligible, is equal to the E_k change of the ethanol. Thus,

$$q_{C_2H_5OH} = q_{H_2O}$$

$$m_{C_2H_5OH} \times c_{C_2H_5OH} \Delta t_{C_2H_5OH} = m_{H_2O} \times c_{H_2O} \times \Delta t_{H_2O}$$

$$c_{C_2H_5OH} = \frac{m_{H_2O} \times c_{H_2O} \times \Delta t_{H_2O}}{m_{C_2H_5OH} \times \Delta t_{C_2H_5OH}}$$

$$= \frac{50.7\text{ g} \times 4.19\frac{\text{J}}{\text{g°C}} \times (49.2 - 38.4)\text{°C}}{41.8\text{ g} \times (38.4 - 15.8)\text{°C}}$$

$$= 2.43\frac{\text{J}}{\text{g°C}}$$

The answer is A. The specific heat capacity of many substances is less than that of water.

NR4. 95.2

From the graph, $H°_{f\,(BaO_{2(s)})} = -648.7\text{ kJ / mol.}$

From the Chemistry 30 Data Booklet (page 6), $H°_{f\,(BaO_{(s)})} = -553.5\text{ kJ / mol.}$

The enthalpy change for the reaction given

$BaO_{(s)} + \frac{1}{2}O_{2(q)} \rightarrow BaO_{2(s)}$ is calculated using Hess's Law

$$\Delta H°_{net} = \Sigma nH°_{f\,(\text{products})} - \Sigma nH°_{f\,(\text{reactants})}$$

$$= \left(1\text{ mol} \times \left\{-648.7\frac{\text{kJ}}{\text{mol}}\right\}\right) - \left(1\text{ mol} \times \left\{-553.5\frac{\text{kJ}}{\text{mol}}\right\}\right)$$

$$= -95.2\text{ kJ}$$

The enthalpy change of the reaction is –95.2 kJ.

16. C

This is a simple E_k calculation as follows:

$q = mc\Delta t$

$$= 1.20 \times 10^6\text{ g} \times 4.19\frac{\text{J}}{\text{g°C}} \times (40.0 - 12.0)\text{°C}$$

$$= 1.41 \times 10^8\text{ J}$$

Clearly 1.41×10^8 J of energy must be supplied.

17. A

When water evaporates, it undergoes a change in phase from liquid to gas:

$H_2O_{(l)} \rightarrow H_2O_{(g)}$

When this phase change occurs, energy must be absorbed to break intermolecular bonds. Thus, the water on the player's skin undergoes an endothermic phase change.

Alternatives B and D are clearly wrong because evaporation is a phase change.

18. C

The high specific heat capacity of water requires the body to absorb a considerable amount of heat energy in order to change temperature to any significant extent.

Since water is not melted, vaporized, or formed from hydrogen and oxygen in the body, alternatives A, B, and D do not apply.

Copyright Protected

19. C

If there is no change in temperature, $\Delta t = 0$, then no E_k change is involved in this change (q or $\Delta E_k = mc\Delta t$).

Instead, the evaporation of water is an increase in potential energy that is readily estimated as follows.

$$\Delta H_{vap} = nH_{vap}$$
$$= 10.0\ \text{g} \times \frac{\text{mol}}{18.02\ \text{g}} \times (+40.8\ \text{kJ/mol})$$
$$= +22.6\ \text{kJ}$$

During evaporation, energy is absorbed to break intermolecular bonds between the liquid water molecules as they are converted into a gas.

NR5. 16.5

The answer to this problem is easily obtained using simple proportions:

342.34 g (1 mol) of sucrose yields 5 640.3 kJ of energy so

1.00 g yields

$$\Delta H = \frac{1.00\ \text{g}}{342.34\ \text{g}} \times 5\ 640.3\ \text{kJ} = 16.5\ \text{kJ}$$

Alternatively,

$$H_{rxn(C_{12}H_{22}O_{11(aq)})} = -5\ 640.3\ \text{kJ}$$
$$\Delta H_{rxn} = nH_{rxn}$$
$$= 1.00\ \text{g} \times \frac{\text{mol}}{342.34\ \text{g}} \times (-5\ 640.3\ \text{kJ/mol})$$
$$= -16.5\ \text{kJ}$$

Some 16.5 kJ of energy are available when 1.00 g of sucrose reacts.

NR6. 37.2

Mercury melts at –38.8°C and boils at 357°C, so for the temperature change given, liquid mercury is being warmed. If a sample of matter only changes temperature, it undergoes a change in E_k only. So:

$$q = mc\Delta t$$
$$= 3.21\ \text{g} \times 0.138\ \text{J/g°C} \times (101.2\text{°C} - 17.3\text{°C})$$
$$= 37.2\ \text{J}$$

20. C

All reactions that lose energy to their surroundings, exothermic reactions, have products with lower formation enthalpy than their reactants.

Only alternatives A and C depict exothermic reactions. The enthalpy change in alternative A is about –2 000 kJ, while in alternative C, it is about –3 000 kJ. The size of the activation energy hump is not a factor here. The main flaw in alternatives B and D is that the total molar enthalpies of formation of the reactants is not 0 kJ.

21. B

A change that causes the surroundings to warm up is, by definition, exothermic. In addition, if the substance does not experience a change in temperature, it is likely undergoing a phase change.

Condensation is an exothermic process because energy is released to the surroundings as intermolecular bonds are formed (in molecular substances, the situation is more complex for ionic compounds and metals/alloys) as a gas becomes liquid at the boiling point.

Alternative A is a poor choice because melting is an endothermic process. Heat energy is absorbed to break intermolecular bonds when a solid becomes a liquid at the melting point.

Alternative C is not a viable option because the temperature of the substance would change. An increase in potential energy of the substance would cause a decrease in the temperature of the surroundings so alternative D is wrong.

Not for Reproduction

22. B

It is nuclear reactions that occur in breeder reactors. In a nuclear reaction, the reactants and products involve different *elements*. Only alternative B fits this description.

The processes in alternatives A and D are chemical reactions, while in alternative C, the process is a phase change.

NR7. 2, 4, 3, 1

Reaction 1 is the formation of glucose.

Reaction 2 is nuclear fusion—a process in which small nuclei combine to form a larger nucleus.

Reaction 3 is photosynthesis—the process whereby plants convert carbon dioxide and water into oxygen and glucose.

Reaction 4 is nuclear fission—a process where large nuclei are split up to form two or more smaller nuclei.

23. A

By definition, all the elements in their standard states have zero enthalpy of formation. $O_{2(g)}$ is the only element of the choices available.

24. D

It is $CO_{2(g)}$ from the combustion of fossil fuels that is the prime culprit in what scientists now call the anthropogenic/runaway greenhouse effect. Higher levels of $CO_{2(g)}$ and other gases in the atmosphere are responsible for trapping ever-increasing quantities of infrared radiation in Earth's atmosphere.

It is chlorine atoms in the stratosphere that are destroying the ozone layer; oxygen and water or hydrogen ions that are responsible for the corrosion / oxidation of metals; and $CO_{2(g)}$ is not a toxin, though it will cause suffocation.

25. B

Amphiprotic entities can donate or accept protons in a Brønsted-Lowry neutralization. Typically, an amphiprotic entity appears on both sides of an acid-base table (see page 11 in the Chemistry 30 data book).

Of the choices available, only $H_2O_{(l)}$ fits the requirements. The answer is B.

26. B

Generally speaking, the energy per mole involved in common processes decreases in the order $H_{nuclear} > H_{chemical} > H_{phase} > \Delta E_k$.

Alternatives B and C involve phase changes, while alternative A is a nuclear change, and alternative D is a chemical change.

Since fewer intermolecular bonds need be broken when water fuses than when water vaporizes, alternative B represents the least energy per mole.

27. B

Photosynthesis is the means whereby plants and some other organisms absorb energy from the sun and store it as glucose and other carbohydrates. Processes that absorb heat energy to proceed are endothermic.

28. A

All nuclear and chemical processes involve the making and breaking of bonds. The net enthalpy change of a process is the difference between the energy absorbed to break bonds in the reactants and the energy released to make bonds in the products. Nuclear reactions are accompanied by much greater enthalpy changes than chemical reactions simply because the bonds made and broken in nuclear processes are so much stronger.

29. C

The heating curve shown illustrates the changes in temperature and phase of a sample of air warmed from below the boiling point of nitrogen, when the air sample is liquid, to above the boiling point of oxygen whereupon the air sample is gaseous.

The plateau regions B, D, and F correspond to the boiling points of nitrogen, argon, and oxygen, respectively. At these points, potential energy is absorbed to vaporize each respective component by breaking weak intermolecular bonds between the nitrogen, argon, or oxygen molecules. Regions A, C, E, and G correspond to warming periods when the air sample is gaining in kinetic energy. The answer is C.

30. D

The water molecules in the perspiration are produced at body temperature. Thus, the water molecules must warm up by gaining kinetic energy before potential energy is absorbed to break all the intermolecular bonds during vaporization.

Translational, rotational, and vibrational kinetic energy describe how the total kinetic energy of a collection of molecules is distributed. Alternative D is the only option that correctly identifies E_p and E_k.

31. A

When ammonium nitrate dissolves, energy is absorbed by the reaction (an endothermic reaction) and this is what causes the water (the surroundings) to cool down. On the other hand, when calcium chloride dissolves, the reaction loses energy (an exothermic reaction) and the water (the surroundings) warms up.

Alternatives B and C contradict themselves. A hot pack should contain an exothermic process. Clearly alternative A is most suitable (Alternative D indicates that ammonium nitrate would be a suitable *cold* pack ingredient).

32. A

The products of an endothermic process have more potential energy than the reactants, while the products of an exothermic process have less potential energy than the reactants. Remember, the dissolving of $CaCl_{2(s)}$ is exothermic. Alternatives C and D do not fit the description. Alternative B is suggestive, but it represents the dissolving of ammonium chloride as exothermic when it is, in fact, endothermic (it cools its surrounding). Alternative A is the only logical choice.

33. B

The reaction representing cellular respiration can be written as

$$C_6H_{12}O_{6(aq)} + 6O_{2(g)} \rightarrow 6CO_{2(g)} + 6H_2O_{(g)}$$

Cellular respiration releases energy stored in glucose in what is clearly an exothermic reaction. Given that hydrocarbon combustion is the primary means of producing energy to heat homes or produce electricity, it too must be an exothermic process. Consider the burning of natural gas:

$$CH_{4(g)} + 2O_{2(q)} \rightarrow CO_{2(4)} + 2H_2O_{(q)}$$

Therefore, statement II is incorrect.

In methane combustion, the oxidation number of C increases from –4 to + 4. During cellular respiration, the oxidation number of carbon rises from 0 to +4. In both processes, the oxidation number of oxygen decreases from 0 to –2. Clearly, cellular respiration and hydrocarbon combustion are reduction-oxidation processes. Thus, statement III is correct.

While many students may not know the precise structure of glucose, it is not difficult to see that C–H bonds are broken when glucose and methane react with oxygen. In addition, the C=O bonds of carbon dioxide are evident in both reactions. Clearly, statement I is correct. The answer is B.

(Alternatively, the answer cannot include statement II – this rules out all but alternative B.)

Not for Reproduction

34. B

Using the short form of Hess's Law, namely

$\Delta H^\circ_{net} = \Sigma nH^\circ_{f\,(Products)} - \Sigma nH^\circ_{f\,(Reactants)}$

We can substitute to get:

$$-562.0\text{ kJ} = \left(2\text{ mol} \times \left\{\frac{-54.8\text{ kJ}}{\text{mol}}\right\} + 2\text{ mol} \times H^\circ_f\text{ W}\right) - \left(1\text{ mol} \times \left\{\frac{-22.5\text{ kJ}}{\text{mol}}\right\} + 3\text{ mol} \times \left\{\frac{+78.3\text{ kJ}}{\text{mol}}\right\}\right)$$

Rearranging this equation gives us :

$$2\text{ mol} \times H^\circ_f\text{W} = -562.0\text{ kJ} + 212.4\text{ kJ} + 109.6\text{ kJ}$$

$$2\text{ mol} \times H^\circ_f\text{W} = -240.0\text{ kJ}$$

$$H^\circ_f\text{W} = -120.0\text{ kJ / mol}$$

The standard molar heat/enthalpy of formation of substance W is –120.0 kJ/mol.

35. C

The balanced combustion reaction for ethanol is $C_2H_5OH_{(l)} + 3O_{2(g)} \rightarrow 2CO_{2(g)} + 3H_2O_{(g)}$

The enthalpy change can be obtained from $\Delta H^\circ_{net} = \Sigma nH^\circ_{f\,(products)} - \Sigma nH^\circ_{f\,(reactants)}$, as follows

$$\Delta H^\circ_{net} = \left(2\text{ mol} \times \left\{\frac{-393.5\text{ kJ}}{\text{mol}}\right\} + 3\text{ mol} \times \left\{\frac{-241.8\text{ kJ}}{\text{mol}}\right\}\right)$$

$$-\left(1\text{ mol} \times \left\{\frac{-277.1\text{ kJ}}{\text{mol}}\right\}\right) = -1235.3\text{ kJ}$$

(Alternatively, ethanol is a fuel. The endothermic choices in alternatives A and D are incorrect. Alternative B does not give a balanced equation and it makes $H_2O_{(l)}$.)

NR8. 1, 2, 3, 6

A simple calorimetric equation would most likely be used to estimate the molar enthalpy of combustion of the ethanol.

An equation like: $nH = (mc\Delta t)_{H_2O}$

where n = the number of moles of ethanol consumed
H = the molar enthalpy of combustion of ethanol
m = the mass of the water
c = the specific heat capacity of liquid
Δt = the maximum temperature change of the water

The initial and final temperatures of the aluminum calorimeter and the water can be assumed to be the same, so data point 1 is needed. The mass of water will be the difference in calorimeter data: points 3 and 2. The mass change of the ethanol, data point 6, will give n, the number of moles of ethanol burned.

NR9. 1.04

Using the formula

$nH = mc\Delta t$

and rearranging it to give

$$H = \frac{mc\Delta t}{n}$$

we substitute to get

$$H = \frac{\left(0.500\text{ kg} \times 4.19\frac{\text{kJ}}{\text{kg}} \times {}^\circ\text{C}\right) \times (91.0^\circ\text{C} - 25.0^\circ\text{C})}{(0.133\text{ mol})}$$

$$= 1.04 \times 10^3\text{ kJ / mol}$$

An estimated molar enthalpy of combustion of the ethanol is –1.04 MJ/mol.

Note: $10^3\text{ kJ} = 1\text{ MJ}$, and the reaction is exothermic (–) because energy is lost by the reaction. The heat lost warmed the water.

Copyright Protected

36. C

The $H^\circ_{f\,(C_2H_5OH_{(l)})} = -277.1\,\text{kJ}$

The formation reaction of ethanol is

$$2C_{(s)} + 3H_{2(g)} + \frac{1}{2}O_{2(g)} \rightarrow C_2H_5OH_{(l)}$$

The negative sign in the formation enthalpy signifies that energy is lost (we can say *produced*) when ethanol forms from its elements.

Clearly,

$$2C_{(s)} + 3H_2 + \frac{1}{2}O_{2(g)} \rightarrow C_2H_5OH_{(l)} + 277.1\,\text{kJ}$$

The answer must be C.

Note: Alternative A represents an endothermic reaction, alternative B is the combustion of ethanol, and alternative D represents the "acidity" of ethanol in water, which is negligible given the extremely small *K* value.

NR10. 1.70

The equation given in the information box indicates that 850.0 kJ of heat energy is released when 2 mol of $NaAlO_{2(aq)}$ is produced. When 4.00 mol of $NaAlO_{2(aq)}$ is generated, twice as much energy will be released or

$$\Delta H = \frac{4.00\,\text{mol}}{2.00\,\text{mol}} \times (-850.0\,\text{kJ}) = -1.70\,\text{MJ}$$

The heat released is 1.70 MJ.

37. D

For a reaction in a simple calorimeter,

$nH = mc\Delta t$ where

n = the number of moles of reactant
H = the molar enthalpy of the reaction for the reactant
m = the mass of water warmed or cooled by the reaction
c = the specific heat capacity of liquid water
Δt = the temperature change of the water in the calorimeter

Thus, $H = \dfrac{mc\Delta t}{n}$

$$= \frac{0.120\,\text{kg} \times 4.19\frac{\text{kJ}}{\text{kg}} \times {}^\circ\text{C} \times (20.2 - 17.8)^\circ\text{C}}{\left(12\,\text{g} \times \frac{\text{mol}}{132.16\,\text{g}}\right)}$$

= 13 kJ/mol

Since the calorimeter cooled down, the reaction is endothermic. The experimental molar enthalpy of solution of ammonium sulfate is +13 kJ/mol. (The positive sign indicates that the reaction gained 13 kJ.)

Not for Reproduction

38. A

The combustion reaction of butane is

$$C_4H_{10(g)} + \frac{13}{2}O_{2(g)} \rightarrow 4CO_{2(g)} + 5H_2O_{(g)}$$

Using
$\Delta H°_{net} = \Sigma nH°_{f\,(Products)} - \Sigma nH°_{f\,(Reactants)}$
We get

$$\Delta H°_{net} = 4\text{ mol} \times \left\{\frac{-393.5\text{ kJ}}{\text{mol}}\right\} + 5\text{ mol} \times \left\{\frac{-241.8\text{ kJ}}{\text{mol}}\right\} - \left(1\text{ mol} \times \left\{\frac{-126.5\text{ kJ}}{\text{mol}}\right\}\right)$$

$$= -2\,656.5\text{ kJ}$$

The molar enthalpy of combustion of butane is –2 656.5 kJ/mol (one mole of butane burned).

You can now use $\Delta H = nH$ to calculate the heat released when 1.00 g of butane burns.

$$\Delta H = nH = \left(1.00\text{ g} \times \frac{\text{mol}}{58.14\text{ g}}\right) \times \left(-2656.5\frac{\text{kJ}}{\text{mol}}\right)$$

$$= -45.7\text{ kJ}$$

The heat released when 1.00 g of butane burns is 45.7 kJ.

NR11. 3.15

When a sample of matter is warmed (only), it undergoes an E_k change as given by $q = mc\Delta t$.

In this case,

$$q = 2.03\text{ g} \times \frac{0.444\text{ J}}{\text{g°C}} \times (375 - 25.0)\text{°C}$$

$$= 315 \text{ or } 3.15 \times 10^2\text{ J}$$

39. B

The equation given is akin to cellular respiration—the metabolism of carbohydrate to obtain/release energy. Energy is written as a product of the reaction so alternative B is the answer.

Written Response

1. a) ***Measurements***

- mass or volume of water
- mass of $Cu_{(s)}$ calorimeter
- initial temperature of water
- highest temperature of water
- initial mass of candle
- final mass of candle

b)

Heat produced by combustion = Heat absorbed by water + Heat absorbed by calorimeter

$$nH = mc\Delta t + mc\Delta t$$

n = moles of wax burned (m/M)
H = molar enthalpy of combustion
m = mass of water/copper
c = specific heat capacity of water/copper
Δt = temperature change of water/copper

c. *Improvements for product materials:*

- use of a bomb calorimeter
- protect the flame from air currents (e. g., surround it with a cylinder)
- include m and c for thermometer
- place in centre of calorimeter
- insulate calorimeter/ use stirrer
- t_i is as many °C below room temp as t_f above room temp
- do several trials
- calorimeter that conducts heat better than copper

Not for Reproduction

ANSWERS AND SOLUTIONS
CHEMICAL ENERGETICS – UNIT TEST 1

1. D	**NR2. 1 3 2 1**	**9. A**	**15. C**	**21. D**
2. B	**6. C**	**10. A**	**16. A**	**22. C**
3. C	**7. B**	**11. C**	**17. D**	**23. D**
4. C	**NR3. 1.19**	**12. C**	**18. D**	
5. B	**8. C**	**13. A**	**19. C**	
NR1. 40.8 or 44.0	**NR4. 13.2**	**14. D**	**20. B**	

1. D

The combustion of methane is an exothermic process. This means that the product molecules have some 802.3 kJ ($\Delta H°$ combustion) less potential energy than the reactant molecules. Distractors A, B, and C would all tend to increase—they comprise the kinetic energy of the products, which will be higher at normal reaction temperature.

2. B

For any substance, $\Delta E_k \propto \Delta t$. In the diagram shown, only regions I-II, III-IV, and V-VI correspond to E_k changes. Region I-II (below melting point) corresponds to warming ice. Region V-VI (above boiling point) corresponds to warming steam. Region III-IV (between boiling point and melting point) corresponds to warming liquid water.

3. C

Most metals do not melt in the 20.0°C to 50.0°C range, so it is likely that absorbed energy is kinetic energy only. In this case,

$q = mc\Delta t$

so $c = \dfrac{q}{m\Delta t} = \dfrac{178\text{ J}}{25.0\text{ g} \times 30.0°\text{C}} = 0.237\dfrac{\text{J}}{\text{g°C}}$

The specific heat capacity of the metal sample is $0.237\dfrac{\text{J}}{\text{g°C}}$ (The metal is probably silver.)

4. C

The total energy change in going from point X to point Y is: $\Delta E_{Total} = nH_{fusion} + mc\Delta t$

Characteristic properties 1, 2, and 5 are unnecessary to calculate ΔE_{Total}—the compound vaporizes beyond point Y. Characteristic property 3 is required to calculate ΔE_{Total}—it is needed to calculate the energy to warm the liquid compound from 20°C to 120°C (point Y). Characteristic property 5 is needed to calculate the energy required to melt the unknown at 20°C.

5. B

Generally speaking, $H_{nuclear} >> H_{chemical} > H_{phase}$. Reaction B, α emission, is a nuclear process, while distractor A represents a phase change and distractors C and D represent chemical reactions.

NR1. 40.8 or 44.0

Page 3 of the Chemistry Data Booklet has the equation $H_2O_{(l)} \rightarrow H_2O_{(g)}$, H = + 40.8 kJ. Vaporization is the phase change from liquid to gas that occurs at the boiling point of a substance. Thus, 40.8 kJ/mol is the energy required breaks intermolecular bonds (in the case of a substance such as water).

Copyright Protected

NR2. 1 3 2 1

The sublimation of dry ice ($CO_{2(s)} \rightarrow CO_{2(g)}$) and the condensation of water ($H_2O_{(g)} \rightarrow H_2O_{(l)}$) involve the breaking/making of bonds between molecules, therefore, intermolecular bonds.

When hydrogen atoms fuse to form helium,

$4\,{}^{1}_{1}H \rightarrow {}^{4}_{2}He + 2\,{}^{0}_{1}e$ bonds are made/broken within atomic nuclei, therefore, intranuclear bonds. When gasoline burns in an automobile engine,

$$2C_8H_{18(g)} + 25O_{2(g)} \rightarrow 16CO_{2(g)} + 18H_2O_{(g)}$$

bonds are made/broken within molecules, therefore, intramolecular bonds.

6. C

Energy is released from plant material when it rots, is burned, or is eaten—all of which are chemical changes. A chemical change occurs when the products of a process have a different chemical composition from the reactants, e.g.

$$C_6H_{12}O_6 + 6O_2 \rightarrow 6CO_2 + 6H_2O$$

7. B

Recall that an exothermic reaction loses heat to its surroundings. This means that energy is a reaction product and can also be communicated as a negative enthalpy change, $\Delta H <$ 0kJ. Equation I fits this description. In reaction III, + 110.5 kJ on the product side is equal to $\Delta H = -110.5$ kJ, i.e., $\Delta H < 0$. Therefore, reaction III is also exothermic. Reactions in which energy is a reactant (communicated as a positive enthalpy change, $\Delta h > 0$ kJ) are endothermic reactions. Reactions II and IV are endothermic.

NR3. 1.19

Be careful here: this question only asks for the energy involved, **not** the molar enthalpy of the reaction. Since the heat capacity of the calorimeter is quoted, the enthalpy change is readily computed:

$$\Delta H = C\Delta t = 228\frac{\text{J}}{°\text{C}} \times (21.6 - 16.4°\text{C})$$

$$= 228 \text{ J/°C} \times 5.2° \text{ C} = 1.2 \times 10^3 \text{ J or } 1.2 \text{ kJ}$$

Before rounding, the three-digit answer is 1.19 kJ.

8. C

Neither the division on the thermometer (I) nor the room temperature (IV) are manipulated variables in the experiment (I limits the precision of the responding variable, and the effect of IV is severely limited/controlled by the insulation). Only the mass of the water (II) and the mass of the copper sample (III) are suitable as manipulated variables.

NR4. 13.2

The enthalpy of solidification of the copper is equivalent to the kinetic energy change of the calorimeter.

$$n_{\text{Cu}}H_{solidification} = (mc\Delta t)_{calorimeter}$$

$$H_{solidification} = \frac{(mc\Delta t)_{calorimeter}}{n_{\text{Cu}}}$$

$$= \frac{(0.200\text{kg})(4.19\frac{\text{kJ}}{\text{g°C}})(17.34 - 11.23)°\text{C}}{24.6\text{g} / 63.55\frac{\text{g}}{\text{mol}}}$$

$$= 13.2\frac{\text{kJ}}{\text{mol}}$$

The molar enthalpy/heat of solidification of copper is –13.2 kJ/mol.

Not for Reproduction

9. A

We need only apply the equation $\Delta H_{solution} = nH_{solution}$ to this problem. Thus,

$$\Delta H_{solution} = n_{\text{NaOH}} H_{solution}$$
$$= \left(\frac{25.0\text{g}}{40.00\frac{\text{g}}{\text{mol}}}\right)\left(-44.6\frac{\text{kJ}}{\text{mol}}\right)$$
$$= -27.9 \text{ kJ}$$

The answer signifies that 27.9 kJ of energy are released to the calorimeter.

10. A

Simple stoichiometric calculations show that, in this excess-limiting problem, 24.0g of $C_{(s)}$ are sufficient to make 0.666 mol of propane ($C_3H_{8(g)}$) while 10.0 g of $H_{2(g)}$ are enough to prepare 1.24 mol of propane. Clearly, the $H_{2(g)}$ is in excess, and the enthalpy released depends on the amount of propane predicted for the $C_{(s)}$ available.

$$3C_{(s)} + 4H_{2(g)} \rightarrow C_3H_{8(g)}$$
$$\Delta H_f^{\circ} = -103.8 \text{ kJ}$$
$$n_{C_{(s)}} = \frac{24.0 \text{ g}}{12.01\frac{\text{g}}{\text{mol}}} = 2.00 \text{ mol}$$
$$n_{C_3H_{8(g)}} = \frac{1}{3} n_{C_{(s)}} = \frac{1}{3}(2.00 \text{ mol}) = 0.666 \text{ mol}$$
$$\Delta H_f^{\circ} = nH_f^{\circ} = (0.666 \text{ mol})\left(-103.8\frac{\text{kJ}}{\text{mol}}\right)$$
$$= -69.1 \text{ kJ}$$

The maximum heat liberated by the reaction is 69.1 kJ.

11. C

When rewritten, the balanced equation with whole number coefficients that includes an energy term is

$$Al_4C_{3(s)} + 12H_2O_{(l)} \rightarrow 4\,Al(OH)_{3(s)} + 3CH_{4(g)} + 1\,763.0 \text{ kJ}.$$

If the equation were rewritten to represent one mole of $CH_{4(g)}$, the energy produced would be precisely one-third of 1 763.0 kJ; i.e., 587.7 kJ on the product side.

Alternatively:

$$H_{reaction}(CH_{4(g)}) = \frac{\Delta H_{reaction}}{n_{CH_4}}$$
$$= \frac{-1\,763.0 \text{ kJ}}{3 \text{ mol}} = -587.67 \text{ kJ}$$

This corresponds to 587.7 kJ on the product side of the appropriately balanced equation.

12. C

A cold pack feels cold because the reaction occurring within it absorbs kinetic energy from its surroundings. Formally speaking, when $NH_4NO_{3(s)}$ dissolves, more potential energy is **absorbed** in breaking ionic bonds within the salt than is **released** in forming bonds (ion dipole attractions) between water molecules and the NH_4^+ and NO_3^- ion, respectively.

Any reaction that cools its surroundings for this reason is an endothermic reaction. (Exothermic reactions warm their surroundings because more energy is released in forming bonds within the products than is absorbed to break bonds within the reactants).

13. A

If an industrial process is exothermic it produces energy—energy that may be used to offset the amount of fuel that must be burned to keep the process warm.

Copyright Protected

14. D

A reaction that loses/releases energy is said to be exothermic. The energy profile of such a reaction is as follows:

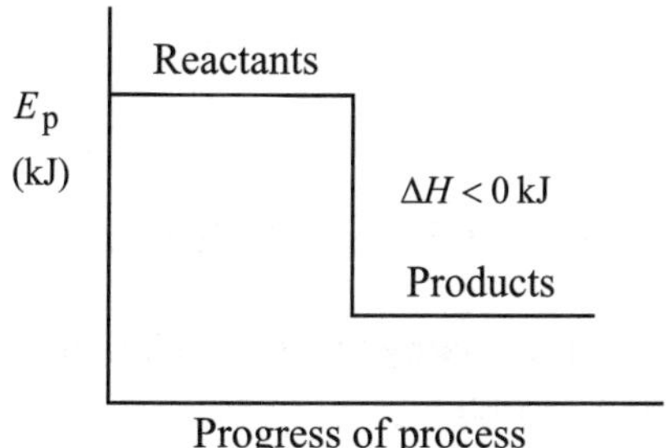

Clearly, the reactants have more E_p than do the products.

15. C

Hess' Law states that the enthalpy change for a reaction is the difference in enthalpy between the products and the reactants. In equation form, we write:

$$\Delta H_{net} = \Sigma nH^\circ_f(\text{products}) + \Sigma nH^\circ_f(\text{reactants})$$
$$= (-640\text{kJ}) - (-560\text{kJ})$$
$$= -80 \text{ kJ}$$

The enthalpy change for the reaction is –80 kJ.

16. A

The information box refers to "the energy change for the dissolving of ammonium nitrate." Clearly, the energy change can only represent an enthalpy of solution.

17. D

Hess's Law might otherwise be interpreted as "no matter what reaction pathway is broken between reactant X and product W, the enthalpy change for the reaction is the difference in formation enthalpies of X and W!"

Alternative A has no bearing on thermodynamics, while alternatives B and C cannot be derived from the information given (it is not an enthalpy diagram). Put another way, if the route $X \rightarrow Y \rightarrow Z \rightarrow W$ was the catalysed alternative to direct reaction, $X \rightarrow W$, the enthalpy change would be the same!

18. D

For any reaction
$$\Delta H^\circ_{net} = \Sigma nH^\circ_f(products) - \Sigma nH^\circ_f(reactants)$$

So

$$\Sigma nH^\circ_f(H_2SO_{4(aq)}) = \Delta H^\circ_{net} + \Sigma nH^\circ_f(reactants)$$
$$= -227.8 \text{ kJ} + (1 \text{ mol} \times [-395.7 \tfrac{\text{kJ}}{\text{mol}}] +$$
$$1 \text{ mol} \times [-285.8 \tfrac{\text{kJ}}{\text{mol}}])$$
$$+ (1 \text{ mol} \times H^\circ_f[H_2SO_{4(aq)}])$$
$$= -909.3 \text{ kJ}$$
$$H^\circ_f(H_2SO_{4(aq)}) = -909.3 \tfrac{\text{kJ}}{\text{mol}}$$

19. C

Reaction I represents cellular respiration in cell mitochondria, and reaction II represents the complete combustion of glucose to gaseous products. In both reactions, carbon is oxidized (its oxidation number increases from 0 to +4). Simple ΔH°_{net} calculations and/or common sense tell us that both reactions are exothermic. When one mole of $H_2O_{(g)}$ is produced, the amount of energy released is 44.0 kJ less than when one mole of $H_2O_{(l)}$ is produced.

20. B

When one mole of water vapour is produced from its elements, 241.8 kJ of heat energy is released to the surroundings (Note: $H_2O_{(l)}$ is amphiprotic so alternative A is correct. $H_2O_{(l)}$ lies on both sides of a standard electrode potential table so alternative C is correct. Alternative D, also correct, is part of the modified Arrhenius definition of acids).

21. D

Historically speaking, the reaction of a compound or element with oxygen is referred to as oxidation. Moreover, the oxidation number of tin increases from 0 to +2, which signifies a loss of 2 moles of e^- per mole of $Sn_{(s)}$. Therefore, the tin is oxidized! The $H_{f\,(SnO_{(s)})} = -285.8 \frac{kJ}{mol}$, an exothermic formation reaction.

22. C

When $SO_{3(g)}$ dissolves, energy is released to the surroundings (an exothermic reaction/energy is a product of the reaction) and causes an increase in temperature. In addition, as $H_2SO_{4(aq)}$ is formed, the solution will become acidic and the pH will drop.

23. D

The statement (i) does not mention which chemical contributes to global warming, therefore, it is not scientific; (ii) makes no mention of cost, therefore, it is not economic; and (iii) contains no reference to nation states/levels of government, therefore, it is not political.

The statement does refer to a serious environmental/ecological problem facing the planet as a consequence of increasing reliance on fossil fuel combustion for energy to fuel industrial growth.

Written Response

1. **a)** $C_{12}H_{22}O_{11(s)} + 12O_{2(g)} \rightarrow$

$12CO_{2(g)} + 11H_2O_{(l)}$

$$\Delta E_p = 12(-393.5\text{ kJ}) + 11(-285.8\text{ kJ}) - (-2225.5\text{ kJ})$$

The molar enthalpy for the oxidation of sucrose is –5640.3 kJ/mol.

b) $\left(\frac{6.84+6.75+6.79}{3}\right)\text{g}\left(\frac{1\text{ mol}}{342.34\text{ g}}\right)5\,640.3\text{kJ/mol}$

$= 112$ kJ

c) E_p diagram for $C_{12}H_{22}O_{11(s)}$

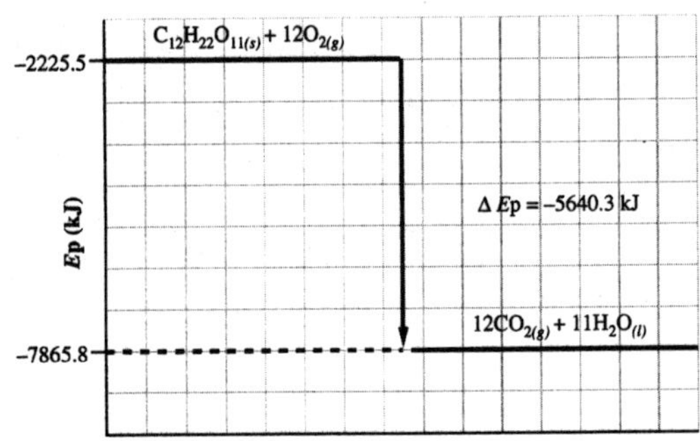

Copyright Protected

2. **a)** $\Delta H_1 = [-1\,914.0\text{kJ} + 2(-241.8\text{kJ})] - [-1\,129.7\text{kJ} + 4(-271.1\text{kJ})]$

$= -183.5$ kJ (–271.5 kJ for water liquid)

$\Delta H_2 = -2\,112.9 \text{ kJ} - (1\,914.0 \text{ kJ}) = -198.9 \text{ kJ}$

$\Delta H_{net} = -183.5 \text{ kJ} + (-198.9 \text{ kJ}) = -382.4 \text{ kJ}$

$$\frac{2.00 \times 10^6 \text{g}}{352.03 \text{ g / mol}} \times \frac{1}{1} \times 382.4 \text{ kJ / mol} = 2.17 \text{ GJ}$$

(2.19 GJ for U-235 with M = 349 g/mol)

b) Advantages:

- nuclear reactors do not add to the greenhouse effect, acid rain, etc.
- Canada has a lot of uranium ore
- high-energy density
- use of radioscopes
- preservation of existing fuels for other usage
- low cost of fuel

Disadvantages:

- nuclear fuel wastes are difficult to dispose of
- reactors cause thermal pollution
- possible catastrophic accidents
- high cost of technology/plant set-up/staff expertise
- high cost of decommissioning of nuclear plants
- military use of byproducts
- non-renewable

Copyright Protected

ANSWERS AND SOLUTIONS
REDUCTION–OXIDATION – UNIT REVIEW

1. C	**12. D**	**21. C**	**32. B**
2. B ‡	**NR3. 16.4**	**NR7. 8.05**	**33. B**
3. C	**NR4. 0.31 ‡ ‡**	**22. B**	**34. B**
4. A	**13. A**	**23. D**	**NR9. 2, 3, 1, 4++**
5. A	**14. C**	**24. A**	**35. D**
6. D	**NR5. 2 1 2 1**	**NR8. 1.10**	**36. C**
NR1. 1356	**15. A**	**25. A**	**NR10. 56.2***
7. C	**16. A**	**26. A**	**37. A**
8. B	**17. D**	**27. A**	**38. D**
9. A	**18. C**	**28. B**	**39. A**
10. C	**19. B**	**29. A**	**40. C**
NR2. 1.50	**NR6. 3142**	**30. D**	**41. D**
11. D	**20. B**	**31. B**	**42. B****

1. ‡ If MC1 is
   A, then MC2 is C
   B, then MC2 is D
   C, then MC2 is B
   D, then MC2 is A

2. ‡ ‡NR4 = NR3 × 0.01875

3. ++ accept 2, 3, 1, 3

4. * If MC36 is
   A or B, then NR10 is 22.5
   C or D, then NR10 is 56.2*

5. ** If MC41 is
   A, then MC42 is C
   B, then MC42 is D
   C, then MC42 is A
   D, then MC42 is B*

1. C

In most electrochemical cells, the strongest reducing agent present is oxidized at the anode. When brine is electrolyzed, although $H_2O_{(l)}$ is predicted to be the strongest reducing agent, it is the chloride ion that is oxidized/loses electrons at the anode. The oxidation of the chloride ion, a faster reaction than the oxidation of water, is made possible in part by the excess applied potential typical for electrolytic cells (an overpotential).

Alternatives A and B are reductions.

Not for Reproduction

2. B

Chlorine bleaches litmus paper (and litmus solution)—an observation that is best remembered from a laboratory demonstration.

Alternative A, the test for $O_{2(g)}$, is correct for those who picked D in MC 1.

Alternative C, the litmus effect of bases, corresponds to A in MC 1.

Alternative D, the reaction of a $Na_{(s)}$ (a very strong reducing agent) with water, corresponds to option B in MC 1.

3. C

As ethanol is oxidized by a dichromate ion, strong acid is consumed (reactant $H^{+}_{(aq)}$) and weak acid is produced ($CH_3COOH_{(aq)}$). Accordingly, the product solution is expected to be less acidic than the reactant solution. A less acidic solution has a higher pH. Clearly, the answer is C.

4. A

The oxidation number (ON) changes in the reaction are as follows (the O and H atoms are unaffected in the reaction):

$$5\overset{-2}{C}_2H_5OH_{(l)} + 4\overset{+7}{Mn}O_4^{-}{}_{(aq)} + 12H^{+}_{(aq)} \rightarrow$$

$$5\overset{0}{C}H_3\overset{0}{C}OOH_{(aq)} + 4\overset{2+}{Mn}{}^{2+}_{(aq)} + 11H_2O_{(l)}$$

Since the ON of C increases from –2 to +2, the C atoms have lost e^- and been oxidized. This means that the ethanol the reducing agent. The Mn in $MnO_4^{-}{}_{(aq)}$ undergoes a decrease in oxidation number from +7 to +2 because each Mn has gained $5e^-$. As is typical, the acidified $MnO_4^{-}{}_{(aq)}$ is the oxidizing agent.

No entities have the ONs +8, +10, or +28, so alternatives B and D are incorrect. The ONs in alternative C refer to $Mn^{2+}{}_{(aq)}$ and C in $CH_3COOH_{(aq)}$, neither of which is the oxidizing agent.

5. A

By definition, voltaic cells "host" a spontaneous chemical reaction that converts chemical energy into electrical energy. It is in electrolytic cells that the application of electrical energy forces a non-spontaneous reaction: a reaction that converts electrical energy into chemical energy.

6. D

On a reduction half-reaction table, the strongest reducing agent is the entity on the right side of the table that has the lowest reduction potential/electrode potential. It is obvious from the table below that aluminum would be the strongest reducing agent.

Entity	$E°_R$ (V)
$I^{-}{}_{(aq)}$	+0.54
$Br_{2(aq)}$	+0.85 (an oxidizing agent)
$H_2O_{(l)}$	+1.23
$Al_{(s)}$	–1.66

Copyright Protected

NR1. 1 3 5 6

Only those processes in which the oxidation numbers of two or more reactant atoms change over the course of the reaction can be considered reduction-oxidation reactions. In reactions 2 and 4, none of the atoms involved undergoes a change in oxidation number.

In reaction 1, the ONs of Fe and Cr change.

In reaction 3, the ONs of N and O change.

In reaction 5, the ONs of Sn and N change.

In reaction 6, the ONs of Pb and S change.

7. C

It is logical to assume that $CaMoO_{4(s)}$ is a salt of $Ca^{2+}{}_{(s)}$ and $MoO_4{}^{2-}{}_{(s)}$. All the ONs in a polyatomic ion add up to the charge on that ion. Thus (call the ON of Mo *x*; the ON of O is –2, as usual):

$$x - 4(-2) = -2$$

$$x = +6$$

The ON of Mo in $MoO_4{}^{2-}{}_{(s)}$ is +6.

8. B

The half-reactions that occur when iron is oxidized are

Cathode:

$$O_{2(g)} + 2H_2O_{(l)} + 4e^- \rightarrow 4OH^-{}_{(aq)}$$

$$E°_R = +0.40\text{ V}$$

Anode:

$$2Fe_{(s)} \rightarrow 2Fe^{2+}{}_{(aq)} + 4e^-$$

$$E°_R = -0.45\text{ V}$$

$$E°_{net} = E°_R\ cathode - E°_R\ anode$$

$$= +0.40\text{ V} - (-0.45\text{ V})$$

$$= +0.85\text{ V}$$ The answer is B.

Note: when the anode half-reaction is doubled, its $E°_R$ is left untouched. Alternatives A and C refer to nonspontaneous reactions—rust formation is spontaneous. Alternative D is what results if the $E°_R$ for the anode half-reaction is doubled. When a half-cell is doubled, twice as much reaction occurs but the potential energy per coulomb of electrons produced (the $E°_R$) does not change.

9. A

When zinc is alloyed/mixed with iron, it is the zinc (the stronger reducing agent) that will be oxidized and thus act as an anode.

10. C

A water droplet sitting on a metal surface acts both as a salt bridge and the electrolyte for each region (anodic and cathodic). A salty water droplet would act as a higher conductivity salt bridge/electrolyte. Clearly, alternative C is the best answer.

Not for Reproduction

NR2. 1.50

Under standard conditions, the half-cell reactions for the reaction of $Au^{3+}{}_{(aq)}$ with $H_{2(g)}$ are:

	$E°_R$
Cathode: $Au^{3+}{}_{(aq)} + 3e^- \rightarrow Au_{(s)}$	+1.50 V
Anode: $H_{2(g)} \rightarrow 2H^+{}_{(aq)} + 2e^-$	0.00 V

$E°_{net} = E°_R\ cathode - E°_R\ anode$

$$= +1.50\text{ V} - 0.00\text{ V}$$
$$= +1.50\text{ V}$$

The cell potential for the reaction is 1.50V. It is not necessary to compute the net cell reaction. When multiples of the half-reactions are employed, their $E°_R$ values are left untouched.

11. D

More often than not, metal ions act as oxidizing agents and metal elements act as reducing agents. A spontaneous reduction–oxidation reaction is predicted when, on a reduction half-reaction table, the oxidizing agent lies above the reducing agent.

In diagrammatic form, the following locations of OA and RA are evident from the reactions:

First Reaction	Second Reaction	Third Reaction	Fourth Reaction	Fifth Reaction
$X_{(s)}$	$X^{2+}{}_{(aq)}$	$D^+{}_{(aq)}$	$D_{(s)}$	$Z_{(s)}$
$Z^{3+}{}_{(aq)}$	$D_{(s)}$	$A_{(s)}$	$Z^{3+}{}_{(aq)}$	$A^{2+}{}_{(aq)}$

The reduction half-reaction table likely from these pieces of evidence is:

$X^{2+}{}_{(aq)} + 2e^-$ ”$X_{(s)}$

$D^+{}_{(aq)} + e^-$ ”$D_{(s)}$

$Z^{3+}{}_{(aq)} + 3e^-$ ”$Z_{(s)}$

$A^{2+}{}_{(aq)} + 2e^-$ ”$A_{(s)}$

The oxidizing agents (left side) arranged in order from strongest to weakest correspond to answer D.

12. D

A five-step redox prediction method will provide the net reaction. The species present are:

$\overset{OA}{K^+{}_{(aq)}}, \overset{SOA}{MnO_4{}^-{}_{(aq)}}, \overset{OA}{H^+{}_{(aq)}}, \underset{SRA}{H_2O_{2(l)}}, \overset{OA}{\underset{RA}{H_2O_{(l)}}}$

Reduction:

$$2MnO_4{}^-{}_{(aq)} + 16H^+{}_{(aq)} + 10e^- \rightarrow 2Mn^{2+}{}_{(aq)} + 8H_2O_{(l)}$$

Oxidation:

$$5H_2O_{2(l)} \rightarrow 5O_{2(g)} + 10H^+{}_{(aq)} + 10e^-$$

Net Redox Reaction:

$$2MnO_4{}^-{}_{(aq)} + 6H^+{}_{(aq)} + 5H_2O_{2(l)} \rightarrow 2Mn^{2+}{}_{(aq)} + 8H_2O_{(l)} + 5O_{2(g)}$$

This is the spontaneous net reaction, and it corresponds to alternative D.

NR3. 16.4

The volumes for each trial are:

Trial	Volume of $KMnO_{4(aq)}$
I	17.39 mL
II	16.3mL
III	16.5mL
IV	16.4mL

The average volume of $KMnO_{4(aq)}$ added is the average of those volumes obtained in trials 2 to 4. The average is 16.4 mL.

NR4. 0.31

A stoichiometric calculation based on equation A, B, C or D in MC 12 proceeds as follows:

$$n_{MnO^-_4} = 16.4\text{ mL} \times \frac{0.15\text{ mol}}{\text{L}} = 2.5\text{ mmol}$$

$$n_{H_2O_2} = \frac{5}{2} n_{MnO^-_4} = \frac{5}{2} \times 2.5\text{ mmol} = 6.5\text{ mmol}$$

$$[H_2O_{2(aq)}] = \frac{6.5\text{ mmol}}{20.0\text{ mL}} = 0.31\frac{\text{mol}}{\text{L}}$$

The hydrogen peroxide concentration is $0.31\frac{\text{mol}}{\text{L}}$.

(Whatever answer was obtained in NR3, the answer to NR4 = 0.01875 × NR3.)

13. A

A molecule/ion/compound has been reduced when the oxidation number of an atom within that molecule/ion/compound decreases as a result of a chemical reaction.

In alternative A, the oxidation number of carbon decreases from +4 in $CO_{2(g)}$ to 0 in $C_6H_{12}O_{6(aq)}$.

In alternative B, there are no changes in oxidation number, while in alternatives C and D, the oxidation number of carbon increases as the carbon is oxidized.

14. C

The electrolysis of molten (liquid) sodium chloride is represented as follows:

$$2Na^+_{(l)} + 2Cl^-_{(l)} \rightarrow 2Na_{(l)} + Cl_{2(g)}$$

The strongest oxidizing agent in the molten $NaCl_{(l)}$ is $Na^+_{(l)}$, and the strongest reducing agent is $Cl^-_{(l)}$ (see page 9 – Chemistry 30 Data Booklet).

In any cell, reduction occurs at the cathode while oxidation occurs at the anode. Within any cell, anions migrate to the anode and cations migrate to the cathode. It is obvious that the answer is C.

Alternative A is wrong since reduction occurs at the cathode. Alternatives B and D cannot apply since water is not present.

NR5. 2 1 2 1

The reaction may be balanced in two ways:

Using half-reactions:

$$(i)\begin{cases} Al_{(s)} \rightarrow AlO^-_{2\,(aq)} \\ NO^-_{2\,(aq)} \rightarrow NH_{3(g)} \end{cases}$$

$$(ii)\begin{cases} Al_{(s)} + 2H_2O_{(l)} \rightarrow AlO^-_{2\,(aq)} \\ NO^-_{2\,(aq)} \rightarrow NH_{3(g)} + 2H_2O_{(l)} \end{cases}$$

$$(iii)\begin{cases} Al_{(s)} + 2H_2O_{(l)} \rightarrow AlO^-_{2\,(aq)} + 4H^+_{(aq)} \\ NO^-_{2(aq)} + 7H^+_{(aq)} \rightarrow NH_{3(g)} + 2H_2O_{(l)} \end{cases}$$

$$(iv)\begin{cases} Al_{(s)} + 2H_2O_{(l)} \rightarrow AlO^-_{2(aq)} + 4H^+_{(aq)} + 3e^- \\ NO^-_{2\,(aq)} + 7H^+_{(aq)} + 6e^- \rightarrow NH_{3(g)} + 2H_2O_{(l)} \end{cases}$$

$$(v)\ 2H_2O_{(l)} + NO^-_{2\,(aq)} + 2Al_{(s)} \rightarrow NH_{3(g)} + 2AlO^-_{2\,(aq)} + H^+_{(aq)}$$

Using oxidation numbers:

$$(i)\ \_\,H_2O_{(l)} + \underline{1}\overset{+3}{NO^-_{2\,(aq)}} + \underline{2}\overset{0}{Al_{(s)}} \rightarrow \underline{1}NH_{3(g)} + \underline{2}AlO^-_{2\,(aq)} + \_\,H^+_{(aq)}$$

$$\frac{\text{gain } 6e^-/N}{\times 1} \qquad \frac{\text{loss } 3e^-/Al}{\times 2}$$

$$(ii)\ \underline{2}H_2O_{(l)} + \underline{1}NO^-_{2\,(aq)} + \underline{2}Al_{(s)} \rightarrow \underline{1}NH_{3(g)} + \underline{2}AlO^-_{2\,(aq)} + \underline{1}H^+_{(aq)}$$

15. A

The common five step table method (use page 9 of the Data table) gives the answer with little difficulty.

(*i*) Species list:

	OA	*SOA*	*OA* / *OA*
$Cu_{(s)}$	$H^{+}_{(aq)}$	$SO_4{}^{2-}_{(aq)}$	$H_2O_{(l)}$
SRA			*RA*

(*ii*) Reduce the SOA

$$4H^{+}_{(aq)} + SO_4{}^{2-}_{(aq)} + 2e^{-} \rightarrow H_2SO_{3(aq)} + H_2O_{(l)}$$

(*iii*) Oxidize the SRA

$$Cu_{(s)} \rightarrow Cu^{2+}_{(aq)} + 2e^{-}$$

(*iv*) Balance the electrons lost and gained and make the net reaction.

$$Cu_{(s)} + SO_4{}^{2-}_{(aq)} + 4H^{+}_{(aq)} \rightarrow Cu^{2+}_{(aq)} + H_2SO_{3(aq)} + H_2O_{(l)}$$

(*v*) The reaction is non-spontaneous, but as the question indicates, the reaction occurs with concentrated sulfuric acid.

Alternatives B and C might occur if hydrosulfuric acid, $H_2S_{(aq)}$, were present. Alternative D might occur if a weaker oxidizing acid like $HCl_{(aq)}$ were present.

16. A

Simple stoichiometric calculation gives the answer to this question.

$$\underset{}{Cu^{2+}_{(aq)}} + \underset{\substack{100\ \text{C/s} \\ 24.0\ \text{hrs}}}{2e^{-}} \rightarrow \underset{\substack{m=? \\ 63.55\ \text{g/mol}}}{Cu_{(s)}}$$

$$n_{e^-} = \frac{100\ \text{C/s} \times (24.0 \times 3600)\text{s}}{9.65 \times 10^{4}\ \text{C/mol}} = 89.5\ \text{mol}$$

$$n_{Cu} = \tfrac{1}{2} n_{e^-} = \tfrac{1}{2} \times 89.5\ \text{mol} = 44.8\ \text{mol}$$

$$m_{Cu} = 44.8\ \text{mol} \times 63.55\ \text{g/mol} = 2.84 \times 10^{3}\ \text{g}$$

The mass of copper likely produced will be 2.84 kg.

17. D

The oxidation number of copper in $CuO_{(s)}$ and $Cu^{2+}_{(aq)}$ is +2. In fact, no atom in the reaction undergoes a change in oxidation number, making it plain that this is not a reduction–oxidation reaction. Thus, the copper in copper (II) oxide is neither oxidized nor reduced.

18. C

An atom is reduced if its oxidation number decreases over the course of a reduction–oxidation reaction.

The oxidation number of gold changes from 0 (in $Au_{(s)}$) to +3 (in $HAuCl_{4(aq)}$). The gold atoms are oxidized.

The oxidation number of nitrogen changes from +5 (in $HNO_{3(aq)}$) to +4 (in $NO_{2(g)}$). Clearly, nitrogen atoms are reduced in the reaction.

The oxidation numbers of hydrogen and chlorine remain unchanged throughout the reaction.

Copyright Protected

19. B

See question 18. For every three moles of electrons lost by each mole of gold atoms (oxidation number increased by 3), some three moles of nitric acid must gain one mole of electrons each.

Alternatively, the reaction can be balanced using:

Oxidation numbers:

$$i.\ \_\overset{0}{Au}_{(s)} + \_\overset{+5}{HNO}_{3(aq)} + \_HCl_{(aq)} \rightarrow$$

$$\underset{\times 1}{\text{loss } 3e^-/\text{Au}} \qquad \underset{\times 3}{\text{gain } 1e^-/\text{N}}$$

$$\_\overset{+3}{HAuCl}_{4(aq)} + \_H_2O_{(l)} + \_\overset{+4}{NO}_{2(g)}$$

$$ii.\ \underline{1}Au_{(s)} + \underline{3}HNO_{3(aq)} + \underline{4}HCl_{(aq)} \rightarrow \underline{1}HAuCl_{4(aq)} + \underline{3}H_2O_{(l)} + \underline{3}NO_{2(g)}$$

Half reactions:

$$(i)\begin{cases} Au_{(s)} + HCl_{(aq)} \rightarrow HAuCl_{4(aq)} \\ HNO_{3(aq)} \rightarrow H_2O_{(l)} + NO_{2(g)} \end{cases}$$

$$(ii)\begin{cases} Au_{(s)} + 4HCl_{(aq)} \rightarrow HAuCl_{4(aq)} + 3H^+_{(aq)} \\ H^+_{(aq)} + HNO_{3(aq)} \rightarrow H_2O_{(l)} + NO_{2(g)} \end{cases}$$

$$(iii)\begin{cases} Au_{(s)} + 4HCl_{(aq)} \rightarrow HAuCl_{4(aq)} + 3H^+_{(aq)} + 3e^- \\ e^- + H^+_{(aq)} + HNO_{3(aq)} \rightarrow H_2O_{(l)} + NO_{2(g)} \end{cases}$$

$$(iv)\ Au_{(s)} + 3HNO_{3(aq)} + 4HCl_{(aq)} \rightarrow HAuCl_{4(aq)} + 3H_2O_{(l)} + 3NO_{2(g)}$$

NR6. 3 1 4 2

The order in which the metal ions are reduced will essentially be the same as when the ions are listed from strongest to weakest oxidizing agent.

The ions, when listed from strongest to weakest oxidizing agent, are: $Fe^{3+}_{(aq)}$, $Pb^{2+}_{(aq)}$, $Cd^{2+}_{(aq)}$, and $Fe^{2+}_{(aq)}$; therefore, the answer is 3, 1, 4, and 2.

Oxidizing agents are found on the left side of a reduction half-reaction table. Oxidizing agents are reduced over the course of an oxidation–reduction reaction.

20. B

In a disproportionation (also called an auto-oxidation) the oxidation number of one atom in a reactant both increases and decreases over the course of an oxidation reduction reaction.

In the reaction given in alternative B, the oxidation number of chlorine changes from 0 (in $Cl_{2(aq)}$) to +1 (in $HOCl_{(aq)}$) and to -1 (in $Cl^-_{(aq)}$).

In alternatives A, C and D the oxidation numbers of two reactant entities change. This renders these reactions as regular oxidation–reduction processes.

21. C

From the given half-reactions, the net reaction is

$$3C_{(s)} + 6O^{2-}_{(aq)} + 4Al^{3+}_{(aq)} \rightarrow 3CO_{2(g)} + 4Al_{(s)}$$

$$n_{C_{(s)}} = 1.00\text{ kg} \times \frac{\text{mol}}{12.01\text{ g}} = 0.0833\text{ kmol}$$

$$n_{Al_{(s)}} = \tfrac{4}{3} n_{C_{(s)}} = \tfrac{4}{3} \times 0.0833\text{ kmol} = 0.111\text{ kmol}$$

$$m_{Al_{(s)}} = 0.111\text{ kmol} \times 26.98\text{ g/mol} = 3.00\text{ kg}$$

The mass of aluminum expected per kilogram of carbon consumed is 3.00 kg.

NR7. 8.05

When sodium reacts with oxygen, the net reduction oxidation reaction is

$$4Na_{(s)} + O_{2(g)} \rightarrow 2Na_2O_{(s)}$$

The oxidation half-reaction of this process is

$$Na_{(s)} \rightarrow Na^+_{(s)} + e^-$$

$$n_{e^-} = 0.350\text{ mol}$$

$$n_{Na} = \tfrac{1}{1} n_{e^-} = 0.350\text{ mol}$$

$$m_{Na} = 0.350\text{ mol} \times 22.99\text{ g/mol} = 8.05\text{ g}$$

The mass of sodium that will react is 8.05 g.

Not for Reproduction

22. B

The energy stored in a battery is in the form of chemical potential energy.

Vibrational, rotational, and translational kinetic energy depend on a sample of matter's temperature.

23. D

Cells that produce energy are voltaic cells. Cells that function when an electric current is applied to them are electrolytic cells.

The battery provides energy to drive the starter motor and once the engine is running, its alternator puts energy back in as it recharges the battery. Thus, the answer is D.

24. A

From electrode potentials, it is clear that the silver half- cell ($E°_R = +0.80$ V) is the anode, and the dichromate half cell ($E°_R = +1.33$ V) is the cathode. (If redox couples are present, the half-cell with the highest reduction potential is the half-cell with the greatest potential to host a reduction reaction.) The half-reactions are:

Cathode:

$$Cr_2O_7^{2-}{}_{(aq)} + 14H^+{}_{(aq)} + 6e^- \rightarrow 2Cr^{3+}{}_{(aq)} + 7H_2O_{(l)}$$

Anode:

$$6Ag_{(s)} \rightarrow 6Ag^+_{(aq)} + 6e^-$$

Net cell reaction:

$$Cr_2O_7^{2-}{}_{(aq)} + 14H^+{}_{(aq)} + 6Ag_{(s)} \rightarrow 2Cr^{3+}{}_{(aq)} + 6Ag^+{}_{(aq)} + 7H_2O_{(l)}$$

Alternatives B, C, and D have charges that are not balanced.

NR8. 1.10

The net cell nomenclature of the apparatus is $Cu_{(s)} / Cu^{2+}{}_{(aq)} // Zn^{2+}{}_{(aq)} / Zn_{(s)}$

The cathode of the cell is the copper half-cell; it has the highest reduction potential, $E°_{RC} = +0.34$ V. The zinc half-cell is the anode with $E°_{RA} = -0.76$ V.

The net cell potential, under standard conditions, is readily calculated

$$\begin{aligned} E°_{net} &= E°_{RC} - E°_{RA} \\ &= +0.34 \text{ V} - (-0.76 \text{ V}) \\ &= +1.10 \text{ V} \end{aligned}$$

The net cell potential is +1.10 V.

25. A

An oxidation involves the loss of electrons and the oxidation half-reaction has electrons on the product side.

Only alternatives A and C are oxidations (apparently), but alternative C is *not balanced.* Thus, the answer is A.

26. A

In any reduction–oxidation reaction, the strongest oxidizing agent is reduced. Using oxidation numbers, the strongest oxidizing agent is identified as that entity that contains an atom whose oxidation number decreases over the course of the reaction.

The oxidation number of nickel decreases from +4 (in $NiO_{2(s)}$) to +2 (in $Ni(OH)_{2(s)}$), which indicates that the nickel was reduced in the cell. That makes $NiO_{2(s)}$ the strongest oxidizing agent.

Copyright Protected

27. A

In all electrochemical cells, the anions flow through the electrolyte to the anode. Evidently, the anode in the cell shown is the $X_{(s)} / X^{2+}{}_{(aq)}$ half-cell.
Thus, the hydrogen half cell is the cathode, and the half-reaction occurring there will be the reduction of $H^+_{(aq)}$, as follows:

$$2H^+{}_{(aq)} + 2e^- \rightarrow H_{2(g)} \qquad E°_{RC} = 0.00\ V$$

With fewer $H^+{}_{(aq)}$ ions in the cathode, as the cell operates, the cathode pH is destined to rise (a less acidic half-cell).

Since, in all cells, electrons flow from the anode to the cathode, it is obvious that in the cell shown, electrons will flow from $X_{(s)}$ to the inert electrode and pH in the hydrogen half-cell will increase—answer A.

28. B

See solution 27.

For all cells, $E°_{net} = E°_{RC} = E°_{RA}$

where $E°_{RC}$ = cathode reduction potential and $E°_{RA}$ = anode reduction potential.

$$+0.45\ V = 0.00\ V - E°_{R\,X_{(s)}/X^{2+}{}_{(aq)}}$$

$$E°_{R\,X_{(s)}/X^{2+}{}_{(aq)}} = 0.00\ V - 0.45\ V = -0.45\ V$$

Upon consulting page 9 of the Data Table, you will see that the reduction potential of an iron half-cell is –0.45 V. The answer is B.

29. A

The net cell reaction of a propane fuel cell and the combustion reaction of propane in a bomb calorimeter are one and the same, namely:

$$C_3H_{8(g)} + 5O_{2(g)} \rightarrow 3CO_{2(g)} + 4H_2O_{(l)}$$

The enthalpy change of this reaction is readily computed using Hess' Law, as follows:

$$\Delta H°_{net} = \Sigma nH°_{f(Products)} - \Sigma nH°_{f(Reactants)}$$
$$= [3\ mol \times (-393.5\ kJ/mol) + 4\ mol \times (-285.8\ kJ/mol)] - [1\ mol \times (-103.8\ kJ/mol)]$$
$$\Delta H_{C(C_3H_{8(g)})} = -2219.9\ kJ$$

The correct answer is A.

Alternative C includes the enthalpy change when $4H_2O_{(g)}$ is produced. Alternative B incorrectly quotes the enthalpy change for the formation of propane. Alternative D has the equation that results from adding the half-reactions without properly balancing the electrons lost and gained.

30. D

The anode/oxidation half-reaction is:

$$C_3H_{8(g)} + 6H_2O_{(l)} \rightarrow 3CO_{2(g)} + 20H^+{}_{(aq)} + 20e^-$$

Thus 15.7 g of propane, $C_3H_{8(g)}$, are consumed at the anode and:

$$n_{C_3H_8} = 15.7\ g \times \frac{mol}{44.11\ g} = 0.356\ mol$$

Some 0.356 mol of propane are consumed at the anode.

Not for Reproduction

31. B

The combustion of propane is described by

$$C_3H_{8(g)} + 5O_{2(g)} \rightarrow 3CO_{2(g)} + 4H_2O_{(g)}$$

Cellular respiration is described by

$$C_6H_{12}O_{6(aq)} + 6O_{2(g)} \rightarrow 6CO_{2(g)} + 6H_2O_{(l)}$$

In both cases, oxygen (the ultimate oxidizing agent, if you like) oxidizes carbon from an oxidation number of $-\frac{8}{3}$ (in $C_3H_{8(g)}$) or 0 (in $C_6H_{12}O_{6(aq)}$) to +4 (in $CO_{2(g)}$).

Propane is burned as a fuel source in all manner of applications, while glucose is "burned" in cell mitochondria to provide metabolic energy and heat. Both reactions are exothermic. Clearly, B is the correct answer.

32. B

The oxidation number of aluminum in its element is 0. In $NaAlO_{2(aq)}$, aluminum is in the ion $AlO_2^-{}_{(aq)}$. Since the oxidation number of oxygen is routinely –2, in a compound or polyatomic ion such as this, the oxidation number of aluminum must be +3. The answer is B.

33. B

The oxidation numbers in $(CH_2O)_{n(s)}$ all add up to zero. The oxidation numbers of hydrogen and oxygen are +1 and –2, respectively, and this gives the oxidation number of carbon as 0. In $CO_{2(g)}$, the oxidation number of carbon is +4. Overall, the oxidation number of carbon increases from 0 to +4.

Evidently, the carbon in $(CH_2O)_{n(s)}$ lost electrons in the ATAD process. The loss of electrons is called oxidation. (An atom with a higher oxidation number is more oxidized!)

34. B

In answering this question, some important points must be noted

- A reduction–oxidation reaction will be spontaneous if its strongest oxidizing agent lies above its strongest reducing agent in a reduction half-reaction table.
- The reduced species in a reaction is the oxidizing agent (OA).
- The oxidized species in a reaction is the reducing agent (RA).
- The atom/entity that undergoes a reduction in oxidation number has been oxidized.

In reactions 1 and 3, the oxidizing agents $U^{3+}{}_{(aq)}$ and $Y^{3+}{}_{(aq)}$, (they were both reduced) must lie above the reducing agent $La_{(s)}$, and thus $La^{3+}{}_{(aq)}$ in a reduction half-reaction table. In the second reaction, the oxidizing agent $Y^{3+}{}_{(aq)}$ must lie below the reducing agent $U_{(s)}$ in a reduction half-reaction table.

Thus, we can construct a table as follows:

$$U^{3+}{}_{(aq)} + 3e^- \rightarrow U_{(s)}$$

$$Y^{3+}{}_{(aq)} + 3e^- \rightarrow Y_{(s)}$$

$$La_{(s)} + 3e^- \rightarrow La_{(s)}$$

The oxidizing agents, listed from strongest to weakest, are $U^{3+}{}_{(aq)}$, $Y^{3+}{}_{(aq)}$, and $La^{3+}{}_{(aq)}$

Copyright Protected

NR9. 2 3 1 4

It is best to construct a reduction–oxidation net reaction here.

Species List:

$$\underset{SRA}{Sn_{(s)}} \quad \overset{OA}{Ni^{2+}_{(aq)}} \quad \overset{OA}{\underset{RA}{H_2O_{(l)}}}$$

Reduction Half:

$$NO_3^-{}_{(aq)} + 2H^+_{(aq)} + e^- \rightarrow NO_{2(g)} + H_2O_{(l)}$$

Oxidation Half:

$$Sn_{(s)} \rightarrow Sn^{2+}_{(aq)} + 2e^-$$

Reduction (Spontaneous) Net:

$$2NO_3^-{}_{(aq)} + 4H^+_{(aq)} + Sn_{(s)} \rightarrow$$
$$NO_{2(g)} + 2H_2O_{(l)} + 2Sn^{2+}_{(aq)}$$

In this reaction, the tin is oxidized, the nitrate ion is reduced, the nickel (II) ion does not react (too weak an OA), and the hydrogen ion reacts but its oxidation number is +1 before and after reaction.

35. D

A sacrificial anode, to be effective, must be a suitably stronger if it is to be oxidized preferentially. In most applications, $Mg_{(s)}$ and $Zn_{(s)}$ serve this purpose well. Copper, on the other hand, is a weaker reducing agent than iron and so it will not oxidize as readily as the iron. In fact, the iron will be anodic relative to the copper and will corrode more effectively!

Alternatives B and C would only apply if $Cu_{(s)}$ were a stronger reducing agent than $Fe_{(s)}$. Alternative A is most unlikely because $Cu_{(s)}$ is a much stronger reducing agent than is $Cl^-_{(aq)}$.

36. C

The nomenclature of the voltaic cell illustrated is
$C_{(s)}|MnO_4^-{}_{(aq)}, H^+_{(aq)}, Mn^{2+}_{(aq)}||Cu^{2+}_{(aq)}, SO_4^{2-}{}_{(aq)}|Cu_{(s)}$

The half-cell with the higher reduction potential, $C_{(s)}|MnO_4^-{}_{(aq)}, H^+_{(aq)}, Mn^{2+}_{(aq)}$ is the cathode. Thus, we can proceed to formulate the net cell reaction.

Cathode: $MnO_4^-{}_{(aq)}, 8H^+_{(aq)} + 5e^- \rightarrow$
$$MnO^{2+}_{(aq)} + 4H_2O_{(l)}$$

Anode: $Cu_{(s)} \rightarrow Cu^{2+}_{(aq)} + 2e^-$

Net Cell Reaction:
$$2MnO_4^-{}_{(aq)} + 16H^+_{(aq)} + 5Cu_{(s)} \rightarrow$$
$$2Mn^{2+}_{(aq)} + 8H_2O_{(l)} + 5Cu^{2+}_{(aq)}$$

$$E°_{net} = E°_{RC} - E°_{RA} = +1.51V\ !\ 0.34V$$
$$= +1.17V.$$

Alternative C is the answer

Note: the reactions in alternatives A and B are not balanced, while the $E°_{net}$ in alternative D is the result of an arithmetic error.

NR10. 56.2

A stoichiometric calculation using the balanced equation in alternative C of MC 36 (or alternative D) is as follows:

$$n_{cu} = \frac{5}{2} n_{Mno_4^-} = \frac{5}{2} \times 0.354 \text{ mol}$$

$$m_{cu} = \frac{5}{2} \times 0.354 \text{ mol} \times \frac{63.55 \text{ g}}{\text{mol}} = 56.2 \text{ g}$$

Note: If incorrect alternatives A or B in MC 36 were chosen, then

$$m_{cu} = \frac{1}{1} \times 0.354 \text{ mol} \times \frac{63.55 \text{ g}}{\text{mol}} = 22.5 \text{ g}$$

Since MC 36 and NR 6 are linked, an answer of 56.2 (linked to C, D in MC36) or 22.5g (linked to A, B in MC36) will be marked as correct.

37. A

The copper half-cell houses the strongest reducing agent in the system. Thus, the copper half-cell is the anode. Electrons will thus flow from the anode, $Cu_{(s)}$, to the cathode—the $C_{(s)}$ rod. Alternative A is the answer. In this cell, anions will migrate through the porous cup toward the copper electrode and cations will migrate to the carbon rod. Since sulfate ions are not included in the net cell reactions (correct or incorrect), their concentration will be unaffected.

38. D

Since $MnO_4^-{}_{(aq)}$ is the oxidizing agent, it will be reduced at the cathode. Alternative D is clearly the answer.

Alternatives A, B, and C are consistent with proper operation of the illustrated cell.

39. A

In the given reduction half-reaction table, the reducing agents lie on the right side and get stronger proceeding down the table. The lowest entity on the right side of the table is $V^{2+}{}_{(aq)}$.

40. C

A species list of the cell constituents is as follows:

$$\underset{\text{SRA}}{Al_{(s)}},\ \overset{\text{OA}}{Na^+_{(aq)}}\ \overset{\text{SOA}}{O_{2(g)}}\ \ \underset{\text{RA}}{\overset{\text{OA}}{H_2O_{(l)}}}\underset{\text{RA}}{OH^-_{(aq)}}$$

Taken together, $O_{2(g)}$ and $H_2O_{(l)}$ are the strongest oxidizing agent, so they will be reduced as the cell operates. The answer in this system is C.

41. D

The species list for the cell illustrated shows that $O_{2(g)}$ and $H_2O_{(l)}$ are the strongest oxidizing agents. Thus, the reduction half-reaction will involve the reduction of $O_{2(g)}$ with $H_2O_{(l)}$ as follows:

$$O_{2(g)} + 2\,H_2O_{(l)} + 4\,e^- \rightarrow 4\,OH^-{}_{(aq)}$$

Alternatives A and B are the reduction of the weaker oxidizing agents in the cell, and alternative C is unlikely in a cell with $NaOH_{(aq)}$ as its electrolyte.

42. B

The net cell potential of the voltaic cell with an aluminum anode $E°_{RA} = -1.66$ V and an $O_{2(l)}$, $H_2O_{(l)}$ cathode $E°_{RC} = +0.40$ V is

$$\begin{aligned} E°_{net} &= E°_{RC} - E°_{RA} = +0.40\text{ V} - (-1.66\text{ V}) \\ &= +2.06\text{ V} \end{aligned}$$

NR11. 6.18

When three cells with a potential of +2.06V are connected in series (head-to-tail, if you like), the voltage generated is tripled to give +0.18 V (from alternative B in MC42).

If you chose A in MC42, the answer here is +7.08 V.

If you chose C in MC42, the answer here is +2.49 V.

If you chose D in MC42, the answer here is –3.15 V.

NR12. 0.44

The two half-reactions in the equation given are:

Cathode Half: $2\ RhCl_6^{3-} + 6e^- \rightarrow 2Rh_{(s)}$
$E°_{RC} = ?$

Anode Half: $3\ Zn_{(s)} \rightarrow 3\ Zn^{2+}_{(aq)} + 6e^-$
$E°_R = -0.7611\ V$

Thus, $E°_{net} = E°_{RC} - E°_{RA}$

or

$$E°_{RC} = E°_{net} - E°_{RA}$$
$$= +1.20\ V + (-0.76\ V) = +0.44\ V$$

The cathode potential is +0.44 V.

Written Response

The samples that follow represent only one valid approach to each of the problems. During the diploma examination marking session, provision is made for considering various approaches the student may have used.

1. **a)** The anode is zinc metal. The change in oxidation number is from 0 to +2.

b) $t = \frac{n_{e-} \times F}{I}$

$$t = \frac{\frac{2}{1}(10.0\ g / 65.38\ g/mol)(9.65 \times 10^4\ C/mol)}{0.300\ A}$$

$$t = 9.84 \times 10^4\ s \times \frac{h}{3\ 600\ s}$$

$$t = 27.3\ h$$

c) Zinc chloride because it will operate at −12°C and it is cheaper per unit time for the life of the battery
$\left(\frac{5.7}{2.5}\right) 95¢ = \$2.17$
vs. $2.25
(cost is 38¢/h Vs. 39¢/h for the alkaline cell) or Alkaline because it will operate at −12°C and it creates less waste since one cell lasts over twice as long as the zinc chloride, thus half the waste will be generated.

2. **a)**

$$2(CrO_4^{2-}{}_{(aq)} + 4H_2O_{(l)} + 3e^- \rightarrow Cr(OH)_{3(s)} + 5OH^-_{(aq)})$$
$$3(Fe_{(s)} \rightarrow Fe^{2+}_{(aq)} + 2e^-)$$
$$2CrO_4^{2-}{}_{(aq)} + 8H_2O_{(l)} + 3Fe_{(s)} \rightarrow 2Cr(OH)_{3(s)} + 10\ OH^-_{(aq)} + 3Fe^{2+}_{(aq)}$$

b)

$$n_{e^-} = \frac{(3.00\ C/s)(48.0\ h)(3600\ s/h)}{9.65 \times 10^4\ C/mol} = 5.37\ mol$$

$$n_{Fe} = \frac{1}{2} n_{e^-} = 2.69\ mol$$

$$m_{Fe} = 2.69\ mol\ (55.85\ g/mol) = 150\ g$$

$$\Delta m_{anode} = 400 - 150 = 250\ g$$

c)

An aluminum anode would last longer than iron because a smaller mass of aluminum would be consumed under the same circumstances. Any metal with a lower ratio of molar mass-to-ion charge would be valid because less anode mass would be consumed.

$$mass_{Al} = \frac{(3.00 C/s)\ (26.98\ g/mol) \left(\frac{1}{3}\right) (48.0\ h)\ (3600\ s/h)}{9.65 \times 10^4\ C/mol}$$

$= 48.3$ g used (**vs** 150 g of $Fe_{(s)}$)

Copyright Protected

ANSWERS AND SOLUTIONS
REDUCTION–OXIDATION – UNIT TEST 2

1. A	8. D	15. C	21. A	NR10. 3.46 †
2. D	9. B	16. B	22. D	28. A
3. C	10. C	17. A	23. C	29. A
4. A	11. D	NR5. 1.89	24. D	30. D
5. B	12. A	18. B	25. A	31. D
6. D	13. A	19. B	26. B	32. D
NR1. 3.04*	14. C	NR6. 4 6 3 1	NR8. 4 3 8 6	NR11. 5 2 3 4
NR2. 2.37**	NR3. 2 3 4 3	20. C	27. A	
7. A	NR4. 2 4 1 5	NR7. 1467	NR9. 2.15	

Note: *If MC 6 is A, then NR1 is 0.80
B, then NR1 is 0.34
C, then NR1 is 0.13
D, then NR1 is 2.37

**If MC 6 is A, then NR2 is 12.5
B, then NR2 is 7.94
C, then NR2 is 12.5
D, then NR2 is 3.04

†NR10 = $\frac{9.65}{6}$ × NR9

1. A

A reaction is spontaneous if it has a positive E_{net} / E°_{net}—a condition possible when, in a reduction half-reaction table, the strongest oxidizing agent lies above the strongest reducing agent.

In the first equation, $S^{2+}_{(aq)}$ (the SOA/the reduced species) must lie above $T_{(s)}$ (the SRA/the oxidized species) in a reduction half-reaction table. In the second equation, $R^{3+}_{(aq)}$ (the SOA/the reduced species) must lie below $T_{(s)}$ (the SRA/the oxidized species) in a reduction half-reaction table (the reaction is non-spontaneous).

In the third equation, $R^{3+}_{(aq)}$ (the SOA/the reduced species) must lie above $V_{(s)}$ (the SRA/the oxidized species) in a reduction half-reaction table.

From this information, we get the mini-reduction half-reaction table:

$$S^{2+}_{(aq)} + 2e^- \rightarrow S_{(s)}$$

$$T^{+}_{(aq)} + e^- \rightarrow T_{(s)}$$

$$R^{3+}_{(aq)} + 3e^- \rightarrow R_{(s)}$$

$$V^{2+}_{(aq)} + 2e^- \rightarrow V_{(s)}$$

The OAs, listed strongest to weakest, are:

$$S^{2+}_{(aq)}, T^{+}_{(aq)}, R^{3+}_{(aq)}, V^{2+}_{(aq)}$$

Distractors C and D offer unlikely answers since they list/rank reducing agents.

Not for Reproduction

2. D

Electroplating, if it occurs, always does so at the **cathode** of a cell (voltaic **or** electrolytic) where, typically, a metal cation is reduced to its element.

(The anode is the site of oxidation.)

3. C

One of the half-reactions that occurs at the cathode is:

$$Cr_2O_7{}^{2-}{}_{(aq)} + 14H^+{}_{(aq)} + 6e^- \rightarrow Cr^{3+}{}_{(aq)} + 7H_2O_{(l)}$$

This half-reaction consumes $H^+{}_{(aq)}$ ions—clearly the solution pH will rise accordingly (toward 7).

(Note $H_2Cr_2O_{7(aq)} - H^+{}_{(aq)}$ is $Cr_2O_7{}^{2-}{}_{(aq)}$.

It is an SOA, so it will be reduced. The process occurring in an electrolytic cell is endo-energetic/endergonic, so the potential energy of the products exceeds that of the reactants. Oxidation would occur at the $Pb_{(s)}$ electrode—it is the anode.)

4. A

$Cr^{3+}{}_{(aq)}$, an oxidizing agent, lies below $Cd_{(s)}$, $Sn_{(s)}$, and $Pb_{(s)}$. Only $Al_{(s)}$ lies below $Cr^{3+}{}_{(aq)}$ in the reduction half-reaction table—an arrangement necessary for spontaneous reaction.

5. B

When zinc metal is oxidized, it loses electrons and forms zinc ions, $Zn^{2+}{}_{(aq)}$. The relevant oxidation reaction is the reverse of the reduction at $E° = -0.76$ V on page 9 of the Chemistry Data Booklet.

Note: $Zn^{2+}{}_{(aq)}$ would seem to be the more likely product.

6. D

The reducing agents $Pb_{(s)}$ and $Mg_{(s)}$ lie below $H^+{}_{(aq)}$ in the reduction half-reaction table, and both would be expected to react spontaneously with $HCl_{(aq)}$. Though E°_{net} values do not specify the rate of redox reaction, it is the $Mg_{(s)}$ that reacts more vigorously with the acid. The reaction is predicted as follows:

	SOA		OA	
$Mg_{(s)}$	$H^+{}_{(aq)}$	$Cl^-{}_{(aq)}$	$H_2O_{(l)}$	$Pb_{(s)}$
SRA		RA	RA RA	RA

		E°_R
Reduction:	$2H^+{}_{(aq)} + 2e^- \rightarrow H_{2(g)}$	0.00V
Oxidation:	$Mg_{(s)} \rightarrow Mg^{2+}{}_{(aq)} + 2e^-$	–2.37V
Net Reaction:	$2H^+{}_{(aq)} + Mg_{(s)} \rightarrow H_{2(g)} + Mg^{2+}{}_{(aq)}$	

NR1. 3.04

A stoichiometric calculation is all that is needed to answer the question.

$Mg_{(s)}$	+ $2H^+{}_{(aq)}$	→	H_2 + $Mg^{2+}{}_{(aq)}$
m = ?			0.250 L
24.31 g/mol			1.00 mol/L

$$n_{H^+} = 0.250\,\text{L} \times \frac{1.00\,\text{mol}}{\text{L}} = 0.250\,\text{mol}$$

$$n_{Mg} = \frac{1}{2} n_{H^+} = \frac{1}{2} \times 0.250\,\text{mol} = 0.125\,\text{mol}$$

$$m_{Mg} = 0.125\,\text{mol} \times \frac{24.31\,\text{g}}{\text{mol}} = 3.04\,\text{g}$$

The mass of $Mg_{(s)}$ consumed is 3.04 g.

If A was chosen for MC4, some 27.0 g of $Ag_{(s)}$ could be consumed but only 12.50 g strips were reacted—the answer would be 12.5 g. Similarly, if C was chosen for MC4, some 25.9 g of $Pb_{(s)}$ could react. The answer would again be 12.5 g. If B was chosen for MC4, the mass of copper consumed would be 7.94 g.

NR2. 2.37

$$E^\circ_{net} = E^\circ_{RC} - E^\circ_{RA} = 0.00\text{ V} - (-2.37\text{ V}) = +2.37\text{ V}$$

Faculty of

SCIENCE

University of Alberta

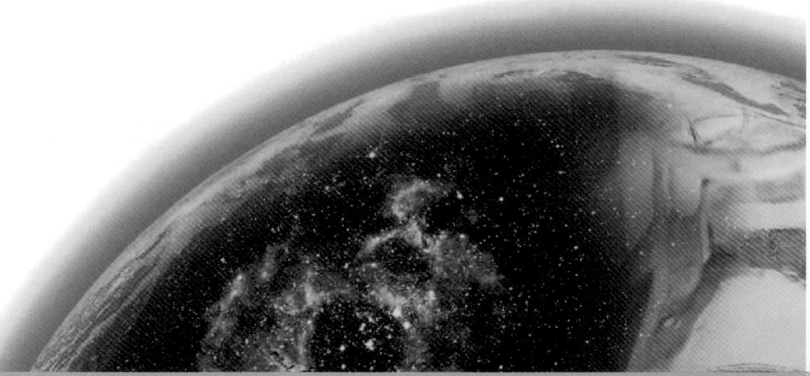

Your science career begins at the U of A Faculty of Science

With close to 60 degrees in over 40 subject areas, the Faculty of Science at the U of A offers some of the best undergraduate Science programs in North America. Our Faculty is internationally recognized for its teaching and research excellence – **Explore what we have to offer!**

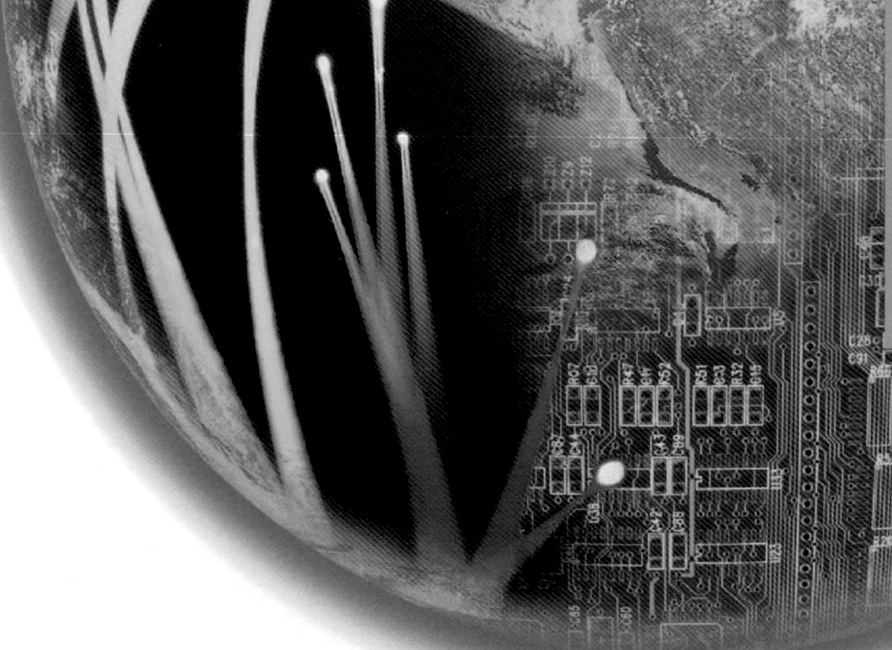

CW 223 Biological Sciences Building
University of Alberta
Edmonton, Alberta T6G 2E9
Tel: (780) 492-4758
E-mail: dean.science@ualberta.ca
www.science.ualberta.ca

www.science.ualberta.ca

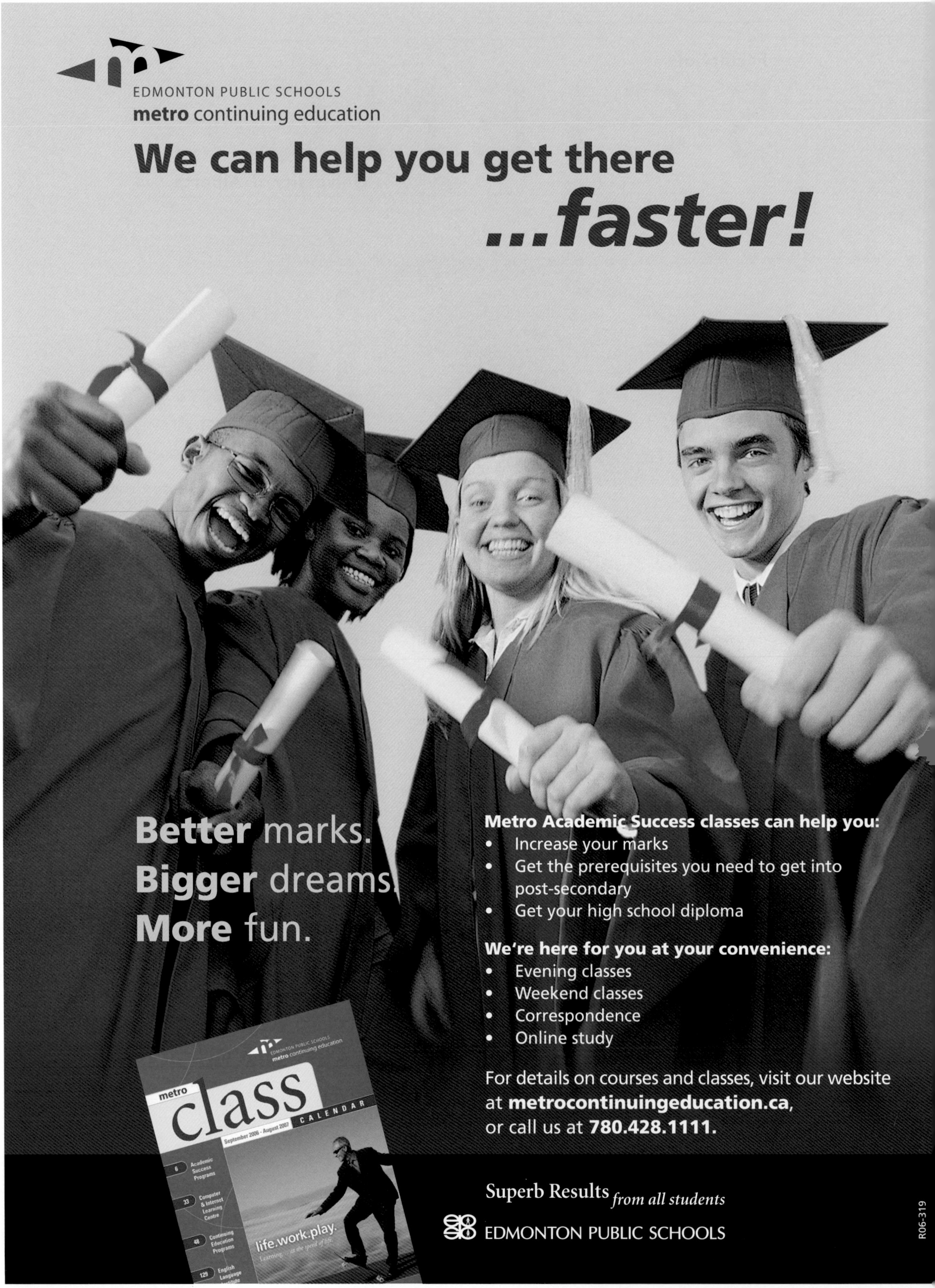

We can help you get there ...faster!

Better marks.
Bigger dreams.
More fun.

Metro Academic Success classes can help you:

- Increase your marks
- Get the prerequisites you need to get into post-secondary
- Get your high school diploma

We're here for you at your convenience:

- Evening classes
- Weekend classes
- Correspondence
- Online study

For details on courses and classes, visit our website at **metrocontinuingeducation.ca**, or call us at **780.428.1111.**

metro class CALENDAR
September 2006 - August 2007
life.work.play.

Superb Results *from all students*
EDMONTON PUBLIC SCHOOLS

R06-319

Engineering

ITS THE APPLICATION OF THE PRINCIPLES OF MATH AND SCIENCE TO SOLVING REAL-LIFE PROBLEMS.

- We are Canada's second largest Engineering program offering degrees in Chemical (including Computer Process Control, Oil Sands and Biomedical), Civil (including Environmental), Computer (including Software), Electrical (including Biomedical), Engineering Physics (including Nanoengineering), Materials (including Biomedical), Mechanical, Mining and Petroleum Engineering.
- We offer co-op work experience program opportunities to over 1100 students.
- We have extensive scholarships available to our students.
- Engineering provides a state of the art teaching and learning environment and award winning professors.

ARE YOU READY FOR THE CHALLENGE?

Contact Us:

E6-050 ETLC
University of Alberta
Edmonton, AB T6G 2V4
Phone: **(780) 492-3320** or **1-800-407-8354**
Fax: (780) 492-0500
E-mail: **info@engineering.ualberta.ca**
www.engineering.ualberta.ca

Social Work

SHARE OUR VISION

You envision a better world, one free of discrimination, poverty, abuse and oppression. A world where people of different genders, abilities and ethnicities have equal opportunities and rights. A world where people in crisis have the support and counsel they need to heal and move forward.

Through a career in **social work**, you can help create that better world. Social workers partner with communities, groups, families and individuals to make positive changes. They promote diversity, equality, and social justice. They help people and communities help themselves.

At the University of Calgary's Faculty of Social Work, we provide students with the skills and knowledge needed to excel in the profession of social work. Your first two years at U of C can focus on any discipline; then you can transfer into Social Work in your third year.

Make the Faculty of Social Work your next step toward making a world of difference. www.fsw.ucalgary.ca

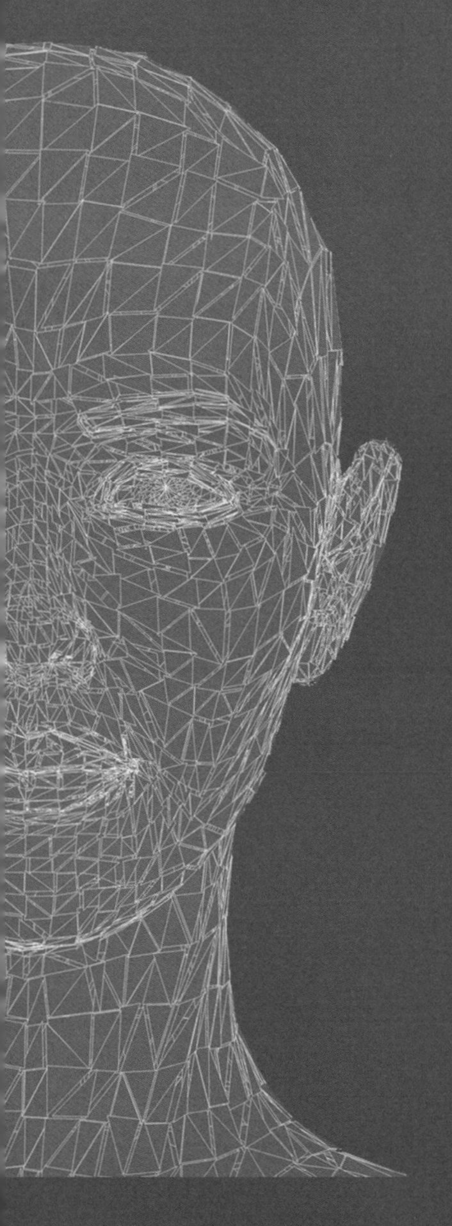

SCHULICH:
THE NEW FACE OF
ENGINEERING EXCELLENCE

U OF C
THIS IS NOW

The school with the best engineering scholarships in Canada.

> The Engineering School of 'FIRST CHOICE'
> Canada's Largest Internship Program
> Located in Canada's Engineering Capital
> Award-winning Women in Engineering Program
> Strong focus on design & innovation

www.schulich.ucalgary.ca

We're everywhere.

Information technology is more than computers and programming. IT is a driving force for progress in industries such as oil and gas, health care, and global communications. IT is even helping biologists predict the spread of disease among trees.

Where will you make your mark? Invent information security technologies that will ensure people's privacy. Visualize oil reserves so they can be discovered and managed for future generations. Or build a database that could be instrumental in treating and finding cures for cancer.

Join us to embark on a meaningful IT career. **Your future starts here:** www.cpsc.ucalgary.ca

UofC THIS IS NOW

You're curious about the world

UNIVERSITY OF
CALGARY
FACULTY OF
SCIENCE

You want to use the latest technology to advance your career. At the University of Calgary, you will learn from world-class researchers who generate the latest knowledge in petroleum geology, information security, astrophysics and forward looking fields like quantum computing. From biochemistry and statistics to water quality and resource management, you will acquire the problem-solving skills that will help you succeed in the oil and gas, agricultural, pharmaceutical, environmental science and financial industries.

www.science.ucalgary.ca

World-class research + hands-on learning
+ international opportunities + work experience
= Knowledge that will advance your career

UOFC
THIS IS NOW

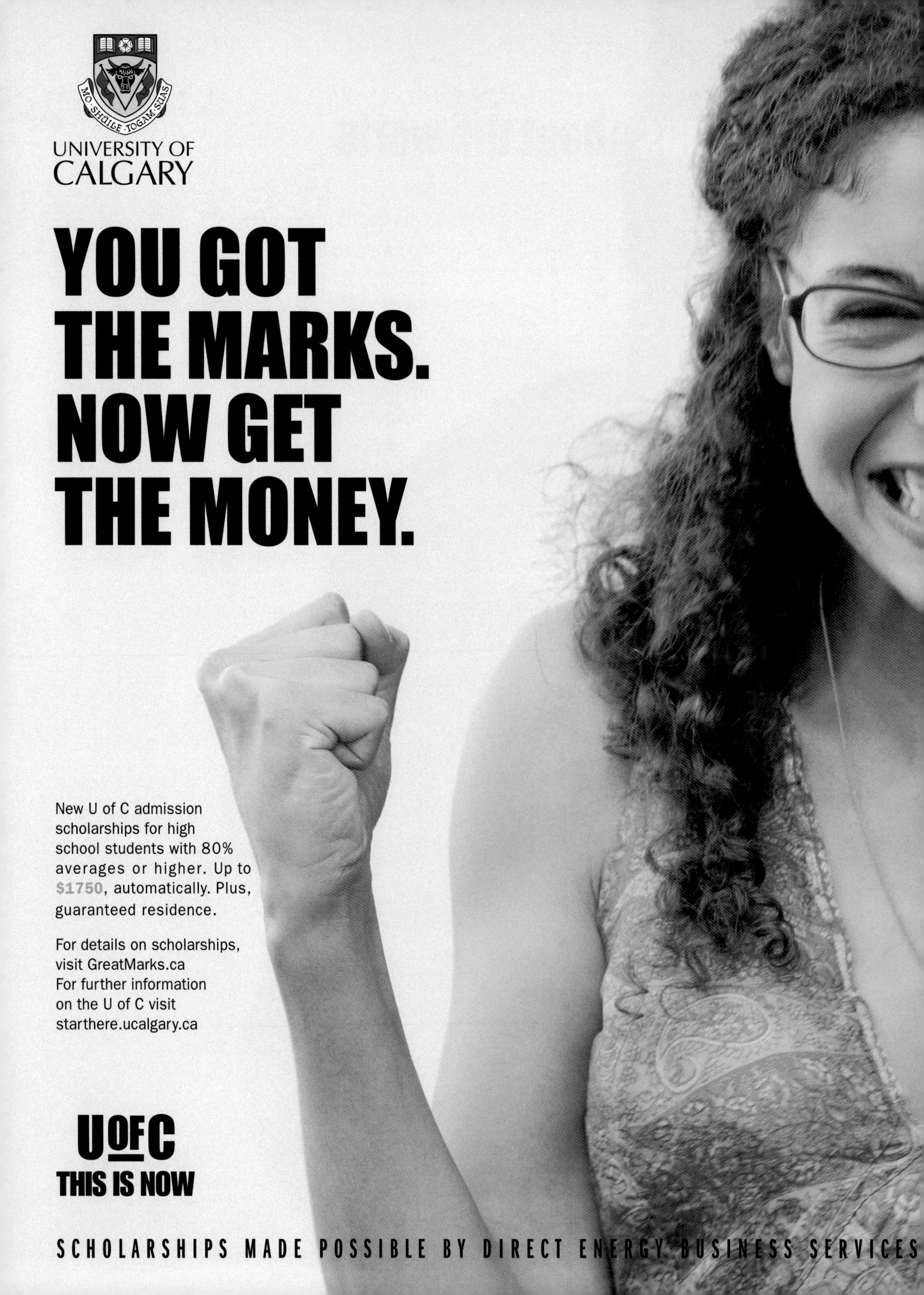

UNIVERSITY OF
CALGARY

YOU GOT THE MARKS. NOW GET THE MONEY.

New U of C admission scholarships for high school students with 80% averages or higher. Up to $1750, automatically. Plus, guaranteed residence.

For details on scholarships, visit GreatMarks.ca
For further information on the U of C visit starthere.ucalgary.ca

UOFC
THIS IS NOW

SCHOLARSHIPS MADE POSSIBLE BY DIRECT ENERGY BUSINESS SERVICES

DIPLOMAX

Grade 12 Diploma Exam Tutorials

in Edmonton

Castle Rock
Research Corp

Castle Rock Guarantees:

- Highly-qualified, enthusiastic, and experienced instructors
- Preparation for Part A and Part B sections of each exam
- Students enrolled in a first session of Biology, Chemistry, Physics, or Math may attend a second session of the same subject at no extra cost
- Complete student satisfaction with their Diploma exam result – or take the same course for free, at any time in the future

Students have taken over 18,000 courses with Castle Rock since 1995

information and online registration

www.castlerockresearch.com

780.448.0631

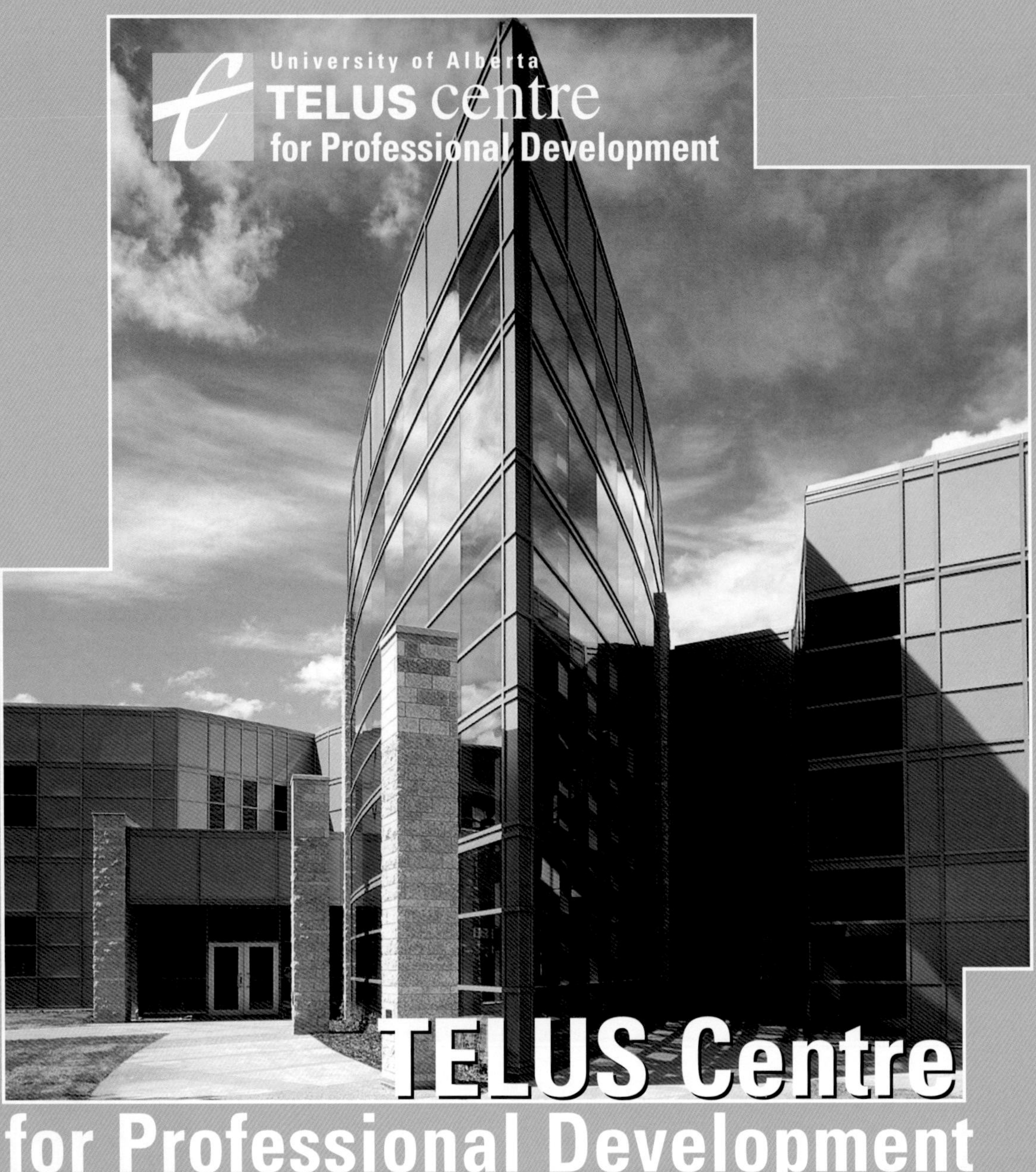

for Professional Development

Located on the University of Alberta campus, this state-of-the-art facility offers you:

- the ultimate setting for meetings, conferences, videoconferences, training sessions and business receptions/dinners for up to 300 people
- technology-enhanced rooms for various types of presentations
- underground parking and easy access to downtown Edmonton

University of Alberta ■ 87 Avenue & 111 Street ■ Edmonton, Alberta, Canada T6G 2R1
Phone: (780) 492-8000 ■ Fax: (780) 492-8200 ■ Toll free: (866) 492-8000
teluscentre@ualberta.ca ■ www.teluscentre.com

... inspire generations

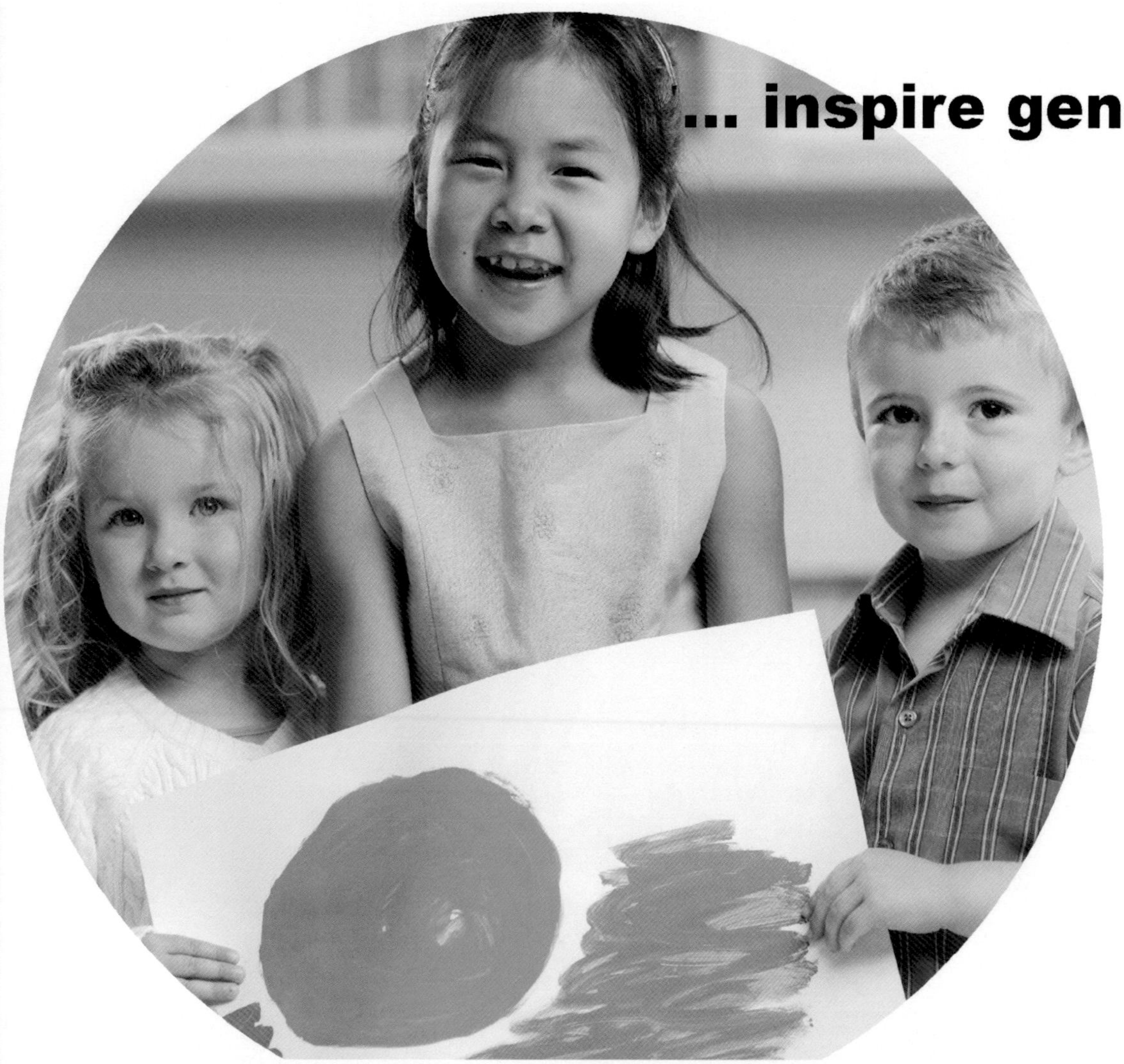

University of Alberta EDUCATION

The largest, the first and the most diverse education faculty in the country

Undergraduate Degrees

- Elementary Education (K-6)
- Secondary Education (7-12)
- Combined Degrees (5 years) in Native Studies, Physical Education and Recreation, Science, Music, and Science in Human Ecology
- After Degree (2 years)

Admissions Information

- Application deadline is March 1
- No direct admission from high school
- Students complete a minimum of 8 half-courses before applying to the Faculty of Education

Undergraduate Student Services 1-107 Education North Building
Phone: (780) 492-3659 www.education.ualberta.ca/uss/

Our pre-service teachers thrive in a research environment related to current teaching practice.

THE BEAR CHILDREN'S FUND

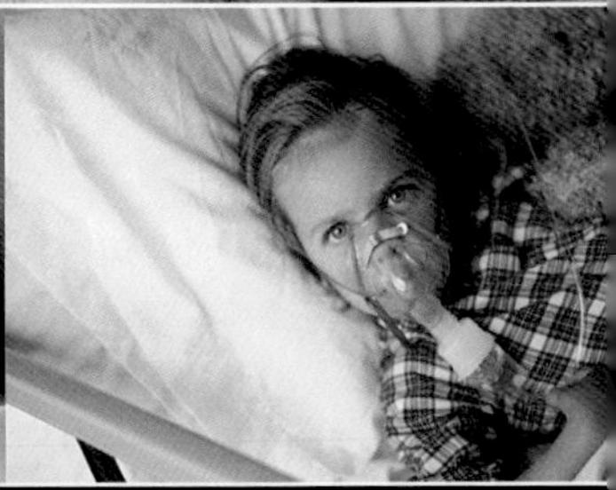

Think of it as 'Tough Love'

Since 1992, The Bear has been giving back to Edmonton's kids through The Bear Children's Fund. In the years since the Fund's inception, over $1,300,000 has been directed back into the greater Edmonton community and its charities. To make the Fund work requires the dedication of both management and staff, who have volunteered thousands of hours of their time to this worthwhile cause. As a rock station, The Bear may be loud, but it's proud too. Proud to be a part of a community as generous as Edmonton.

To apply for grants from the Bear Children's Fund please visit **www.thebearrocks.com**

Alberta Committee for Citizens with Disabilities | Alberta Ros
Chapter | Alberta Special Olympics | Arbutus Volunteer Foundatio
Belmont Elementary School | Ben Calf Robe Native Elementa
& Junior High Catholic School | Bent Arrow Traditional Healir
Society | Boyle Street Co-op Playground | Boys & Girls Club
Edmonton | Canadian Progress Club | Century Services In
Stollery Children's Hospital Foundation | Children's Heart Socie
City Centre Education Project | CNIB | Cross Cancer Institu
Early Head Start Program | Edmonton City Police D.A.R.
Program | Edmonton Food Bank | Edmonton Garrison Base Fur
Edmonton Jaycees | Edmonton School Lunch Program | Edmonto
Spring Board & Platform Diving Club | Employabilities | EMS Soc
Club | Firefighter's Burn Unit | Fort Saskatchewan Boys & Gi
Club | Friends of Rosecrest | Garden Valley Pony Club | Glenros
Rehabilitation Hospital | Griesbach School Council | Inner Ci
Youth Development Association | Head First Foundation | Hug-
Bear Express | Kid's Kottage | Kinsmen Club of St. Albert | Mansio
Youth Drop-In Centre for Teens | McCauley Community After Scho
Care Association | Morinville Panthers | New York City Police
Fire Widows' & Children's Benefit | Northern Alberta Brain Inju
Society | Norwood Community Centre | Nottingham Playgrour
Association | Parents Empowering Parents | P.A.R.T.Y. Progra
Project Literacy | Queen Mary Park School | Rainbow Socie
Ronald McDonald House | Royal Alexandra Hospital | Southwest Ar
Council of Community Leagues | St. Michael's School | St. Patrick
School (Edmonton) Parents Society | Terra Association | Uncles
Large | Various Trust Funds & Confidential Donations | Westvie
Regional Health Authority Youth Health Centre | Wetaskiwin Hea
Start Society | Yellowhead Youth Centre | Youth Emergency Shelt
Society | Skills Woodcroft Respite Home | Royal Alexandra Hospit
NICU Family Room (Bear Den) | Brightview Elementary Scho

The Answer is Digital School.

Autodesk
Authorized Training Center

CAD Technician Training | Computer Aided Drafting | Continuing Education | Distance Learning

Digital School's focused CAD Programs get you working fast.

Do you like to draw, sketch, or design? Do you want to know how things are made? If you do, then AutoCAD is for you!

In fact, CAD Technicians enjoy exciting careers with great income potential and are sought after by companies in Alberta and throughout North America. Digital School's certified instructors pride itself in delivering current, customizable Autodesk software training to meet individual and corporate needs on a flexible and convenient schedule.

Make your ideas possible with Digital School.

"Our corporate objective at Challenger Geomatics Ltd. is to provide innovative, professional services to our clients. We are impressed with the students from Digital School and we look forward to talking with them about employment opportunities within our company."
Tim Harding, VP Operations, Edmonton

www.digitalschool.ca email: info@digitalschool.ca

#304, 10205-101 Street, Edmonton, Alberta T5J 4H5 Phone (780) 414-0200

"You're Hired!"

Academy of Learning can help you get the training for a new Career that gets you hired!

- Business Administration
- Medical Office Assistant / Unit Clerk Specialty *
- Government of Alberta Health Care Aide *
- Dental Administrative Assistant *
- Computerized Payroll Accounting
- Network Security Specialist *
- Retail Pharmacy Technician *
- Office Administration
- Web Designer
- Network Administrator
- Payroll Administrator
- Computerized Accounting
- PC Support Specialist
- Web and Applications Developer *
- Insurance Advisor *
- and more!

* May not be available at all locations.

Consumers' Choice Award™ 2002 - 2006 For Business Excellence

www.academyoflearning.ab.ca

Financial assistance may be available to qualified applicants.

Simply a BETTER Way to Learn!

Airdrie .... (403) 912-3430
Calgary Central .... (403) 282-3166
Calgary Northeast .... (403) 569-8973
Calgary South .... (403) 252-8973
Edmonton Downtown .... (780) 424-1144
Edmonton South .... (780) 433-7284
West Edmonton Mall .... (780) 496-9428
High River .... (403) 652-2116
Lethbridge .... (403) 329-3244
Medicine Hat .... (403) 526-5833
Red Deer .... (403) 347-6676

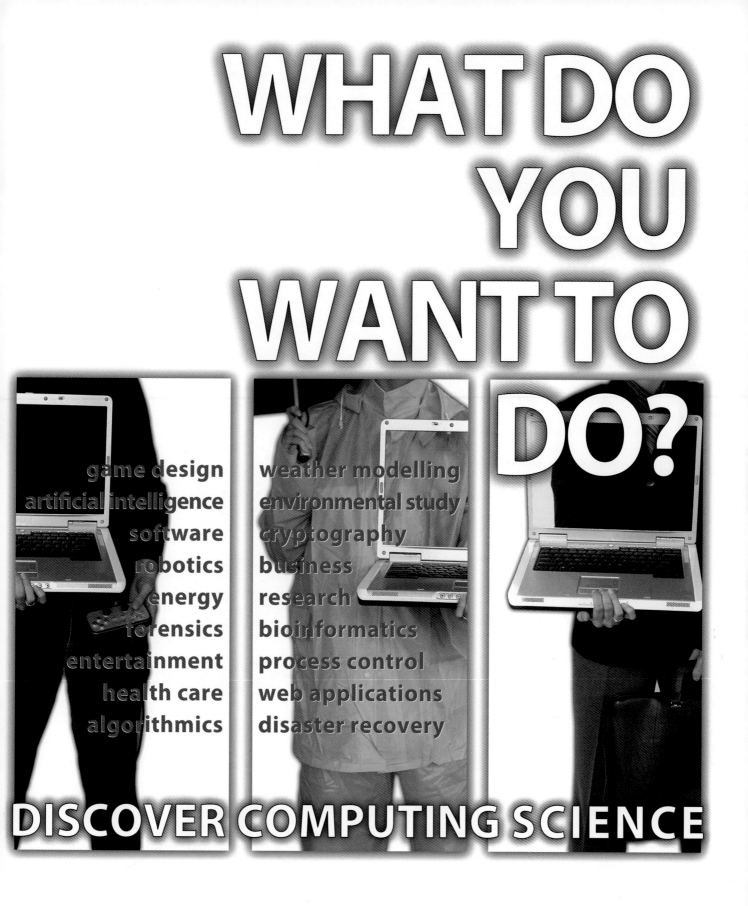

WHAT DO YOU WANT TO DO?

game design
artificial intelligence
software
robotics
energy
forensics
entertainment
health care
algorithmics

weather modelling
environmental study
cryptography
business
research
bioinformatics
process control
web applications
disaster recovery

DISCOVER COMPUTING SCIENCE

DEPARTMENT OF
COMPUTING SCIENCE

www.cs.ualberta.ca info@cs.ualberta.ca

Castle Rock Research is a Promise Builder

Castle Rock
Research Corp

Alberta's Promise thanks **Castle Rock Research** for their ongoing support of children and youth in Alberta. Their donation of *The Key* study guides to students attending Edmonton Public schools shows their commitment to children and youth and the value of giving back to the community.

"We feel honoured to participate in the education initiatives of Alberta's Promise with the shared goal of making Alberta the best place to raise our children."

Gautam Rao, President

Castle Rock Research Corp.

Alberta's Promise is a movement by caring community partners to create opportunities for our children to be successful, healthy and happy.

Alberta's Promise

Pulling Together for Children and Youth

2520 AMEC Place | 801 - 6th Avenue SW | Calgary | AB | T2P 3W2 | Tel 403-297-7500 | Toll free 1-866-313-7500
www.albertaspromise.org

Copyright Protected

7. A

Chlorine reacts with iodide as follows:

$$\underset{\text{SOA}}{Cl_{2(g)}} \quad \underset{\text{SRA}}{I^-_{(aq)}} \quad \overset{\text{OA}}{\underset{\text{RA}}{H_2O_{(l)}}}$$

Reduction: $Cl_{2(g)} + 2e^- \rightarrow 2Cl^-_{(aq)}$

Oxidation: $2I^-_{(aq)} \rightarrow I_{2(s)} + 2e^-$

Net: $Cl_{2(g)} + 2I^-_{(aq)} \rightarrow 2Cl^-_{(aq)} + I_{2(s)}$

The reddish-brown colour is due to the production of $I_{2(s)}$. Clearly, it is the $I^-_{(aq)}$ ions that are oxidized.

8. D

Since, in the balanced reaction given, the **ratios** of Al to O and Si to O do not change in going from reactants to products, the reaction is unlikely to be redox in nature. No protons are present in the reactants **or** the products, so the process cannot be a Brønsted–Lowry acid-base reaction.

9. B

The iron in the reaction is changed from iron (II) in $FeS_{2(s)}$ to iron (III) in $Fe_2O_{3(s)}$. Thus, iron's oxidation number changes from +2 to +3.

Note: in $FeS_{2(s)}$, the oxidation number of sulfur is –1.

10. C

The process given can be broken down to

Reduction $Cl_{2(g)} + 2e^- \rightarrow 2Cl^-_{(g)}$

Oxidation $2Na_{(g)} \rightarrow 2Na^+_{(g)} + 2e^-$

Note: A and D represent oxidation half-reactions, while B is quite impossible.

11. D

When the oxidation numbers of all the reaction entities are considered:

$$2\overset{+6}{Cr}\overset{-2}{O}_{3(s)} + \overset{+1}{H_2}\overset{-2}{O}_{(l)} \rightarrow 2\overset{+1}{H^+_{(aq)}} + \overset{+6}{Cr_2}\overset{-2}{O}{}_7^{2-}{}_{(aq)}$$

it becomes obvious that no redox reaction has occurred (A is wrong) because the oxidation number of chromium is unchanged.

Note that a solution with H^+ ions will have a $pH < 7$.

12. A

The sum of the oxidation numbers of all the atoms in bicarbonate ion is –1. So,

$ON_C + ON_H + 3ON_O = -1$

or $ON_C + 1 - 6 = -1$

$ON_C = +4.$

Note: The terms oxidation number and oxidation state are, more often than not, used interchangeably.

13. A

The oxidation number of N in $NO_3^-{}_{(aq)}$ is +5. The oxidation number of N in $NO_{(g)}$ is +2. Clearly, the oxidation number of nitrogen decreases by 3 in the reaction given.

Note: There is no need to consider the coefficients of $NO_3^-{}_{(aq)}/NO_{(g)}$ to determine the oxidation number change.

14. C

The oxidation numbers of O and H do not change in this reaction. The oxidation number of chlorine decreases from 0 to –1, which signifies a reduction. The oxidation number of sulfur increases from +2 to +6. Through the following process, we come to the balanced oxidation half-reaction:

$$S_2O_3{}^{2-}{}_{(aq)} \rightarrow SO_4{}^{2-}{}_{(aq)}$$

$$S_2O_3{}^{2-}{}_{(aq)} \rightarrow 2SO_4{}^{2-}{}_{(aq)}$$

$$5H_2O_{(l)} + S_2O_3{}^{2-}{}_{(aq)} \rightarrow 2SO_4{}^{2-}{}_{(aq)}$$

$$5H_2O_{(l)} + S_2O_3{}^{2-}{}_{(aq)} \rightarrow 2SO_4{}^{2-}{}_{(aq)} + 10H^+{}_{(aq)}$$

$$5H_2O_{(l)} + S_2O_3{}^{2-}{}_{(aq)} \rightarrow 2SO_4{}^{2-}{}_{(aq)} + 10H^+{}_{(aq)} + 8e^-$$

Note: Half-reactions given in alternatives B and D are reductions, while the reaction given in alternative A is not balanced!

NR3. 2 3 4 3

The reaction can be balanced by inspection, by making half-reactions, or by using oxidation numbers.

By Making Half-Reactions

Reduction Half-Reaction:

$$V_2O_{5(s)} \rightarrow 2VO_{(s)}$$

$$V_2O_{5(s)} \rightarrow 2VO_{(s)} + 3H_2O_{(l)}$$

$$6H^+{}_{(aq)} + V_2O_{5(s)} \rightarrow 2VO_{(s)} + 3H_2O_{(l)}$$

$$6e^- + 6H^+{}_{(aq)} + V_2O_{5(s)} \rightarrow 2VO_{(s)} + 3H_2O_{(l)}$$

Oxidation Half-Reaction:

$$Mn_{(s)} \rightarrow MnO_{2(s)}$$

$$2H_2O_{(l)} + Mn_{(s)} \rightarrow MnO_{2(s)}$$

$$2H_2O_{(l)} + Mn_{(s)} \rightarrow MnO_{2(s)} + 4H^+{}_{(aq)}$$

$$2H_2O_{(l)} + Mn_{(s)} \rightarrow MnO_{2(s)} + 4H^+{}_{(aq)} + 4e^-$$

Net Reaction:

$$(6e^- + 6H^+{}_{(aq)} + V_2O_{5(s)} \rightarrow 2VO_{(s)} + 3H_2O_{(l)}) \times 2$$

$$(2H_2O_{(l)} + Mn_{(s)} \rightarrow MnO_{2(s)} + 4H^+{}_{(aq)} + 4e^-) \times 3$$

$$2V_2O_{5(s)} + 3Mn_{(s)} \rightarrow 4VO_{(s)} + 3MnO_{2(s)}$$

By Using Oxidation Numbers

$$2V_2\overset{+5}{O}_{5(s)} + 3\overset{0}{Mn}_{(s)} \rightarrow 4V\overset{+2}{O}_{(s)} + 3Mn\overset{+4}{O}_{2(s)}$$

gain $3e^-/V$; gain $6e^-/V2O5(s)$; $\times 2$

loss $4e^-/Mn_{(s)}$; $\times 3$

NR4. 2 4 1 5

The oxidation number of oxygen in each of the nitrogen oxides is –2 (it is the more electronegative atom). Assume that the oxidation number of N in each compound is x. Thus:

Compound	Sum of ONs		ON_N
$NO_{(g)}$	$x - 2 = 0$	$\Rightarrow$	$x = +2$
$NO_{2(g)}$	$x - 4 = 0$	$\Rightarrow$	$x = +4$
$N_2O_{(g)}$	$2x - 2 = 0$	$\Rightarrow$	$x = +1$
$N_2O_{5(g)}$	$2x - 10 = 0$	$\Rightarrow$	$x = +5$

Copyright Protected

15. C

	E°_R
$Fe^{2+}{}_{(aq)} + 2e^- \rightarrow Fe_{(s)}$	–0.45V
$Ga^{3+}{}_{(aq)} + 3e^- \rightarrow Ga_{(s)}$	?
$Zn^{2+}{}_{(aq)} + 2e^- \rightarrow Zn_{(s)}$	–0.76V
$Mg^{2+}{}_{(aq)} + 2e^- \rightarrow Mg_{(s)}$	–2.37V

A list-and-label method can be used to predict the net redox reaction:

$$\underset{}{\overset{\text{SOA}}{MnO_4^-{}_{(aq)}}} \quad \overset{\text{OA}}{H^+{}_{(aq)}} \quad \underset{\text{SRA}}{H_2O_{2(aq)}} \quad \underset{\text{RA}}{\overset{\text{OA}}{H_2O_{(l)}}} \quad \overset{\text{OA}}{K^+{}_{(aq)}}$$

$$(MnO^{4-}{}_{(aq)} + 8H^+{}_{(aq)} + 5e^- \rightarrow Mn^{2+}{}_{(aq)} + 4H_2O_{(l)}) \times 2$$

$$(H_2O_{2(l)} \rightarrow O_{2(g)} + 2H^+{}_{(aq)} + 2e^-) \times 5$$

$$2MnO_4{}^-{}_{(aq)} + 6H^+{}_{(aq)} + 5H_2O_{2(l)} \rightarrow 2Mn_2{}^+{}_{(aq)} + 5O_{2(g)} + 8H_2O_{(l)}$$

A straightforward stoichiometric calculation yields the answer:

$$n_{MnO_4^-} = (17.00 \text{ mL})(0.0080 \tfrac{\text{mol}}{\text{L}}) = 0.14 \text{ mmol}$$

$$n_{H_2O_2} = \tfrac{5}{2} \times n_{MnO_4^-} = \tfrac{5}{2} \times 0.14 \text{ mmol} = 0.34 \text{ mmol}$$

$$[H_2O_{2(l)}] = \frac{0.34 \text{ mmol}}{11.33 \text{ mL}} = 0.030 \frac{\text{mol}}{\text{L}}$$

The reducing agent concentration is 3.0×10^{-2} mol / L.

16. B

The reduction half reaction of $Sn^{2+}{}_{(aq)}$ is $Sn^{2+}{}_{(aq)} + 2e^- \rightarrow Sn_{(s)}$ for which $E^\circ_R = -0.14V$.

17. A

In a comparison of several electrochemical cells, the most rational experimental design would likely have some of the following variables.

Controlled variable(s):
- electrolyte concentration

Manipulated variable:
- metal/metallic ion in each electrode and the responding variable would be the cell potential voltage.

NR5. 1.89

It is obvious from the given information that reaction I (the oxidation) is the anode half-reaction, while reaction II (the reduction) is the cathode half-reaction. Thus,

$$E^\circ_{net} = E^\circ_{RC} - E^\circ_{RA}$$

$$+1.40V = -0.49V - E^\circ_{RA}$$

$$E^\circ_{RA} = -0.49 \text{ V} - (+1.40 \text{ V}) = -1.89 \text{ V}$$

The reduction potential of half-reaction I is –1.89 V.

Not for Reproduction

18. B

In the cell diagram, the electron flow makes the zinc electrode the cathode of this voltaic cell (positive E°_{net}). Therefore, the $Q_{(s)}$ electrode is the anode. The anode half-cell holds the most readily oxidized entity (in other words, the strongest reducing agent is in this cell). Obviously, $Zn_{(s)}$ is a weaker reducing agent than is $Q_{(s)}$.

Normally, it is the electrode of a voltaic cell that has the highest reduction potential that is the cathode. Alternative A is incorrect.

If $Q^{2+}{}_{(aq)}$ were the stronger oxidizing agent in the cell, the electron flow would enter the $Q_{(s)}$ electrode/cathode—alternative D is incorrect.

If the reduction potential of $Q^{2+}{}_{(aq)} / Q_{(s)}$ were greater than that of copper it would react spontaneously with copper, and zinc and it would be the cathode of the voltaic cell in the diagram. This is plainly not so—alternative C is incorrect.

19. B

It's always useful to compare several characteristics of electrolytic and voltaic cells:

Characteristic	Voltaic Cell	Electrolytic Cell
E°_{net}	positive	negative
Spontaneity	spontaneous	non spontaneous
Energy Input/ Output	produces energy /electricity	consumes energy/ electricity
Electrode Process	reduction at cathode oxidation at anode	reduction at cathode oxidation at anode
Process	produces electricity from chemical reaction	needs electrical energy to effect chemical reaction

From this table, we see that the only correct statement made about electrolytic cells is B.

NR6. 4 6 3 1

For the cell given:
$Cu_{(s)} / Cr^{2+}{}_{(aq)} // Ni^{2+}{}_{(aq)} / Ni_{(s)}$, the cathode ($E^{\circ}_{\text{RC}} = +0.34$ V) is the copper half-cell and the anode is the nickel half-cell. Thus,

- the cathode is the copper electrode—4
- the external circuit joins the electrodes—6
- the oxidizing agent is the copper (II) ion—3
- the anode is the nickel electrode—1

(5 is the salt bridge and 2 is the weakly oxidizing electrolyte at the anode)

20. C

We know that $E^{\circ}_{net} = E^{\circ}_{RC} - E^{\circ}_{RA}$, and $E^{\circ}_{RC} = +0.34$ V, since $Cu^{2+}{}_{(aq)}$ is reduced—a process that happens at the cathode. Thus,

$$\begin{aligned} E^{\circ}_{RA} &= E^{\circ}_{RC} - E^{\circ}_{net} \\ &= (+0.34\text{ V}) - (-0.20\text{ V}) \\ &= +0.14\text{ V} \end{aligned}$$

Looking at page 9 of the Chemistry Data Booklet, we see that the only appropriate oxidation that will occur is
$H_2S_{(aq)} \rightarrow S_{(s)} + 2H^{+}{}_{(aq)} + 2e^{-}$

Note: The answer cannot be B because the anode half-reaction must be an oxidation.

NR7. 1 4 6 7

It is obvious that insulated containers (2) and a thermometer (5) are needed for a calorimetry experiment. Similarly, pH paper (3) and a buret (8) are needed for investigating acid–base chemistry. To make a voltaic cell, the necessary materials in the list are electrodes (1), porous boundary (a porous cup or a 'U'-tube) (4), suitable electrolytes (6), and an external circuit (the relevant wires and a voltmeter) (7).

Copyright Protected

21. A

Use an appropriate mini-reduction half-reaction table from the evidence given with select reduction potentials from "Standard Electrode Potentials" in the Chemistry 30 Data Booklet.

The reduction potential of $Ga^{3+}_{(aq)}$ must lie between –0.45 V and –0.76 V. Only answer A fits this requirement.

22. D

By definition, a spontaneous E°_{net} is positive. The answer can only be D. A cell with an $E^{\circ}_{net} < 0V$ is electrolytic in nature, i.e. energy must be supplied to force a non-spontaneous reaction to proceed.

23. C

Ordinarily, $Mg_{(s)}$ might be produced from the reduction of $Mg^{2+}_{(aq)}$ at the cathode of the electrolytic cell. However, $H_2O_{(l)}$ is a stronger oxidizing agent than is $Mg^{2+}_{(aq)}$ and the likely products at the cathode are $H_{2(g)}$ and $OH^{-}_{(aq)}$. (**Note:** Alternatives B and D are incorrect because $Mg^{2+}_{(aq)}$ is an oxidizing agent. Alternative A is incorrect because $Cl^{-}_{(aq)}$ is a reducing agent.)

In most electrolyses of aqueous solutions, $H_2O_{(l)}$ is reduced and/or oxidized. The most common means of avoiding this is through the electrolysis of molten salts. $Mg_{(s)}$ is produced from electrolysis of $MgCl_{2(l)}$ in a Downs Cell.

24. D

The relative positions of the half-cell potentials in a standard electrode potential table remain unchanged no matter what electrode is chosen as a standard. The E°_R of the $Ni^{2+}_{(aq)}/Ni_{(s)}$ redox couple will always lie 0.60 V below the E°_R of the $Cu^{2+}_{(aq)}/Cu_{(s)}$ redox couple. Thus, if the E°_R of $Cu^{2+}_{(aq)}/Cu_{(s)}$ becomes 0.00 V, the E°_R of $Ni^{2+}_{(aq)}/Ni_{(s)}$ will be –0.60 V (electrode potentials below the standard line are always negative reduction potentials). Alternatively, whatever change is necessary to convert a reduction potential relative to the $H_{2(g)},H^{+}_{(aq)}/Pt_{(s)}$ standard to 0.00 V must be applied equally to all other electrode potentials; e.g.,

	E°_R (re: $H_{2(g)}, H^{+}_{(aq)}/PT_{(s)}$)		E°_R (re: $Cu^{2+}_{(aq)}/CU_{(s)}$)
$Cu^{2+}_{(aq)}/Cu_{(s)}$	+034 V	$\xrightarrow{\text{subtract 0.34 V}}$	0.00 V
$Ni^{2+}_{(aq)}/Ni_{(s)}$	–026 V	$\xrightarrow{\text{subtract 0.34 V}}$	–0.60 V

25. A

Although the temperature is not specified, the cell shown is standard. In cell nomenclature, the cell is written as $Zn_{(s)}/Zn^{2+}_{(aq)}//Cu^{2+}_{(aq)}/Cu_{(s)}$. The cathode is the copper half-cell (contains SOA, has highest reduction potential) and the anode is the zinc half-cell.

$$E^{\circ}_{net} = E^{\circ}_{RC} - E^{\circ}_{RA}$$
$$= (+034\text{ V}) - (-0.76\text{ V})$$
$$= +1.10\text{ V}$$

The net cell potential is +1.10 V.

26. B

Electroplating occurs when a metal ion is reduced at the cathode of an electrochemical cell. Thus, during the nickel stage, the following cathode half-reaction will occur: $Ni^{2+}{}_{(aq)} + 2e^- \rightarrow Ni_{(s)}$. The nickel ions will gain electrons and be plated at the cathode.

NR8. 4 3 8 6

Since electroplating occurs at the cathode and the car bumper is to be plated, the cathode is 4. In all electrochemical cells, electrons flow from the anode to the cathode. The electron flow is arrow 3. In all electrochemical cells, the net electric field within the cell causes cations to migrate to the cathode. The cation flow is arrow 8. The only anion (negative ion) in the cell is the nitrate ion, 6.

27. A

For the cell $Cd_{(s)} / Cd^{2+}{}_{(aq)} // Ag^+{}_{(aq)} / Ag_{(s)}$, the cadmium electrode is the anode. Thus, the anode half-reaction can be employed in a stoichiometric calculation:

$$Cd_{(s)} \rightarrow Cd^{2+}_{(aq)} + 2e^-$$

m = ?   6.00 A(C/s)
112.41 g/mol   2.00 h

$$n_{e^-} = \frac{It}{F} = \frac{6.00\ C/s \times 2.00\ h \times 3600\ s/n}{9.65 \times 10^4\ C/mol\ e^-}$$

$$= 0.448\ mol$$

$$n_{Cd} = \frac{1}{2} n_{e^-} = \frac{1}{2} \times 0.448\ mol = 0.224\ mol$$

$$m_{Cd} = 0.228\ mol \times \frac{112.41\ g}{mol} = 25.2\ g$$

Corrosion occurs at the anode, so the anode mass decreases by 25.2 g.

Alternatively, $m_{Cd} = \frac{It}{F} \times \frac{A_{Cd}}{V_{Cd}}$

$$= \frac{6.00\ c/s \times 2.00\ h \times 3600\ s/h \times 117.41\ \frac{g}{mol}}{9.65 \times 10^4\ C/mol\ e^- \times 2}$$

$$= 25.2\ g$$

Note: The cathode mass increases by 48.3g through the electroplating of silver.

NR9. 2.15

Some simple half-cell stoichiometry provides the answer:

$$Cr^{2+}{}_{(aq)} + 2e^- \rightarrow Cr_{(s)}$$

$n_{Cr^{2+}} = ?$ 112 g, $52.00\ \frac{g}{mol}$

$$n_{Cr} = \frac{112\ g}{52.00\ \frac{g}{mol}} = 2.15\ mol$$

$$n_{Cr^{2+}} = \frac{1}{1} \times n_{Cr} = \frac{1}{1} \times 2.15\ mol = 2.15\ mol$$

Some 2.15 mol of $Cr^{2+}{}_{(aq)}$ must be reduced at the bumper.

NR10. 3.46

$$n_{e^-} = \frac{2}{1} \times n_{Cr} = \frac{2}{1} \times 2.15\ mol = 4.30\ mol$$

Since $n_{e^-} = \frac{It}{F}$, then $t = \frac{Fn_{e^-}}{I}$, so

$$t = \frac{(9.65 \times 10^4\ \frac{C}{mol})(4.30\ mol)}{2000\ \frac{C}{s}} = 207\ s$$ or

$$t = 207\ s \times \frac{1\ min}{60\ s} = 3.46\ min.$$

28. A

For a metal to be more anodic than iron, it must be a stronger reducing agent than iron. Only $Mg_{(s)}$ is a stronger reducing agent than $Fe_{(s)}$.

Copyright Protected

29. A

Sometimes it is necessary to use tabled half-reactions to predict a redox reaction.

SOA

$Na_{(s)}$ $H_2O_{(l)}$

SRA RA

The net reaction is spontaneous because the SOA lies above the SRA in a reduction half-reaction table.

Reduction: $2\,H_2O_{(l)} + 2\,e^- \rightarrow H_{2(g)} + 2\,OH^-_{(aq)}$

Oxidation: $2\,Na_{(s)} \rightarrow 2\,Na^+_{(aq)} + 2\,e^-$

Net Reaction: $2\,H_2O_{(l)} + 2\,Na_{(s)} \rightarrow H_{2(g)} + 2\,Na^+_{(aq)} + 2\,OH^-_{(aq)}$

This reaction produces hydroxide ions, which will result in a reaction mixture pH greater than 7.

Note: It is $H^+_{(aq)}$ not $H_{2(g)}$ that contributes to solution pH.

30. D

Distractors A and B are not redox reactions (A illustrates a precipitation reaction while B is an acid–base neutralization). Alternative C represents the combustion of natural gas. Alternative D is incorrect because it illustrates the cellular respiration of glucose in cell mitochondria.

31. D

Historically speaking, the reaction of a compound or element with oxygen is referred to as oxidation. Moreover, the oxidation number of tin increases from 0 to +2—this signifies a loss of 2 moles of e^- per mole of $Sn_{(s)}$—so the tin is oxidized!

The $H^\circ_{f\,(SnO_{(s)})} = -285.8\,\frac{kJ}{mol}$ —an exothermic formation reaction.

NR11. 5 2 3 4

Reaction 1 is an acid–base neutralization. Reaction 2 is cellular respiration—a biological redox reaction common to plant and animal cells. Reaction 3 is a spontaneous non-biological redox reaction ($Ni^{2+}_{(aq)}$, the OA, lies above $Fe_{(s)}$, the RA, on page 9 of the Chemistry Data Booklet, $E^\circ_{net} = +0.19$ V) Reaction 4 is a non-spontaneous, non-biological redox reaction ($Co^{2+}_{(aq)}$, the OA, lies below $Fe^{2+}_{(aq)}$, the RA, on page 9 of the Chemistry Data Booklet, $E^\circ_{net} = -1.05$ V). Reaction 5 is the photosynthesis reaction—a biological redox reaction common to plants.

ANSWERS AND SOLUTIONS
ACIDS AND BASES – UNIT REVIEW

NR1. 29.9	14. B	28. C	41. D
1. C	15. A	29. D	42. D
2. D	16. B	30. B	43. A
3. A	17. D	NR8. 2.28 #	NR12. 3.26
4. B	18. B	NR9. 11.3	44. D
NR2. 2.41 *	19. D	31. B	45. A
5. A	20. A	32. A	46. B
6. D	21. C	33. B	47. D
7. B	22. B	34. D	NR13. 10.8
8. A	23. C	35. D	48. C
9. C	NR5. 8.38 or 8.37 ‡	36. C	49. C
10. B	24. A	37. A	50. D
11. C	25. C	NR10. 4213	51. A
NR3. 2.56 †	NR6. 0.50 §	38. A	
NR4. 0.13	26. B ‖	NR11. 3.49	
12. D	27. B	39. B	
13. A	NR7. 4123	40. C	

* If MC4 is
- A, then NR2 is 0.08
- B, then NR2 is 2.41
- C, then NR2 is 4.74
- D, then NR2 is 4.82

‡ If MC23 is
- A, then NR5 is 12.1
- B, then NR5 is 11.6
- C, then NR5 is 8.38 or 8.37
- D, then NR5 is 8.87, 8.88

‖ If MC25 is
- A, then MC 26 is D
- B, then MC 26 is C
- C, then MC 26 is B
- D, then MC 26 is A

† If MC11 is
- A, then NR3 is 6.48
- B, then NR3 is 2.98
- C, then NR3 is 2.56
- D, then NR3 is 5.44

§ If MC25 is
- A, then NR6 is 0.26
- B, then NR6 is 0.48
- C, then NR6 is 0.50
- D, then NR6 is 0.70

If MC 30 is
- A, then NR 8 is 2.55
- B, then NR 8 is 2.28
- C, then NR 8 is 1.59
- D, then NR 8 is 3.15

NR1. 29.9

The stoichiometric method gives the answer.

$NaOH_{(aq)} + HCl_{(aq)} \rightarrow NaCl_{(aq)} + H_2O_{(l)}$

10.0 mL $V_{HCl} = ?$

2.57 mol/L 0.860 mol/L

$$n_{NaOH} = 10.0\text{ mL} \times \frac{2.57\text{ mol}}{\text{L}} = 25.7\text{ mmol}$$

$$n_{HCl} = \frac{1}{1} n_{NaOH} = \frac{1}{1} \times 25.7\text{ mmol} = 25.7\text{ mmol}$$

$$V_{HCl} = 25.7\text{ mmol} \times \frac{\text{L}}{0.860\text{ mol}} = 29.9\text{ mL}$$

Some 29.9 mL of $HCl_{(aq)}$ are required to neutralize the caustic soda.

1. C

When a strong base is neutralized by a strong acid (here it is $NaOH_{(aq)}$ and $HCl_{(aq)}$), the equivalence point pH is 7. This is because the strongest acid and base in the product species is $H_2O_{(l)}$. The best indicator has a colour change range that overlaps the equivalence point. Only bromothymol blue (6.0–7.6, yellow to blue) is suitable.

Alternative D (1,3,5-trinitrobenzene) would change colour too early (too high a pH range), while alternatives A and B (methyl violet and bromocresol green) would change colour too late (too low a pH range).

2. D

Catalysts/enzymes increase the rates of chemical/biochemical reactions by providing alternate pathways from the reactants to the products that have lower activation energies than uncatalysed reactions. Low levels or a complete absence of alcohol dehydrogenase would cause the metabolism of alcohol to occur more slowly than normal.

Alternatives A, B, and C would only apply if you had high levels of the enzyme.

3. A

Acetic acid is a weak acid with a K_a value of 1.8×10^{-5} mol/L. This means that at 0.83 mol/L, the extent of reaction with water described by:

$$CH_3COOH_{(aq)} + H_2O_{(l)} \text{”} \quad CH_3COO^-_{(aq)} + H_3O^+_{(aq)}$$

is considerably less than 50%.

Thus:

$$[CH_3COOH_{(aq)}] >> [CH_3COO^-_{(aq)}] = [H_3O^+_{(aq)}]$$

Only answer A, which is true for all weak acids is correct.

Copyright Protected

4. B

For the acetic/ethanoic acid in vinegar, the $[H^+{}_{(aq)}]$ is best calculated as follows:

$$CH_3COOH_{(aq)} \text{"} H^+{}_{(aq)} + CH_3COO^-{}_{(aq)}$$

Initially	$0.83\frac{\text{mol}}{\text{L}}$	—	—
Equilibrium	$0.83 - x$	x	x

$$K_a = \frac{[H^+{}_{(aq)}][CH_3COO^-{}_{(aq)}]}{[CH_3COOH^-{}_{(aq)}]}$$

$$K_a = \frac{x^2}{0.83 - x} \qquad \text{But } \frac{0.83}{K_a} \cong 5\times10^4$$

$$\text{So } K_a \cong \frac{x^2}{0.83}$$

$$x = \sqrt{0.83 \times K_a}$$

$$x = 3.9\times10^{-3}\ \frac{\text{mol}}{\text{L}} = [H^+{}_{(aq)}]$$

The acid concentration of the vinegar is $3.9\times10^{-3}\ \frac{\text{mol}}{\text{L}}$.

If the quadratic method is used, the answer is ~0.2% lower. (Brønsted–Lowry, modified Arrhenius, or dissociation as shown all give the same answer.)

NR2. 2.41

$$pH = -\log[H^+{}_{(aq)}]$$

$$= -\log\left(3.9\times10^{-3}\ \frac{\text{mol}}{\text{L}}\right) = 2.41$$

The number of decimal places in the pH correspond to the number of significant digits in the $[H^+{}_{(aq)}]$: two. Whatever method is used to compute $[H^+{}_{(aq)}]$, the pH is the same and if the answer to MC4 is kept in the calculator or if 3.9×10^{-3} is entered, there is still no difference in the answer.

If A was chosen in MC4, the answer is 0.08.

If C was chosen in MC4, the answer is 4.74.

If D was chosen in MC4, the answer is 4.82.

5. A

At a pH of 2.37, phenolphthalein is colourless (colourless below 8.2). The colour will be that of bromocresol green (pH 3.8 to 5.4, yellow to blue). The solution will be yellow.

Not for Reproduction

6. D

The better theory to use in explaining weak acid–base reactions is Brønsted–Lowry theory.

The major species present are $\overset{SA}{CH_3COOH_{(aq)}}$, $Na^+_{(aq)}$, $\underset{SB}{\overset{A}{HCO_3^-{}_{(aq)}}}$, and $\underset{B}{\overset{A}{H_2O_{(l)}}}$.

The predicted net equation is

$$CH_3COOH_{(aq)} + HCO^-_{3(aq)} \overset{>50\%}{"} CH_3COO^-_{(aq)} + H_2CO_{3(aq)}$$

But $H_2CO_{3(aq)}$ is essentially $CO_{2(l)}$ in water, and loss of $CO_{2(g)}$ leads to near quantitative reaction, which is written as

$$CH_3COOH_{(aq)} + HCO_3^-{}_{(aq)} \rightarrow CH_3COO^-_{(aq)} + CO_{2(g)} + H_2O_{(l)}$$

Alternative A is unlikely since no strong acid is present. Alternative B makes no sense because the enthanoic acid is the strongest one present. Alternative C is not a net ionic equation (no ions, Na^+ is a spectator ion).

7. B

Conjugate acid–base pairs are different by one H^+. The conjugate acid–base pairs for the reaction given are ($HNO_{2(aq)}$, $NO_2^-{}_{(aq)}$) and ($H_3BO_{3(aq)}$, $H_2BO_3^-{}_{(aq)}$). The answer can only be B.

8. A

In a typical acid–base strength table, amphiprotic entities appear in both the acid and the conjugate base columns. More formally, amphiprotic entities can lose or gain H^+ ion in a Brønsted–Lowry neutralization reaction. Whichever reaction occurs is contingent on the other reactant. The only species that works here is $H_2BO_3^-{}_{(aq)}$, answer A.

9. C

For the generic equilibrium $aA + bB$ " $cC + dD$, the equilibrium constant expression is $K_c = \frac{[C]^c[D]^d}{[A]^a[B]^b}$, where K_c is the concentration equilibrium constant; *a*, *b*, *c*, and *d* are the equation coefficients of A, B, C, and D; and [A], [B], [C], and [D] are the concentrations of reactants A and B and products C and D.

Solid reactants/products are never included in a *K* expression. Only when two or more liquids are present are pure liquid reactants/products included in a *K* expression.

For the reaction:

$$HC_6H_5O_{(aq)} + H_2O_{(l)} " C_6H_5O_{(aq)} + H_3O^-_{(aq)}$$

is

$$K_a = \frac{[C_6H_5O^-{}_{(aq)}][H_3O^+{}_{(aq)}]}{[HC_6H_5O_{(aq)}]}$$

10. B

For the reaction

$$H_2O_{(l)} + HC_6H_5O_{(aq)} " C_6H_5O^-_{(aq)} + H_3O^-_{(aq)}$$

Initially	$6.44\times10^{-2}\ \frac{mol}{L}$	—	—
Equilibrium	$6.44\times10^{-2} - x$	x	x

$$K_a = \frac{x^2}{6.44\times10^{-2} - x} \text{ but}$$

$$x = [H^+{}_{(aq)}] = 10^{-pH} = 10^{-5.60}$$

$$K_a = \frac{(10^{-5.60})^2}{6.44\times10^{-2} - 10^{-5.60}} = 9.8\times10^{-11}\ \frac{mol}{L}$$

The answer is B, whether or not the value of *x* in the denominator is included!

Copyright Protected

11. C

$$K_{bC_6H_5O^-(aq)} = \frac{K_w}{K_{aC_6H_5OH}}$$

$$= \frac{1.0\times10^{-14}}{1.3\times10^{-10}}\ \frac{mol}{L}$$

$$= 7.7\times10^{-5}\ \frac{mol}{L}$$

The K_b for $C_6H_5O^-{}_{(aq)}$ has a value of 7.7×10^{-5}. Typically, solutions of the conjugate bases of weak acids are basic.

NR3. 2.56

An equilibrium calculation is needed to compute the pOH of the solution.

$$C_6H_5O^-{}_{(aq)} + H_2O_{(l)} \text{”} C_6H_5OH_{(aq)} + OH^-{}_{(aq)}$$

Initially	$0.10\frac{mol}{L}$	—	—	—
Equilibrium	$0.10-x$	—	x	x

$$K = \frac{x^2}{1.10-x} \cong \frac{x^2}{0.10} \text{ since } \frac{1.10\text{ mol/L}}{K_b} > 1000$$

$$[OH^-_{(aq)}] = x = \sqrt{0.10\times K_b} = 2.8\times10^{-3}\text{ mol/L}$$

$$pOH = -\log[OH^-{}_{(aq)}]$$
$$= -\log(2.7\times10^{-3}\text{ mol/L})$$
$$= 2.56$$

The pOH is the same whether the recorded answer in MC 11 is used or the numbers are kept in the calculator.

If A was chosen in MC 11:

$$[OH^-{}_{(aq)}] = \sqrt{1.1\times10^{-12}\times0.10} = 3.3\times10^{-7}\ \frac{mol}{L}$$

and pOH = 6.48

If B was chosen in MC 11:

$$[OH^-{}_{(aq)}] = \sqrt{1.1\times10^{-5}\times0.10} = 1.0\times10^{-3}\ \frac{mol}{L}$$

and pOH = 2.98

If D was chosen in MC 11:

$$[OH^-{}_{(aq)}] = \sqrt{1.3\times10^{-10}\times0.10} = 3.6\times10^{-6}\ \frac{mol}{L}$$

and pOH = 5.44

Not for Reproduction

NR4. 0.13

The neutralization of a strong acid by a strong base is exothermic. The point at which the exothermic reaction ceases is the maximum of the titration curve, corresponding to a volume of $NaOH_{(aq)}$ of 30.0 mL. A simple stoichiometry completes the question.

$$HCl_{(aq)} + NaOH_{(aq)} \rightarrow NaCl_{(aq)} + H_2O_{(l)}$$

20.0 mL   30.0 mL

$0.20 \frac{\text{mol}}{\text{L}}$ $[NaOH_{(aq)}] = ?$

$$n_{HCl} = 20.0\ \text{mL} \times \frac{0.20\ \text{mol}}{\text{L}} = 4.0\ \text{mmol}$$

$$n_{NaOH} = \frac{1}{1} n_{HCl} = \frac{1}{1} \times 4.0\ \text{mmol} = 4.0\ \text{mmol}$$

$$[NaOH_{(aq)}] = \frac{4.0\ \text{mmol}}{30.0\ \text{mL}}$$

$$= 0.13 \frac{\text{mol}}{\text{L}}$$

The $[NaOH_{(aq)}]$ molar concentration is $0.13 \frac{\text{mol}}{\text{L}}$.

12. D

At most normal concentrations, weak acids, no matter how many protons they have, behave as if they were monoprotic acids. Thus, the equation that best represents the equilibrium of $H_3PO_{4(aq)}$ in water is

$$H_3PO_{4(aq)} + H_2O_{(l)} "H_2PO_4^-{}_{(aq)} + H_3O^+{}_{(aq)}$$

13. A

The pH of an equivalence point is the pH of the middle of a steep drop or rise on a pH curve. The second equivalence point on the pH curve shown is at a pH of 10. Of the indicator choices given, only option A, phenolphthalein, is suitable.

Bromothymol blue, methyl red, and methyl orange all change colour at too low/early a pH range.

14. B

Buffers maintain the pH of a system at a relatively constant value when small amounts of strong acid $(H_3O^+{}_{(aq)})$ or strong base $(OH^-{}_{(aq)})$ are added. A simple Brønsted–Lowry prediction will give a likely equation here.

The species list is:

$$\underset{}{\overset{SA}{H_3O^+{}_{(aq)}}}\quad \underset{B}{\overset{A}{H_2PO_4^-{}_{(aq)}}}\quad \underset{SB}{\overset{A}{HPO_4^{2-}{}_{(aq)}}}\quad \underset{B}{\overset{A}{H_2O_{(l)}}}$$

The net reaction is: $H_3O^+{}_{(aq)} + HPO_4^{2-}{}_{(aq)} \rightarrow H_2O_{(l)} + H_2PO_4^-{}_{(aq)}$

An equilibrium sign may be used, but this equilibrium probably favours the products so much as to be a quantitative reaction.

15. A

A solution is basic when its pH exceeds 7 (and its $[OH^-{}_{(aq)}]$ exceeds $10^{-7} \frac{\text{mol}}{\text{L}}$).

$$[H^+{}_{(aq)}] = 10^{-pH} = 10^{-7.40} = 4.0 \times 10^{-8} \frac{\text{mol}}{\text{L}}$$

The solution is basic and has an $[H^+{}_{(aq)}]$ of $4.0 \times 10^{-8} \frac{\text{mol}}{\text{L}}$.

Copyright Protected

16. B

If the substances released by the bathers increase the water's pH, this means that they decrease the $[H_3O^+_{(aq)}]$ and increase the $[OH^-_{(aq)}]$. The increase in $[OH^-_{(aq)}]$ will cause a shift away from the side of the equilibrium that contains $HClO_{(aq)}$. Since it is undissociated $HClO_{(aq)}$ that kills the bacteria and the algae, lower concentrations of it will be more favourable to bacterial growth.

17. D

By definition, buffers maintain the pH of a system relatively constant when small amounts of $H_3O^+_{(aq)}$ or $OH^-_{(aq)}$ are added.

The continual addition of acid or base to a buffered system will eventually destroy the buffer by completely neutralizing either the basic or acidic half of the buffer.

18. B

A buffer is composed of a weak acid–base conjugate pair, hence alternatives C and D are not buffers.

Option B is clearly the best answer because it is a buffer formed, in part, from $CO_{2(g)}$ dissolved in blood plasma.

19. D

At equilibrium, the rate of formation of reactants is equal to the rate of formation of products; i.e., the rates of forward and reverse reactions are equal. D is the answer.

Thus, alternatives B and C are quite wrong. Alternative A refers to the size of the equilibrium constant, not the rates of reaction.

20. A

Different volumes of the same solution will have the same chemical properties (same conductivity, same reactivity to $Mg_{(s)}$, same pH/$[H_3O^+_{(aq)}]$, and so on). One drop of methyl red in beaker II will result in a more dilute, lighter red colour than in beaker I. The same number of moles of $Mg^-_{(aq)}$ will be present in twice the volume of solution.

21. C

Except at extremely low concentrations, weak acids tend to react with water/dissociate less than 100%.

More often than not, the concentration of unreacted acid exceeds the concentration of $H_3O^+_{(aq)}$ and conjugate base produced.

For $0.100\frac{\text{mol}}{\text{L}}$ $HCOOH_{(aq)}$, only about 4% of the acid reacts with water to produce $H_3O^+_{(aq)}$ and $HCOO^-_{(aq)}$ (calculated using either a quadratic or an approximation method.) That is about 96%.

Alternatives B and D would only occur if the percentage of reaction of $HCOOH_{(aq)}$ was 50% and not 4%.

22. B

The pH of the equivalence point when a monoprotic acid is neutralized by a strong base is critically dependent on the basicity the conjugate base produced.

That said, solution of most weak conjugate bases will have a pH above 7 (probably just above 7) when produced at the equivalence point of a weak acid strong base titration.

Orange IV (red to yellow, pH = 1.4 to 2.8) and methyl red (red to yellow, pH + 4.8 to 6.0) change colour too early to be suitable for indicating the equivalence point. Indigo carmine (blue to yellow, 11.4 to 13.00) would only change colour in solutions with comparable concentrations of $OH^-_{(aq)}$ to the $NaOH_{(aq)}$ being added in the titration. That is, it would change colour too late in the titration.

Cresol red (yellow to red, pH = 7.2 to 8.8) in alternative B is most definitely the best indicator for "catching" the equivalence point.

(A calculation of the equivalence point—essentially the pH of $0.0500 \frac{\text{mol}}{\text{L}}$ $HCOO^-_{(aq)}$—is 8.22.

23. C

$NaHCOO_{(aq)}$ is a weak base whose basicity is best described by the equation below.

$HCOO^-_{(aq)} + H_2O_{(l)}$ "$HCOOH_{(aq)} + OH^-_{(aq)}$

A simple equilibrium calculation using the K_b of $HCOO^-_{(aq)}$ and the concentration of the base will give $[OH^-_{(aq)}]$.

First $K_{b_{HCOO}} = \frac{K_w}{K_{a_{HCOOH}}}$

$= \frac{1.0 \times 10^{-14}}{1.8 \times 10^{-4}} \frac{\text{mol}}{\text{L}}$

$= 5.6 \times 10^{-11} \frac{\text{mol}}{\text{L}}$

	$HCOO^-_{(aq)}$ +	$H_2O_{(l)}$ "	$HCOOH_{(aq)}$ +	$OH^-_{(aq)}$
Initially	$0.10 \frac{\text{mol}}{\text{L}}$	—	—	—
Equilibrium	$0.10 - x$	—	x	x

$K_b = \frac{x^2}{0.10 - x} \cong \frac{x^2}{0.10}$ since $\frac{K_b}{[HCOO^-_{(aq)}]} >> 1000$

$x = [OH^-_{(aq)}] = \sqrt{0.10\ \text{mol/L} \times 5.6 \times 10^{-11}\ \text{mol/L}}$

$[OH^-_{(aq)}] = 2.4 \times 10^{-6} \frac{\text{mol}}{\text{L}}$

(Using a quadratic method yields the same answer.)

Copyright Protected

NR5. 8.38 or 8.37

$$\text{pOH} = -\log[\text{OH}^-_{(aq)}]$$
$$= -\log\left(2.4\times10^{-6}\ \frac{\text{mol}}{\text{L}}\right)$$
$$= 5.62$$
$$\text{pH} = 14.00 - 5.62$$
$$= 8.38$$

The solution pH is 8.38. (If the answer to MC 23 is retained in the calculator, a value of 8.37 is obtained.)

The answer is 12.1 if alternative A in MC23 was chosen.

The answer is 11.6 if alternative B in MC23 was chosen.

The answer is 8.88 if alternative D in MC23 was chosen.

24. A

A catalyst, by definition, has no effect on the position of an equilibrium since it provides an alternate pathway from the reactants to the products and vice versa with lower activation energies. A catalyst simply shortens the time it takes for a system to reach equilibrium that has the same equilibrium constant, K_{eq}.

In addition, catalysts have no effect on the enthalpy change of an overall reaction. The ΔH_{rxn} is dependent on the difference in enthalpy of the products and reactants and is independent of the route taken to transform the reactants into the products.

25. C

On a pH titration curve, the equivalence point of an acid–base titration is the middle point of that region of the graph where a steep rise or drop in pH occurs. (For those of you who have studied calculus, this midpoint is a point of inflexion.)

On the graph shown, only point III is suitable – the answer is C.

At point II, the acid is yet to be completely neutralized. At point IV, the pH of the solution is governed entirely by the solution volume and the excess $OH^-_{(aq)}$ from the titrant.

Point I is essentially the pK_a point. At this stage, the$[CH_3COOH_{(aq)}]$remaining is equal to the $[CH_3COO^-_{(aq)}]$produced and $[H^+_{(aq)}] = K_a$. Ideally, the pH at this point should be 4.74, but in the measured graph, it is a little low (~5% lower).

Not for Reproduction

NR6. 0.50

At the equivalence point (III) on the graph, the volume of 0.20 mol/L added is 25 mL. A simple acid–base stoichiometric calculation gives the answer.

$$NaOH_{(aq)} + CH_3COOH_{(aq)} \rightarrow NaCH_3COO_{(aq)} + H_2O_{(l)}$$

2.5 mL 10.0 mL

$0.20\frac{\text{mol}}{\text{L}}$ $[CH_3COOH_{(aq)}] = ?$

$$n_{NaOH} = 25\text{ mL} \times 0.20\frac{\text{mol}}{\text{L}} = 5.0\text{ mmol}$$

$$n_{CH_3COOH} = \tfrac{1}{1} n_{NaOH} = \tfrac{1}{1} \times 5.0\text{ mmol} = 5.0\text{ mmol}$$

$$[CH_3COOH_{(aq)}] = \frac{5.0\text{ mmol}}{10.0\text{ mL}} = 0.50\text{ mol/L}$$

The acid concentration is 0.50 mol/L.

The $[CH_3COOH_{(aq)}] = 0.26\frac{\text{mol}}{\text{L}}$ if alternative A in MC25 was chosen.

The $[CH_3COOH_{(aq)}] = 0.48\frac{\text{mol}}{\text{L}}$ if alternative B in MC25 was chosen.

The $[CH_3COOH_{(aq)}] = 0.70\frac{\text{mol}}{\text{L}}$ if alternative D in MC25 was chosen.

26. B

The best choice of acid–base indicator gives an endpoint (colour change range) that overlaps the equivalence point pH on a pH curve.

Since point III (pH ~ 9.0) is the correct equivalence point, the indicator of choice is phenolphthalein (colourless to red, pH = 8.2 to 10.0).

If A (point I, pH ~ 4.5) was chosen in MC25, the suitable indicator is bromocresol green (yellow to blue, pH = 3.8 to 5.4).

If B (point II, pH ~ 7.0) was chosen in MC25, the suitable indicator is bromothymol blue (yellow to blue, pH = 6.0 to 7.6).

If D (point IV, pH ~ 12.7) was chosen in MC25, the suitable indicator is indigo carmine (Blue to yellow, pH = 11.4 to 13.0).

27. B

Rearranging K_{eq} to isolate $[C_2H_5OH_{(g)}]$ gives

$$[C_2H_5OH_{(g)}] = K_{eq}[C_2H_{4(g)}][H_2O_{(g)}]$$

$$= 300.0\frac{\text{L}}{\text{mol}} \times \frac{115\text{ mol}}{5000\text{ L}} \times \frac{110\text{ mol}}{5000\text{ L}}$$

$$= 0.152\frac{\text{mol}}{\text{L}}$$

If the amounts of $C_2H_{4(g)}$ and $H_2O_{(g)}$ are used, instead of their concentrations, it is not possible to get the correct answer.

Copyright Protected

NR7. 4 1 2 3

When weak acids and bases react, the products are favoured (>50% reaction) when the weak acid lies above the weak base in an acid–base table (see page 11 of the Data Booklet).

When acids and bases react, the reactants are favoured (<50% reaction) when the weak acid lies below the weak base in an acid–base table (see Data Booklet).

With the three reactions given:

- $HNO_{2(aq)}$ lies above $HCOO^-{}_{(aq)}$ in an acid–base table.
- $HN_{3(aq)}$ lies above $OBr^-{}_{(aq)}$ in an acid–base table.
- $HN_{3(aq)}$ lies below $HCOO^-{}_{(aq)}$ in an acid–base table.

Using this information, we can construct a "mini" acid–base table as follows:

Acid	Number	Conjugate Base
$HNO_{2(aq)}$	4	$NO_2^-{}_{(aq)}$
$HCOOH_{(aq)}$	1	$HCOO^-{}_{(aq)}$
$HN_{3(aq)}$	2	$N_3^-{}_{(aq)}$
$HOBr_{(aq)}$	3	$OBr^-{}_{(aq)}$

The acids, listed from strongest to weakest, are $HNO_{2(aq)}$, $HCOOH_{(aq)}$, $HN_{3(aq)}$, $HOBr_{(aq)}$.

28. C

In the reaction given, there is complete neutralization of the acid by the base.

Thus, the mole ratio of the base to the acid will indicate the number of protons removed.

$$\frac{n_{KOH}}{n_{ACID}} = \frac{150 \text{ mL} \times 0.10 \text{ mol/L}}{50 \text{ mL} \times 0.10 \text{ mol/L}} = 3.00$$

Some three moles of $KOH_{(aq)}$ are required to neutralize one mole of acid. The likely formula of the acid is $H_3X_{(aq)}$.

29. D

The most likely species list when lactic acid (comparable in strength to methanoic acid, judging from its K_a) reacts with sodium bicarbonate in the dough is:

$$\underset{SB}{\overset{A}{HCO_3^-{}_{(aq)}}},\ \overset{SA}{HC_3H_5O_{3(aq)}},\ \underset{B}{\overset{A}{H_2O_{(l)}}}$$

The net acid–base reaction is:

$$HCO_3^-{}_{(aq)} + HC_3H_5O_{3(aq)} \xrightleftharpoons{>50\%} H_2CO_{3(aq)} + C_3H_5O_{3(aq)}$$

and this reverts to the simpler

$$HCO_3^-{}_{(aq)} + HC_3H_5O_{3(aq)} \rightarrow H_2O_{(l)} + CO_{2(g)} + C_3H_5O_3^-{}_{(aq)}$$

A quantitative reaction arrow is not unreasonable when one considers that loss of $CO_{2(g)}$ into the dough as it rises might shift the equilibrium to completion.

Alternatives A and C are unlikely since no strong acid is present and alternative B has bicarbonate acting as the strongest acid in the system that reacts with lactate ion, which is not a major species. Since both entities in alternative B are also very weak, quantitative reaction is unlikely.

Not for Reproduction

30. B

An equilibrium calculation will give the $[H^+{}_{(aq)}]$ with little difficulty.

$$HC_3H_5O_{3(aq)} + H_2O_{(l)} \text{"} H_3O^+{}_{(aq)} + C_3H_5O_3^-{}_{(aq)}$$

Initially	0.20 mol/L	—	—	—
Equilibrium	0.20 − x	—	x	x

$K = \dfrac{x^2}{0.20 - x} \cong \dfrac{x^2}{0.20}$ since $\dfrac{[HC_3H_5O_{3(aq)}]}{K_a} >$ 1000

So $x = [H_3O^+{}_{(aq)}] = \sqrt{0.20K_a}$

$$= \sqrt{0.20 \text{ mol/L} \times 1.4 \times 10^{-4} \text{ mol/L}}$$

$$= 5.3 \times 10^{-3} \text{ mol/L}$$

The $[H_3O^+{}_{(aq)}]$ of the lactic acid solution is 5.3×10^{-3} mol/L. (The quadratic method gives 5.2×10^{-3} mol/L .)

NR8. 2.28

Using the recorded answer for B in MC30:

$pH = -\log(5.3 \times 10^{-3} \text{ mol / L}) = 2.28$

The lactic acid solution pH is 2.28.

(If the answer to MC30 is calculated using a shortcut or a quadratic method and retained in the calculator, the pH is still 2.28.)

The answer is 2.55 if alternative A in MC30 was chosen.

The answer is 1.59 if alternative C in MC30 was chosen.

The answer is 3.15 if alternative D in MC30 was chosen.

NR9. 11.3

A good rule of thumb when analyzing titration data is to average the three closest volumes of titrant added (called titres) that are within a range of 0.2 mL.

The volume of $NaOH_{(aq)}$ added = Final burette reading – initial burette reading.

Trial	1	2	3	4
Vol. of $NaOH_{(aq)}$ (mL)	12.1	11.3	11.4	11.2

The average volume of $NaOH_{(aq)}$ is

$$\frac{11.3 \text{ mL} + 11.4 \text{ mL} + 11.2 \text{ mL}}{3} = 11.3 \text{ mL}$$

31. B

When phosphoric acid is titrated to the second equivalence point, two protons have been removed quantitatively and the conjugate produced is $HPO_4^{2-}{}_{(aq)}$.

A stoichiometric calculation based on either Brønsted–Lowry theory or Arrhenius theory will give the answer.

Use either

$$H_3PO_{4(aq)} + 2OH^-{}_{(aq)} \rightarrow HPO_4^{2-}{}_{(aq)} + 2H_2O_{(l)}$$

or

$$H_3PO_{4(aq)} + 2NaOH_{(aq)} \rightarrow Na_2HPO_{4(aq)} + 2H_2O_{(l)}$$

$$n_{NaOH} = 11.3 \text{ mL} \times 0.125 \frac{\text{mol}}{\text{L}} = 1.41 \text{ mmol}$$

$$n_{H_3PO_4} = \tfrac{1}{2} n_{NaOH} = \tfrac{1}{2} \times 1.41 \text{ mmol} = 0.706 \text{ mmol}$$

$$[H_3PO_{4(aq)}] = \frac{0.706 \text{ mmol}}{10.00 \text{ mL}} = 0.0706 \text{ mol/L}$$

The $[H_3PO_{4(aq)}]$ is 0.0706 mol/L **or** 70.6 mmol/L

Copyright Protected

32. A

In most 0.10 mol/L weak acid solutions, the percentage of reaction with water is much less than 50%. (A quick equilibrium calculation gives a percentage reaction of 23% at 25°C for 0.10 mol/L $H_3PO_{4(aq)}$). The equilibrium equation can be written and interpreted as follows.

	$H_3PO_{4(aq)}$	$+ H_2O_{(l)}$	”$H_3O^+_{(aq)}$	$+ H_2PO_4^-{}_{(aq)}$
Initially	0.1mol/L	—	—	—
Equilibrium	$0.10 - x$	—	x	x

Since x amounts to less than half the initial concentration of $H_3PO_{4(aq)}$, we can say that

$[H_3PO_{4(aq)}] > [H_3O^+_{(aq)}] = [H_2PO_4^-{}_{(aq)}]$

The only way that $HPO_4^{2-}{}_{(aq)}$ can make an appearance is when $H_2PO_4^-{}_{(aq)}$ reacts with water.

$H_2PO_4^-{}_{(aq)} + H_2O_{(l)}$ ”$HPO_4^{2-}{}_{(aq)} + H_3O^+_{(aq)}$

However, the K_a for this equilibrium is 6.3×10^{-8} mol/L, and the $H_2PO_4^-{}_{(aq)}$ is the product in an equilibrium with a K_a value of 7.0×10^{-3} mol/L. To a good approximation, the $[HPO_4^{2-}{}_{(aq)}]$ from this second equilibrium is about 6.3×10^{-8} mol/L (the same value as K_a). In other words, the $[HPO_4^{2-}{}_{(aq)}]$ is so close to zero as to be negligible. Generally speaking, most polyprotic acids behave as if they were monoprotic when on their own in an aqueous solution.

33. B

A solution of ammonium chloride contains $NH_4^+{}_{(aq)}$, $Cl^-{}_{(aq)}$ and $H_2O_{(e)}$. The ammonium ion is a weak acid in the Relative Strengths of Acids and Base table. Chloride ion is a weaker base than water. The most likely Brønsted–Lowry reaction in this solution (reactants favoured) is

$NH_4^+{}_{(aq)} + H_2O_{(l)}$ ° $NH_{3(aq)} + H_3O^+{}_{(aq)}$

Evidently, a solution of ammonium ions will be slightly acidic.

34. D

In the reaction given, the oxidizing agent is $O_{2(g)}$ (the oxidation number of O in $O_{2(g)}$ decreases from 0 to –2) while the reducing agent is the $(CH_2O)_{n(s)}$ (the sludge reacted with the oxidizing agent). Alternatives B and C are thus incorrect. Buffers are weak acid–base conjugate pairs. Enzymes are, by definition, biological catalysts.

35. D

The change in hydronium ion concentration is given by

$[H_3O^+{}_{(aq)}]$(pH 6.80) $-$ $[H_3O^+{}_{(aq)}]$(pH 7.00)

$[H_3O^+{}_{(aq)}] = 10^{-pH}$

Therefore, the change in hydronium ion concentration is

$10^{-6.80} - 10^{-7.00}$

$= 1.6 \times 10^{-7}$ mol/L $- 1.0 \times 10^{-7}$ mol/L

$= 5.8 \times 10^{-8}$ mol/L

36. C

The equivalence points in any pH titration curve are located in the middle of any very steep rise or drop in the curve. The middle of the steep rise in the curve illustrated is at pH 7.

Not for Reproduction

37. A

The pH of the equivalence point on a pH titration curve depends on the acidity/basicity of the conjugate produced during neutralization. Given that the equivalence point on the curve shown is at pH7, the sample on the experiment was strong (i.e., completely dissociated). In addition, the curve starts at a low pH and rises to equivalence. Clearly, the curve illustrates the addition of a strong base (in the burette) to a strong acid sample (in the Erlenmeyer flask).

NR10. 4 2 1 3

Obviously, the nitric acid solution will be the least basic—it is a strong acid after all!

The $Ba(OH)_{2(aq)}$ solution will be the most basic solution because it is a strong base. The two remaining entities are basic in aqueous solution and, according to the Relative Strengths of Acids and Bases Table, hydrogen carbonate ion is more basic than nitrite ion.

The solution basicities in order from most to least basic are $Ba(OH)_{2(aq)} > NaHCO_{3(aq)} > NaNO_{2(aq)} > HNO_{3(aq)}$

38. A

If pH = 3.00, then $[H_3O^+_{(aq)}] = 10^{-3.00}$
1.0×10^{-3} mol/L

So,

$$[OH^-_{(aq)}] = \frac{kw}{[H_3O^+_{(aq)}]} = \frac{1.0 \times 10^{-14}}{1.0 \times 10^{-3}} \text{ mol/L}$$

$$= 1.0 \times 10^{-11} \text{ mol/L}$$

Alternatively pOH =! 14.00 ! pH

$$= 14.00 - 3.00 = 11.00$$

Thus $[OH^-_{(aq)}] = 10^{-pOH} = 10^{-11.00}$ mol/L

$$= 1.0 \times 10^{-11}$$

NR11. 3.49

We need only apply the equation for calculating pH here.

$$pH = -\log[H_3O^+_{(aq)}]$$
$$= -\log(3.2 \times 10^{-4} \text{mol/L}) = 3.49$$

39. B

Thymol blue is blue in the pH range 2.8 to 8.0. Litmus is red up to a pH of 4.5. Methyl red is red up to a pH of 4.8. Methyl orange, however, is orange in the range 3.2 to 4.4—a much narrower range than the other indicators.

40. C

A Brønsted–Lowry net acid–base reaction favours the products when the strongest acid reactant in the system lies above the strongest base reactant in a Relative Strengths of Acids and Bases Table. According to the Brønsted–Lowry theory, acids lose protons and bases gain protons.

For alternative A, $NH_4^+{}_{(aq)}$ (acid) lies below $H_2PO_4^-{}_{(aq)}$ (base); therefore, reactants favoured.

For alternative B, $HCN_{(aq)}$ (acid) lies below $HS^-_{(aq)}$ (base); therefore, reactants favoured.

For alternative D, $HSO_4^-{}_{(aq)}$ (acid) lies below $HSO_3^-{}_{(aq)}$ (base); therefore, reactants favoured.

For alternative C, $HCO_3^-{}_{(aq)}$ (acid) lies above $HBO_3^-{}_{(aq)}$ (base); therfore, products favoured.

41. D

The best buffers are composed of weak conjugate acid base pairs. Only alternative D is suitable.

Copyright Protected

42. D

The original solution pH of the base is 14.00. $[H_3O^+_{(aq)}] = 10^{-pH} = 10^{-14.00} = 1.0 \times 10^{-14}$ mol/L. The rest of the data provided are quite irrelevant!

43. A

Buffers maintain a relatively constant system pH when small amounts of $H_3O^+_{(aq)}$ or $OH^-_{(aq)}$ are added to them. The acid half of the buffer neutralizes added base, while the base half neutralizes added acid.

When hydrochloric acid is added to the buffer given, the species list is

SA A

$H_3O^+_{(aq)}$, $Cl^-_{(aq)}$, $H_2PO_4^-{}_{(aq)}$,

B B

A

$HPO_4^{2-}{}_{(aq)}$

SB

The net acid–base reaction is (alternative A):

$$H_3O^+_{(aq)} + HPO_4^{2-}{}_{(aq)} \circ H_2O_{(l)} + H_2PO_4^-{}_{(aq)}$$

Alternatives B and D ignore the fact that $HCl_{(aq)}$ reacts completely in water to produce $H_3O^+_{(aq)}$ and $Cl^-_{(aq)}$. In alternative C, $H_2PO_4^-{}_{(aq)}$ is **not** the strongest base in the system!

NR12. 3.26

Since acetylsalicylic acid is monoprotic, one mole of acid is neutralized by one mole of $NaOH_{(aq)}$. So

$$n_{ASA} = \frac{1}{1} n_{NaoH} = \frac{1}{1} \times 20.1\,\text{mL} \times \frac{0.900\,\text{mol}}{\text{L}}$$

$$= 1.81\,\text{mmol}$$

$$m_{ASA} = 1.81\,\text{mmol} \times \frac{180.17\text{g}}{\text{mol}} = 3.26$$

(ASA = acetylsalicylic acid)

Please note that this mass corresponds to about ten normal–strength aspirin tablets—a possible overdose.

44. D

The Law of Mass Action defines the equilibrium constant expression for $aA + bB \circ cC + dD$

as $K_{eq} = \dfrac{[C]^c \times [D]^d}{[A]^a \times [B]^b}$

Thus, for $2\,H_2S_{(g)} + 3\,O_{2(g)} \circ 2\,H_2O_{(g)} + 2\,SO_{2(g)}$

$$K_{eq} = \frac{[H_2O_{(g)}]^2\,[SO_{2(g)}]^2}{[H_2S_{(g)}]^2\,[O_{2(g)}]^3}$$

Not for Reproduction

45. A

The conjugate base of any entity/chemical is that species produced when a proton, H^+, is lost. Thus, the conjugate base of $H_2SO_{3(aq)}$ is $HSO_3{}^-{}_{(aq)}$.

Simply by looking at the Relative Strengths of Acids and Bases Table in the table at the back of the Key, you will find the same answer!

Note: $SO_3{}^{2-}{}_{(aq)}$ is the conjugate base of $HSO_3{}^-{}_{(aq)}$, $OH^-{}_{(aq)}$ is the conjugate base of $H_2O_{(l)}$, and $H_2O_{(l)}$ is the conjugate base of $H_3O^+{}_{(aq)}$.

46. B

The equilibrium constant expression for reaction II is $K_{eq} = \dfrac{[SO_{3(g)}]^2}{[SO_{2(g)}]^2\,[O_{2(g)}]}$

When rearranged for $[O_{2(g)}]$,

$$[O_{2(g)}] = \frac{[SO_{3(g)}]^2}{[SO_{2(g)}]^2\,K_{(eq)}}$$

We can substitute the values given to get

$$[O_{2(g)}] = \frac{(0.840\ \text{mol/L})^2}{(0.361\ \text{mol/L})^2(13.0\ \text{L/mol})}$$

$$[O_{2(g)}] = 0.416\ \text{mol/L}$$

The answer is B. Common arithmetic errors and/or ill-formulated K_{eq} expressions give the other answers.

47. D

Le Châtelier's Principle, simply stated, is: when a system at equilibrium is stressed, the system readjusts to minimize the effect(s) of that stress.

The reaction given is exothermic (alternative A). Raising the system temperature would shift the equilibrium to the left because heat is a product of this reaction.

Alternative B, adding a catalyst, would only decrease the time taken for the system to reach equilibrium and not increase the concentrations of reactants or products.

Alternative C, removing $SO_{2(g)}$(a reactant), would cause equilibrium to shift left to replace the lost $SO_{2(g)}$.

Only alternative D, adding $NO_{2(g)}$ (a reactant), would cause the equilibrium to shift to the right and make more $SO_{3(g)}$ (and $NO_{(g)}$).

NR13. 10.8

Since pH + pOH = 14.00 for aqueous solutions under standard condition,

pOH = 14.00 – pH = 14.00 – 3.2 = 10.8

Copyright Protected

48. C

Solution volume has no bearing on pH. We need only use the acid concentration in calculating pH.

For a strong acid, $[H_3O^+{}_{(aq)}] = [\text{acid}]$

For a weak acid, $[H_3O^+{}_{(aq)}] \cong \sqrt{K_a[acid]}$

when the $\frac{[\text{acid}]}{K_a} > 1000.$

However, if, for a weak acid $\frac{[\text{acid}]}{K_a} < 1000$

a quadratic method must be employed to get a more accurate $[H_3O^+{}_{(aq)}]$.

For the acids given:

Acid	[Acid](mol/L)	Approximate pH
$H_2S_{(aq)}$	1.00×10^{-2}	4.48
$H_2SO_{3(aq)}$	1.00×10^{-4}	4.00 or slightly lower
$H_2SO_{4(aq)}$	1.00×10^{-3}	3.00 or slightly lower
$H_2SO_{4(aq)}$	1.00×10^{-4}	4.00 or slightly lower

The $H_2SO_{3(aq)}$ here at this very low concentration is 100% dissociated, and the $HSO_3{}^-{}_{(aq)}$ conjugate is also some 2% dissociated.

49. C

Thymol blue in its blue form ($Tb^{2-}{}_{(aq)}$, pH > 9.6) will turn red when it is added to 0.10 mol/L $H_2SO_{4(aq)}$ (pH = 1.00 or slightly lower).

Since $H_2SO_{4(aq)}$ is a strong acid, it will react completely with the $Tb^{2-}{}_{(aq)}$ to make $H_2Tb_{(aq)}$. Thymol blue is red below pH = 1.2.

Thymol blue is yellow in the pH range 2.8 to 8.0, where the predominant species is HTb.

50. D

If biomagnification of heavy metals in wildlife will decrease because of a decision to reduce sulfur dioxide emissions, then that decision exemplifies an environmental perspective.

51. A

Combustion of fossil fuels (hydrocarbons) produces $CO_{2(g)}$.

Cellular Respiration:

$$C_6H_{12}O_{6(aq)} + 6O_{2(g)} \rightarrow 6CO_{2(g)} + 6H_2O_{(g)}$$

Catalytic converters in cars convert $CO_{2(g)}$ to $CO_{2(g)}$ in exhaust emissions (this is not the primary function of a catalytic converter, but it is a reaction they encourage).

Photosynthesis is described by the equation

$$6CO_{2(g)} + 6H_2O_{(l)} \rightarrow C_6H_{12}O_{6(aq)} + 6O_{2(g)}.$$

Not for Reproduction

Written Response

1. **Valid stresses:**

- add $NO_{2(g)}$
- remove $N_2O_{4(g)}$
- increase pressure or decrease volume
- lower temperature

Sample Procedure:

- observe the colour of the gas in a $NO_{2(g)} - N_2O_{4(g)}$ equilibrium tube at room temperature
- the bulb could now be put in a cold water bath and the colour change observed

Explanation of Le Châtelier's Principle

- when the bulb is put in the cold water, it will turn a lighter brown because the removal of energy will make the exothermic reaction predominate, which will make the equilibrium shift to produce more $N_2O_{4(g)}$ (colourless)

Predicted Evidence

- brown colour diminishes
- temperature increases
- pressure decreases

2. **Factors Causing the Changes**

The photos illustrate the damage that is caused by air pollutants, specifically acid rain. The burning of fossil fuels in industry and transportation creates a variety of oxides such as $NO_{2(g)}$, $CO_{2(g)}$, and $SO_{2(g)}$. These oxides react with water in the air to form acids such as $HNO_{3(aq)}$, $H_2SO_{4(aq)}$, $H_2CO_{3(aq)}$, etc. These acids are flushed from the atmosphere by rain and snow, etc., thus coming in contact with stone building materials such as limestone $CaCO_{3(s)}$.

Possible Reactions:

$$H_2SO_{4(aq)} + CaCO_{3(s)} \rightarrow$$

$$SO_4{}^{2-}{}_{(aq)} + CO_{2(g)} + H_2O_{(l)} + Ca^{2+}{}_{(aq)}$$

$$2HNO_{3(aq)} + CaCO_{3(s)} \rightarrow$$

$$2NO_3{}^{-}{}_{(aq)} + H_2O_{(l)} + CO_{2(g)} + Ca^{2+}{}_{(aq)}$$

This neutralization process between the acid rain and the limestone gradually breaks down the stone structure. If one considers the statue to be made of metal, then the possible reaction between acid rain and the statue is

$$O_{2(g)} + 4H^{+}{}_{(aq)} + 2Fe_{(s)} \rightarrow 2Fe^{2+}{}_{(aq)} + 2H_2O_{(l)}$$

Ways to Address the Problem:

Governments have reacted to the damages caused by acid rain by imposing tighter regulations on emissions from automobiles and factories. They also encourage use of rapid transit to reduce vehicle emissions in cities. Industry and government are researching alternate energy sources to replace fossil fuel combustion.

or

To reduce corrosion of the statue, it could be painted or covered to reduce exposure from the elements. Perhaps statues in the future could be made of inert materials.

Copyright Protected

3. Experimental Design

A number of factors could be tested regarding the effectiveness of the antacids. Sample Factor to Study: Using the same dose of active ingredient, determine which antacid neutralizes the most acid.

- Obtain the recommended amount of each antacid.
- Dissolve each antacid in 40 mL of deionized water. Add 2 to 3 drops of bromothymol blue indicator.
- Titrate the antacid with a strong acid ($HCl_{(aq)}$) of known concentration until a colour change occurs.
- Record the volume of $HCl_{(aq)}$ required for the pH to reach 7.

Controlled Variables

Dose of antacid sample

Concentration of acid, $HCl_{(aq)}$

pH at end point

Data Table

Record the volume and concentration of acid added until there is some indication (pH, colour, bubbles) of when to stop.

Sample ID	Mass of Antacid	Vol. of Acid	mass/acid (if mass not same)

Factor Considerations

Mass of sample used, i.e., one big pill to swallow

Liquid versus solid—ease of use

Low solubility so that the antacid does not react before it hits the stomach

Cost factor, taste, toxicity, rate of reaction, or how exothermic

Possible side effects of ingredients:

Producing $H_2CO_{3(aq)}$ → more "gas" due to $CO_{2(g)}$ evolved

$Mg(OH)_{2(s)}$ or $CaCO_{3(s)}$
→ needed for strong bones
→ magnesium causes diarrhea

$Mg^{2+}{}_{(aq)}$ → causes diarrhea

$Al(OH)_{3(s)}$ → linked to Alzheimer's disease

$Na^{+}{}_{(aq)}$ → heart problems

Not for Reproduction

ANSWERS AND SOLUTIONS
ACIDS AND BASES – UNIT TEST 3

1. D	9. D	NR3. 8.52	23. D	28. C
2. C	10. C	NR4. 34.5	24. A	29. A
3. B	11. D	17. D	25. B	30. D
4. C	12. D	18. C	NR6. 6.51 or 6.63	31. A
5. B	13. D	19. A	NR7. 3.26**	
6. C	14. B	20. D	NR8. 4231	
7. C	15. B	21. B	NR9. 1.47	
NR1. 1423	16. B	22. B	26. C	
8. C	NR2. 2.64	NR5. 9.13*	27. A	

Notes: *If MC22 is A, then NR5 is 0.53
B, then NR5 is 9.13
C, then NR5 is 28.7
D, then NR5 is 0.08

**NR7 = (NR6)/2 = 3.26

1. D

Solutions with a sour taste are typically acidic solutions. Of the alternatives available, only $CH_3COOH_{(aq)}$ fits this category ($NH_{3(aq)}$ and $NaOH_{(aq)}$ are bases that are present in the conjugate base column of the acid–base table in the Data Table). $HCO^{-}{}_{(aq)}$ in $NaHCO_{3(aq)}$, though amphiprotic (capable of donating/losing a proton in a Brønsted–Lowry neutralization), is a basic solution. This results from the fact that, in water, the magnitude of the K_b for $HCO_3^-{}_{(aq)}$, 2.3×10^{-8}, is nearly 500 times the magnitude of its K_a value: 4.7×10^{-11}.

2. C

Lemon juice contains citric acid and generally has a pH 7 like most normal food stuffs.

Note: alternatives A and D refer to basic substances while B refers to a neutral solution, but lemon juice is sour!

3. B

Brønsted–Lowry acids lose/donate protons during neutralization while bases accept/remove protons during neutralization.

Moreover, in the equilibrium shown, the conjugate acid–base pairs are $(NH_4^+{}_{(aq)}, NH_{3(aq)})$ and $(H_2O_{(l)}, OH^-{}_{(aq)})$. Clearly, $NH_4^+{}_{(aq)}$ and $H_2O_{(l)}$ are the Brønsted–Lowry acids asked for.

The presence of the bases $HN_{(aq)}$ or $OH^-{}_{(aq)}$ in distractors A, C, and D render them incorrect.

4. C

The conjugate base of $N_2H_5^+{}_{(aq)}$, by definition, will have one less proton. $N_2H_{4(aq)}$ is the conjugate base of $N_2H_5^+{}_{(aq)}$.

Note: $N_2H_6^{2+}{}_{(aq)}$ is the conjugate acid of $N_2H_5^+{}_{(aq)}$.

Copyright Protected

5. B

If $HCO_3^-{}_{(aq)}$ reacts as an acid, it loses a proton and becomes $CO_3^{2-}{}_{(aq)}$. In addition, it reacts with those bases that lie above its acid location in an acid–base table to favour the reactants in equilibrium neutralizations.

Only $HPO_4^{2-}{}_{(aq)}$ satisfies these requirements in acting as a base.

The equilibrium in alternative A favours the products while the equilibrium in C and D shows $HCO_3^-{}_{(aq)}$ acting as a base.

6. C

When $Na_2CO_{3(s)}$ is completely neutralized, $H_2CO_{3(aq)}$ is produced. This, in turn, decomposes to $CO_{2(g)}$ and $H_2O_{(l)}$, the former being the likely source of the bubbles. Clearly, adding acid to carbonate ions would produce $CO_{2(g)}$. The empirical property that corresponds to an acid, of the four possibilities given, is that it would turn litmus red.

Alternatives A, B, and D are empirical properties of bases.

7. C

When weak acids and bases react, the reactants are favoured when the acid lies below the base in a common acid–base table and the products are favoured when the acid lies above the base in an acid–base table. Evidently, hypobromous acid, $HBrO_{(aq)}$, lies below the bases $HCO_3^-{}_{(aq)}$, $HS^-{}_{(aq)}$ and $OCl^-{}_{(aq)}$ in the acid–base table but above $H_2BO_3^-{}_{(aq)}$ in the table. A "mini" acid–base table constructed from the given evidence follows.

Acid	Conjugate Base
$H_2CO_{3(aq)}$	$HCO_3^-{}_{(aq)} + H^+{}_{(aq)}$
$H_2S_{(aq)}$	$HS^-{}_{(aq)} + H^+{}_{(aq)}$
$HOCl_{(aq)}$	$OCl^-{}_{(aq)} + H^+{}_{(aq)}$
$HBrO_{(aq)}$	$OBr^-{}_{(aq)} + H^+{}_{(aq)}$
$H_3BrO_{3(aq)}$	$H_2BrO_3^-{}_{(aq)} + H^+{}_{(aq)}$

$HBrO_{(aq)}$ lies below hypochlorous acid, $HOCl_{(aq)}$.

NR1. 1 4 2 3

According to the Brønsted–Lowry Theory, the acid in a neutralization loses/donates an H^+, while a base accepts the H^+. When it loses its proton, an acid becomes its conjugate base: $HSO_4^-{}_{(aq)}$ is the acid (1) and $SO_4^{2-}{}_{(aq)}$ is its conjugate base (4). When a base gains an H^+ it becomes its conjugate acid: $HCOO^-{}_{(aq)}$ is the base (2) and $HCOOH_{(aq)}$ is the conjugate acid (3).

8. C

The four electrolytes to choose from are all weak acids. It is the strongest of these weak acids that will dissociate/react with water/ionize the most to produce the solution most capable of conducting an electric current. The strongest acid is $HF_{(aq)}$—it lies higher than the other three in the acid base table (Chemistry Data in the back of ***THE KEY***).

Not for Reproduction

9. D

The acid most likely to have the lowest pH will be the strongest acid (higher $[H^+_{(aq)} / H_3O^+_{(aq)}]$ means lower pH). However, $H_2SO_{4(aq)}$ is diprotic while $HNO_{3(aq)}$ is monoprotic. Below 1.0 mol/L, calculations show that $H_2SO_{4(aq)}$ will have the lower pH.

10. C

Methyl red is yellow above pH = 6.0

Phenol red is yellow below pH = 6.6

Bromocresol green is blue above pH = 5.4

Phenolphthalein is colorless below pH = 8.2

Evidently, the solution pH lies in the 6.0 to 6.6 range, so the answer can only be A or C. At pH = 6.0, bromothymol blue will likely be yellow; therefore, C is correct.

11. D

A solution of dissolved calcium carbonate ions is basic: $CO_3^{2-}{}_{(aq)}$ ions lie on the base side of the acid–base table, and $Ca^{2+}{}_{(aq)}$ ions do not undergo hydrolysis to produce $H_3O^+{}_{(aq)}$. As sulfurous acid reacts with the dissolved carbonate in the lake water, the pH drops slightly and then remains relatively constant. This is characteristic of buffering as noted in the pH titration: the $HCO_3^-{}_{(aq)}$, formed as

$H_2SO_{3(aq)} + CO_3^{2-}{}_{(aq)} \text{"} HSO_3^-{}_{(aq)} + HCO_3^-{}_{(aq)}$

is amphiprotic and can act as a buffer on its own, or, as the conjugate acid–base pair ($HCO_3^-{}_{(aq)}$, $CO_3^{2-}{}_{(aq)}$), it could act as a buffer.

12. D

For any reaction

$\Delta H^\circ_{net} = \Sigma nH^\circ_f(\text{products}) - \Sigma nH^\circ_f(\text{reactants})$

So

$\Sigma nH^\circ_f(H_2SO_{4(aq)}) = \Delta H^\circ_{net} + \Sigma nH^\circ_f(\text{reactants})$

$= -227.8 \text{ kJ} + (1 \text{ mol} \times (-395.7 \frac{\text{kJ}}{\text{mol}})) + (1 \text{ mol} \times (-285.8 \frac{\text{kJ}}{\text{mol}}))$

$1 \text{ mol} \times H^\circ_f(H_2SO_{4(aq)}) = -909.3 \text{ kJ}$

$H^\circ_f(H_2SO_{4(aq)}) = -909.3 \frac{\text{kJ}}{\text{mol}}$

13. D

When strong acid is added to a buffer system, it is the base component of the buffer that neutralizes the acid thus:

$H_3O^+{}_{(aq)} + HCO_3^-{}_{(aq)} \rightarrow H_2O_{(l)} + H_2CO_{3(aq)}$

loses H^+ (acid) gains H^+ (base)

14. B

Since pH + pOH = 14.00

then pOH = 14.00 – 3.45 = 10.55

$[OH^-{}_{(aq)}] = 10^{-\text{pOH}} = 10^{-10.55}$

$= 2.8 \times 10^{-11} \text{ mol/L}$

The hydroxide ion concentration is 2.8×10^{-11} mol/L.

15. B

The acid equilibrium reaction for hydrazoic acid is

$HN_{3(aq)} + H_2O_{(l)} \text{"} H_3O^+{}_{(aq)} + N_3^-{}_{(aq)}$

for which the K_a expression is

$$K_a = \frac{[H_3O^+{}_{(aq)}][N_3^-{}_{(aq)}]}{[HN_{3(aq)}]}$$

Copyright Protected

16. B

Since the K_a for the hydrazoic acid equilibrium is very much less than one, the extent of the reaction with water will be less than 50%. In this situation, the concentration of unreacted molecular acid, $[HN_{3(aq)}]$, is greater than the concentration of hydronium or azide ion.

In all aqueous solution at normal concentrations, $[H_2O_{(l)}] >> [\text{solute}]$.

NR2. 2.64

For the equilibrium

$$HN_{3(aq)} \rightleftharpoons H^+{}_{(aq)} + N_{3(aq)}^-$$

	$HN_{3(aq)}$	$H^+{}_{(aq)}$	$N_{3(aq)}^-$
Initially:	0.28 mol/L	—	—
At equilibrium:	$0.28 - x$	x	x

$$K_a = \frac{x^2}{0.28 - x} \cong \frac{x^2}{0.28} \quad \text{since } \frac{[HN_3]}{K_a} > 1000$$

$$X = [H^+{}_{(aq)}] = \sqrt{K_a(0.28)}$$

$$[H^+{}_{(aq)}] = \sqrt{1.9 \times 10^{-5}\ \frac{\text{mol}}{\text{L}} \times 0.28\ \frac{\text{mol}}{\text{L}}}$$

$$= 2.3 \times 10^{-3}\ \text{mol/L}$$

$$\text{pH} = -\log(2.3 \times 10^{-3}\ \text{mol/L})$$

$$= 2.64$$

Whether a quadratic or approximation method is used to compute the $[H^+{}_{(aq)}]$, the pH is 2.64.

NR3. 8.52

A stoichiometric calculation will provide the answer.

$$NaOH_{(aq)} + HN_{3(l)} \rightarrow NaN_{3(aq)} + H_2O_{(l)}$$

6.00 mol/L 2.20 kg

$V_{NaOH} = ?$ 43.04 g/mol

$$n_{HN_3} = 2.20\ \text{kg} \times \frac{\text{mol}}{43.04\ \text{g}} = 51.1\ \text{mol}$$

$$n_{NaOH} = \frac{1}{1} n_{HN_3} = \frac{1}{1} \times 51.1\ \text{mol} = 51.1\ \text{mol}$$

$$V_{NaOH} = 51.1\ \text{mol} \times \frac{\text{L}}{6.00\ \text{mol}} = 8.52\ \text{L}$$

Some 8.52 L of 6.00 mol/L $NaOH_{(aq)}$ are required to completely neutralize 2.20 kg of $HN_{3(l)}$.

NR4. 34.5

A simple equilibrium calculation is all that is necessary to answer this question.

$$N_{2(g)} + H_{2(g)} \rightleftharpoons 2NH_{3(g)}$$

	$N_{2(g)}$	$H_{2(g)}$	$2NH_{3(g)}$
Initially:	80.0 mol	90.0 mol	0 mol
Change:	$-x$	$-3x$	$+2x$
Equilibrium:	$80.0 - x$	$90.0 - 3x$	$2x$

At equilibrium $n_{NH_3} = 37.0\ \text{mol} = 2x$

Therefore $x = 18.5\ \text{mol}$

Consequently $n_{H_2} = 90.0\ \text{mol} - 3x$

$= 90.0\ \text{mol} - 3(18.5\ \text{mol})$

$= 34.5\ \text{mol}$

Upon first acquaintance, the pressure and temperature suggest a more complicated question—calculating K_{eq}—however, this was not asked and so this data is irrelevant.

Not for Reproduction

17. D

The given equilibrium has energy as a product:

$H_{2(g)} + F_{2(g)} \rightleftharpoons 2HF_{(g)} + 542.2\ \text{kJ}$

Cooling the reaction vessel would remove heat energy, which the equilibrium would replace by shifting to the right to make yet more $HF_{(g)}$ (incidentally, the value of K_{eq} would increase).

Note that total system pressure changes (alternative C) would have no effect since there are equal moles of gaseous products and reactants. Removing $H_{2(g)}$ or adding $HF_{(g)}$ would effect the opposite equilibrium shift to that asked for, so alternatives A and B are incorrect.

18. C

For a weak conjugate acid–base pair ($HA_{(aq)}$, $A^-_{(aq)}$)

$K_{a(HA)_{(aq)})} \times K_{b(A^-{(aq)})} = K_w$

Thus, $K_{bF^-} = \dfrac{K_w}{K_{aHF}}$

$= \dfrac{1.0 \times 10^{-14}\ (\text{mol/L})^2}{6.6 \times 10^{-4}\ \text{mol/L}}$

$= 1.5 \times 10^{-11}\ \text{mol/L}$

The value of the K_b of $F^-_{(aq)}$ is 1.5×10^{-9} mol/L. Alternatively, the K_b of $F^-_{(aq)}$ is unlikely to equal K_w alternative D), the K_a of $HF^-_{(aq)}$ (alternative A), or be greater than 1 (alternative B).

19. A

A weak acid–weak base neutralization reaction favours the products (> 50% reaction) when the weak acid is located above the weak base in an acid–base table.

Alternatives B, C, and D all illustrate equilibria that favour the reactants; i.e., < 50% reaction.

20. D

What the question really asks is which of the entities is amphiprotic (and would appear on both sides of an acid–base table). Only $H_2BO_3^-{}_{(aq)}$ can both donate and accept protons.

Alternative A is an acid only, and B is a base only. Alternative C has a proton but that proton is held by a strong covalent bond to C and is not lost in aqueous solution.

21. B

In a closed system, chemical equilibrium is established when, for a reversible process, reaction proceeds in both the forward and reverse direction in such a way that the amounts of products and reactants are constant.

It is rarely the case that the mass or number of moles of products and reactants are equal, so alternatives C and D are incorrect.

22. B

Simply put, $[NO_{2(g)}] = \dfrac{0.734\ \text{mol}}{2.00\ \text{L}} = 0.367\dfrac{\text{mol}}{\text{L}}$

NR5. 9.13

For the equilibrium $2NO_{2(g)} \rightleftharpoons N_2O_{4(g)}$,

$K = \dfrac{[N_2O_{4(g)}]}{[NO_{2(g)}]^2}$ Substituting in the value from MC22 (this can vary), we then find the equilibrium concentration and substitute it into the equation, giving us

$K = \dfrac{(0.125\frac{\text{mol}}{\text{L}})}{(0.117\frac{\text{mol}}{\text{L}})^2} = 9.13\frac{\text{L}}{\text{mol}}$

The value of the equilibrium constant for the reaction is 9.13 (a three–digit answer).

Copyright Protected

23. D

In basic soil, $H_2PO_4{}^-{}_{(aq)}$ would in all likelihood react as a Brønsted–Lowry acid: it would lose one of its protons to form $HPO_4{}^{2-}{}_{(aq)}$.

Weak acids tend to lose one proton only in most common situations.

24. A

Bromothymol blue is yellow in acidic media with a pH ≤ 6. The amphiprotic entities offered are:
$HSO_4{}^-{}_{(aq)}, HCO_3{}^-{}_{(aq)}$ and $H_2O_{(l)}$
($OCl^-{}_{(aq)}$ is basic only).

Solutions of $NaHCO_{3(aq)}$ are basic (since $K_{a(HCO_3{}^-{}_{(aq)})} < K_{b(HCO_3{}^-{}_{(aq)})}$) with a $pH > 7$.

Solutions of $HSO_4{}^-{}_{(aq)}$ are acidic since $K_{a(HSO_4{}^-{}_{(aq)})} > K_{b(HSO_4{}^-{}_{(aq)})}$ with a $pH < 7$.

Only $NaHSO_{4(aq)}$ could react with bromothymol blue to produce a yellow colour. $H_2O_{(l)}$ (neutral, pH = 7) would render bromothymol blue a green colour.

25. B

$CO_{2(g)}$ in water and $H_2CO_{3(aq)}$ would exacerbate the young child's acidosis since they are both acidic. Since blood is buffered, $H_2O_{(l)}$ would have little or no effect on the child's blood pH. $HCO_3{}^-{}_{(aq)}$ is basic ($K_{b(HCO_3{}^-{}_{(aq)})} > K_{a(HCO_3{}^-{}_{(aq)})}$) and applied in suitable concentration, it would raise the child's blood pH. Moreover $HCO_3{}^-{}_{(aq)}$ is biocompatible!

NR6. 6.51 or 6.63

The volumes of titrant used in trials 1 to 4 are, respectively, 6.99 mL, 6.52 mL, 6.51 mL, and 6.51 mL. The most reliable titrant volume is the average of the three consecutive trials within 0.2 mL of each other.

The average titrant volume is

$$\frac{(6.52 + 6.51 + 6.51)\text{ mL}}{3} = 6.51\text{ mL}$$

NR7. 3.26

A stoichiometric calculation is all that is required here.

$$\begin{array}{llll} NaOH_{(aq)} & + HNO_{3(aq)} & \rightarrow NaNO_{3(aq)} & + HOH_{(aq)} \\ & 6.51\text{ mL} & 10.0\text{ mL} & \\ & 0.00500 & [HNO_{3(aq)}] = \text{ mol/L} & \end{array}$$

$$n_{NaOH} = 6.51\text{ mL} \times \frac{0.00500\text{ mol}}{\text{L}} = 0.0326\text{ mmol}$$

$$n_{HNO_3} = \frac{1}{1} n_{NaOH} = \frac{1}{1} \times 0.0326\text{ mmol} = 0.0326\text{ mmol}$$

$$[HNO_{3(aq)}] = \frac{0.0326\text{ mmol}}{10.0\text{ mL}} = 0.00326\text{ mol/L} = 3.26\text{ mmol/L}$$

The $HNO_{3(aq)}$ molar concentration is 3.26 mmol/L.

Not for Reproduction

NR8. 4 2 3 1

When polyprotic acids are titrated with strong base, they lose protons one at a time to form amphiprotic conjugates that are usually still capable of neutralizing the strong base. This polyprotic family of acids, when ordered from most to least acidic, are:

$$H_4A_{(aq)} > H_3A^-_{(aq)} > H_2A^{2-}_{(aq)} > HA^{3-}_{(aq)}$$

(The higher negative charge on the conjugates formed following proton loss causes the remaining protons to be more tightly bound and thus less acidic.) Brønsted–Lowry theory indicates that at any one stage in a series of neutralizations, it is the strongest acid present that is neutralized. So $H_4A_{(aq)}$ reacts before $H_3A^-_{(aq)}$, which reacts before $H_2A^{2-}_{(aq)}$, which in turn reacts before $HA^{3-}_{(aq)}$.

NR9. 1.47

A sophisticated acid–base stoichiometric calculation provides the answer.

$$HCl_{(aq)} + NaOH_{(aq)} \rightarrow NaCl_{(aq)} + H_2O_{(l)}$$

$$\underset{\text{20 drops}}{[HCl_{(aq)}] = ?} \quad \underset{\text{26 drops}}{[NaOH_{(aq)}] = 1.13\ \frac{mol}{L}}$$

$$n_{NaOH_{(aq)}} = 26\ \text{drops} \times 1.13\ \frac{mol}{L}$$

$$n_{HCl_{(aq)}} = \frac{1}{1} \times n_{NaOH_{(aq)}} = 26\ \text{drops} \times 1.13\ \frac{mol}{L}$$

$$[HCl_{(aq)}] = \frac{26\ \text{drops} \times 1.13\ \frac{mol}{L}}{20\ \text{drops}} = 1.47\ \frac{mol}{L}$$

If you find the above solution uncomfortable/difficult to handle, simply substitute "mL" for "drops" and the same answer will be obtained.

26. C

Since pH + pOH = 14.00, the given solution's pH is 10.8.

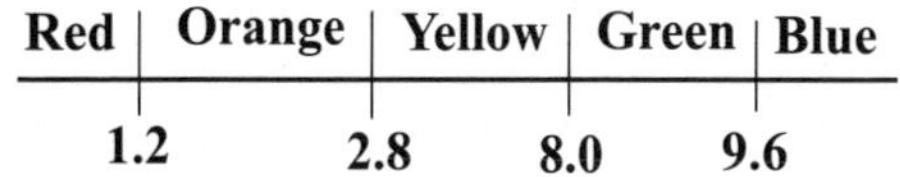

At this pH, thymolphthalein is blue (bromocresol green is blue). The solution is basic; therefore, it is unlikely to satisfy two empirical observations that characterize acids—alternatives A and B.

27. A

The colour ranges of thymol blue are given on the following number line.

A 1.0 mol/L $NaOH_{(aq)}$ solution has a pH of 14.00. Continuous addition of 1.0 mol/L $HCl_{(aq)}$ will ultimately lower the pH to below 1.2. Obviously then, the indicator colour will start as blue and change to green, yellow, orange, and finally red, in that order.

Alternative B corresponds to the indicator colours as 1.0 mol/L $NaOH_{(aq)}$ is added to a 1.0 mol/L $HCl_{(aq)}$ solution containing the indicator.

28. C

The most suitable choice of indicator has an indicator endpoint/colour change range that overlaps or occurs slightly after the equivalence point on a pH titration plot of an acid–base reaction. The most suitable indicator in this titration is chlorophenol red. Phenolphthalein would produce an early endpoint while methyl violet would produce a very late endpoint. Methyl orange would suffice as an indicator but would still produce a relatively late endpoint when compared with chlorophenol red.

29. A

A definite purple colour from these two indicators would result when bromothymol blue is blue and phenolphthalein is pink (pH 10). At pH values below 8.2, the phenolphthalein would be colourless and the solution would be blue.

30. D

Homeostatic pH maintenance is accomplished by buffering in the red blood cells and the blood plasma.

31. A

A buffer contains a weak conjugate acid–base pair. Only alternative A is viable (equimolar means equal molar concentration).

Alternatives B, C, and D all contain strong acids only because $Cl^-_{(aq)}$ and $ClO_4^-{}_{(aq)}$ are weaker bases than water.

Written Response

1. The pH of the sample is zero or less since methyl violet is yellow at a pH of zero or less. Hence, the only acids with pHs of zero or less and with a concentration of 1.0 mol/L are $HClO_{4(aq)}$, $HI_{(aq)}$, $HBr_{(aq)}$, $HCl_{(aq)}$, $H_2SO_{4(aq)}$, and $HNO_{3(aq)}$.
(–log 1 = 0.00 = pH)

Silver ions cause precipitate to form in all the strong acids with exception of $HNO_{3(aq)}$ and $HClO_{4(aq)}$.

Of these acids, only two are strong enough oxidizing agents to react spontaneously with copper metal. These are $HClO_{4(aq)}$ and $HNO_{3(aq)}$.

$$ClO_4^-{}_{(aq)} + 8H^+_{(aq)} + 8e^- \rightarrow Cl^-_{(aq)} + 4H_2O_{(l)}$$

$$Cu_{(s)} \rightarrow Cu^{2+}_{(aq)} + 2e^-$$

$$4Cu_{(s)} + ClO_4^-{}_{(aq)} + 8H^+_{(aq)} \rightarrow Cl^-_{(aq)} + 4H_2O_{(l)} + 4Cu^{2+}_{(aq)}$$

$$Cu_{(s)} \rightarrow Cu^{2+}_{(aq)} + 2e^-$$

$$2NO_3^-{}_{(aq)} + 4H^+_{(aq)} + Cu_{(s)} \rightarrow Cu^{2+}_{(aq)} + 2NO_{2(g)} + 2H_2O_{(l)}$$

Thus, the acid is most likely $HNO_{3(aq)}$ since it is the only acid that reacts with $Cu_{(s)}$ to produce a gas ($NO_{2(g)}$) and produce blue solution ($Cu^{2+}{}_{(aq)}$).

2. *Procedure*:

- obtain several samples of the acid
- using water baths at a variety of temperatures, warm or cool the acid sample
- record the temperature and the pH of the various acid samples

Variables:

controlled—same acid, concentration of acid

manipulated—temperature

responding—pH

Calculations:

$$[H_3O^+{}_{(aq)}] = [A^-{}_{(aq)}] = 10^{-pH}$$

$$K_a = \frac{[H_3O^+{}_{(aq)}][A^-{}_{(aq)}]}{[HA_{(aq)}]}$$

KEY STRATEGIES FOR SUCCESS ON EXAMS

Copyright Protected

NOTES

Not for Reproduction

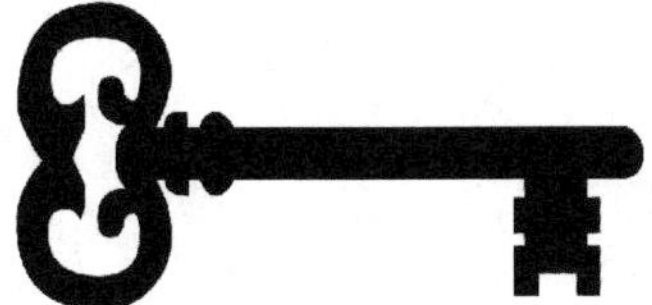

KEY STRATEGIES FOR SUCCESS ON EXAMS

There are many different ways to assess your knowledge and understanding of course concepts. Depending on the subject, your knowledge and skills are most often assessed through a combination of methods which may include performances, demonstrations, projects, products, and oral and written tests. Written exams are one of the most common methods currently used in schools. Just as there are some study strategies that help you to improve your academic performance, there are also some test writing strategies that may help you to do better on unit test and year-end exams. To do your best on any test, you need to be well prepared. You must know the course content and be as familiar as possible with the manner in which it is usually tested. Applying test writing strategies may help you to become more successful on exams, improve your grades, and achieve your potential.

🕮 STUDY OPTIONS FOR EXAM PREPARATION

Studying and preparing for exams requires a strong sense of self-discipline. Sometimes having a study buddy or joining a study group

- helps you to stick to your study schedule
- ensures you have others with whom you can practice making and answering sample questions
- clarifies information and provides peer support

It may be helpful to use a combination of individual study, working with a study buddy, or joining a study group to prepare for your unit test or year-end exam. Be sure that the study buddy or group you choose to work with is positive, knowledgeable, motivated, and supportive. Working with a study buddy or a study group usually means you have to begin your exam preparation earlier than you would if you are studying independently.

Tutorial classes are often helpful in preparing for exams. You can ask a knowledgeable student to tutor you or you can hire a private tutor. Sometimes school jurisdictions or individual schools may offer tutorials and study sessions to assist students in preparing for exams. Tutorial services are also offered by companies that specialize in preparing students for exams. Information regarding tutorial services is usually available from school counsellors, local telephone directories, and on-line search engines.

Copyright Protected

Exam Question Formats

There is no substitute for knowing the course content. To do well in your course you need to combine your subject knowledge and understanding with effective test writing skills. Being familiar with question formats may help you in preparing for quizzes, unit tests or year-end exams. The most typical question formats include multiple choice, numerical response, written response, and essay. The following provides a brief description of each format and suggestions for how you might consider responding to each of the formats.

Multiple Choice

A multiple choice question provides some information for you to consider and then requires you to select a response from four choices, often referred to as distracters. The distracters may complete a statement, be a logical extension or application of the information. In preparing for multiple choice questions you may wish to focus on:

- studying concepts, theories, groups of facts or ideas that are similar in meaning; **compare and contrast their similarities and differences**; ask yourself "How do the concepts differ?", "Why is the difference important?", "What does each fact or concept mean or include?" "What are the exceptions?"
- **identifying main ideas, key information**, formulas, concepts, and theories, where they apply and what the **exceptions** are
- memorizing important definitions, examples, and applications of key concepts
- learning to **recognize *distracters*** that may lead you to apply plausible but incorrect solutions, and ***three and one splits*** where one answer is obviously incorrect and the others are very similar in meaning or wording
- **using active reading techniques** such as underlining, highlighting, numbering, and circling important facts, dates, basic points
- making up your own multiple choice questions for practice

Not for Reproduction

Numerical Response

A numerical response question provides information and requires you to use a calculation to arrive at the response. In preparing for numerical response questions you may wish to focus on:

- memorizing formulas and their applications
- completing chapter questions or making up your own for practice
- making a habit of **estimating the answer** prior to completing the calculation
- paying special **attention to accuracy** in computing and the use of significant digits where applicable

Written Response

A written response question requires you to respond to a question or directive such as "explain", "compare", contrast". In preparing for written response questions you may wish to focus on:

- ensuring your response **answers the question**
- recognizing **directing words** such as "list", "explain", "define"
- providing **concise answers** within the time limit you are devoting to the written response section of the exam
- identifying subject content that lends itself to short answer questions

Essay

An essay is a lengthier written response requiring you to identify your position on an issue and provide logical thinking or evidence that supports the basis of your argument. In preparing for an essay you may wish to focus on:

- examining **issues** that are relevant or related to the subject area or **application of the concept**
- comparing and contrasting two points of view, articles, or theories
- considering the merits of the opposite point of view
- identifying **key concepts**, principles or ideas
- providing **evidence**, examples, and **supporting information** for your viewpoint
- preparing two or three essays on probable topics
- **writing an outline** and essay within the defined period of time you will have for the exam
- understanding the "marker's expectations"

Copyright Protected

KEY TIPS FOR ANSWERING COMMON EXAM QUESTION FORMATS

Most exams use a variety of question formats to test your understanding. You must provide responses to questions ranging from lower level, information recall types to higher level, critical thinking types. The following information provides you with some suggestions on how to prepare for answering multiple choice, written response and essay questions.

MULTIPLE CHOICE

Multiple choice questions often require you to make fine distinctions between correct and nearly correct answers so it is imperative that you:

- begin by answering only the questions for which you are certain of the correct answer
- read the question stem and formulate your own response before you read the choices available
- read the directions carefully paying close attention to words such as "mark ***all*** correct", "choose the ***most*** correct" and "choose the ***one best*** answer"
- use active reading techniques such as underlining, circling, or highlighting critical words and phrases
- watch for superlatives such as "all", "every", "none", "always" which indicate that the correct response must be an undisputed fact
- watch for negatives such as "none", "never", "neither", "not" which indicate that the correct response must be an undisputed fact
- examine all of the alternatives in questions which include "all of the above" or "none of the above" as responses to ensure that "all" or "none" of the statements apply *totally*
- be aware of distracters that may lead you to apply plausible but incorrect solutions, and 'three and one splits' where one answer is obviously incorrect and the others are very similar in meaning or wording
- use information from other questions to help you
- eliminate the responses you know are wrong and then assess the remaining alternatives and choose the best one
- guess if you are not certain

Not for Reproduction

WRITTEN RESPONSE

Written response questions usually require a very specific answer. In answering these questions you should:

- underline key words or phrases that indicate what is required in your answer such as "three reasons", "list", or "give an example"
- write down rough, point-form notes regarding the information you want to include in your answer
- be brief and only answer what is asked
- reread your response to ensure you have answered the question
- use the appropriate subject vocabulary and terminology in your response
- use point form to complete as many questions as possible if you are running out of time

ESSAY

Essay questions often give you the opportunity to demonstrate the breadth and depth of your learning regarding a given topic. In responding to these questions it may be helpful to:

- read the question carefully and underline key words and phrases
- make a brief outline to organize the flow of the information and ideas you want to include in your response
- ensure you have an introduction, body, and conclusion
- begin with a clear statement of your view, position, or interpretation of the question
- address only one main point or key idea in each paragraph and include relevant supporting information and examples
- assume the reader has no prior knowledge of your topic
- conclude with a strong summary statement
- use appropriate subject vocabulary and terminology when and where it is applicable
- review your essay for clarity of thought, logic, grammar, punctuation, and spelling
- write as legibly as you can
- double space your work in case you need to edit it when you proof read your essay
- complete the essay in point form if you run short of time

Copyright Protected

KEY Tips for Responding to Common 'Directing' Words

There are some commonly used words in exam questions that require you to respond in a predetermined or expected manner. The following provides you with a brief summary of how you may wish to plan your response to exam questions that contain these words.

- **Evaluate** (to assess the worth of something)
  - Determine the use, goal, or ideal from which you can judge something's worth
  - Make a value judgment or judgments on something
  - Make a list of reasons for the judgment
  - Develop examples, evidence, contrasts, and details to support your judgments and clarify your reasoning

- **Discuss** (usually to give pros and cons regarding an assertion, quotation, or policy)
  - Make a list of bases for comparing and contrasting
  - Develop details and examples to support or clarify each pro and con
  - On the basis of your lists, conclude your response by stating the extent to which you agree or disagree with what is asserted

- **Compare and Contrast** (to give similarities and differences of two or more objects, beliefs, or positions)
  - Make a list of bases for comparing and contrasting
  - For each basis, judge similarities and differences
  - Supply details, evidence, and examples that support and clarify your judgment
  - Assess the overall similarity or difference
  - Determine the significance of similarity or difference in connection with the purpose of the comparison

- **Analyze** (to break into parts)
  - Break the topic, process, procedure, or object of the essay into its major parts
  - Connect and write about the parts according to the direction of the question: describe, explain, criticize

- **Criticize** (to judge strong and weak points of something)
  - Make a list of the strong points and weak points

Not for Reproduction

- Develop details, examples, and contrasts to support judgments
- Make an overall judgment of quality

- **EXPLAIN** (to show causes of or reasons for something)
  - In Science, usually show the process that occurs in moving from one state or phase in a process to the next, thoroughly presenting details of each step
  - In Humanities and often in Social Sciences, make a list of factors that influence something, developing evidence for each factor's potential influence

- **DESCRIBE** (to give major features of something)
  - Pick out highlights or major aspects of something
  - Develop details and illustrations to give a clear picture

- **ARGUE** (to give reasons for one position and against another)
  - Make a list of reasons for the position
  - Make a list of reasons against the position
  - Refute objections to your reasons for and defend against objections to your reasons opposing the position
  - Fill out reasons, objections, and replies with details, examples, consequences, and logical connections

- **COMMENT** (to make statements about something)
  - Calls for a position, discussion, explanation, judgment, or evaluation regarding a subject, idea, or situation
  - Is strengthened by providing supporting evidence, information, and examples

- **DEMONSTRATE** (to show something)
  - Depending upon the nature of the subject matter, provide evidence, clarify the logical basis of something, appeal to principles or laws as in an explanation, supply a range of opinion and examples

- **SYNTHESIZE** (to invent a new or different version)
  - Construct your own meaning based upon your knowledge and experiences
  - Support your assertion with examples, references to literature and research studies

(Source: http://www.counc.ivic.ca/learn/program/hndouts/simple.html)

Copyright Protected

TEST ANXIETY

Do you get test anxiety? Most students feel some level of stress, worry, or anxiety before an exam. Feeling a little tension or anxiety before or during an exam is normal for most students. A little stress or tension may help you rise to the challenge but too much stress or anxiety interferes with your ability to do well on the exam. Test anxiety may cause you to experience some of the following in a mild or more severe form:

- "butterflies" in your stomach, sweating, shortness of breath, or a quickened pulse
- disturbed sleep or eating patterns
- increased nervousness, fear, or irritability
- sense of hopelessness or panic
- drawing a "blank" during the exam

If you experience extreme forms of test anxiety you need to consult your family physician. For milder forms of anxiety you may find some of the following strategies effective in helping you to remain calm and focused during your unit tests or year-end exams.

- Acknowledge that you are feeling some stress or test anxiety and that this is normal
- Focus upon your breathing, taking several deep breaths
- Concentrate upon a single object for a few moments
- Tense and relax the muscles in areas of your body where you feel tension
- Break your exam into smaller, manageable, achievable parts
- Use positive self-talk to calm and motivate yourself. Tell yourself, "I can do this if I read carefully/start with the easy questions/focus on what I know/stick with it/. . ." instead of saying, "I can't do this."
- Visualize your successful completion of your review or the exam
- Recall a time in the past when you felt calm, relaxed, and content. Replay this experience in your mind experiencing it as fully as possible.

Not for Reproduction

KEY STRATEGIES FOR SUCCESS BEFORE AN EXAM – A CHECKLIST

Review, review, review. That's a huge part of your exam preparation. Here's a quick review checklist for you to see how many strategies for success you are using as you prepare to write your unit tests and year-end exams.

KEY Strategies for Success Before an Exam	*Yes*	*No*
Have you been attending classes?		
Have you determined your learning style?		
Have you organized a quiet study area for yourself?		
Have you developed a long-term study schedule?		
Have you developed a short-term study schedule?		
Are you working with a study buddy or study group?		
Is your study buddy/group positive, knowledgeable, motivated and supportive?		
Have you registered in tutorial classes?		
Have you developed your exam study notes?		
Have you reviewed previously administered exams?		
Have you practiced answering multiple choice, numerical response, written response, and essay questions?		
Have you analyzed the most common errors students make on each subject exam?		
Have you practiced strategies for controlling your exam anxiety?		
Have you maintained a healthy diet and sleep routine?		
Have you participated in regular physical activity?		

Copyright Protected

KEY STRATEGIES FOR SUCCESS DURING AN EXAM

Doing well on any exam requires that you prepare in advance by reviewing your subject material and then using your knowledge to respond effectively to the exam questions during the test session. Combining subject knowledge with effective test writing skills gives you the best opportunity for success. The following are some strategies you may find useful in writing your exam.

- Managing Test Anxiety
  - Be as prepared as possible to increase your self-confidence.
  - Arrive at the exam on time and bring whatever materials you need to complete the exam such as pens, pencils, erasers, and calculators if they are allowed.
  - Drink enough water before you begin the exam so you are hydrated.
  - Associate with positive, calm individuals until you enter the exam room.
  - Use positive self-talk to calm yourself.
  - Remind yourself that it is normal to feel anxious about the exam.
  - Visualize your successful completion of the exam.
  - Breathe deeply several times.
  - Rotate your head, shrug your shoulders, and change positions to relax.

- While the information from your crib notes is still fresh in your memory, write down the key words, concepts, definitions, theories or formulas on the back of the test paper before you look at the exam questions.
  - Review the entire exam.
  - Budget your time.
  - Begin with the easiest question or the question that you know you can answer correctly rather than following the numerical question order of the exam.
  - Be aware of linked questions and use the clues to help you with other questions or in other parts of the exam.

If you "blank" on the exam, try repeating the deep breathing and physical relaxation activities first. Then move to visualization and positive self-talk to get you going. You can also try to open the 'information flow' by writing down anything that you remember about the subject on the reverse side of your exam paper. This activity sometimes helps you to remind yourself that you do know something and you are capable of writing the exam.

Not for Reproduction

GETTING STARTED

Managing Your Time

- Plan on staying in the exam room for the full time that is available to you.
- Review the entire exam and calculate how much time you can spend on each section. Write your time schedule on the top of your paper and stick as closely as possible to the time you have allotted for each section of the exam.
- Be strategic and use your time where you will get the most marks. Avoid spending too much time on challenging questions that are not worth more marks than other questions that may be easier and are worth the same number of marks.
- If you are running short of time, switch to point form and write as much as you can for written response and essay questions so you have a chance of receiving partial marks.
- Leave time to review your paper asking yourself, "Did I do all of the questions I was supposed to do?", "Can I answer any questions now that I skipped over before?", "Are there any questions that I misinterpreted or misread?"

Using the Five Pass Method

- **Browsing Stage** – Scan the entire exam noting the format, the specific instructions and marks allotted for each section, which questions you will complete and which ones you will omit if there is a choice.
- **The First Answering Pass** – To gain confidence and momentum, answer only the questions you are confident you can answer correctly and quickly. These questions are most often found in the multiple choice or numerical response sections of the exam. Maintain a brisk pace; if a question is taking too long to answer, leave it for the Second or Third Pass.
- **The Second Answering Pass** – This Pass addresses questions which require more effort per mark. Answer as many of the remaining questions as possible while maintaining steady progress toward a solution. As soon as it becomes evident the question is too difficult or is tasking an inordinate amount of time, leave it for the Third Answering Pass.
- **The Third Answering Pass** – During the Third Answering Pass you should complete all partial solutions from the first two Passes. Marks are produced at a slower rate during this stage. At the end of this stage, all questions should have full or partial answers. Guess at any multiple choice questions that you have not yet answered.
- **The Final Review Stage** – Use the remaining time to review the entire exam, making sure that no questions have been overlooked. Check answers and calculations as time permits.

Copyright Protected

Using the Three Pass Method

- **Overview** – Begin with an overview of the exam to see what it contains. Look for 'easy' questions and questions on topics that you know thoroughly.
- **Second Pass** – Answer all the questions that you can complete without too much trouble. These questions help to build your confidence and establish a positive start.
- **Last Pass** – Now go through and answer the questions that are left. This is when you begin to try solving the questions you find particularly challenging.

KEY EXAM TIPS FOR SELECTED SUBJECT AREAS

The following are a few additional suggestions you may wish to consider when writing exams in any of the selected subject areas.

English Language Arts

Exams in English Language Arts usually have two components, writing and reading. Sometimes students are allowed to bring approved reference books such as a dictionary, thesaurus and writing handbook into the exam. If you have not used these references on a regular basis, you may find them more of a hindrance than a help in an exam situation. In completing the written section of an English Language Arts exam:

- plan your essay
- focus on the issue presented
- establish a clear position using a thesis statement to direct and unify your writing
- organize your writing in a manner that logically presents your views
- support your viewpoint with specific examples
- edit and proof read your writing

In completing the reading section of an English Language Arts exam:

- read the entire selection before responding
- use titles, dates, footnotes, pictures, introductions, and notes on the author to assist you in developing an understanding of the piece presented
- when using line references, read a few lines before and after the identified section

Not for Reproduction

MATHEMATICS

In some instances, the use of calculators is permitted (or required) to complete complex calculations, modeling, simulations, or to demonstrate your use of technology. It is imperative that you are familiar with the approved calculator and the modes you may be using during your exam. In writing exams in mathematics:

- use appropriate mathematical notation and symbols
- clearly show or explain all the steps involved in solving the problem
- check to be sure you have included the correct units of measurement and have rounded to the appropriate significant digit
- use appropriate labelling and equal increments on graphs

SCIENCES

In the Sciences written response and open-ended questions usually require a clear, organized, and detailed explanation of the science involved in the question. You may find it helpful to use the acronym **STEEPLES** to organize your response to these types of questions. STEEPLES stands for **S**cience, **T**echnological, **E**cological, **E**thical, **P**olitical, **L**egal, **E**conomical, and **S**ocial aspects of the issue presented. In writing exams in the sciences:

- use scientific vocabulary to clearly explain your understanding of the processes or issues
- state your position in an objective manner
- demonstrate your understanding of both sides of the issue
- clearly label graphs, diagrams, tables, and charts using accepted conventions
- provide all formulas and equations

SOCIAL STUDIES, HISTORY, GEOGRAPHY

Exams in these courses of study often require you to take a position on an issue and defend your point of view. Your response should demonstrate your understanding of both the positive and negative aspects of the issue and be supported by well-considered arguments and evidence. In writing exams in Social Studies, History or Geography, the following acronyms may be helpful to you in organizing your approach.

- **SEE** – stands for **S**tatement, **E**xplanation, **E**xample. This acronym reminds you to couple your statement regarding your position with an explanation and then an example.

Copyright Protected

- **PERMS** – stands for **P**olitical, **E**conomic, **R**eligious or moral, **M**ilitary, and **S**ocietal values. Your position statement may be derived from or based upon any of these points of view. Your argument is more credible if you can show that recognized authorities such as leaders, theorists, writers or scientists back your position.

SUMMARY

Writing exams involves a certain amount of stress and anxiety. If you want to do your best on the exam, *there is no substitute for being well prepared.* Being well prepared helps you to feel more confident about your ability to succeed and less anxious about writing tests. In preparing for unit or year-end exams remember to:

- use as many senses as possible in preparing for exams
- start as early as possible set realistic goals and targets
- take advantage of study buddies, study groups, and tutorials
- review previously used exams
- study with positive, knowledgeable, motivated, and supportive individuals
- practice the material in the format in which you are to be tested
- try to simulate the test situation as much as possible
- keep a positive attitude
- end your study time with a quick review and then do something different before you try to go to sleep on the night before the exam
- drink a sufficient amount of water prior to an exam
- stay in the exam room for the full amount of time available
- try to relax by focusing on your breathing

If you combine your best study habits with some of the strategies presented here, you may increase your chances of writing a strong exam and maximizing your potential to do well.

DIPLOMA EXAMINATIONS

A GUIDE TO WRITING THE DIPLOMA EXAMINATION

The *Diploma Examinations* section contains the June 2001 and January 2002 diploma examinations. The questions presented here are distinct from those in the Unit Review section. It is recommended that students work carefully through these exams as they are reflective of the format and difficulty **level of the final exam that students are likely to encounter**.

THE KEY contains detailed answers that illustrate the problem-solving process for every question in this section.

When writing practice exams, students are encouraged to simulate actual Diploma Exam conditions. This will help students become:

- *aware of the mental and physical stamina required to sit through an entire exam*
- *familiar with the exam format and how the course content is tested*
- *aware of any units or concepts that are troublesome or require additional study*
- *more successful in managing their review effectively*

To simulate the exam conditions, students should:

- *use an alarm clock or other timer to monitor the time allowed for the exam*
- *select a quiet writing spot away from all distractions*
- *place their picture ID on the desk or table where the exam is being written*
- *assemble the appropriate materials that are allowed for writing the exam such as pens, HB pencils, calculator, dictionary*
- *use "test wiseness" skills*
- *complete as much of the exam as possible within the allowable time*

In writing the practice exam, students should:

- *read instructions, directions, and questions carefully*
- *organize writing time according to the exam emphasis on each section*
- *highlight key words*
- *think about what is being asked*
- *plan their writing; once complete, proof for errors in content, spelling, grammar*
- *watch for bolded words such as most, least, best*
- *in multiple-choice questions, cross out any choices students know are incorrect*
- *if possible, review all responses upon completion of the exam*

Copyright Protected

NOTES

Not for Reproduction

JANUARY 2002 DIPLOMA EXAM

Use the following information to answer the first question.

An oven provides a constant supply of 15 kJ/min of energy to heat a solid substance. The temperature changes of the substance are graphed below.

Temperature–Time Graph

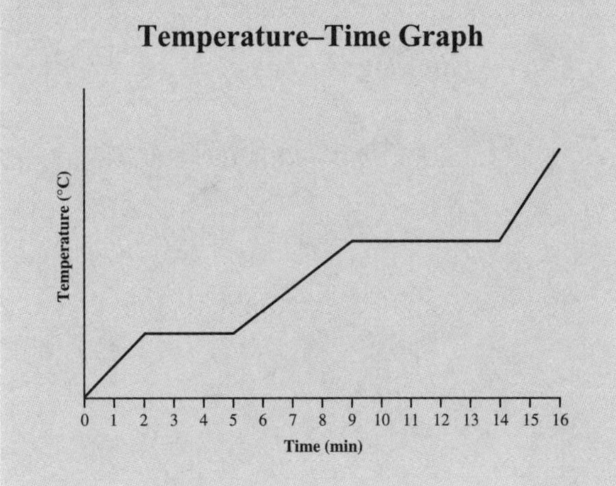

1. According to the graph, between 2 min and 5 min, the

   A. kinetic energy of the sample increased by 45 kJ

   B. potential energy of the sample increased by 45 kJ

   C. kinetic energy and potential energy of the sample increased in equal amounts

   D. kinetic energy of the sample decreased as the potential energy increased by 45 kJ

Use the following inf... que...

The main ingredient in rubb... isopropyl alcohol, $CH_3CH(OH...$ Isopropyl alcohol acts as a disin... flammable and volatile (evaporates... room temperature).

2. When rubbing alcohol is placed on skin, the skin immediately feels

   A. warmer because evaporation is endothermic

   B. warmer because evaporation is exothermic

   C. cooler because evaporation is endothermic

   D. cooler because evaporation is exothermic

Use the following information to answer the next two questions.

In an experiment, 115.24 g of isopropyl alcohol at 20.1°C was mixed with 56.31 g of water at 50.3°C. After thermal equilibrium was reached, the temperature of the mixture was 36.5°C.

3. The energy lost by the water was

   A. 3.26 kJ

   B. 8.61 kJ

   C. 11.9 kJ

   D. 26.2 kJ

Use your recorded answer from ***Multiple Choice 3*** *to answer* ***Numerical Response 1.***

Numerical Response

1. The experimental specific heat capacity of isopropyl alcohol is __________ J/(g • °C). (Record your **three-digit** answer.)

Copyright Protected

...the following information to answer the next two questions.

Methanol ($CH_3OH_{(l)}$), known commercially as both methyl hydrate and gas line antifreeze, is widely used as a solvent. Some properties of methanol are listed below.

melting point	–94.0°C
boiling point	65.0°C
specific heat capacity (liquid)	2.55 J/(g • °C)
molar heat of fusion	2.16 kJ/mol
molar heat of vaporization	34.4 kJ/mol
molar heat of combustion	–638.1 kJ/mol

4. A sample of methanol is heated at a constant rate from 25°C to 75°C. A temperature–time graph that depicts the heating of methanol is

A.

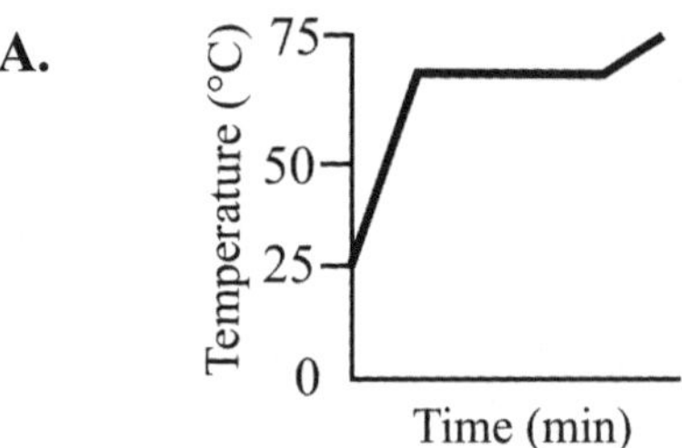

B.

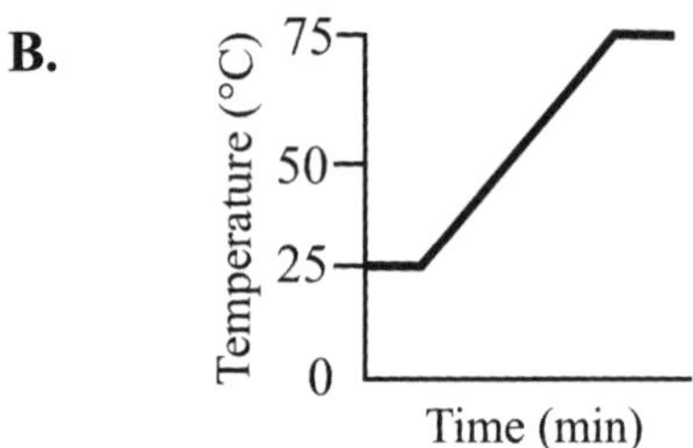

C.

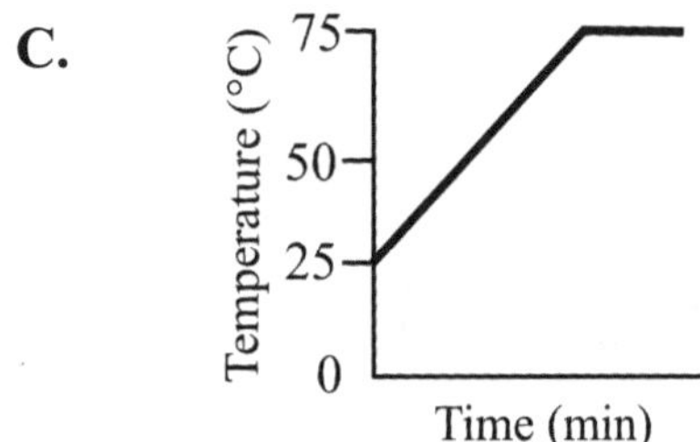

D.

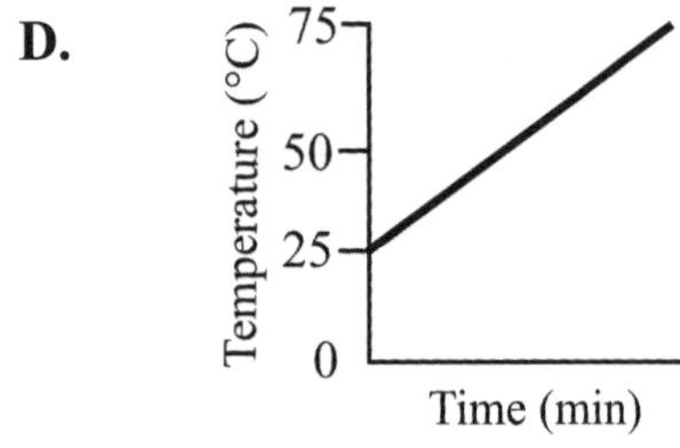

5. The energy required to vaporize 1.00 L (793 g) of methanol at its boiling point is

A. 1.10 kJ

B. 131 kJ

C. 851 kJ

D. 1.07×10^3 kJ

Use the following reaction equations to answer the next question.

Reaction Equations

1	$H_{2(g)} + \frac{1}{2}O_{2(g)} \rightarrow H_2O_{(g)}$
2	$CH_{4(g)} + 2\,O_{2(g)} \rightarrow CO_{2(g)} + 2\,H_2O_{(g)}$
3	${}^{2}_{1}H + {}^{2}_{1}H \rightarrow {}^{4}_{2}He$
4	$CH_3OH_{(l)} + \frac{3}{2}O_{2(g)} \rightarrow CO_{2(g)} + 2\,H_2O_{(g)}$

Numerical Response

2. The reactions represented above, when their enthalpy changes are ranked from largest to smallest according to magnitude, the order of the equations is

_____, _____, _____, and _____.

Numerical Response

3. When 0.500 g of peanut oil was burned, the temperature of 0.950 kg of water in a calorimeter increased by 4.60°C. The enthalpy of combustion of the peanut oil was

If + record **1** in first space.

If – record **2** in first space.

_____ _____ _____ • _____

Note: The placement of the decimal is provided for you.

Not for Reproduction

Use the following information to answer the next two questions.

A student using a computer-based laboratory (CBL) temperature probe attempted to determine the amount of energy released by a commercial heat pack. The student activated the heat pack and placed it in an insulated calorimeter containing 1.00 kg of water at 11.30°C. A graph of the results obtained is given below.

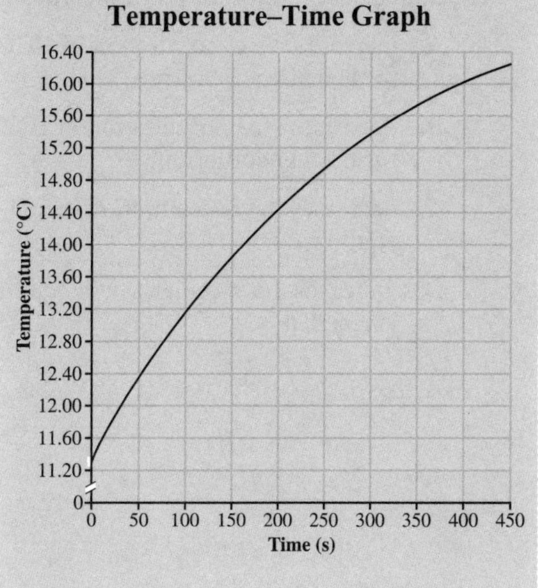

6. To more accurately determine the total heat released by the heat pack, the student should

   A. use more water

   B. use a larger heat pack

   C. start with colder water

   D. collect results for a longer period

7. If the energy change of the plastic container is not considered, the calculated energy change for the water from 0 s to 200 s is

   A. 13.0 kJ

   B. 14.4 kJ

   C. 60.3 kJ

   D. 838 kJ

Use the following information to answer the next question.

The following diagram illustrates the formation enthalpies of $V_{(s)}$, $Cl_{2(g)}$, and a selection of their compounds.

Formation Enthalpies of Vanadium Chlorides

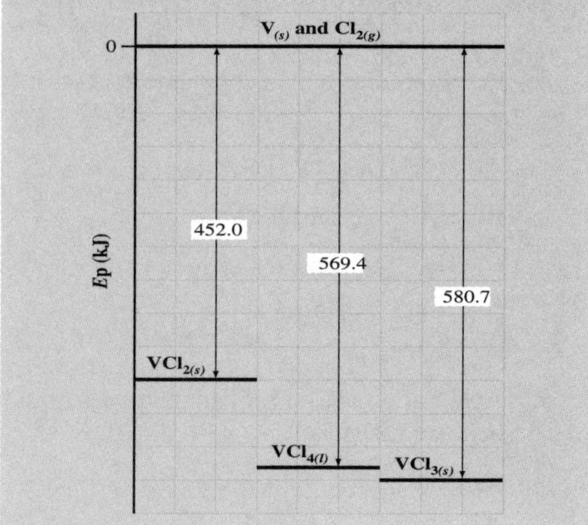

Numerical Response

4. The amount of energy absorbed when 0.350 mol of $VCl_{4(l)}$ decomposes to form $VCl_{2(s)}$ and $Cl_{2(g)}$ is ____ kJ.
(Record your **three-digit** answer.)

Use the following information to answer the next question.

In beer, dissolved carbon dioxide forms carbonic acid, which ionizes in water according to the equation

$$H_2CO_{3(aq)} + H_2O_{(l)} \approx HCO_3^-{}_{(aq)} + H_3O^+{}_{(aq)}$$

8. In this equilibrium, a conjugate acid–base pair is

A. $H_2CO_{3\,(aq)}$ and $HCO_3^-{}_{(aq)}$

B. $H_2CO_{3\,(aq)}$ and $H_3O^+{}_{(aq)}$

C. $H_2CO_{3\,(aq)}$ and $H_2O_{(l)}$

D. $H_2O_{(l)}$ and $HCO_3^-{}_{(aq)}$

9. Acid rain in the form of sulphuric acid could be neutralized by

A. $NaCl_{(s)}$

B. $CaCO_{3(s)}$

C. $NaHSO_{4(aq)}$

D. $CH_3COOH_{(aq)}$

Use the following information to answer the next question.

Apple growers in British Columbia's Okanagan Valley are coping with trees that are stunted and have blistered bark as a result of a dramatic increase in the acidity of the region's soil. Nitrogen fertilizers are one of the main causes of the high acidity level of the soil.

10. To solve this problem, Agriculture Canada has suggested that apple growers work lime into the soil in their orchards because lime is

A. a base

B. an acid

C. a neutral ionic compound

D. a neutral molecular compound

Use the following information to answer the next question.

Blood pH is influenced by the concentration of buffers and gas solutes, such as carbon dioxide, which is formed during cellular respiration. In red blood cells, the enzyme carbonic anhydrase catalyzes the equilibrium

$$CO_{2(aq)} + H_2O_{(l)} \xrightleftharpoons{\text{carbonic anhydrase}} HCO_3^-{}_{(aq)} + H^+{}_{(aq)}$$

11. In this equilibrium, carbonic anhydrase

A. increases the concentration of $HCO_3^-{}_{(aq)}$ formed at equilibrium

B. decreases the concentration of $HCO_3^-{}_{(aq)}$ formed at equilibrium

C. decreases the concentration of $CO_{2(g)}$ at equilibrium

D. increases the speed at which equilibrium is reached

Not for Reproduction

Use the following information to answer the next question.

A buffer system present in some of Alberta's lakes consists of $HCO_3^-{}_{(aq)}$ and $CO_3^{2-}{}_{(aq)}$, as represented by the equilibrium
$HCO_3^-{}_{(aq)} + H_2O_{(l)} \rightleftharpoons H_3O^+{}_{(aq)} + CO_3^{2-}{}_{(aq)}$

12. The graph that best represents the titration of the $CO_3^{2-}{}_{(aq)} - HCO_3^-{}_{(aq)}$ buffer with $NaOH_{(aq)}$ is

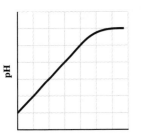

A.

pH

Volume of $NaOH_{(aq)}$ (mL)

B.

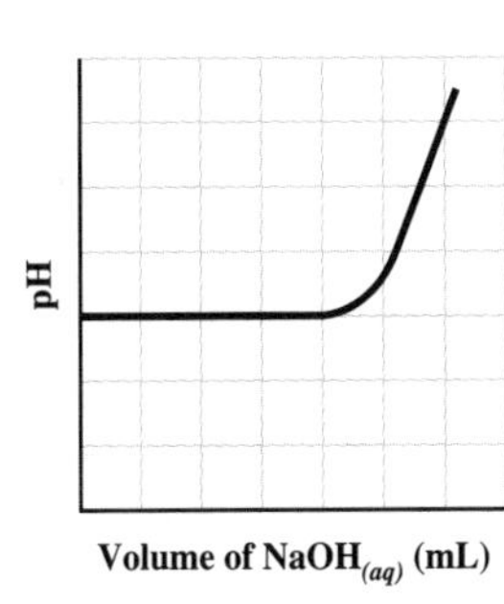

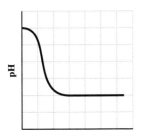

C.

pH

Volume of $NaOH_{(aq)}$ (mL)

D.

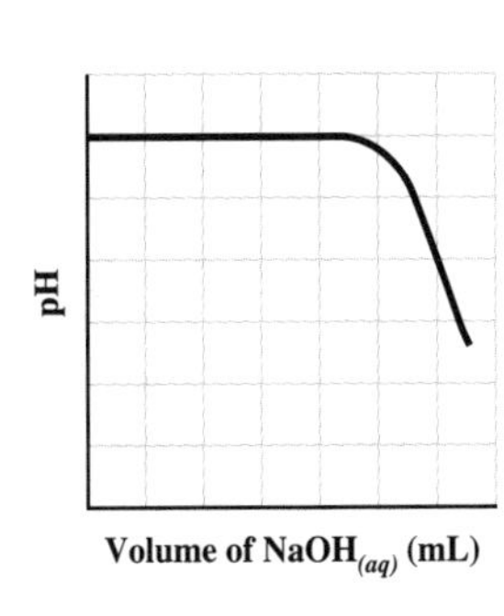

Use the following diagram to answer the next question.

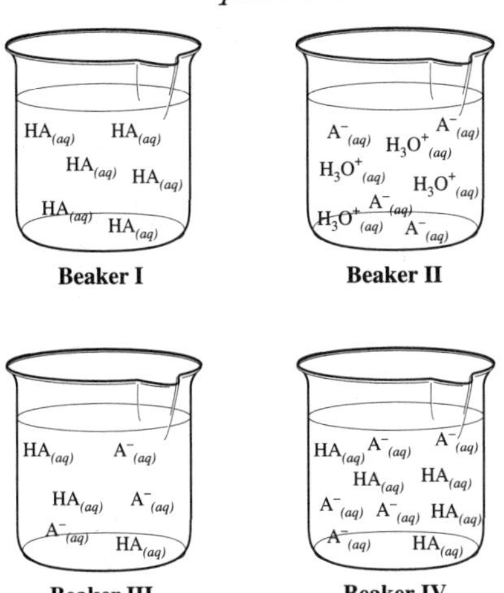

13. The beakers that best represent a buffer solution in which $HA_{(aq)}$ is a weak acid are those labelled

A. I and II

B. I and III

C. II and III

D. III and IV

Copyright Protected

Use the following information to answer the next question.

Oxoacids of Chlorine

Acid	K_a
$HClO_{4(aq)}$	very large
$HClO_{3(aq)}$	5.1×10^{2}
$HClO_{2(aq)}$	1.1×10^{-2}
$HClO_{(aq)}$	2.9×10^{-8}

14. Acids are classified as either strong or weak. Of the acids listed above, only

A. $HClO_{(aq)}$ is a strong acid

B. $HClO_{4(aq)}$ is a strong acid

C. $HClO_{4(aq)}$ and $HclO_{3(aq)}$ are strong acids

D. $HClO_{4(aq)}$, $HclO_{3(aq)}$, and $HclO_{2(aq)}$ are strong acids

Use the following information to answer the next question.

A technician performed a titration to determine the concentration of a 27.0 mL sample of $NaOH_{(aq)}$. A few drops of phenol red indicator were added to the base, which was then titrated with a 0.24 mol/L solution of $HCl_{(aq)}$ until the indicator changed colour from red to orange.

Volume of Acid Used

Final buret reading (mL)	25.8
Initial buret reading (mL)	7.8

Numerical Response

5. The concentration of the $NaOH_{(aq)}$ solution was __________ mol/L.
(Record your **three-digit** answer.)

Use the following information to answer the next three questions.

To determine the identity of a compound, a student dissolved 0.72 g of the compound in enough water to make a 25 mL solution. This solution was titrated with a 0.20 mol/L standardized solution. The student used a pH meter to collect data during the titration and then plotted the data on the graph below.

Titration of the Solution

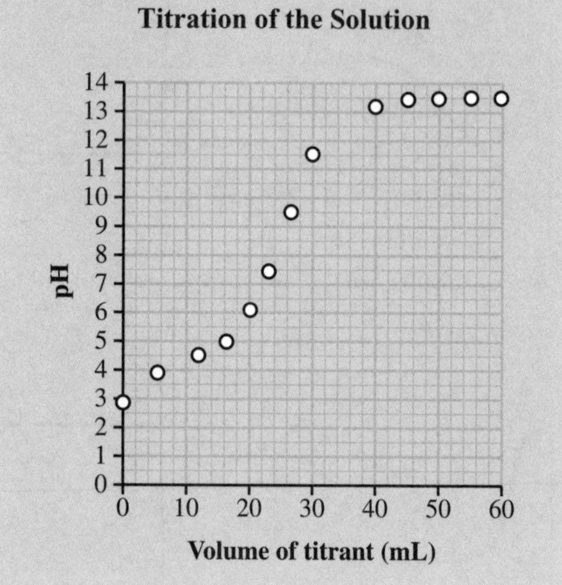

15. This titration likely involved a

A. strong base added to a strong acid

B. strong base added to a weak acid

C. strong acid added to a strong base

D. strong acid added to a weak base

16. The pH of the solution at the equivalence point for this titration is approximately

A. 4.5

B. 8.5

C. 11.5

D. 13.5

Not for Reproduction

17. For this titration, a suitable indicator and its corresponding colour change are

A. phenolphthalein and colourless to pink

B. indigo carmine and blue to yellow

C. thymol blue and blue to yellow

D. phenol red and red to yellow

Numerical Response

6. The K_b for the conjugate base of the ammonium ion, expressed in scientific notation, is ________ $\times 10^{-5}$.

Use the following equilibrium information to answer the next question.

For the equilibrium $PCl_{5(g)} \rightleftharpoons PCl_{3(g)} + Cl_{2(g)}$ the equilibrium constant at two temperatures is given below.

Temperature	K_{eq}
227°C	2.24
486°C	33.3

18. According to this information, as the temperature of the system increases, the equilibrium shifts

A. left and the reaction is exothermic

B. left and the reaction is endothermic

C. right and the reaction is exothermic

D. right and the reaction is endothermic

Use the following information to answer the next question.

A source of hydrogen for the Haber process is "syngas," which is produced by a reaction of methane and water at 1 000°C.

$$CH_{4(g)} + H_2O_{(g)} + \text{heat} \xrightleftharpoons[]{\text{Nickel Catalyst}} CO_{(g)} + 3\,H_{2(g)}$$

Numerical Response

7. If, at equilibrium, the $[CH_{4(g)}] = 2.97$ mol/L, $[H_2O_{(g)}] = 7.94$ mol/L, $[CO_{(g)}] = 5.45$ mol/L, and $[H_{2(g)}] = 2.10$ mol/L, then the K_{eq} is

__________.

(Record your **three-digit** answer.)

Copyright Protected

Use the following information to answer the next question.

Manipulations of an Equilibrium System

$CH_{4(g)} + H_2O_{(g)} + heat \approx CO_{(g)} + 3\,H_{2(g)}$

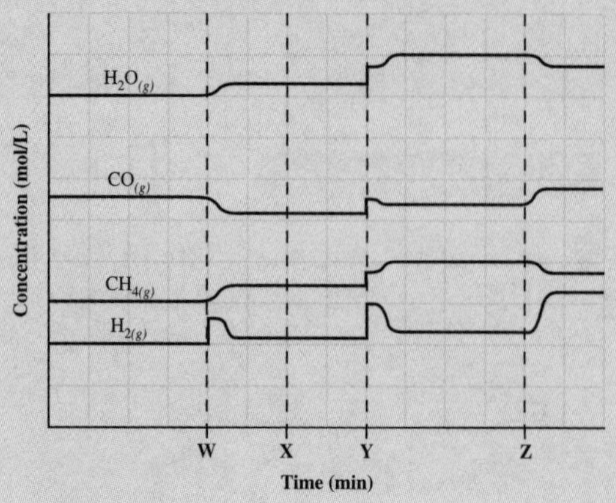

$H_2O_{(g)}$
$CO_{(g)}$
$CH_{4(g)}$
$H_{2(g)}$
Concentration (mol/L)
W X Y Z
Time (min)

Stresses

1 Addition of heat
2 Addition of neon while a constant volume is maintained
3 Addition of hydrogen
4 Pressure increased by decreasing the volume

Numerical Response

8. Match each of the stresses identified above with the letter on the graph that indicates the time at which the stress was applied.

Stress applied: _____ _____ _____ _____
Time: W X Y Z

Use the following information to answer the next three questions.

The beautiful patterns of butterfly wings, the stripes on zebra pelts, and the myriad of colours of tropical fish all result from oscillating chemical reactions. These chemical reactions can be studied in a much simpler form in the laboratory. In 1958, the Russian chemist B.P. Belousoz discovered a complex reaction sequence in which the concentration of reactants and products oscillated over time.

Unbalanced Reaction Equations

I $\_H^+_{(aq)} + \_BrO_2^-{}_{(aq)} + \_BrO_3^-{}_{(aq)} \approx \_BrO_{2(aq)} + \_H_2O_{(l)}$

II $\_Ce^{3+}_{(aq)} + \_BrO_{2(aq)} \approx \_Ce^{4+}_{(aq)} + \_BrO_2^-{}_{(aq)}$

III $\_BrO_2^-{}_{(aq)} \approx \_BrO_3^-{}_{(aq)} + \_BrO^-_{(aq)}$

Numerical Response

9. When reaction equation I is balanced with lowest whole number coefficients, the coefficient of

$H^+_{(aq)}$ is ______ $BrO2^-{}_{(aq)}$ is ______

$BrO_3^-{}_{(aq)}$ is ______ $BrO_{2(aq)}$ is ______

19. In reaction III, the bromine in $BrO_2^-{}_{(aq)}$

A. undergoes oxidation only

B. undergoes reduction only

C. both loses and gains protons

D. both loses and gains electrons

20. If the $[H^+_{(aq)}]$ in reaction I is 0.020 mol/L, then the pH and pOH are, respectively,

A. 1.05 and 12.95

B. 1.40 and 12.60

C. 1.70 and 12.30

D. 2.00 and 12.00

Not for Reproduction

Use the following information to answer the next question.

Common household bleach is an aqueous solution that contains approximately 5% sodium hypochlorite. The equilibrium involved in the production of bleach from chlorine can be represented by the reaction equation

$Cl_{2(g)} + 2\,OH^-_{(aq)} \rightleftharpoons ClO^-_{(aq)} + Cl^-_{(aq)} + H_2O_{(l)}$

21. In the production of bleach, the reduction half-reaction is

A. $Cl_{2(g)} + 2\,e^- \rightarrow 2\,Cl^-_{(aq)}$

B. $2\,Cl^-_{(aq)} \rightarrow Cl_{2(g)} + 2\,e^-$

C. $4\,OH^-_{(aq)} \rightarrow O_{2(g)} + 2\,H_2O_{(l)} + 4\,e^-$

D. $ClO^-_{(aq)} + H_2O_{(l)} + 2\,e^- \rightarrow Cl^-_{(aq)} + 2\,OH^-_{(aq)}$

22. A student has one coin made of copper and one coin made of nickel. Which of the following solutions could the student use to demonstrate which of these metals is the stronger reducing agent?

A. $Hg^{2+}_{(aq)}$

B. $Fe^{3+}_{(aq)}$

C. $Fe^{2+}_{(aq)}$

D. $Sn^{4+}_{(aq)}$

Use the following information to answer the next two questions.

The oil that Syncrude mines from the Athabasca Tar Sands contains large amounts of undesirable sulphur. To remove most of the sulphur, Syncrude uses a chemical process known as the Claus process, which results in a low-sulphur "sweet" crude oil. Two steps involved in the Claus process are shown below.

Step I

$$H_2S_{(g)} + \frac{3}{2}O_{2(g)} \xrightarrow{950°C\text{–}1200°C} SO_{2(g)} + H_2O_{(g)} \qquad \Delta H = -518\text{ kJ}$$

Step II

$$SO_{2(g)} + 2\,H_2S_{(g)} \xrightarrow[\text{catalyst}]{170°C\text{–}370°C} 3\,S_{(l)} + 2\,H_2O_{(g)} \qquad \Delta H = -93\text{ kJ}$$

Syncrude solidifies and stores approximately 1.36 Gg of sulphur per day.

23. The net equation and enthalpy of reaction for the Claus process are

A. $3\,H_2S_{(g)} + \frac{3}{2}O_{2(g)} \rightarrow 3\,S_{(l)} + 3\,H_2O_{(g)}$ $\Delta H = +425$ kJ

B. $3\,H_2S_{(g)} + \frac{3}{2}O_{2(g)} \rightarrow 3\,S_{(l)} + 3\,H_2O_{(g)}$ $\Delta H = -611$ kJ

C. $3\,H_2S_{(g)} + \frac{3}{2}O_{2(g)} \rightarrow 3\,S_{(l)} + 3\,H_2O_{(g)}$ $\Delta H = -704$ kJ

D. $2\,H_2S_{(g)} + O_{2(g)} \rightarrow 2\,S_{(l)} + 2\,H_2O_{(g)}$ $\Delta H = -425$ kJ

24. As the $H_2S_{(g)}$ forms $S_{(l)}$, the sulphur atoms

A. gain 2 e^- and are oxidized

B. lose 2 e^- and are oxidized

C. gain 2 e^- and are reduced

D. lose 2 e^- and are reduced

Copyright Protected

Use the following information to answer the next two questions.

If $H_2S_{(g)}$ is released into the atmosphere, it dissolves in atmospheric water to form hydrosulphuric acid. The ionization of $H_2S_{(aq)}$ can be represented by the equilibrium

$$H_2S_{(aq)} + H_2O_{(l)} \rightleftharpoons HS^-_{(aq)} + H_3O^+_{(aq)}$$

25. The K_a expression for this ionization is

A. $K_a = \dfrac{[H_2S_{(aq)}]}{[HS^-_{(aq)}][H_3O^+_{(aq)}]}$

B. $K_a = \dfrac{[H_2S_{(aq)}][H_2O_{(l)}]}{[HS^-_{(aq)}][H_3O^+_{(aq)}]}$

C. $K_a = \dfrac{[HS^-_{(aq)}][H_3O^+_{(aq)}]}{[H_2S_{(aq)}][H_2O_{(l)}]}$

D. $K_a = \dfrac{[HS^-_{(aq)}][H_3O^+_{(aq)}]}{[H_2S_{(aq)}]}$

26. The $[H_3O^+_{(aq)}]$ in a 0.050 mol/L $H_2S_{(aq)}$ solution is

A. 5.5×10^{-9} mol/L

B. 7.4×10^{-5} mol/L

C. 3.3×10^{-4} mol/L

D. 0.10 mol/L

Use the following information to answer the next four questions.

Poisonous oxalic acid is found in non-toxic concentrations in vegetables such as spinach and rhubarb. Manufacturers of spinach juice are required to analyze the concentration of oxalic acid to avoid problems that could arise from unexpectedly high concentrations of oxalic acid. The reaction of oxalic acid with acidified potassium permanganate can be represented by the following equation.

$$5\,HOOCCOOH_{(aq)} + 2\,MnO_4{}^-_{(aq)} + 6\,H^+_{(aq)} \rightarrow 2\,Mn^{2+}_{(aq)} + 8\,H_2O_{(l)} + 10\,CO_{2(g)}$$

27. If 15.0 mL of oxalic acid solution is completely reacted with 20.0 mL of 0.0015 mol/L acidified permanganate solution, then the oxalic acid concentration will be

A. 8.0×10^{-4} mol/L

B. 2.4×10^{-3} mol/L

C. 5.0×10^{-3} mol/L

D. 6.0×10^{-3} mol/L

28. A technician reacting oxalic acid with acidified potassium permanganate is **not** likely to observe

A. an increase in electrical conductivity

B. a visible colour change

C. a slight increase in pH

D. the formation of a gas

29. Acidic permanganate solutions and acidic dichromate solutions are often used in redox titrations because they are strong

A. reducing agents that change colour when they are oxidized

B. oxidizing agents that change colour when they are reduced

C. reducing agents that change colour when the acid is neutralized

D. oxidizing agents that change colour when the acid is neutralized

Not for Reproduction

30. When oxalic acid is titrated with $NaOH_{(aq)}$, the titration curve that would be predicted is

A.

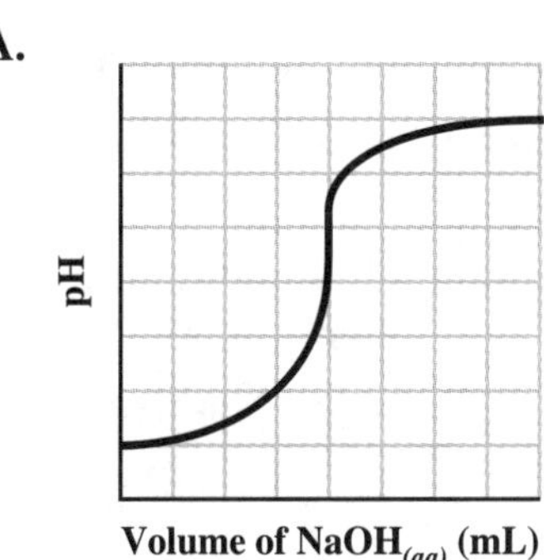

B.

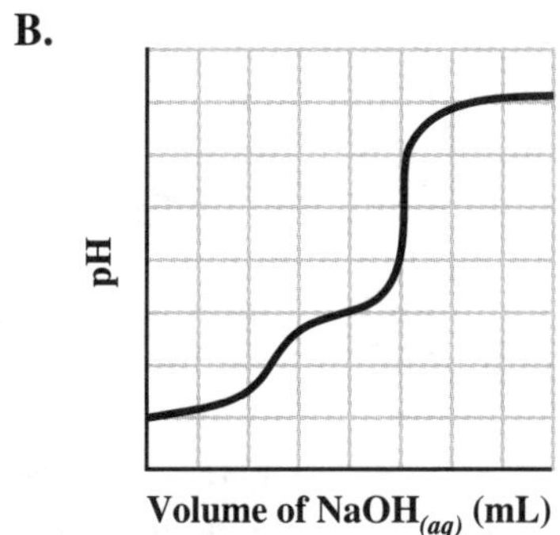

C.

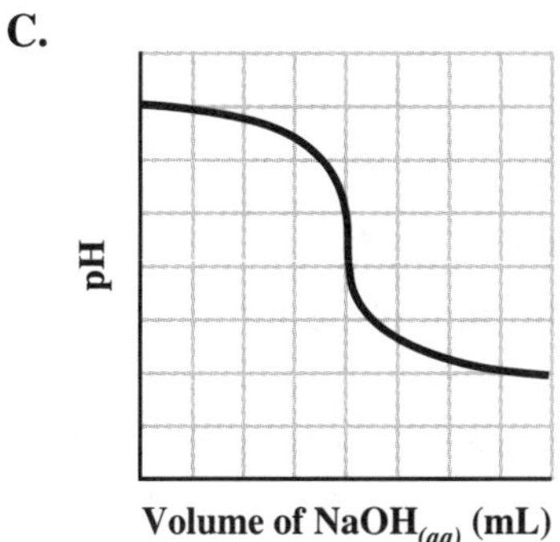

D.

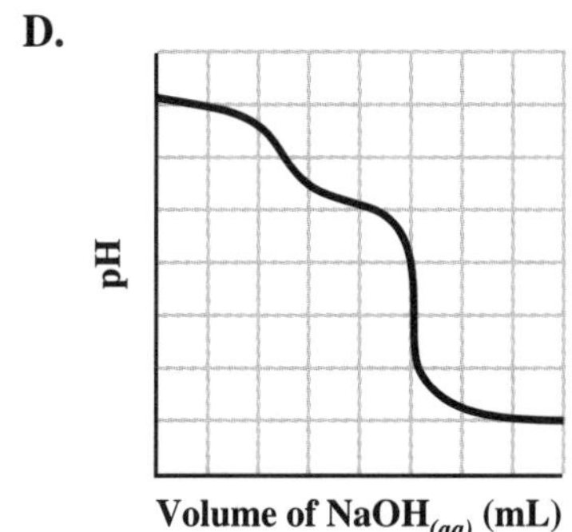

Use the following information to answer the next two questions.

Alfred Nobel was the first person to patent a process to commercially produce dynamite. Dynamite contains nitroglycerine, $C_3H_5(NO_3)_{3(l)}$, an explosive compound that when absorbed by a support material, becomes safer to handle and transport. Nitroglycerine can undergo an explosive decomposition, as represented by the equation

$$4\,C_3H_5(NO_3)_{3(l)} \rightarrow 12\,CO_{2(g)} + 10\,H_2O_{(g)} + 6\,N_{2(g)} + O_{2(g)}$$

31. In the decomposition equation, the product species that would have an oxidation state of zero are

A. hydrogen and nitrogen

B. carbon and hydrogen

C. nitrogen and oxygen

D. carbon and oxygen

32. Reactions producing carbon dioxide cause concern among environmentalists because $CO_{2(g)}$ is

A. a poisonous gas

B. a major greenhouse gas

C. a major contributor to acid rain

D. an important component of combustion

Use the following information to answer the next question.

Tiny iron filings are added as a mineral supplement to many breakfast cereals in minute quantities. The iron can be collected by mixing the cereal with water and placing it in a bag with a powerful magnet. When the bag is shaken the magnet collects the tiny iron filings. Once ingested, the iron reacts with the hydrochloric acid in the stomach. The iron is then converted into a form that can be absorbed by the body.

33. In the stomach, the reaction between hydrochloric acid and iron occurs because the

A. iron donates protons to the acid

B. acid donates electrons to the iron

C. iron accepts protons from the acid

D. acid accepts electrons from the iron

Use the following information to answer the next two questions.

Electronic circuit boards can be made by etching a copper board that is coated with plastic on one side. A special masking tape is applied to the surface of the copper board in the shape of the desired circuit pattern. The circuit board is then etched by reacting it with $FeCl_{3(aq)}$ to remove the unwanted copper.

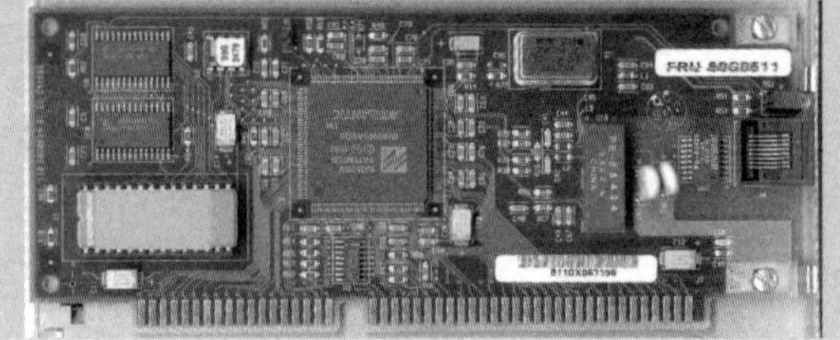

34. The net equation for the spontaneous reaction that occurs when the circuit board is immersed in $FeCl_{3(aq)}$ is

A. $Fe^{2+}_{(aq)} + Cu_{(s)} \rightarrow Cu^{2+}_{(aq)} + Fe_{(s)}$

B. $Cu^{+}_{(aq)} + Fe^{2+}_{(aq)} \rightarrow Fe^{3+}_{(aq)} + Cu_{(s)}$

C. $2\,Fe^{3+}_{(aq)} + Cu_{(s)} \rightarrow Cu^{2+}_{(aq)} + 2Fe^{2+}_{(aq)}$

D. $2\,Fe^{3+}_{(aq)} + 3\,Cu_{(s)} \rightarrow 3\,Cu^{2+}_{(aq)} + 2\,Fe_{(s)}$

35. In this reaction, the copper acts as the

A. oxidizing agent and is oxidized

B. oxidizing agent and is reduced

C. reducing agent and is oxidized

D. reducing agent and is reduced

Use the following information to answer the next question.

Electrochemical Cell

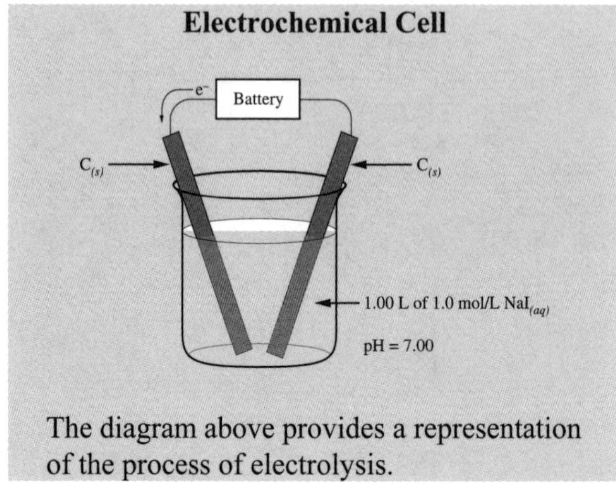

The diagram above provides a representation of the process of electrolysis.

36. Which of the following statements describes what happens during the operation of this cell?

A. Chemical energy is converted to electrical energy.

B. Electrical energy is converted to chemical energy.

C. Electrons flow toward the anode.

D. Plating takes place at the anode.

37. A solution containing a metal ion with a 3+ charge was electrolyzed by a 5.0 A current for 10.0 min. If 1.19 g of the metal was electroplated, then the metal was likely

A. indium

B. scandium

C. aluminum

D. potassium

Not for Reproduction

Use the following information to answer the next question.

A voltaic cell capable of lighting a small light bulb can be made by placing copper and zinc strips in a lemon.

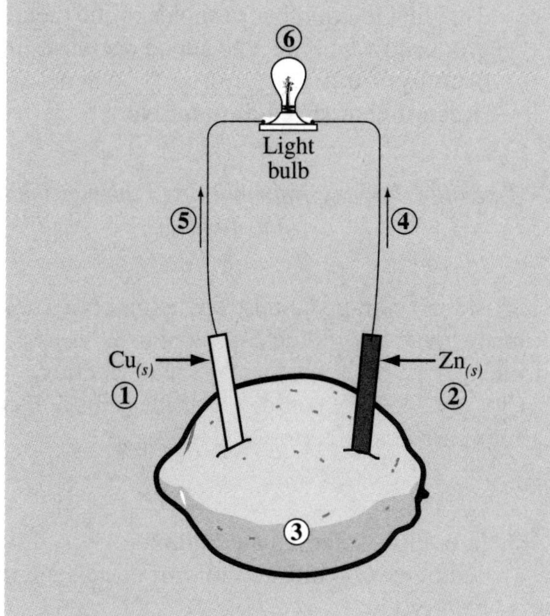

Numerical Response

10. Identify the part of the voltaic cell, as numbered above, that corresponds to each of the descriptors listed below.

Anode __________
Cathode __________
Electron flow __________
Electrolyte __________

Use the following information to answer the next question.

A possible alternative to the internal combustion engine used in present-day automobiles is an electric motor powered with energy supplied by an aluminum–air battery, which uses a sodium hydroxide solution as an electrolyte. When air is bubbled through the sodium hydroxide solution, the half-reaction that occurs at the cathode is

$$O_{2(g)} + 2\,H_2O_{(l)} + 4\,e^- \rightarrow 4\,OH^-_{(aq)}$$

38. The reduction potential for this half-reaction is

A. −0.40 V

B. +0.40 V

C. −0.70 V

D. +0.70 V

Use the following information to answer the next question.

Some car manufacturers have designed an anticorrosion system that sends a weak electric current from the battery to the frame of the car. The current provides a source of electrons, which reduces corrosion of the steel frame.

39. Which of the following methods could **not** be used as an alternative to the method of corrosion prevention described above?

A. Galvanize the steel frame with zinc.

B. Coat the steel frame with inert plastic polymers.

C. Use a paint that prevents contact of the steel frame with the environment.

D. Bolt sacrificial anodes made of copper to the steel frame.

Copyright Protected

Use the following information to answer the next three questions.

To determine the identity of an unknown metallic ion in a solution, a student designed the voltaic cell shown below.

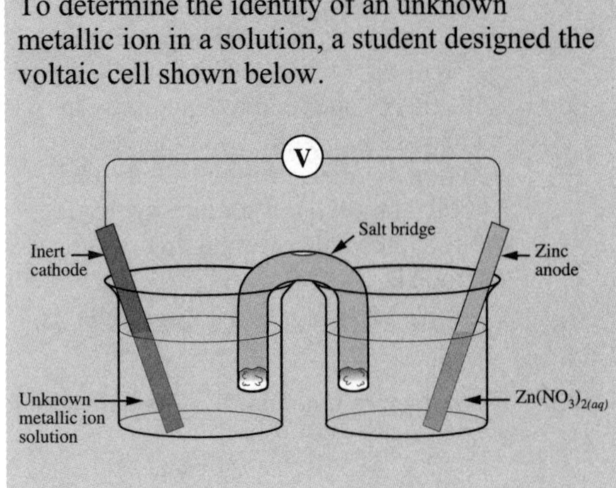

40. The student chose zinc for the anode because zinc

A. gains electrons easily

B. can be easily reduced

C. is an oxidizing agent

D. is a reducing agent

41. If the cell generates a voltage of +1.24 V under standard conditions, the half-reaction occurring at the cathode will have an electrode potential of

A. +2.00 V

B. –2.00 V

C. +0.48 V

D. –0.48 V

42. If the zinc anode loses 200 g of mass during the operation of the cell, then the number of moles of electrons transferred is

A. 1.53 mol

B. 3.06 mol

C. 6.12 mol

D. 12.2 mol

Use your recorded answer from ***Multiple Choice 42*** *to answer* ***Numerical Response 11.****

Numerical Response

11. If the charge on the unidentified metal ion is 3+, then the number of moles of the metal produced when the zinc anode decreases in mass by 200 g is ____________ mol. (Record your **three-digit** answer.)

Use the following information to answer the next question.

Most lead storage batteries in automobiles are made up of six voltaic cells connected in series. Each of the cells consists of a lead electrode ($Pb_{(s)}$), a lead (IV) oxide electrode ($PbO_{2(s)}$), and sulphuric acid electrolyte ($H_2SO_{4(aq)}$).

43. In cold weather, an automobile will sometimes be difficult to start because in the battery, the

A. ions in the electrolyte move very slowly

B. atoms in the lead plate move very slowly

C. concentration of the electrolyte decreases

D. concentration of the lead (IV) oxide decreases

Not for Reproduction

Use the following information to answer the next question.

A 0.532 mol/L solution of $Ce^{4+}_{(aq)}$ was used to titrate a 25.0 mL sample of $Sn^{2+}_{(aq)}$.

Volume Used	
Final buret reading (mL)	43.5
Initial buret reading (mL)	12.6

The half-reaction for cerium(IV) can be represented by

$$Ce^{4+}_{(aq)} + e^- \rightarrow Ce^{3+}_{(aq)} \quad E^\circ = +1.61 \text{ V}$$

Numerical Response

12. The $[Sn^{2+}_{(aq)}]$ of the sample, expressed in scientific notation, is __________ $\times 10^{-1}$ mol/L.
(Record your **three-digit** answer.)

Use the following information to answer the next question.

Some pacemakers use specialized lithium cells as a power source. The half-reactions and electrode potentials in these cells are

$$2\,SOCl_{2(aq)} + 4\,e^- \rightarrow 4\,Cl^-_{(aq)} + S_{(s)} + SO_{2(aq)} \quad E^\circ = +0.36 \text{ V}$$

$$Li^+_{(aq)} + e^- \rightarrow Li_{(s)} \quad E^\circ = -3.04 \text{ V}$$

44. The net equation and potential of this lithium cell are

A. $2\,SOCl^{2(aq)} + Li^+_{(aq)} \rightarrow 4\,Cl^-_{(aq)} + S_{(s)} + SO_{2(aq)} + Li_{(s)}$ $E^\circ_{net} = +3.40$ V

B. $2\,SOCl_{2(aq)} + 4\,Li^+_{(aq)} \rightarrow 4\,Cl^-_{(aq)} + S_{(s)} + SO_{2(aq)} + 4\,Li_{(s)}$ $E^\circ_{net} = +2.68$ V

C. $2\,SOCl_{2(aq)} + Li_{(s)} \rightarrow 4\,Cl^-_{(aq)} + S_{(s)} + SO_{2(aq)} + Li^+_{(aq)}$ $E^\circ_{net} = +2.68$ V

D. $2\,SOCl_{2(aq)} + 4\,Li_{(s)} \rightarrow 4\,Cl^-_{(aq)} + S_{(s)} + SO_{2(aq)} + 4\,Li^+_{(aq)}$ $E^\circ_{net} = +3.40$ V

Use the following information to answer the next question.

$HOCl_{(aq)}$, a weak acid, is the active ingredient used in the disinfecting of swimming pools. It can be formed by adding $Ca(OCl)_{2(s)}$ tablets to pool water.

The pH of a swimming pool should be kept between 7.2 and 7.8 so that the equilibrium $[HOCl_{(aq)}]$ is optimal. Phenol red is used by lifeguards to test pH. Based on the test results with phenol red, a lifeguard may

- adjust the pH by adding $Na_2CO_{3(s)}$
- adjust the pH by adding $HCl_{(aq)}$
- not do anything

Written Response—15%

1. **a)** Write the net ionic equation that illustrates the formation of $HOCl_{(aq)}$ when $Ca(OCl)_{2(s)}$ tablets are added to a swimming pool.

b) Identify two characteristics of this system, or of any system, at equilibrium.

c) Based on the indicator colour, the lifeguard may choose any one of the three different courses of action. Relate each indicator colour to a course of action.

Copyright Protected

Use the following information to answer the next question.

A space shuttle uses more than one type of rocket fuel. The two solid rocket boosters use a fuel mixture of aluminum and ammonium perchlorate that reacts according to the equation

$$\underbrace{3Al_{(s)} + 3NH_4ClO_{4(s)}}_{\text{solid fuel}} \rightarrow Al_2O_{3(s)} + AlCl_{3(s)} + 3NO_{(g)} + 6H_2O_{(g)}$$

In the three main shuttle engines, a mixture of hydrogen and oxygen form a second fuel. The hydrogen and oxygen are carried as compressed liquids in a large tank adjoining the shuttle and react to produce energy according to the reaction

$$H_{2(g)} + \frac{1}{2}O_{2(g)} \rightarrow H_2O_{(g)}$$

Relevant Heats of Formation

H_f° of $NH_4ClO_{4(s)}$ = –295.3 kJ/mol

H_f° of $AlCl_{3(s)}$ = –705.6 kJ/mol

2. Compare the two rocket fuels as energy sources for powering the space shuttle. Your response should also include the calculated energy released for each fuel, an analysis of the energy-to-mass ratio for each fuel, and any environmental concerns related to each fuel.

Not for Reproduction

JUNE 2001 DIPLOMA EXAMINATION

1. Which of the following equations is associated with the largest energy change per mole of fluorine?

   A. $F_{2(g)} \rightarrow F_{2(l)}$

   B. ${}^{19}_{9}F + {}^{4}_{2}He \rightarrow {}^{1}_{0}n + {}^{22}_{11}Na$

   C. $2\,F_{2(g)} + 2\,H_2O_{(l)} \rightarrow O_{2(g)} + 4\,HF_{(aq)}$

   D. $CH_{4(g)} + 2\,Cl_{2(g)} + 2\,F_{2(g)} \rightarrow CCl_2F_{2(g)} + 2\,HCl_{(g)} + 2\,HF_{(g)}$

2. Which of the following molecular properties is a main component of the potential energy of matter?

   A. Vibrational motion

   B. Intramolecular bonding

   C. Movement from place to place

   D. Rotation about the molecules' centre of mass

3. When one mole of sodium bicarbonate is formed from its elements, 947.7 kJ of heat energy is released into the surroundings. This enthalpy change can be represented as

   A. $Na_{(s)} + \frac{1}{2}H_{2(g)} + C_{(s)} + \frac{3}{2}O_{2(g)} \rightarrow NaHCO_{3(s)} + 947.7\text{ kJ}$

   B. $Na_{(s)} + \frac{1}{2}H_{2(g)} + C_{(s)} + \frac{3}{2}O_{2(g)} + 947.7\text{ kJ} \rightarrow NaHCO_{3(s)}$

   C. $Na^{+}_{(aq)} + HCO_3{}^{-}_{(aq)} \rightarrow NaHCO_{3(s)} + 947.7\text{ kJ}$

   D. $Na^{+}_{(aq)} + HCO_3{}^{-}_{(aq)} + 947.7\text{ kJ} \rightarrow NaHCO_{3(s)}$

Use the following information to answer the next question.

Cold packs are commonly used by athletes to reduce swelling caused by injury. The packs consist of two plastic pouches: an inner pouch that contains a chemical and an outer pouch that contains water. When the inner pouch is broken, the chemical and water mix, which causes the pack to feel cold.

Statements

1 Ice is considerably less expensive than are commercial cold packs.

2 Ammonium nitrate is commonly used in cold packs because its heat of solution is endothermic.

3 The disposal of cold packs poses a landfill concern.

4 Durability and flexibility are design requirements for the plastic outer pouch.

Numerical Response

1. The statements above that reflect an ecological, scientific, economic, and technological perspective are, respectively, _____ , _____ , _____ , and _____.

Numerical Response

2. The energy released when 1.00 mol of $AgI_{(s)}$ is formed from its elements is __________ kJ.
(Record your **three-digit** answer.)

Use the following information to answer the next two questions.

Glucose is a biological fuel used by cells to satisfy the energy needs of plants and animals. The overall reaction for the metabolism of glucose is represented by the **unbalanced** equation

$$\_\_C_6H_{12}O_{6(s)} + \_\_O_{2(g)} \rightarrow \_\_CO_{2(g)} + \_\_H_2O_{(l)}$$

4. The balanced equation and the enthalpy change for the cellular respiration of glucose can be represented as

   A. $C_6H_{12}O_{6(s)} + O_{2(g)} \rightarrow CO_{2(g)} + H_2O_{(l)} + 593.8$ kJ

   B. $C_6H_{12}O_{6(s)} + 6\ O_{2(g)} + 2\,802.7\text{ kJ} \rightarrow 6\ CO_{2(g)} + 6\ H_2O_{(l)}$

   C. $C_6H_{12}O_{6(s)} + 6\ O_{2(g)} \rightarrow 6\ CO_{2(g)} + 6\ H_2O_{(l)} + 2\,802.7$ kJ

   D. $C_6H_{12}O_{6(s)} + 6\ O_{2(g)} \rightarrow 6\ CO_{2(g)} + 6\ H_2O_{(l)} + 2\,538.7$ kJ

5. If solid glucose is completely burned in the flame of a Bunsen burner, the enthalpy change is

   A. greater than it is during cellular respiration because the production of $H_2O_{(g)}$ releases more energy than does the production of $H_2O_{(l)}$

   B. less than it is during cellular respiration because the production of $H_2O_{(g)}$ releases less energy than does the production of $H_2O_{(l)}$

   C. the same as it is in the body because the enthalpy change is independent of the state of the products

   D. the same as it is in cellular respiration because they are identical processes

6. When 1.65 g of ethanol ($CH_3CHO_{(l)}$) is burned in a calorimeter to produce $H_2O_{(l)}$ and $CO_{2(g)}$, 44.7 kJ of heat energy is produced. According to this experimental data, the molar enthalpy of combustion of ethanol is

   A. $+1.52 \times 10^3$ kJ/mol

   B. -76.6 kJ/mol

   C. -165 kJ/mol

   D. -1.19×10^3 kJ/mol

Numerical Response

3. A student heated a 120.0 g sample of $H_2O_{(l)}$ from 21.0°C to 32.5°C by adding 5.93 kJ of energy. The student then used this data to calculate the specific heat capacity of water and compared it with the standard value. The experimental percentage difference was __________ %. (Record your **three-digit** answer.)

Use the following equation to answer the next question.

$$2\ C_2H_{2(g)} + 5\ O_{2(g)} \rightarrow 4\ CO_{2(g)} + 2\ H_2O_{(g)}$$
$$\Delta H = -2\,511.0 \text{ kJ}$$

Numerical Response

4. The amount of energy released by the combustion of 100 g of $C_2H_{2(g)}$ is __________ MJ.
(Record your **three-digit** answer.)

Not for Reproduction

Use the following information to answer the next question.

Many insects and small animals have unique defence systems. Bombardier beetles fight off predators with a hot chemical spray. This spray consists of solutions of hydroquinone ($C_6H_4(OH)_{2(aq)}$), hydrogen peroxide ($H_2O_{2(aq)}$), and enzymes, which are secreted by the beetles' glands.

Reaction Equations Related to Spray Formation

I $2\,H_2O_{(l)} + O_{2(g)} \rightarrow 2\,H_2O_{2(aq)}$ $\Delta H = +189.2$ kJ

II $H_2O_{(l)} \rightarrow H_{2(g)} + \frac{1}{2}O_{2(g)}$ $\Delta H = +285.8$ kJ

III $C_6H_4(OH)_{2(aq)} \rightarrow C_6H_4O_{2(aq)} + H_{2(g)}$ $\Delta H = +177.0$ kJ

A chemical reaction that occurs in order to produce the hot chemical spray can be represented by the equation

$C_6H_4(OH)_{2(aq)} + H_2O_{2(aq)} \rightarrow C_6H_4O_{2(aq)} + 2\,H_2O_{(l)}$

hydroquinone quinone

7. The heat of reaction for the production of this hot chemical spray is

A. – 489.2 kJ

B. – 203.4 kJ

C. – 82.4 kJ

D. + 12.2 kJ

Use the following equations to answer the next question.

Energy Reaction Equations

I $C_6H_{12}O_{6(aq)} + 6\,O_{2(g)} \rightarrow 6\,CO_{2(g)} + 6\,H_2O_{(l)}$ + energy

II ${}^1_1H + {}^3_1H \rightarrow {}^4_2He$ + energy

III $6\,CO_{2(g)} + 6\,H_2O_{(l)}$ + energy $\rightarrow C_6H_{12}O_{6(aq)} + 6\,O_{2(g)}$

8. The energy reactions above involve the conversion of energy for metabolic (body) processes. The chronological order of these reactions is

A. I, III, and II

B. III, II, and I

C. II, III, and I

D. II, I, and III

9. The total enthalpy change associated with the conversion of 1.00 Mg of water at 20.0°C into steam at 250.0°C could be calculated by using the formula

A. [1.00 Mg × 4.19 J/(g • °C) × 80.0°C] + [(1.00 Mg/18.02 g/mol) × 40.8 kJ/mol]

B. [1.00 Mg × 2.01 J/(g • °C) × 230.0°C] + [(1.00 Mg/18.02 g/mol) × 40.8 kJ/mol]

C. [1.00 Mg × 4.19 J/(g • °C) × 80.0°C] + [(1.00 Mg/18.02 g/mol) × 40.8 kJ/mol] + [1.00 Mg × 4.19 J/(g • °C) × 150.0°C]

D. [1.00 Mg × 4.19 J/(g • °C) × 80.0°C] + [(1.00 Mg/18.02 g/mol) × 40.8 kJ/mol] + [1.00 Mg × 2.01 J/(g • °C) × 150.0°C]

Copyright Protected

Use the following information to answer the next three questions.

At the Wascana Gas Plant in Balzac, Alberta, environmental and economic concerns have resulted in the development of an efficient process for the removal of sulphur from sour gas, which is a mixture of hydrocarbons and $H_2S_{(g)}$. In the first step of the process, one-third of the $H_2S_{(g)}$ reacts with $O_{2(g)}$ to produce $SO_{2(g)}$. In the second step of the process, the $SO_{2(g)}$ produced reacts with the remaining $H_2S_{(g)}$ to form elemental sulphur and water.

Step I $2\ H_2S_{(g)} + 3\ O_{2(g)} \equiv 2\ H_2O_{(g)} + SO_{2(g)}$

Step II $2\ H_2S_{(g)} + SO_{2(g)} \equiv 2\ H_2O_{(g)} + 3\ S_{(s)}$

Overall equation $H_2S_{(g)} + O_{2(g)} \equiv 2\ H_2O_{(g)} + 2\ S_{(s)}$

To maximize the amount of sulphur removed from the sour gas, the gas plant engineers apply Le Châtelier's Principle.

10. According to the overall equilibrium equation above, the amount of sulphur removed may be increased by

A. adding a catalyst

B. removing water vapour

C. increasing the volume of the system

D. increasing the temperature of the system

11. As $H_2S_{(g)}$ forms $S_{(s)}$, the oxidation number of sulfur

A. changes from 0 to –2 and sulfur is reduced

B. changes from –2 to 0 and sulfur is oxidized

C. decreases by 2 and hydrogen sulfide acts as the reducing agent

D. stays the same because the sulfur is neither oxidized nor reduced

Use the following information to answer the next question.

The sulphur produced in step II is initially produced in liquid form. As it cools, it is converted from a liquid state to a solid state as represented by the equation

$$S_{(l)} \rightarrow S_{(s)}$$

12. In terms of energy, this conversion is

A. endothermic, releases heat, and has a positive ΔH

B. exothermic, releases heat, and has a negative ΔH

C. exothermic, absorbs heat, and has a negative ΔH

D. endothermic, absorbs heat, and has a positive ΔH

Use the following information to answer the next three questions.

At one time, an *aq*ueous solution of formaldehyde called formalin ($CH_2O_{(aq)}$) was used as a disinfectant and as a tissue preservative. Today, formalin is commonly used in the industrial preparation of plastics and resins. Formalin can be produced by reacting methanol with acidified potassium dichromate, as represented by the following **unbalanced** equation.

$$\_CH_3OH_{(l)} + \_Cr_2O_7{}^{2-}{}_{(aq)} + \_H^+{}_{(aq)} \rightarrow \_CH_2O_{(aq)} + \_Cr^{3+}{}_{(aq)} + \_H_2O_{(l)}$$

13. The type of reaction that this equation represents is

A. a Brønsted–Lowry acid–base reaction

B. an oxidation–reduction reaction

C. a formation reaction

D. a combustion reaction

Not for Reproduction

14. When the above equation is balanced, the equation is

A. $CH_3OH_{(l)} + Cr_2O_7{}^{2-}{}_{(aq)} + 14\ H^+{}_{(aq)} \rightarrow CH_2O_{(aq)} + 2\ Cr^{3+}{}_{(aq)} + 7\ H_2O_{(l)}$

B. $3\ CH_3OH_{(l)} + Cr_2O_7{}^{2-}{}_{(aq)} + 14\ H^+{}_{(aq)} \rightarrow 3\ CH_2O_{(aq)} + 2\ Cr^{3+}{}_{(aq)} + 7\ H_2O_{(l)}$

C. $3\ CH_3OH_{(l)} + Cr_2O_7{}^{2-}{}_{(aq)} + 8\ H^+{}_{(aq)} \rightarrow 3\ CH_2O_{(aq)} + 2\ Cr^{3+}{}_{(aq)} + 7\ H_2O_{(l)}$

D. $3\ CH_3OH_{(l)} + Cr_2O_7{}^{2-}{}_{(aq)} + 8\ H^+{}_{(aq)} \rightarrow 3\ CH_2O_{(aq)} + 2\ Cr^{3+}{}_{(aq)} + 8\ H_2O_{(l)}$

*Use your recorded answer for **Multiple Choice 14** to answer **Numerical Response 5.****

Numerical Response

5. When 39.5 kg of methanol is reacted, the mass of formalin produced is ________ kg. (Record your **three-digit** answer.)

15. Iodine solutions, which contain a suspension of $I_{2(s)}$, have a brown colour. Which of the following metals will **not** cause an iodine solution to change colour?

A. $N_{(s)}$

B. $Cu_{(s)}$

C. $Ag_{(s)}$

D. $Mg_{(s)}$

Use the following information to answer the next question.

A sample of $Na_2S_2O_{3(aq)}$ is titrated with acidified $KMnO_{4(aq)}$ to a pink endpoint. One product of this redox reaction is $SO_4{}^{2-}{}_{(aq)}$.

16. A product of the reduction half-reaction is

A. $H^+{}_{(aq)}$

B. $Mn^{2+}{}_{(aq)}$

C. $SO_4{}^{2-}{}_{(aq)}$

D. $S_2O_3{}^{2-}{}_{(aq)}$

Use the following information to answer the next question.

In an experiment, dilute hydrochloric acid was added to a test tube containing several small pieces of zinc metal.

17. Which of the following observations could have been made during this experiment?

A. There was no reaction.

B. A thick white precipitate formed.

C. A colourless gas was produced and the test tube cooled off.

D. colourless gas was produced and the test tube warmed up.

Copyright Protected

Use the following information to answer the next question.

A student used an acidified 6.31×10^{-2} mol/L $KMn04_{(aq)}$ solution to titrate 25.0 mL samples of $Fe^{2+}{}_{(aq)}$ solution of unknown concentration. In the reactions, the $Fe^{2+}{}_{(aq)}$ ion was oxidized to the $Fe^{3+}{}_{(aq)}$ ion. The student completed five trials and summarized the data in a table.

Trial Number	1	2	3	4	5
Final Buret Reading (mL)	17.55	35.65	26.40	42.65	16.85
Initial Buret Reading (mL)	0.30	17.55	10.05	26.40	0.55
Final Colour	purple	purple	pink	pink	Pink

18. According to the student's data, the concentration of $Fe^{2+}{}_{(aq)}$ is

A. 0.206 mol/L **B.** 0.218 mol/L

C. 0.213 mol/L **D.** 0.223 mol/L

19. The half-reaction to which all other half-cell potentials are compared is

A. $Li^{+}{}_{(aq)} + e^{-} \rightarrow Li_{(s)}$

B. $Au^{3+}{}_{(aq)} + 3\,e^{-} \rightarrow Au_{(s)}$

C. $F_{2(g)} + 2\,e^{-} \rightarrow 2\,F^{-}{}_{(aq)}$

D. $2\,H^{+}{}_{(aq)} + 2\,e^{-} \rightarrow H_{2(g)}$

Use the following information to answer the next two questions.

Electronic hobbyists often "etch" circuit boards. In this process, unwanted copper foil is removed from a copper-clad plastic circuit board by immersing the board in a bath of iron(III) chloride solution. The equation for the net reaction is
$Cu_{(s)} + 2\,Fe^{3+}{}_{(aq)} \rightarrow Cu^{2+}{}_{(aq)} + 2\,Fe^{2+}{}_{(aq)}$

20. In the reaction above in which the unwanted copper foil is removed,

A. copper ions are reduced

B. copper atoms are oxidized

C. iron(II) ions act as the oxidizing agent

D. iron(III) ions act as the reducing agent

21. Which of the following statements and corresponding net voltages are correct for this reaction?

A. It is a spontaneous reaction with an $E^{\circ}_{net} = +0.43$ V.

B. It is a spontaneous reaction with an $E^{\circ}_{net} = +1.11$ V.

C. A power supply is required because the $E^{\circ}_{net} = -0.43$ V.

D. A power supply is required because the $E^{\circ}_{net} = -1.11$ V.

Not for Reproduction

Use the following information to answer the next two questions.

Hydrogen–oxygen fuel cells have been used for years in spacecraft and more recently in small-scale power plants to generate electricity. Now, some governments and companies are working together to perfect this type of fuel cell for automobile use, and experiments are currently being conducted with operational prototypes. A diagram of a hydrogen–oxygen fuel cell is shown below.

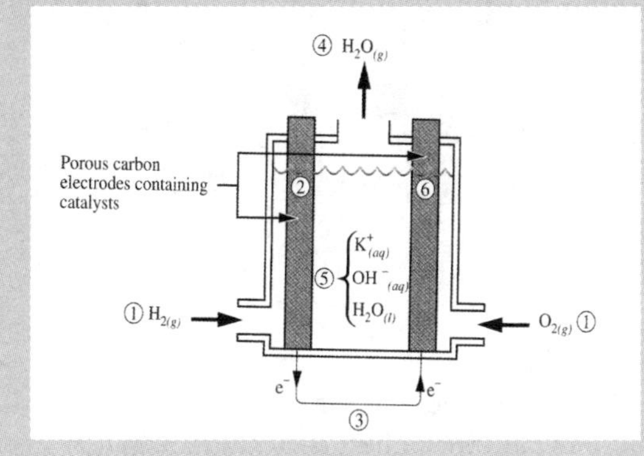

Numerical Response

6. In the diagram above, the anode, the cathode, the electrolyte, and a product of the reaction are labelled, respectively, _____, _____, _____, and _____.

22. From an ecological perspective, a reason why hydrogen–oxygen fuel cells should **not** be used to power automobiles is that

A. hydrogen fuel can be produced through the electrolysis of seawater by using the energy produced from burning fossil fuels

B. cars powered by a hydrogen–oxygen fuel cell would be up to 30% more efficient than cars powered by gasoline

C. water vapour is the primary byproduct of the cell

D. oxygen is readily available from the atmosphere

Use the following information to answer the next two questions.

Copper can be refined (purified) using an apparatus like the one shown below, which is a small-scale version of an industrial apparatus.

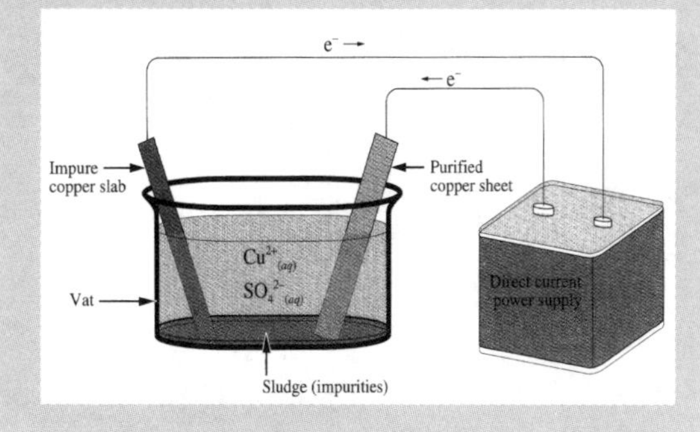

23. In this electrochemical cell, the purified copper sheet acts as the

A. anode and is the site where $SO_4^{2-}{}_{(aq)}$ ions are oxidized

B. cathode and is the site where $SO_4^{2-}{}_{(aq)}$ ions are reduced

C. anode and is the site where $Cu^{2+}_{(aq)}$ ions are oxidized

D. cathode and is the site where $Cu^{2+}_{(aq)}$ ions are reduced

Numerical Response

7. If the direct current power supply produces a steady 3.50 A current, then the time required to deposit 0.100 g of purified copper is __________ s.
(Record your **three-digit** answer.)

Copyright Protected

Use the following information to answer the next three questions.

The silver oxide alkaline cell is a miniature power source used in watches, calculators, hearing aids, and cameras. The construction of this cell is shown in the following diagram.

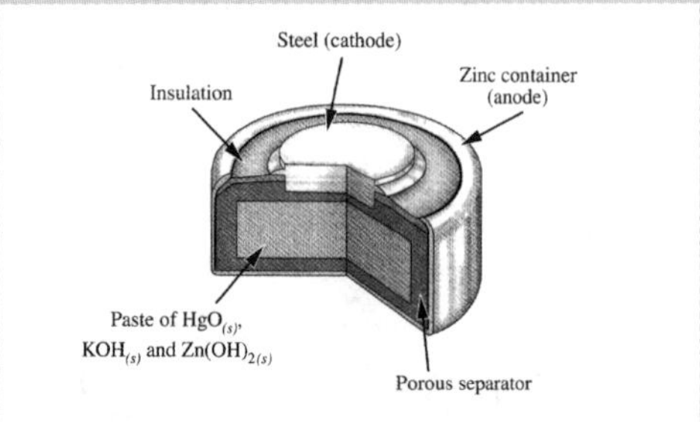

Half-Reactions

$Zn(OH)_{2(s)} + 2\,e^- \rightarrow Zn_{(s)} + 2\,OH^-_{(aq)}$ $\quad E° = -1.25$ V

$Ag_2O_{(s)} + H_2O_{(l)} + 2\,e^- \rightarrow 2\,Ag_{(s)} + 2\,OH^-_{(aq)}$ $\quad E° = +0.34$ V

24. During the discharging of the cell, the substance oxidized is

A. $Zn_{(s)}$

B. $Ag_{(s)}$

C. $H_2O_{(l)}$

D. $Ag_2O_{(s)}$

25. In this cell, the separator must be porous in order to

A. allow migration of ions

B. replenish the electrolyte

C. provide a pathway for electron flow

D. provide a surface on which electron transfer can occur

Numerical Response

8. During discharge, the voltage generated by the cell is +/–__________ V.
(Record your **three-digit** answer.)

Use the following diagram to answer the next question.

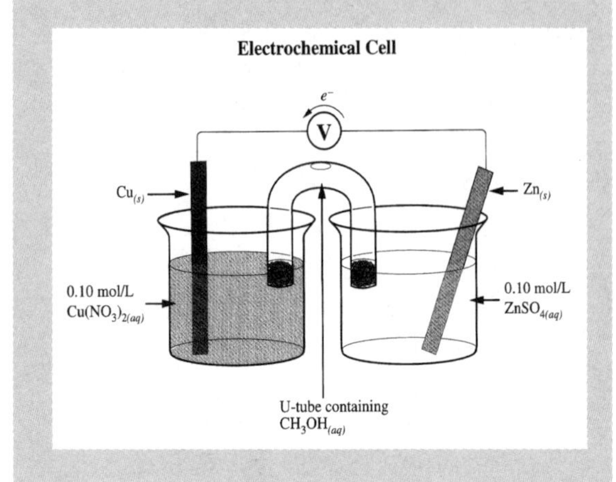

26. The cell in the diagram was constructed and connected by a chemistry student. The voltage of the cell remained at 0.00 V trial after trial. One possible reason for the malfunction of the cell was that the

A. concentrations of the solutions were too low

B. solution in the U-tube was a non-electrolyte

C. redox reaction was non-spontaneous

D. voltmeter was connected backward

Not for Reproduction

Use the following information to answer the next question.

Kawneer, a company in Lethbridge, processes aluminum "logs" for commercial use. The first step in the process involves removing the natural aluminum oxide coating from the logs.

27. Once the protective coating has been removed, the $Al_{(s)}$ surface undergoes a redox reaction with $H_2O_{(l)}$. In this reaction,

A. $H_{2(g)}$ is evolved and the solution becomes basic

B. $O_{2(g)}$ is evolved and the solution becomes basic

C. $H_{2(g)}$ is evolved and the solution becomes acidic

D. $O_{2(g)}$ is evolved and the solution becomes acidic

Use the following information to answer the next question.

In the late 1980s, the Canadian dollar bill was replaced by a coin commonly called the "loonie." The loonie is manufactured from nickel disks that are stamped and then coated with a thin layer of copper (87.5%) and tin (12.5%) to provide the shiny gold-coloured appearance. This layer is applied through an electrolysis process in which the stamped loonie is one of the electrodes and copper metal is the other electrode.

28. If the plating of the loonie occurs in a $Sn^{2+}_{(aq)}$ and $Cu^{2+}_{(aq)}$ solution, then the reaction that occurs at the cathode is

A. $2H_2O_{(l)} + 2e^- \rightarrow H_{2(g)} + 2OH^-_{(aq)}$

B. $2H_2O_{(l)} \rightarrow O_{2(g)} + 4H^+_{(aq)} + 4e^-$

C. $Cu^{2+}_{(aq)} + 2e^- \rightarrow Cu_{(s)}$

D. $Cu_{(s)} \rightarrow Cu^{2+}_{(aq)} + 2e^-$

29. Of the graphs below, the one that best illustrates the relationship between $[H_3O^+_{(aq)}]$ and $[OH^-_{(aq)}]$ in a solution is

A.

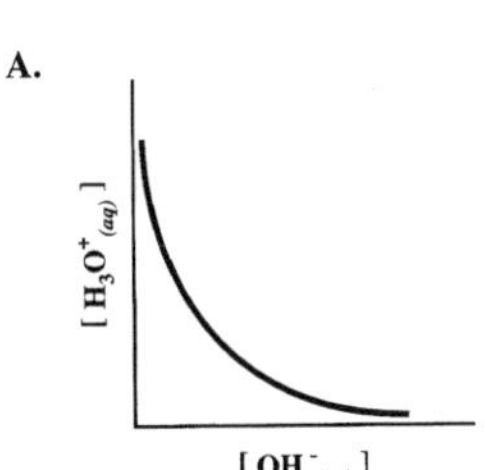

B.

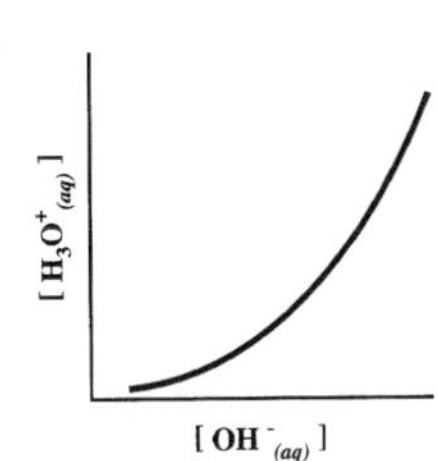

C.

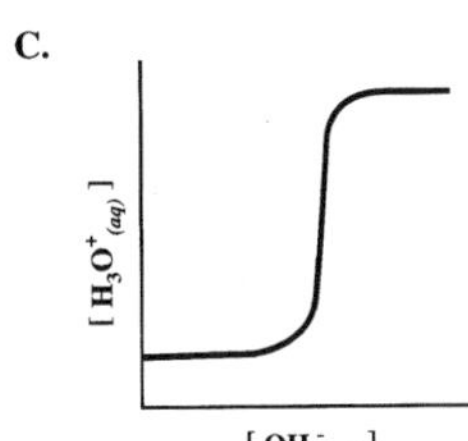

D.

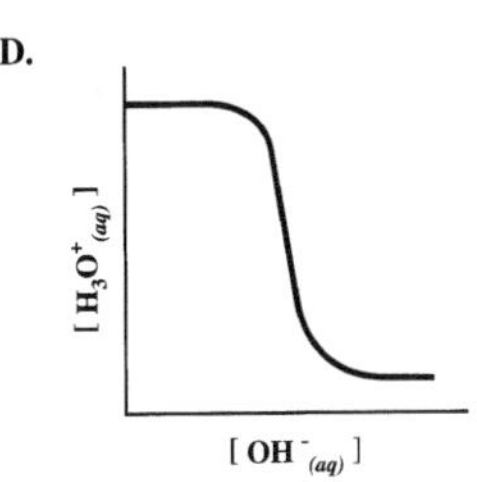

30. If equal moles of acid and base are mixed, then which of the following pairs of species yields a solution with a pH closest to that of pure water at 25°C?

A. $HSO_4^-{}_{(aq)}$ and $OH^-_{(aq)}$

B. $H_2S_{(aq)}$ and $OH^-_{(aq)}$

C. $H_3O^+_{(aq)}$ and $HCO_3^-{}_{(aq)}$

D. $H_3O^+_{(aq)}$ and $OH^-_{(aq)}$

Copyright Protected

Use the following information to answer the next question.

The labels came off four cleaning solution containers found under a kitchen sink. Each of the cleaning solutions was tested with two available indicators, and the following results were recorded.

Cleaning Solution	Bromothymol blue	Phenolphthalein
1	blue	pink
2	blue	colourless
3	green	colourless
4	blue	light pink

Numerical Response

9. Listed in order from lowest to highest pH, the cleaning solutions are, respectively, ______ , ______ , ______ , and ______ .

Use the following information to answer the next four questions.

Prairie Chem Inc. in Edmonton is a bulk manufacturer of concentrated bleach ($NaOCl_{(aq)}$). The bleach reacts with water to form a solution with a pH of 10.87.

$$OCl^-_{(aq)} + H_2O_{(l)} \rightleftharpoons HOCl_{(aq)} + OH^-_{(aq)}$$

31. In this reaction, the substances that act as Brønsted–Lowry acids are

A. $OCl^-_{(aq)}$ and $H_2O_{(l)}$

B. $OCl^-_{(aq)}$ and $HOCl_{(aq)}$

C. $OCl^-_{(aq)}$ and $OH^-_{(aq)}$

D. $H_2O_{(l)}$ and $HOCl_{(aq)}$

32. The substance in the equation above that may act as an amphiprotic species is

A. $OCl^-_{(aq)}$

B. $H_2O_{(l)}$

C. $HOCl_{(aq)}$

D. $OH^-_{(aq)}$

33. The two species in equimolar amounts that could act as a buffer in this bleach solution are

A. $OCl^-_{(aq)}$ and $HOCl_{(aq)}$

B. $HOCl_{(aq)}$ and $OH^-_{(aq)}$

C. $OCl^-_{(aq)}$ and $H_2O_{(l)}$

D. $H_2O_{(l)}$ and $OH^-_{(aq)}$

34. In this bleach solution, the acid–base indicator

A. phenolphthalein would be colourless

B. alizarin yellow R would be orange

C. indigo carmine would be green

D. methyl orange would be red

Use the following information to answer the next question.

A bleach solution can be made by dissolving chlorine gas in a sodium hydroxide solution, as shown by the equation

$$Cl_{2(g)} + 2\ OH^-_{(aq)} \rightleftharpoons ClO^-_{(aq)} + Cl^-_{(aq)} + H_2O_{(l)}$$

35. Mixing a bleach solution with an acid solution can be dangerous because it can cause

A. an increase in pH in the bleach solution

B. a shift in the equilibrium to the products

C. an increase in $Cl_{2(g)}$ concentration in the bleach solution

D. an increase in $Cl^-_{(aq)}$ concentration in the bleach solution

Use the following information to answer the next two questions.

Coal is composed of many organic substances. When coal is mixed with water, acids are formed from the impurities found in the coal. Technicians at Elkview Coal Corporation refer to this mixture of acids as "humic acid."

36. A standard quality-control test involves the titration of monoprotic humic acid with $NaOH_{(aq)}$. If a 10.0 mL sample of a saturated solution of humic acid reacts with 15.9 mL of a 0.100 mol/L $NaOH_{(aq)}$ solution, then the concentration of the acid is

A. 0.0629 mol/L

B. 0.100 mol/L

C. 0.159 mol/L

D. 0.059 mol/L

Use your recorded answer for ***Multiple Choice 36*** *to answer* ***Multiple Choice 37.****

37. If the pH of a specific humic acid sample is 4.50, then the K_a value will be

A. 1.0×10^{-8}

B. 1.6×10^{-8}

C. 1.7×10^{-8}

D. 6.3×10^{-9}

38. Chloroacetic acid ($CH_2ClCOOH_{(aq)}$) has a $K_a = 1.4 \times 10^{-3}$. This acid could best be described as a

A. weak inorganic acid

B. diprotic organic acid

C. weak monoprotic acid

D. strong monoprotic acid

39. In the equation
$HNO_{3(aq)} + N_2H_{4(aq)} \equiv NO_3^-{}_{(aq)} + N_2H_5^+{}_{(aq)}$,
one conjugate acid–base pair is

A. $HNO_{3(aq)}$ and $N_2H_5^+{}_{(aq)}$

B. $HNO_{3(aq)}$ and $N_2H_{4(aq)}$

C. $N_2H_{4(aq)}$ and $N_2H_5^+{}_{(aq)}$

D. $N_2H_{4(aq)}$ and $NO_3^-{}_{(aq)}$

Use the following information to answer the next question.

A 0.500 mol/L solution of hydrazine ($N_2H_{4(aq)}$) contains the following equilibrium concentrations.

$[N_2H_{4(aq)}] = 0.498$ mol/L

$[OH^-{}_{(aq)}] = 2.14 \times 10^{-3}$ mol/L

$[N_2H_5^+{}_{(aq)}] = 2.14 \times 10^{-3}$ mol/L

Numerical Response

10. The K_b for hydrazine, in scientific notation, is $a.bc \times 10^{-d}$. The values of a, b, c, and d are, respectively, _____, _____, _____, and _____.

Copyright Protected

Use the following information to answer the next question.

When equally concentrated solutions of $HNO_{3(aq)}$, $CH_3COOH_{(aq)}$, $HOOCCOOH_{(aq)}$, and $Na_2S_{(aq)}$ were titrated with either a strong acid or strong base, the following titration curves were obtained.

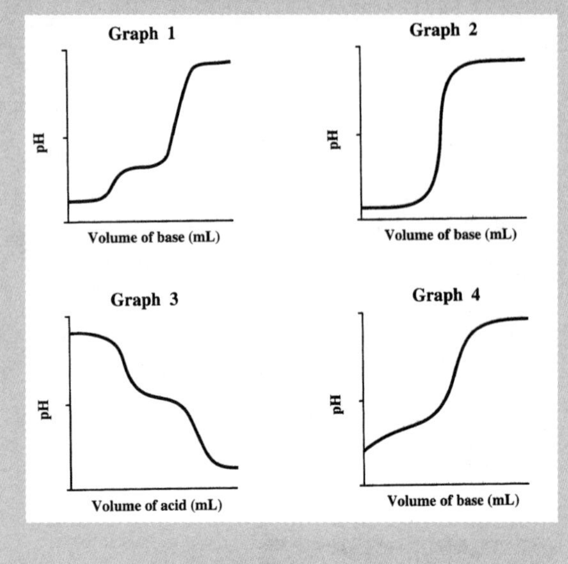

Numerical Response

11. Match each of the graphs, as numbered above, with the corresponding titration species listed below.

$HNO_{3(aq)}$ ______

$CH_3COOH_{(aq)}$ ______

$HOOCCOOH_{(aq)}$ ______

$Na_2S_{(aq)}$ ______

Use the following information to answer the next question.

The burning of methane in a Bunsen burner to produce energy can be represented by the equation

$$CH_{4(g)} + 2\,O_{2(g)} \rightarrow CO_{2(g)} + 2\,H_2O_{(g)}$$

40. A student determined that the reaction represented by the equation above is **not** at equilibrium because

A. the system is open

B. a catalyst is not present

C. the temperature is constant

D. both reactants and products are gases

41. Which of the following chemical changes would have the greatest percentage of products at equilibrium?

A. $AgCl_{(s)} \rightleftharpoons Ag^+_{(aq)} + Cl^-_{(aq)}$ $K_{eq} = 2.0 \times 10^{-10}$

B. $BaCO_{3(s)} \rightleftharpoons Ba^{2+}_{(aq)} + CO_3{}^{2-}_{(aq)}$ $K_{eq} = 5.5 \times 10^{-10}$

C. $HOBr_{(aq)} + H_2O_{(l)} \rightleftharpoons H_3O^+_{(aq)} + OBr^-_{(aq)}$ $K_{eq} = 2.1 \times 10^{-9}$

D. $NH_2OH_{(aq)} + H_2O_{(l)} \rightleftharpoons NH_3OH^+_{(aq)} + OH_{(aq)}$ $K_{eq} = 1.1 \times 10^{-8}$

Not for Reproduction

Use the following information to answer the next question.

The production of paper can involve the reaction of the hydrated aluminum ion $Al(H_2O)_6^{3+}{}_{(aq)}$ with water.

$$Al(H_2O)_6^{3+}{}_{(aq)} + H_2O_{(l)} \rightleftharpoons Al(OH)(H_2O)_5^{2+}{}_{(aq)} + H_3O^+{}_{(aq)}$$

$$K_a = 1.4 \times 10^{-5}$$

42. The acid dissociation expression for this system is

A. $K_a = \dfrac{[Al(OH)(H_2O)_5^{2+}{}_{(aq)}]}{[Al(H_2O)_6^{3+}{}_{(aq)}]}$

B. $K_a = \dfrac{[Al(OH)(H_2O)_5^{2+}{}_{(aq)}][H_3O^+{}_{(aq)}]}{[Al(H_2O)_6^{3+}{}_{(aq)}][H_2O_{(l)}]}$

C. $K_a = \dfrac{[Al(OH)(H_2O)_5^{2+}{}_{(aq)}]}{[Al(H_2O)_6^{3+}{}_{(aq)}][H_2O_{(l)}]}$

D. $K_a = \dfrac{[Al(OH)(H_2O)_5^{2+}{}_{(aq)}][H_3O^+{}_{(aq)}]}{[Al(H_2O)_6^{3+}{}_{(aq)}]}$

*Use your recorded answer for **Multiple Choice 42** to answer **Multiple Choice 43.***

43. The hydronium ion concentration in a 0.585 mol/L $Al(H_2O)_6^{3+}{}_{(aq)}$ solution is

A. 8.2×10^{-6} mol/L

B. 2.4×10^{-5} mol/L

C. 4.9×10^{-3} mol/L

D. 2.9×10^{-3} mol/L

*Use your recorded answer for **Multiple Choice 43** to answer **Numerical Response 12.***

Numerical Response

12. The pH of this aluminum ion solution is _______________.
(Record your **three-digit** answer.)

Use the following information to answer the next question.

Three Important Equilibria in Blood

$HHb^+{}_{(aq)} + O_{2(g)} \rightleftharpoons HbO_{2(aq)} + H^+{}_{(aq)}$
hemoglobin — oxyhemoglobin

$H^+{}_{(aq)} + HCO_3^-{}_{(aq)} \rightleftharpoons H_2CO_{3(aq)}$

$H_2CO_{3(aq)} \rightleftharpoons CO_{2(g)} + H_2O_{(l)}$

44. In blood, the $[H^+{}_{(aq)}]$ could be increased by decreasing the

A. $[CO_{2(g)}]$

B. $[O_{2(g)}]$

C. $[HCO_3^-{}_{(aq)}]$

D. $[H_2CO_{3(aq)}]$

Copyright Protected

Written Response—15%

Use the following information to answer the next question.

Most arenas and curling rinks have artificial ice. Many ice-making plants use ammonia as the refrigerant. The ammonia is circulated in pipes under the ice of the arena or curling rink. For this question, assume that the **only** changes to the ammonia are represented in the equilibrium

$$NH_{3(l)} \rightleftharpoons NH_{3(g)} \qquad \Delta H = +23.3 \text{ kJ}$$

1. **a)** On graph paper, draw and label, as precisely as possible, the graphs that represent the energy changes that occur to the ammonia below the ice surface and to the water on the ice surface as the refrigeration system operates. Assume that the water applied to the ice surface is initially at 20.00°C.

   b) What mass of ammonia must undergo a phase change in order to change 1.00×10^7 g (10.0 kL) of water at 20.00°C to ice at 0.00°C?

Use the following information to answer the next question.

The formation of a pollutant gas, nitrogen monoxide ($NO_{(g)}$), by the reaction of nitrogen with oxygen in a gasoline engine can be affected by changing the combustion temperature within the engine. The equilibrium constant for the production of one mole of $NO_{(g)}$ at 25°C is 1.0×10^{-17}.

2. Explain how an increase in temperature could affect the concentration of the pollutant gas and the equilibrium constant. Your response should also include
   - relevant chemical equation(s) and values from the chemistry data booklet
   - a description of two ways that car manufacturers could reduce the $NO_{(g)}$ emissions in new model vehicles

Not for Reproductio

ANSWERS AND SOLUTIONS
JANUARY 2002 DIPLOMA EXAMINATION

1. B	9. B	NR7. 2.14	28. A	39. D
2. C	10. A	NR8. 3 2 4 1	29. B	40. D
3. A	11. D	NR9. 2 1 1 2	30. B	41. C
NR1. 1.72†	12. B	19. D	31. C	42. C
4. A	13. D	20. C	32. B	NR11. 2.04‡
5. C	14. C	21. A	33. D	43. A
NR2. 3 2 4 1	NR5. 0.16	22. D	34. C	NR12. 3.29
NR3. 2 3 6 6	15. B	23. B	35. C	44. D
6. D	16. B	24. B	36. B	
7. A	17. A	25. D	37. A	
NR4. 41.1	NR6. 1.72 or 1.7	26. B	NR10. 2 1 4 3	
8. A	18. D	27. C	38. B	

Links:

†If MC 3 is
A, then NR 1 is 1.72†
B, then NR 1 is 4.56
C, then NR 1 is 6.30, 6.28
D, then NR 1 is 13.9
For NR 1, 1.72 is always scored as correct regardless of the response to MC3.

‡If MC 42 is
A, then NR 11 is 0.51
B, then NR 11 is 1.02
C, then NR 11 is 2.04‡
D, then NR 11 is 4.07, 4.08
For NR 11, 2.04 is always scored as correct regardless of the response to MC 42.

1. B

During this time interval, no temperature change occurs; therefore, a phase change must be occurring. Phase changes are changes in potential energy.
The energy change is calculated as follows:

$$time = 5 \text{ min} - 2 \text{ min} = 3 \text{ min}$$

$$3 \text{ min} \times 15 \text{ kJ/min} = 45 \text{ kJ}$$

2. C

Evaporation is an endothermic reaction—for example, the molar enthalpy of vapourization of water is +40.8 kJ/mol. Endothermic processes take heat from their surroundings (your skin in this case, making your skin feel cooler).

3. A

This question appears more complex than it really is: we are asked to find only the **energy lost by the water.**

$$E = mc\,\Delta t$$
$$= 0.05631\text{ kg} \times 4.19\frac{\text{kJ}}{\text{kg}\bullet{}^\circ\text{C}} \times (50.3 - 36.5)^\circ\text{C}$$
$$= 3.26\text{ kJ}$$

NR1. 1.72

Heat gained by the C_3H_7OH = the heat lost by the water (3.26 kJ from MC 3)

$$E = m c \Delta t$$

$$3.26 \text{ kJ} = 0.11524 \text{ kg} \times c \times (36.5 - 20.1)\,°\text{C}$$

$$c = 1.72 \text{ kJ/(kg}\bullet°\text{C)} = 1.72 \text{ J/(g}\bullet°\text{C)}$$

4. A

According to the data given, the methanol starts as liquid at 25°C, vapourizes at 65.0°C, and the vapour heats from 65.0°C to 75°C. This corresponds to graph A.

5. C

The methanol is already at its boiling point, so the only energy required is for the phase change.

$$\Delta H = (1\,mol \times -393.5\,kJ/mol + 2\,mol \times -241.8\,kJ/mol) - (1\,mol \times -74.8\,kJ/mol + 0)$$

$$= -802.3\ kJ$$

$$\Delta H = n\text{H}$$

$$= \frac{793 \text{ g}}{32.05 \text{ g/mol}} \times 34.4 \text{ kJ/mol} = 851 \text{ kJ}$$

NR2. 3 2 4 1

We start by determining the energy required for each process:

Reaction 1 ΔH = –241.8 kJ (formation of water vapour)

Reaction 2 $\Delta \text{H} = \sum nH^o_{fp} - \sum nH^o_{fr}$

Reaction 3 nuclear (fusion): much larger energy

Reaction 4 $\Delta \text{H} = \sum nH^o_{fp} - \sum nH^o_{fr}$

$$\Delta\text{H} = (1 \text{ mol} \times -393.5 \text{ kJ/mol} + 2 \text{ mol} \times -241.8 \text{ kJ/mol}) - (1\text{mol} \times -239.0 \text{ kJ/mol} + 0)$$

$$= -638.1 \text{ kJ}$$

Correct order from largest to smallest in magnitude: **3 2 4 1**

NR3. 2 3 6 6

Total energy released by the peanut oil:

$$E = mc\Delta t$$

$$= 0.950 \text{ kg} \times 4.19 \text{ kJ/kg}\bullet°\text{C} \times 4.60\ °\text{C}$$

$$= -18.3 \text{ kJ}$$

The question asks, however, for the kJ/g of peanut oil. 0.500 g of peanut oil are burned. Therefore,

–18.3 kJ/0.500 g = –36.6 kJ/g

Because this is a negative number, record 2 in the first space.

6. D

From the graph, we can see that the temperature still appears to be rising at the top right edge of the graph. Therefore, results should be collected for a longer period of time to more accurately determine the total heat released.

7. A

The energy change for the water is only due to the temperature change. No phase change is involved.

$$E = mc\Delta t$$

$$= 1.00 \text{ kg} \times 4.19 \text{ kJ/(kg}\bullet°\text{C)} \times (14.40 - 11.30)\,°\text{C}$$

$$= 13.0 \text{ kJ}$$

Not for Reproduction

NR4. 41.1

It is necessary to write this equation to solve the question.

The described equation is

$$VCl_{4(l)} \rightarrow VCl_{2(s)} + Cl_{2(g)}$$

Using H_f's from the graph and the formula:

$$\Delta H = \sum nH^o_{fp} - \sum nH^o_{fr}$$

$$\Delta H = 1 \text{ mol} \times -452.0 \text{ kJ/mol} - (1 \text{ mol} \times -569.4 \text{ kJ/mol} + 0)$$

$$= +117.4 \text{ kJ}$$

$$H_{r\ VCl_{4(l)}} = +117.4 \text{ kJ/mol}$$

$$\Delta H = n\,H = 0.350 \text{ mol} \times (+117.4 \text{ kJ/mol})$$

$$= +41.1 \text{ kJ}$$

8. A

Conjugate acids and bases always differ by one proton. When the acid gives away a proton, it becomes a base. This is shown in the acid–base pair in **A**.

9. B

To neutralize an acid, a base is required. The stronger the base, the better the chance of complete neutralization. $CO_3^{2-}{}_{(aq)}$ is the strongest base of the choices given. $NaCl_{(s)}$ (alternative A) is neutral, $NaHSO_{4(aq)}$ (alternative C) is an acid or a very weak base, and $CH_3COOH_{(aq)}$ (alternative D) is an acid. The best choice is **B**.

10. A

Lime's basic nature will buffer the soil against added acid and, therefore, the pH will change less upon exposure to acid rain.

11. D

The question states that carbonic anhydrase catalyzes the reaction. Catalysts do not have any effect on equilibrium concentrations. They affect how quickly a system reaches equilibrium.

12. B

The buffer's pH should remain near constant for a time and then rise rapidly once the acid component of the buffer is completely consumed. The graph that best represents this is shown in **B**.

13. D

A weak acid should have only partial ionization from the un-ionized form, $HA_{(aq)}$. This is illustrated by the solutions in beaker III and beaker IV.

14. C

In this question, it is important for students to consider every answer. $HClO_{4(aq)}$ is definitely a strong acid from its position at the top of the *Relative Strengths of Acids and Bases* chart. The larger the K_a value for an acid, the stronger the acid. $HClO_{3(aq)}$ has a K_a that is larger than that of $HNO_{3(aq)}$, which is a strong acid. Therefore, $HClO_{3(aq)}$ is a strong acid even though it doesn't appear on the chart.

NR5. 0.16

$$NaOH(aq) + HCl(aq) \rightarrow H2O(l) + NaCl(aq)$$

n_2	n_1
27.0 mL	18.0 mL
c = ?	0.24 mol/L

$n_1 = c \bullet v = 0.24 \text{ mol/L} \bullet 18.0 \text{ mL} = 4.3 \text{ mmol}$

$n_2 = 4.3 \text{ mmol} \bullet 1/1 = 4.3 \text{ mmol}$

$[NaOH_{(aq)}] = n/v = 4.3 \text{ mmol}/ 27.0 \text{ mL}$
$= 0.16 \text{ mol/L}$

Copyright Protected

15. B

The endpoint can be read from a titration curve by finding the pH corresponding to the middle of a rapidly rising (or rapidly falling) part of the curve. In this titration, the pH at the endpoint is greater than 7, which indicates the titration of a weak acid with a strong base. The starting pH is not a factor since we do not know what the molar concentration of the acid is.

16. B

From the graph, we can see that the middle of the rapidly rising portion of the titration curve corresponds to a pH of 8.5.

17. A

Phenolphthalein changes from colourless to pink between pH = 8.2 and pH = 10.0. We know that the endpoint of the titration is at pH = 8.5 (from MC16), so **A** is the correct answer.

NR6. 1.72

For any acid/conjugate base pair, their acid equilibrium constant, K_a, and base equilibrium constant, K_b, are related by

$$K_a \times K_b = 1.00 \times 10^{-14} \text{ mol}^2/\text{L}^2$$

$$K_b = \frac{1.00 \times 10^{-14} \text{mol}^2/\text{L}^2}{K_a \text{ for } NH^+_{4(aq)}}$$

$$K_b = \frac{1.00 \times 10^{-14} \text{mol}^2/\text{L}^2}{5.8 \times 10^{-10} \text{mol/L}} = 1.7 \times 10^{-5}$$

Enter on answer sheet as **1.7**, leaving first box blank. Note that Alberta Education also accepted **1.72** as the answer on the diploma exam.

18. D

From the data given, K_{eq} grows with temperature. This means that the concentration of products is increasing and that of the reactant is decreasing. This would indicate that the reaction is endothermic:

energy + $PCl_{5(g)}$ $PCl_{3(g)}$ + $Cl_{2(g)}$

By Le Châtelier's Principle, an increase in temperature would shift the equilibrium to the right.

NR7. 2.14

Something unusual about this question is that water is included in K_{eq} since it is in gas phase. Substituting, we get

$$K_{eq} = \frac{[Co_{(g)}]\bullet[H_{2(g)}]^3}{[CH_{4(g)}]\bullet[H_2O_{(g)}]}$$

$$= \frac{(5.45 \text{ mol/L})(2.10 \text{ mol/L})^3}{(2.97 \text{ mol/L})(7.94 \text{ mol/L})}$$

$$= 2.14$$

NR8. 3 2 4 1

Using Le Châtelier's Principle, the following shifts can be predicted for the stresses.

1 addition of heat: shift right

2 addition of neon gas: no effect. Note that even though the addition of neon would raise the total pressure of the system, it would have no effect on the partial pressures of the substances in equilibrium

3 addition of hydrogen: shift left

4 increase pressure by decreasing volume: shift left since there are fewer moles of gases on the left side of the equation.

Therefore, the correct answer is **3 2 4 1**.

Not for Reproduction

NR9. 2 1 1 2

Balancing by the oxidation-state method:

Br's oxidation states:

+3 +5 +4

2H+(aq) +1BrO2-(aq) +1BrO3 →

2BrO2(aq) +1H2O(l)

changes:

1 e^-/Br 1 e^-/Br

1 e^-/BrO_2^- 1 e^-/BrO_3^-

Enter the answer as **2 1 1 2**

Note that this equation balances relatively easily and it might have been possible to balance it by inspection without a great deal of effort.

Balancing the equation by writing half-reaction equations and adding the half-reactions to make the make the balanced equation could also be done, but it requires quite a lot more work.

19. D

In reaction 3, the Br in $BrO_2^-{}_{(aq)}$, which has an oxidation state of +3, goes to +5 in $BrO_3^-{}_{(aq)}$. This is oxidation (loss of electrons). It also goes to +1 in $BrO^-{}_{(aq)}$. This is reduction (gain of electrons).

20. C

pH is a way of communicating $[H^+{}_{(aq)}]$ and can be calculated by the following formula:

$pH = -\log [H^+{}_{(aq)}]$

$= -\log (0.020 \text{ mol/L}) = 1.70$

pOH can also be used for communication, but is more useful for quickly shifting between $H^+{}_{(aq)}$ and $OH^-{}_{(aq)}$ in calculations.

$pOH = 14.000 - 1.70 = 12.30$

21. A

In **reduction** reactions, the oxidation state decreases. The Cl in $Cl_{2(g)}$ has an oxidation state of 0. The Cl in $Cl^-{}_{(aq)}$ has an oxidation state of –1. Therefore, the correct half-reaction starts with $Cl_{2(g)}$ and ends with $Cl^-{}_{(aq)}$. This is shown in **A**.

22. D

Since $Sn^{4+}{}_{(aq)}$ is between $Cu^{2+}{}_{(aq)}$ and $Ni^{2+}{}_{(aq)}$ on the *Standard Electrode Potentials* chart, it will not react spontaneously with $Cu_{(s)}$, but it will react spontaneously with $Ni_{(s)}$, demonstrating that $Ni_{(s)}$ is the stronger reducing agent.

23. B

$H_2S_{(g)} + 3/2\ O_{2(g)} \rightarrow SO_{2(g)} + H_2O_{(g)}$ $\Delta H = -518$ kJ

$SO_{2(g)} + 2\ H_2S_{(g)} \rightarrow 3\ S_{(l)} + 2\ H_2O_{(g)}$ $\Delta H = -93$ kJ

$3\ H_2S_{(g)} + 3/2\ O_{2(g)} \rightarrow 3\ S_{(l)} + 3\ H_2O_{(g)}$ $\Delta H = -611$ kJ

24. B

The S in $H_2S_{(g)}$ has an oxidation state of –2. The S in $S_{(l)}$ has an oxidation state of 0.

The change is 2 electrons. Since the oxidation state is increasing, this is oxidation, which is defined as a loss of electrons.

Copyright Protected

25. D

$H_2O_{(l)}$ is not part of an equilibrium constant (K_{eq} or K_a or K_b, etc) unless the reaction is occurring in a non-aqueous environment. This is not the case here, so water is not included. Alternative A also does not include $H_2O_{(l)}$, but the numerator and denominator are reversed.

26. B

For weak acids like $H_2S_{(aq)}$, it is necessary to find the $[H_3O^+_{(aq)}]$ using K_a since dissociation or ionization is only partially complete.

	$H_2S_{(aq)} + H_2O_{(l)}$	$HS^-_{(aq)}$ +	$H_3O^+_{(aq)}$
Initial	0.050 mol/L	0	0
Change	$-x$	$+x$	$+x$
Equilibrium	$(0.050 - x)$ mol/L	x	x

$$K_a = \frac{[H_3O^+_{(aq)}]\bullet[HS^-_{(aq)}]}{[H_2S_{(aq)}]}$$

$$1.1\times10^{-7}\text{ mol/L} = \frac{x^2}{(0.050 - x)\text{ mol/L}}$$

Since the initial acid concentration is many times greater than 1 000 times K_a, we can approximate:

$$1.1\times10^{-7}\text{ mol/L} = \frac{x^2}{0.050\text{ mol/L}}$$

$$x = [H_3O^+_{(aq)}] = \sqrt{5.5\times10^{-9}\text{ mol}^2/\text{L}^2} = 7.4\times10^{-5}\text{ mol/L}$$

27. C

This is a redox titration calculation.

$$5\ HOOCCOOH_{(aq)} + 2\ MnO_4^-{}_{(aq)} + 6\ H^+_{(aq)} \rightarrow 2\ Mn^{2+}_{(aq)} + 8\ H_2O_{(l)} + 10\ CO_{2(g)}$$

n_2	n_1
15.0 mL	20.0 mL
$c = ?$	0.0015 mol/L

$n_1 = c \bullet v = 0.0015\text{ mol/L} \bullet 20.0\text{ mL}$
$= 0.030$ mmol

$n_2 = 0.030\text{ mol} \times \frac{5}{2} = 7.5 \times 10^{-2}$ mmol

$$[HOOCCOOH_{(aq)}] = \frac{7.5\times10^{-2}\text{ mmol}}{15.0\text{ mL}}$$

$= 5.0 \times 10^{-3}$ mol/L

28. A

The only way conductivity could change would be if ions reacted to form insoluble compounds or if new products dissociated in different ways to produce more ions.

29. B

Both $MnO_4^-{}_{(aq)}$ and $Cr_2O_7^{2-}{}_{(aq)}$ in the presence of acid are strong oxidizing agents. Both undergo colour changes:

purple $MnO_4^-{}_{(aq)}$ to almost colourless $Mn^{2+}_{(aq)}$

orange $Cr_2O_7^{2-}{}_{(aq)}$ to green $Cr^{2+}_{(aq)}$

Not for Reproduction

30. B

Since oxalic acid, $HOOCCOOH_{(aq)}$, has 2 protons to give away, we would expect a titration curve with two sharp rises, presuming both steps are quantitative. This is shown in the graph in **B**.

31. C

Pure elements have an oxidation state of 0. The only pure elements present are nitrogen and oxygen.

32. B

Carbon dioxide is a greenhouse gas, and this is a major environmental problem. Carbon dioxide does contribute to acid rain, but only in a very minor way when compared with oxides of nitrogen and sulfur.

33. D

In the stomach, the half-reactions are:

$Fe_{(s)} \rightarrow Fe^{2+}_{(aq)} + 2\,e^-$

$2\,H^+_{(aq)} + 2\,e^- \rightarrow H_{2(g)}$

The electrons produced by the iron half-reaction are consumed by the acidic $H^+_{(aq)}$.

34. C

The copper must be oxidized to become soluble $Cu^{2+}_{(aq)}$ and be removed from the circuit board. The half-reactions are:

$2 \times (Fe^{3+}_{(aq)} + e^- \rightarrow Fe^{2+}_{(aq)})$

$(Cu_{(s)} \rightarrow Cu^{2+}_{(aq)} + 2\,e^-)$

$2\,Fe^{3+}_{(aq)} + Cu_{(s)} \rightarrow Cu^{2+}_{(aq)} + 2\,Fe^{2+}_{(aq)}$

35. C

Since copper goes from oxidation state 0 to oxidation state +2, it is oxidized. By definition, it is the reducing agent.

36. B

This cell is undergoing electrolysis as stated in the question. Electrolysis is non-spontaneous and the applied electricity is converted into chemical energy in the products.

37. A

The given information can be used to calculate the molar mass of the metal. This will allow its identification.

$$n_{e^-} = \frac{I \times t}{F} = \frac{5.0\text{A} \times 10.0\text{ min} \times 60\text{ s/min}}{9.65 \times 10^4\text{C/mol}}$$

$$= 0.031\text{ mol}$$

$$n_{metal} = 0.031\text{ mol} \times 1/3 = 0.010\text{ mol}$$

$$M = \frac{m}{n} = \frac{1.19\text{ g}}{0.010\text{ mol}} = 1.1 \times 10^2\text{ g/mol}$$

This is the molar mass of indium.

NR10. 2 1 4 3

$Zn_{(s)}$ is the strongest reducing agent (SRA) and is, therefore, the anode because it is oxidized. $Cu_{(s)}$ is the cathode by process of elimination (it actually functions in this situation as an inert cathode). Electrons flow from the anode to the cathode. The lemon juice is the electrolyte.

Enter your answer as **2 1 4 3**.

38. B

The standard electrode potential or standard reduction potential is read directly from the chart of *Standard Electrode Potentials*. The correct answer is **B**; i.e., +0.40 V.

39. D

$Cu_{(s)}$ is a weaker reducing agent than the $Fe_{(s)}$ in the steel of the car body and frame. The iron would be oxidized more easily than the copper. The copper would therefore have no effect on the corrosion of the steel.

40. D

By definition, the anode is the electrode where oxidation occurs. The substance which gets oxidized is the reducing agent, so the student chose zinc for the anode because he or she knows that zinc is a reducing agent.

41. C

$$E^o_{net} = E^o_{r\ cath} - E^o_{r\ anode}$$

$$+1.24\ \text{V} = \text{E}^{\text{o}}_{\text{rcath}} - (-0.76\ \text{V})$$

$$+0.48\ \text{V} = \text{E}^{\text{o}}_{\text{rcath}}$$

42. C

Number of moles of electrons can be related to number of moles of a substance by Faraday's equation with a balanced half-reaction:

$$n_{\text{Zn}} = \frac{\text{m}}{\text{M}} = \frac{200\ \text{g}}{65.38\ \text{g/mol}} = 3.06\ \text{mol}$$

$$Zn_{(s)} \rightarrow Zn^{2+}_{(aq)} + 2\ e^-$$

3.06 mol

$$n_{e^-} = 3.06\ \text{mol} \times \frac{2}{1} = 6.12\ \text{mol}$$

NR11. 2.04

The 6.12 mol of electrons from MC42 is used to calculate moles of element X using a balanced half-reaction.

$$X^{3+} + 3\ e^- \rightarrow X$$

6.12 mol $\qquad n_X$

$$n_X = 6.12\ \text{mol} \times \frac{1}{3} = 2.04\ \text{mol}$$

43. A

It would seem logical that ions in an electrolyte would move slower at lower temperature. Also, this would be expected to have an effect on reaction rate by redox theory. The other answers are all incorrect because:

—atoms do **not** move in the lead plate
—electrolyte concentration is constant
—lead (IV) oxide cannot change concentration since it was never dissolved.

NR12. 3.29

$$2 \times (Ce^{4+}_{(aq)} + e^- \rightarrow Ce^{3+}_{(aq)})$$

$$Sn^{2+}_{(aq)} \rightarrow Sn^{4+}_{(aq)} + 2\ e^-$$

$$2\ Ce^{4+}_{(aq)} + Sn^{2+}_{(aq)} \rightarrow Sn^{4+}_{(aq)} + 2\ Ce^{3+}_{(aq)}$$

$n_1 \qquad n_2$

30.9 mL $\quad$ 25.0 mL

0.532 mol/L $\quad$ c = ?

$$n_1 = c \cdot v = 0.532\ \text{mol/L} \cdot 30.9\ \text{mL}$$

$$= 16.4\ \text{mmol}$$

$$n_2 = 16.4\ \text{mmol} \times \frac{1}{2} = 8.22\ \text{mmol}$$

$$[Sn^{2+}_{(aq)}] = \frac{n}{v} = \frac{8.22\ \text{mmol}}{25.0\ \text{mL}}$$

$$= 0.329\ \text{mol/L} = 3.29 \times 10^{-1}\ \text{mol/L}$$

Not for Reproduction

44. D

$$2\ SOCl_{2(aq)} + 4\ e^- \rightarrow 4\ Cl^-_{(aq)} + S_{(s)} + SO_{2(aq)}$$
$$4 \times (\ Li_{(s)} \rightarrow Li^+_{(aq)} + e^-)$$

$$2\ SOCl_{2(aq)} + 4\ Li_{(s)} \rightarrow 4\ Li^+_{(aq)} + 4\ Cl^-_{(aq)} + S_{(s)} + SO_{2(aq)}$$

$$E^o_{net} = E^o_{r\ cath} - E^o_{r\ anode}$$
$$= +0.36\ V - (-3.04\ V) = +3.40\ V$$

Written Response

1. a) $OCl^-_{(aq)} + H_2O_{(l)} \equiv HOCl_{(aq)} + OH^-_{(aq)}$

or

$Ca(OCl)_{2(s)} + 2H_2O_{(l)} \equiv 2\ HOCl_{(aq)} + 2\ OH^-_{(aq)} + Ca^{2+}_{(aq)}$

or

$Ca(OH)_{2(s)}$

b) Equilibrium systems have no measurable macroscopic changes in system properties (e.g., pH, temperature, concentration, mass, amount of reactants or products, colour, and pressure all remain constant)
and/or

Equilibrium sytems have dynamic microscopic properties, i.e., rate of forward reaction equals rate of reverse reaction
and/or

Equilibrium sytems are closed systems, i.e. no energy or matter can enter or leave the system

c) $HPr_{(aq)} \rightarrow Pr^-_{(aq)}$
Yellow red
6.6 8.0

The solution with the indicator in yellow form indicates that the pH is less than 6.6. The addition of

$Na_2CO3_{(aq)}$, a base, is required to raise pH.

The solution with the indicator in the red form has a pH that is above 8.0. The addition of $HCl_{(aq)}$, an acid, is required to lower the pH.

The solution with the indicator in orange form indicates that the pH may be in the desired range, which is an acceptable result and need not be adjusted.

Copyright Protected

2. **Energy Comparison**

$3\ Al_{(s)} + 3\ NH_4ClO_{4(s)} \rightarrow$

$Al_2O_{3(s)} + AlCl_{3(s)} + 3\ NO_{(g)} + 6\ H_2O_{(g)}$

$\Delta H = [1\ mol(-1675.7\ kJ/mol) + 1\ mol(-705.6\ kJ/mol) + 3\ mol(+90.2\ kJ/mol) + 6\ mol(-241.8\ kJ/mol)] - [3\ mol(-295.3\ kJ/mol)]$

$\Delta H = -2675.6\ kJ$

(Energy released by the solid rocket fuel is 2675.6 kJ)

$$\frac{2675.6\ kJ}{3\ mol(26.98\ g/mol) + 3\ mol(117.50\ g/mol)}$$

$$H_{2(g)} + \frac{1}{2}O_{2(g)} \rightarrow H_2O_{(g)}$$

$\Delta H = -241.8\ kJ$

(Energy released by the hydrogen-oxygen fuel is 241.8 kJ)

Energy released per gram of $Al_{(s)}$ /$NH_4ClO_{4(s)}$ fuel:

= 6.17 kJ/g fuel (or 6.1729 kJ/g)

Energy released per gram of hydrogen-oxygen fuel:

$$\frac{241.8\ kJ}{1\ mol(2.02\ g/mol) + \frac{1}{2}\ mol(32.00\ g/mol)}$$

= 13.4 kJ/g fuel (or 13.42 kJ/g)

Environmental Concerns

The solid rocket fuel:

- produces $NO_{(g)}$, which is an atmospheric pollutant and precursor to acid rain
- produces solid aluminum compounds, which are atmospheric particulates
- produces $NO_{(g)}$, which can deplete the ozone layer
- uses $Al_{(s)}$, the production of which causes environmental damage

The hydrogen-oxygen fuel:

- is more environmentally friendly because it produces $H_2O_{(g)}$
- requires hydrogen produced directly/indirectly from fossil fuels

ANSWERS AND SOLUTIONS
JUNE 2001 DIPLOMA EXAMINATION

1. B	8. C	19. D	28. C	39. C
2. B	9. D	20. B	29. A	NR10. 9 2 0 6
3. A	10. B	21. A	30. D	NR11. 2 4 1 3
NR1. 3 2 1 4	11. B	NR6. 2 6 5 4	NR9. 3241	40. A
NR2. 61.8	12. B	22. A	31. D	41. D
4. C	13. B	23. D	32. B	42. D
5. B	14. C	NR7. 86.8	33. A	43. D**
6. D	NR5. 37.0	24. A	34. B	NR12. 2.54***
NR3. 2.56 or 2.63	15. C	25. A	35. C	44. C
NR4. 4.82	16. B	NR8. 1.59	36. C	
7. B	17. D	26. B	37. D*	
	18. A	27. A	38. C	

* If MC36 is

A, then MC37 is B
B, then MC37 is A
C, then MC37 is D*
D, then MC37 is C

** If MC42 is

A, then MC43 is A
B, then MC43 is D
C, then MC43 is A
D, then MC43 is D

*** If MC43 is

A, then NR12 is 5.09
B, then NR12 is 4.62
C, then NR12 is 2.31
D, then NR12 is 2.54

1. B

Generally speaking, the energy involved per mole of reactant decreases in the following order: nuclear reaction, chemical reaction, phase change, and then kinetic energy/temperature change. Alternatives C and D give chemical processes where the reactant/product atoms are the same but are grouped in different compounds/molecules. Alternative A is a phase change. Clearly, alternative B, where the reactants and products are of different elements, is a nuclear reaction.

Copyright Protected

2. B

Alternatives A, C, and D refer to vibrational, translational, and rotational kinetic energy. These energies change during temperature changes. Bond energy and potential energy describe the same phenomenon. When gases react, the energy change of the reaction is essentially the difference between the potential energy absorbed to break bonds within the reactants (E_{in}) and the potential energy released to make bonds on the products (E_{out}). For an exothermic reaction, $E_{out} > E_{in}$. For an endothermic reaction, $E_{in} > E_{out}$.

3. A

Exothermic reactions release energy to their surroundings, often as heat. Alternatively, we can say that exothermic reactions produce energy (or, energy is a product term in the reaction, as written). Formation reactions convert elements (single symbol/type of atom/molecule) into compounds.

Alternatives C and D are not formation reactions but rather crystallizations. Alternatives A and B are formation reactions but only A has energy as a product.

NR1. 3 2 1 4

Ecological perspectives concern the effects of processes/products/etc. on the environment; in this case, a landfill concern—statement 3. A scientific perspective covers the explanation or reasoning behind a product/process—statement 2. Economic perspectives deal with the cost of a product/process—statement 1. Technological perspectives centre on aspects of the design/use/convenience/reliability of a product/process—statement 4.

NR2. 61.8

The standard molar heats of formation of many common chemical compounds is given on pages 6 and 7 of the Chemistry Data Booklet. The molar heat of formation of $AgI_{(s)}$ is –61.8 kJ/mol. This means that when 1.00 mol of $AgI_{(s)}$ is formed from its elements, 61.8 kJ of potential energy are released.

4. C

Cellular respiration is the means whereby glucose is metabolized within mitochondria to produce $CO_{2(g)}$, $H_2O_{(g)}$, thermal energy, and metabolic energy (used to convert ADP into ATP).

This reaction is best summarized as
$$C_6H_{12}O_{6(aq)} + 6O_{2(g)} \rightarrow 6CO_{2(g)} + 6H_2O_{(g)}$$

The enthalpy change for this process must be given a negative sign because energy is produced by cellular respiration.

An estimate of the enthalpy change for this net reaction is given by:
$$\Delta H^\circ_{net} = \Sigma n H^\circ_{f(products)} - \Sigma n H_{f(reactants)}$$

$$= \left[6\text{ mol} \times \left(-393.5\frac{\text{kJ}}{\text{mol}}\right) + 6\text{ mol} \times \left(-285.8\frac{\text{kJ}}{\text{mol}}\right)\right] - \left[1\text{ mol} \times \left(-1\ 273.1\frac{\text{kJ}}{\text{mol}}\right)\right]$$

$= -2\ 802.7$ kJ.

Thus, one product of cellular respiration is 2 802.7 kJ of potential energy. Clearly, the answer is C. Alterantive D would be suitable for cellular respiration that forms $H_2O_{(g)}$, alternative A is not balanced, and alternative B is endothermic.

Not for Reproduction

5. B

Every time one mole of $H_2O_{(l)}$ is formed under standard conditions, 285.8 kJ of potential energy are released. Some 44.0 kJ less potential energy (241.8 kJ) is released per mole of $H_2O_{(g)}$ formed.

Within the flame of a Bunsen burner, the more likely form of water produced is $H_2O_{(l)}$. Thus, as glucose burns in a Bunsen flame, less potential energy is released. Evidently, the answer is alternative B.

Note: The enthalpy change of a reaction is critically dependent on the states of the products and reactants. Cellular respiration and complete combustion of glucose are similar but not identical.

6. D

A simple thermodynamic calculation gives the molar enthalpy/heat of combustion of ethanal from the experimental data.

$$\begin{aligned} &\text{Therefore, } \Delta E_p(\text{reaction}) &= &\ \Delta E_k(\text{calorimeter}) \\ &\text{and } \quad \Delta H_{\text{reaction}} &= &\ q_{\text{calorimeter}} \\ &\text{so } \quad nH_{\text{reaction}} &= &\ q_{\text{calorimeter}} \\ &\text{then } \quad H_{\text{reaction}} &= &\ \frac{q_{\text{calorimeter}}}{n_{\text{reactant}}} \end{aligned}$$

$$= \frac{44.7\ \text{kJ}}{\left(1.65\ \text{g} \times \frac{\text{mol}}{44.06\ \text{g}}\right)} = 1.19 \times 10^3\ \text{kJ/mol.}$$

Obviously,

$H_{\text{combustion}}\ (CH_3CHO_{(l)}) = -1.19 \times 10^3$ kJ/mol

since ethanal burned to produce energy.

Alternatively, alternative A is endothermic and thus unsuitable, while alternatives B and C are slightly greater in magnitude than phase changes. Alternative D, the correct answer, is the most promising enthalpy change for a chemical reaction.

NR3. 2.56 or 2.63

For a kinetic energy change (only), the energy involved, q, is readily calculated from:

$q = mc\Delta t$

In this case, $q = 5.93$ kJ, $m = 0.1200$ kg, and $\Delta t = (32.5 - 21.0)°\text{C} = 11.5°\text{C}$.

$$\begin{aligned} \text{Thus, } c &= \frac{q}{m\Delta t} \\ &= \frac{5.93\ \text{kJ}}{0.1200\ \text{kg} \times 11.5°\text{C}} \\ &= \frac{4.30\ \text{kg}}{\text{kg}°\text{C}} \text{ or } 430 \frac{\text{J}}{\text{g}°\text{C}} \end{aligned}$$

The percentage difference is given by

% difference =

$$\frac{\text{reference value} - \text{measured value}}{\text{reference value}} \times 100\%$$

$$= \frac{4.19 \frac{\text{J}}{\text{g}°\text{C}} - 4.30 \frac{\text{J}}{\text{g}°\text{C}}}{4.19 \frac{\text{J}}{\text{g}°\text{C}}} \times 100\%$$

$$= 2.56\%$$

Note: The rules of precision dictate that the answer ought to be 2.5%.

Copyright Protected

NR4. 4.82

Two methods will yield the answer to this problem.

(i) $H_C^{\circ}(C_2H_{2(g)}) = \dfrac{-2\ 511.0\ \text{kJ}}{2\ \text{mol}} = -1\ 255.5\dfrac{\text{kJ}}{\text{mol}}$

So,

$\Delta H = nH = 100\text{g} \times \dfrac{\text{mol}}{26.04\text{g}} \times \left(-1\ 255.5\dfrac{\text{kJ}}{\text{mol}}\right)$

$= -4.82 \times 10^3$ kJ or –4.82 MJ

So, 4.82 MJ of potential energy are released.

(ii) Simple proportions may be used.

Since 2 mol of (52.08 g) of ethyne, $C_2H_{2(g)}$, produce 2 511.0 kJ of potential energy, 100 g of ethyne will release $\Delta H = \dfrac{100\ \text{g}}{52.08\ \text{g}} \times 2511.0\ \text{kJ}$

$= 4.82 \times 10^3$ kJ or 4.82 MJ—the same answer.

7. B

The enthalpy change of the hot chemical spray reaction is obtained by combining
(i) one–half reversed reaction I,
(ii) reaction II reversed, and
(iii) reaction III, unchanged, to give

$H_2O_{2(aq)} \rightarrow H_2O_{(l)} \frac{1}{2}O_{2(g)}$ $\Delta H_{I^-} = -94.6$ kJ

$\frac{1}{2}O_{2(g)} + H_{2(g)} \rightarrow H_2O_{(l)}$ $\Delta H_{II^-} = -285.8$ kJ

$C_6H_4(OH)_{2(aq)} \rightarrow C_6H_4O_{2(aq)} + H_{2(g)}$

$\Delta H_{III} = +177.0$ kJ

Net: $C_6H_4(OH)_{2(aq)} + H_2O_{2(aq)} \rightarrow$
$C_6H_4O_{2(aq)} + 2H_2O_{(l)}$ $\Delta H^{\circ}_{\text{net}}$

$= -203.4$ kJ.

In using Hess's Law in this way, the secret to a solution is to manipulate the given equations to give the **compounds** in the desired reaction in the correct proportions. The elements usually remain in the correct proportions. Always remember that when a reaction is halved, doubled, tripled, etc., the enthalpy change is halved, doubled, tripled, etc. accordingly. If a reaction is reserved/flipped, the enthalpy change associated with it changes sign (from + to – and vice versa).

8. C

The sun (through nuclear fusion—reaction II) drives photosynthesis (production of glucose—reaction III) in plants. This glucose, by various means, is metabolized in mitochondria during cellular respiration (the oxidation of glucose—reaction I). The answer can only be alternative C.

Not for Reproduction

9. D

To answer this problem, a heating curve is needed. The heating curve for converting liquid water at 20.0° C into steam at 250.0° C is as follows:

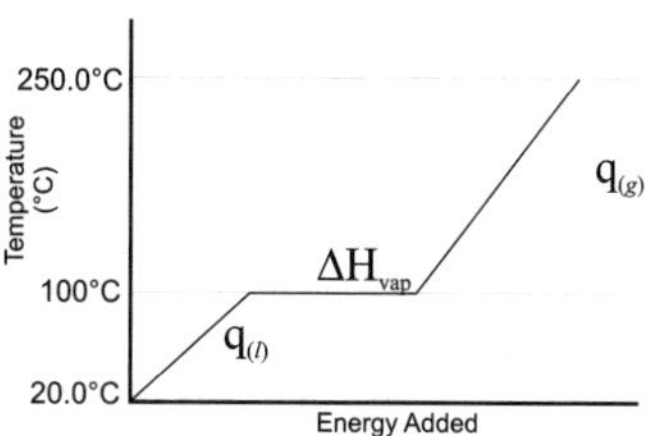

The total energy change, ΔE_{Total}, involved is given by

$$\Delta E_{\text{Total}} = q_{(l)} + \Delta H_{vap} + q_{(g)}$$

$$= \left[1.00\text{ Mg} \times 4.19\frac{\text{J}}{\text{g°C}} \times 80.0\text{°C}\right] + \left[\frac{1.00\text{ Mg}}{18.02\text{g / mol}} \times 40.8\frac{\text{kJ}}{\text{mol}}\right] + \left[1.00\text{ Mg} \times 2.01\frac{\text{J}}{\text{g°C}}\right] \times 150.0\text{° C}$$

Alternatives A and C ignore the different heat capacities of $H_2O_{(l)}$ and $H_2O_{(g)}$. Alternative B neglects the kinetic energy change of the steam.

10. B

Le Châtelier's Principle states that an equilibrium that is stressed in some way readjusts to minimize/counteract the effect(s) of that stress. The presence of a catalyst shortens the time it takes to establish an equilibrium, but it does not affect the equilibrium constant or the equilibrium position. That is, a catalyst will speed up the forward **and** the reverse reactions equally but will not generate more product than is usual at equilibrium. If the volume of an equilibrium is increased, the system's total pressure decreases. Gaseous equilibria counteract this stress by shifting to the side of the reaction with more moles of gas. Steps I and II (and the overall reaction) would be forced to shift left to increase the number of moles of gas and produce less sulfur. The enthalpy change of the overall reaction is – 442.4 kJ (simple calculation). Heating an exothermic equilibrium effects a shift left to absorb the added heat energy and, in this case, we would expect less $S_{(s)}$. When a product (here, $H_2O_{(g)}$) is removed, an equilibrium will shift right to replace that product. In the case of reactions I and II, and the overall reaction, this will lead to increased amounts of sulfur.

11. B

The oxidation number of H, ON_H, in $H_2S_{(g)}$ is +1. Thus, the oxidation number of the ON_s in $H_2S_{(g)}$ is –2. The oxidation number of any atom in its element form is 0 (zero). Clearly, the oxidation number of sulfur changes from –2 to 0, an increase of 2. Or, to put it another way, the sulfur atoms lose $2e^-$ over the course of reaction. The loss of electrons is referred to as oxidation.

Copyright Protected

12. B

When sulfur solidifies, many intermolecular bonds are formed. Since potential energy is **absorbed** to break intermolecular bonds, it must therefore be **released** when intermolecular bonds are **formed**. So, the solidification of sulfur is exothermic; i.e., it releases heat to its surroundings. Exothermic reactions have a negative ΔH value. Only alternative B fits all the requirements.

Alternatives A and C are contradictory, while alternative D applies only to the melting of sulfur, $S_{(s)} \rightarrow S_{(l)}$.

13. B

The reaction shown features no elements or $O_{2(g)}$ as reactants and thus cannot be a formation or combustion reaction. The oxidation numbers of C (in $CH_3OH_{(l)}$) and Cr in ($Cr_2O_7^{2-}$) change over the course of the reaction. The oxidation number of C rises from –2 to 0 ($CH_3OH_{(l)}$ is oxidized) and the oxidation number of Cr decreases from +6 to +3 ($Cr_2O_7{}^{2-}{}_{(aq)}$ is reduced). The answer is B. Brønsted–Lowry acid–base reactions involve the transfer of single protons from the strongest acid to the strongest base in a system. Many more ${}^{+}H_{(aq)}$ are involved in the reaction shown, so alternative A is suggestive, but incorrect.

14. C

The reaction can be balanced using oxidation numbers, as follows.

(i)

$$\overset{-2}{CH_3OH_{(l)}} + \overset{+6}{Cr_2O_7{}^{2-}{}_{(aq)}} + H^+{}_{(aq)} \rightarrow \overset{0}{CH_2O} + \overset{+3}{2Cr^{3+}{}_{(aq)}} + H_2O_{(l)}$$

(the ions of OH have not changed)

(ii)

$$CH_3OH_{(l)} + H^+{}_{(aq)} + Cr_2O_7{}^{2-}{}_{(aq)} \rightarrow CH_2O + Cr^{3+}{}_{(aq)} + H_2O_{(l)}$$

loss $2e^-$/C

gain 3 e^-/Cr

loss $2e^-/CH_3OH_{(l)}$ gain $6e^-/Cr_2O_7{}^{2-}$

(iii)
Clearly, 3 mol of $CH_3OH_{(l)}$ are oxidized per mol of $Cr_2O_7{}^{2-}{}_{(aq)}$ reduced.

$$3CH_3OH_{(l)} + Cr_2O_7{}^{2-}{}_{(aq)} \_\ H^+{}_{(aq)} \rightarrow 3CH_2O_{(l)} + 2Cr^{3+}{}_{(aq)} + \_\ H_2O_{(l)}$$

(iv)
When oxygens are balanced:

$$3CH_3OH_{(l)} + Cr_2O_7{}^{2-}{}_{(aq)} + \text{—}H^+{}_{(aq)} \rightarrow 3CH_2O_{(l)} + 2Cr^{3+}{}_{(aq)} + 7H_2O_{(l)}$$

(v)
When hydrogens are balanced:

$$3CH_3OH_{(l)} + Cr_2O_7{}^{2-}{}_{(aq)} + 8H^+{}_{(aq)} \rightarrow 3CH_2O_{(l)} + 2Cr^{3+}{}_{(aq)} + 7H_2O_{(l)}$$

Not for Reproduction

The reaction can also be balanced by making half–reactions (the ion electron method).

(i) $Cr_2O_7{}^{2-}{}_{(aq)} \rightarrow Cr^{3+}{}_{(aq)}$

$CH_3OH_{(l)} \rightarrow CH_2O_{(l)}$

(ii) $Cr_2O_7{}^{2-}{}_{(aq)} \rightarrow 2Cr^{3+}{}_{(aq)} + 7H_2O_{(l)}$

$CH_3OH_{(l)} \rightarrow CH_2O_{(l)}$

(iii)

$Cr_2O_7{}^{2-}{}_{(aq)} + 14H^+{}_{(aq)} \rightarrow 2Cr^{3+}{}_{(aq)} + 7H_2O_{(l)}$

$CH_3OH_{(l)} \rightarrow CH_2O_{(l)}\ 2H^+$

(iv)

$Cr_2O_7{}^{2-}{}_{(aq)} + 14H^+{}_{(aq)} + 6e^- \rightarrow 2Cr^{3+}{}_{(aq)} + 7H_2O_{(l)}$

$CH_3OH_{(l)} \rightarrow CH_2O_{(l)} + 2H^+{}_{(aq)} + 2e^-$

(v)

$Cr_2O_7{}^{2-}{}_{(aq)} + 14H^+{}_{(aq)} + 6e^- \rightarrow 2Cr^{3+}_{(aq)} + 7H_2O_{(l)}$

$3CH_3OH_{(l)} \rightarrow 3CH_2O_{(l)} + 6H^+{}_{(aq)} + 6e^-$

Net: $Cr_2O_7{}^{2-}{}_{(aq)} + 3CH_3OH_{(l)} + 8H^+{}_{(aq)} \rightarrow 3CH_2O_{(l)} + 2Cr^{3+}{}_{(aq)} + 7H_2O_{(l)}$

No matter how the equation is balanced, only alternative C is correct.

NR5. 37.0

This is a most forgiving question. No matter which of the equations in MC 14 is used in a stoichiometric calculation to determine the mass of methanal/ formalin, the answer will be the same (assuming the correct stoichiometric method).

For the equation in alternative A of MC 14:

$$n_{CH_3OH} = 39.5\ \text{kg} \times \frac{\text{mol}}{32.05\ \text{g}} = 1.23\ \text{kmol}$$

$$n_{CH_2O} = \frac{1}{1} n_{CH_3OH} = \frac{1}{1} \times 1.23\ \text{kmol} = 1.23\ \text{kmol}$$

$$m_{CH_2O} = 1.23\ \text{kmol} \times \frac{30.03\,\text{g}}{\text{mol}} = 37.0\ \text{kg}$$

Some 37.0 kg of $CH_2O_{(l)}$ are expected. For the equations in alternatives B, C, and D of MC 14:

$$n_{CH_3OH} = 39.5\ \text{kg}\ \frac{\text{mol}}{32.05\,\text{g}} = 1.23\ \text{kmol}$$

$$n_{CH_2O} = \frac{3}{3} n_{CH_3OH} = \frac{3}{3} \times 1.23\ \text{kmol} = 1.23\ \text{kmol}$$

$$m_{CH_2O} = 1.23\ \text{kmol} \times \frac{30.03\,\text{g}}{\text{mol}} = 37.0\ \text{kg}$$

The same answer.

Copyright Protected

15. C

What this question asks is which of $Ni_{(s)}$, $Cu_{(s)}$, $Ag_{(s)}$ or $Mg_{(s)}$ will not react spontaneously with $I_{2(s)}$ ($E°_R = +0.54V$). A non-spontaneous reaction occurs when the $E°_{net}$ of the reduction–oxidation process is negative. More simply, a reduction–oxidation will be non-spontaneous if the strongest oxidizing agent in the reaction lies below the strongest reducing agent in a reduction half-reaction/electrode potential table. $Ni_{(s)}$, $Cu_{(s)}$, and $Mg_{(s)}$ are reducing agents that lie below the position of $I_{2(s)}$ (the oxidizing agent) in the table at the back of the Key. The answer is C.

16. B

In the reaction described, the oxidation number of the sulfur increases from +2 (in $S_2O_3^{2-}$) to +6 (in SO_4^{2-}). In other words, the sulfur is oxidized and the oxidizing agent is the acidified permanganate ion. In a redox reaction, it is the oxidizing agent that is **reduced**. The reduction half-reaction of acidified permanganate is:

$$MnO_4{}^-{}_{(aq)} + 8H^+{}_{(aq)} + 5e^- \rightarrow Mn^{2+}{}_{(aq)} + 4H_2O_{(l)}$$

17. D

The diagnostic test for acids is that they react with active metals like $Mg_{(s)}$ or $Zn_{(s)}$ to produce $H_{2(g)}$.

Of the entities in the reaction:

$Zn_{(s)}$, $H^+{}_{(aq)}$, $Cl^-{}_{(aq)}$, and $H_2O_{(l)}$, $Zn_{(s)}$ is the strongest reducing agent and $H^+{}_{(aq)}$ is the strongest oxidizing agent. Moreover, $H^+{}_{(aq)}$ lies above $Zn_{(s)}$ in the reduction half–reaction table (in data pages), so a spontaneous reaction is expected, namely:

$$2H^+{}_{(aq)} + Zn_{(s)} \rightarrow H_{2(g)} + Zn^{2+}{}_{(aq)}$$

Alternative A is clearly wrong, while alternative B is unlikely because $ZnCl_{2(aq)}$ is a high solubility salt (see data pages).

By analogy, given the similar reaction of $Mg_{(s)}$ with $HCl_{(aq)}$, which is exothermic, the reaction of $Zn_{(s)}$ with $HCl_{(aq)}$ is likely exothermic too. The enthalpy change of the reaction cannot be estimated using the table of standard molar heats of formation.

(A recent CRC handbook of Chemistry and Physics estimates that the reaction enthalpy is –154.1 kJ).

Not for Reproduction

18. A

This is obviously a reduction–oxidation reaction/titration analysis because it states: "the $Fe^{2+}_{(aq)}$ ion was oxidized to the $Fe^{3+}_{(aq)}$ ion." Tabulated half–reactions can be combined to give the net redox reaction.

(i)

SoA

OA	OA		OA	OA
$K^{+}_{(aq)}$	$H^{+}_{(aq)}$	$MnO^{-}_{4(aq)}$	$Fe^{2+}_{(aq)}$	$H_2O_{(l)}$
			SRA	RA

Reduction:

$$MnO_4^{-}{}_{(aq)} + 8H^{+}{}_{(aq)} + 5e^{-} \rightarrow Mn^{2+}{}_{(aq)} + 4H_2O_{(l)}$$

Oxidation:

$$5Fe^{2+}{}_{(aq)} \rightarrow 5Fe^{3+}{}_{(aq)} + 5e^{-}$$

Net Reaction:

$$MnO_4^{-}{}_{(aq)} + 8H^{+}{}_{(aq)} + 5Fe^{2+}{}_{(aq)} \rightarrow Mn^{2+}{}_{(aq)} + 5Fe^{3+}{}_{(aq)} + 4H_2O_{(l)}$$

A stoichiometric calculation follows

$$V_{MnO_4^-} = \frac{(16.35 + 16.25 + 16.30)\,\text{mL}}{3}$$

(The volume of titrant is the difference of the initial and final burette readings.)
= 16.30 mL (the average of trials 3 to 5, based on the consecutive volumes).

$$n_{MnO_4^-} = 10.30\text{ mL} \times \frac{0.0631\text{ mol}}{\text{L}} = 1.03\text{ mmol}$$

$$n_{Fe^{2+}} = \frac{5}{1} \times n_{MnO_4^-} = \frac{5}{1} \times 1.03\text{ mmol}$$

$$= 5.14\text{ mmol}$$

$$[Fe^{2+}{}_{(aq)}] = \frac{5.14\,\text{mmoL}}{25.0\,\text{mL}} = 0.206\text{ mol/L}$$

19. D

The standard reference electrode potential, by convention, is the standard hydrogen electrode (SHE: $Pt_{(s)} / H_{2(g)}, H^{+}_{(aq)}$), which is assigned an electrode/reduction potential of 0.00V. This corresponds to the reduction half-reaction illustrated in alternative D.

20. B

In the reaction shown, $Cu_{(s)}$ loses electrons to form Cu^{2+} — the copper atoms are oxidized. Each mole of iron (III) ions gain one mole of e^{-} to form iron (II); the iron (III) ions are reduced. Evidently, the elemental copper acts as a reducing agent while the iron (III) is an oxidizing agent. The $Cu^{2+}_{(aq)}$ and $Fe^{2+}_{(aq)}$ entities are the products of this spontaneous reaction.

21. A

In the reaction, the oxidizing agent, $Fe^{3+}_{(aq)}$, lies above the reducing agent, $Cu_{(s)}$ in the reduction half–reaction/electrode potential table. The half– and net reactions are:

Reduction:

$$2Fe^{3+}{}_{(aq)} + 2e^{-} \rightarrow 2Fe^{2+}{}_{(aq)} \qquad E^{\circ}_{RC} = +0.77\text{V}$$

Oxidation:

$$Cu_{(s)} \rightarrow Cu^{2+}{}_{(aq)} + 2e^{-} \quad E^{\circ}_{RA} = +0.34\text{V}$$

Net Reaction:

$$2Fe^{3+}{}_{(aq)} + Cu_{(s)} \rightarrow 2Fe^{2+}{}_{(aq)} + Cu^{2+}{}_{(aq)}$$

$$E^{\circ}_{net} = +0.43\text{V}$$

$$E^{\circ}_{net} = E^{\circ}_{RC} - E^{\circ}_{RA}$$

The reaction is spontaneous with the E°_{net} shown.

Copyright Protected

NR6. 2 6 5 4

In any cell, electrolytic or voltaic, electrons flow from the anode (the site of oxidation) to the cathode (the site of reduction) in the external circuit. Thus, the anode label is two and the cathode label is six. The electrolyte is commonly between the electrodes, so this is labelled 5. In a hydrogen oxygen fuel cell, the product, coming out of the cell, is water vapour, labelled 4.

(The fuel cell most likely to be used in automobiles is not the kind shown. Rather, the fuel cell being considered has a polymer membrane electrolyte between the electrodes.)

22. A

Alternatives B, C, and D constitute the main factors in favour of hydrogen–oxygen fuel cells; that is, the factors that appear to make them most environmentally/ecologically friendly. Alternative A, on the other hand, is an ecologically unsound reason for using these cells. $CO_{2(g)}$ is a byproduct of fossil–fuel combustion.

23. D

In the electrolytic cell shown, e^- are entering the purified copper sheet (the cathode where reduction of $Cu^{2+}{}_{(aq)}$ occurs to plate $Cu_{(s)}$ on to the electrode).

NR7. 86.8

The half–reaction that forms purified copper is $Cu^{2+}{}_{(aq)} + 2e^- \rightarrow Cu_{(s)}$

$$n_{Cu_{(s)}} = 0.100\text{ g} \times \frac{\text{mol}}{63.55\text{ g}} = 1.57 \times 10^{-3}\text{ mol}$$

$$n_{e^-} = \frac{2}{1} \times n_{Cu} = \frac{2}{1} \times 1.57 \times 10^{-3}\text{ mol}$$
$$= 3.15 \times 10^{-3}\text{ mol}$$

$$t = \frac{n_{e^-}F}{I} = \frac{1.57 \times 10^{-3}\text{ mol} \times 9.65 \times 10^{4}\text{ C/mol}}{3.50\text{ C/s}}$$
$$= 86.8\text{ s}$$

The time required to plate 0.100 g of purified copper is 86.8 s.

24. A

The cathode and anode half–reactions in the silver oxide alkaline cell shown are:

Cathode:

$$Ag_2O_{(s)} + H_2O_{(l)} + 2e^- \rightarrow 2Ag_{(s)} + 2OH^-{}_{(aq)} \quad E^\circ_R = +0.34\text{ V}$$

Anode:

$$Zn_{(s)} + 2OH^-{}_{(aq)} \rightarrow Zn(OH)_{2(s)} + 2e^- \quad E^\circ_R = -1.25\text{ V}$$

Net Cell Reaction:

$$Ag_2O_{(s)} + H_2O_{(l)} + Zn_{(s)} \rightarrow 2Ag_{(s)} + Zn(OH)_{2(s)}$$

The substance oxidized at the anode is the $Zn_{(s)}$.

Not for Reproduction

25. A

The porous separator in most cells serves to prevent contact redox reaction between the anode and cathode half–cells and also to allow ion movement (ion current) to complete the circuit (e^- are the negative charge carriers in the external circuit, while anions are the negative charge carriers in the electrolyte).

NR8. 1.59

The cell shown is voltaic with $E^\circ_{\text{R cathode}} = +0.34$ V and $E^\circ_{\text{R anode}} = -1.25$ V

$$\begin{aligned} E^\circ_{\text{net}} &= E^\circ_{\text{R cathode}} - E^\circ_{\text{R anode}} \\ &= +0.34\text{V} - (-1.25 \text{ V}) = +1.59 \end{aligned}$$

The net cell potential difference is +1.59 V.

26. B

To function normally, the salt bridge in this kind of voltaic cell must be an electrolyte. An electrolyte is a solution/medium capable of allowing the movement of ions through it. Typical electrolytes for salt bridges are inert salt solutions like $KCl_{(aq)}$, $NaCl_{(aq)}$, $NaNO_{3(aq)}$, etc. $CH_3OH_{(aq)}$ is a solution of a molecular compound that does not dissociate to any extent. $CH_3OH_{(aq)}$ is **not** an electrolyte.

27. A

The reaction between fresh $Al_{(s)}$ and $H_2O_{(l)}$ is easily predicted:

		SOA
Species list:	$Al_{(s)}$	$H_2O_{(l)}$
	SRA	RA

Reduction:

$$2\,H_2O_{(l)} + 2e^- \rightarrow H_{2(g)} + 2OH^-_{(aq)}$$

Oxidation:

$$Al_{(s)} \rightarrow Al^{3+}_{(aq)} + 3\,e^-$$

Net Reaction:

$$6H_2O_{(l)} + 2\,Al_{(s)} \rightarrow 3H_{2(g)} + 2\,Al(OH)_{3(s)}$$

This is a spontaneous process ($E^\circ_{\text{net}} = +0.83$ V). Just by looking at the products of the reaction, it should be clear that a gas will be evolved and solution will became basic.

28. C

The plating of loonies is more complex than the question suggests. However, in most cases, the stronger oxidizing agent $Cu^{2+}_{(aq)}$ will most likely be the entity reduced at the cathode according to $Cu^{2+}_{(aq)} + 2e^- \rightarrow Cu_{(s)}$.

The answer is C. Reactions given in B and D are oxidations, so these are unlikely reactions at the cathode, and $H_2O_{(l)}$ (in alternative A) is a much weaker oxidizing agent than $Cu^{2+}_{(aq)}$.

In practice, the potential applied to the loonie plating cell, reduces $S^{2+}_{n(aq)}$ and $Cu^{2+}_{(aq)}$ onto the coin blanks.

29. A

Since $K_w = [H_3O^+_{(aq)}]\ [OH^-_{(aq)}]$, or for graphing purposes $[H_3O^+_{(aq)}] = K_w\left(\frac{1}{OH^-_{(aq)}}\right)$, we have a classic inverse relationship between $[H_3O^+_{(aq)}]$ and $[OH^-_{(aq)}]$ Such relationships always produce hyperbolas—alternative A.

Alternatively, when $[OH^-_{(aq)}]$ is high, $[H_3O^+_{(aq)}]$ is low. When $[OH^-_{(aq)}]$ is low, $[H_3O^+_{(aq)}]$ is high. (Alternatives C and D illustrate graphs that usually have pH on the vertical axis, not $[H_3O^+_{(aq)}]$!)

30. D

When equal moles of acid and base react to produce $H_2O_{(l)}$ as the conjugate or a solution wherein $H_2O_{(l)}$ is the strongest acid and base, then the equivalence point pH will be 7 or very near. The products of alternative A will be $SO_4{}^{2-}{}_{(aq)}$ and $H_2O_{(l)}$ – a weak basic solution.

The products of alternative B will be $HS^-_{(aq)}$ and $H_2O_{(l)}$, yet they will form another basic solution (amphiprotics that lie below $HCO_3^-{}_{(aq)}$ on both sides of the Relative Strengths of Acids and Bases table have pHs above 7 in water). The products of alternative C, $H_2O_{(l)}$ and $H_2CO_{3(aq)}$ will be weakly acidic. The only product of alternative D is $H_2O_{(l)}$.

NR9. 3 2 4 1

In solution 1, bromothymol blue remains blue, and phenolphthalein turns pink; therfore, the pH is above 10.0 (the most basic solution).

In solution 2, bromothymol blue remains blue, and phenolphthalein is colourless; therefore, the pH is $7.6 < pH < 8.2$.

In solution 3, bromothymol blue is green and phenolphthalein is pink; therefore, the pH is $6.0 < pH < 7.6$ (the least basic solution).

In solution 4, bromothymol blue remains blue and phenolophthalein is pink; therefore, the pH is $8.2 < pH < 10.0$.

31. D

Brønsted–Lowry acids are H^+ donators and, as such, must contain at least one H^+ in their formulas. Clearly, $OCl^-_{(aq)}$ cannot be a Brønsted–Lowry acid, so the answer must be D.

32. B

Amphiprotic entities can generally gain H^+ or lose H^+ and act as Brønsted–Lowry bases or acids, respectively. It is often the case that amphiprotic entities can lose or gain H^+ with equal facility. In aqueous solution, it is only those entities resident on both sides of the Relative Strengths of Acids and Bases table that are most capable of being amphiprotic. Of the options available, only $H_2O_{(l)}$ fits the description.

Not for Reproduction

33. A

Buffered solutions do not change pH significantly when small amounts of $H_3O^+_{(aq)}$ or $OH^-_{(aq)}$ are added to them. The best buffer solutions contain weak conjugate acid–base pairs. The only weak conjugate acid–base pair in the choices available is $HOCl_{(aq)}$ and $OCl^-_{(aq)}$.

34. B

Since the pH of the bleach is 10.87, phenolphthalein would be pink, methyl orange would be yellow, indigo carmine would be yellow, and alizarin yellow R would be orange. The answer is B. The entry on the Acid–Base Indicators page of the Chemistry Data Booklet for alizarin yellow R is $HAy_{(aq)}$ 10.1 – 12.0, yellow to red. This is interpreted as:

— Below pH 10.1, alizarin yellow R exists primarily as $HAy^-_{(aq)}$ and this acid form is yellow.
— Above pH 12.0, alizarin yellow R exists primarily as $Ay^-_{(aq)}$, and this base form is red.
— When 10.1 < pH < 12.0, the colours of both the yellow form, $HAy_{(aq)}$, and the red form, $Ay^-_{(aq)}$, mix to lend an orange colour to the solution they are dissolved in.

35. C

The strongest base in the equilibrium, $OH^-_{(aq)}$, will react with added acid (assume $H^+_{(aq)}$) to produce $H_2O_{(l)}$.

Removing the reactant in an equilibrium, according to Le Châtelier's Principle, will cause the equilibrium to shift left to replace the $OH^-_{(aq)}$. At the same time, more $Cl_{2(g)}$ will be produced. Obviously, the answer is C.

Alternatives B and D both concern a shift to the products; i.e., a shift right, not left as expected. If acid is added to a system, a reduction in pH is likely, so alternative A does not work.

36. C

Since humic acid is monoprotic, it is acceptable to give it a shorthand chemical formula such as $Hhum_{(aq)}$ ($HA_{(aq)}$ would also suffice). Now, its neutralization can be written in equation form and a straightforward stoichiometric calculation can be used to gauge its solution concentration as follows:

$$HHum_{(aq)} + NaOH_{(aq)} \rightarrow NaHum_{(aq)} + H_2O_{(l)}$$

10.0 mL   15.9 mL
           0.100 mol/L

$$n_{NaOH} = 15.9\text{ mL} \times 0.100\frac{\text{mol}}{\text{L}} = 1.59\text{ mmol}$$

$$n_{HHum} = \frac{1}{1} \times n_{NaOH} = \frac{1}{1} \times 1.59\text{ mmol} = 1.59\text{ mmol}$$

$$[HHum_{(aq)}] = \frac{1.59\text{ mmol}}{10.0\text{ mL}} = 0.159\text{ mol/L}$$

The humic acid molar concentration is 0.159 mol/L.

Copyright Protected

37. D

For humic acid, we can write

$HHum_{(aq)} + H_2O_{(l)} \circ H_3O^+{}_{(aq)} + Hum^-{}_{(aq)}$

Initially

0.159 mol/L	–	–	–

Change

$-x$	–	$+x$	$+x$

Equilibrium

$0.159 - x$		x	x

therefore

$$K_a = \frac{[H_3O^+{}_{(aq)}][Hum^-{}_{(aq)}]}{[HHum_{(aq)}]}$$

or $$K_a = \frac{x^2}{0.159 - x}$$

but $x = [H_3O^+{}_{(aq)}] = 10^{-pH} = 10^{-4.50}$

Thus $$K_a = \frac{(10^{-4.50})^2}{(0.159 - 10^{-4.50})}$$

This gives a value for K_a of 6.3×10^{-9}. The answer is D. (The same answer results if an approximation is used.)

If MC 36 was A, then MC 37 is B ($K_a = 1.6 \times 10^{-8}$).

If MC 36 was B, then MC 37 is A ($K_a = 1.0 \times 10^{-8}$).

If MC 36 was D, then MC 37 is C ($K_a = 1.7 \times 10^{-8}$).

38. C

Chloroacetic acid is a close relative of acetic/ethanoic acid so we would expect it to dissociate/react in water as follows: $ClCH_2CO_2H_{(aq)} + H_2O_{(l)} \circ ClCH_2CO_2^-{}_{(aq)} + H_3O^+{}_{(aq)}$ The K_a value for this equilibrium (1.4×10^{-3}) indicates that chloroacetic acid is stronger than nitrous acid, weaker than phosphoric acid, and probably comparable to orange IV in strength. Thus, chloroacetic acid is a weak monoprotic acid. It cannot be strong, diprotic, or inorganic.

For those of you who remember some organic chemistry, the structures of acetic and chloroacetic acids are:

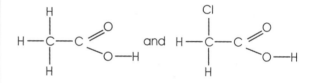

$H_3C{-}C(=O){-}O{-}H$ and $ClH_2C{-}C(=O){-}O{-}H$

In each case, it is the O-bonded H that dissociates (is donated to $H_2O_{(l)}$) in aqueous solution.

39. C

Conjugate acid–base pairs differ only by an H^+ in their respective formulas. The only suitable acid–base pairs in the reaction illustrated are: $HNO_{3(aq)}$, $NO_3^-{}_{(aq)}$ and $N_2H_5^+{}_{(aq)}$, $N_2H_{4(aq)}$. The answer is C. All the other alternatives available differ by more than one H^+ (the acid conjugate always has the extra H^+).

Not for Reproduction

NR 10. 9 2 0 6

We assume that the hydrazine solution is basic because its $[OH^-_{(aq)}]$ is **greater** than 1.0×10^{-7} mol/L by at least four orders of magnitude (a factor of at least 10^4). So, a basic equilibrium is written:

$$N_2H_{4(aq)} + H_2O_{(l)} \circ N_2H_5^+{}_{(aq)} + OH^-{}_{(aq)}$$

therefore $K_b = \dfrac{[N_2H^+_{5(aq)}][OH^-{}_{(aq)}]}{[N_2H_{4(aq)}]}$

Substituting the concentrations provided gives us

$$K_b = \frac{(2.14 \times 10^{-3} \text{ mol / L})(2.14 \times 10^{-3} \text{ mol / L})}{(0.498 \text{ mol/L})}$$

and $K_b = 9.20 \times 10^{-6}$ mol/L

In scientific notation $(a.bc \times 10^{-d})$, a, b, c, and d are 9, 2, 0, and 6.

NR11. 2 4 1 3

The number of equivalence points (steep drops or jumps) in a pH titration curve corresponds to the number of protons quantitatively added to or removed from the sample acid or base.

The pH of an equivalence point is contingent largely on the acidity/basicity of the conjugate produced on neutralization. If a weak acid conjugate is produced on neutralization, the equivalence point pH lies below 7.

If a weak base conjugate is produced, the equivalence point pH lies above 7. If $H_2O_{(l)}$ is the conjugate, the equivalence point pH is 7.

When $HNO_{3(aq)}$ is titrated with a strong base, the Brønsted–Lowry net reaction is $H_3O^+{}_{(aq)} + OH^-{}_{(aq)} \rightarrow 2H_2O_{(l)}$ and the equivalence point pH is 7, there being but one equivalence point. This corresponds to graph 2—of course, the graph will start at low pH and then rise because a base titrant is being added to an acid sample.

When $CH_3COOH_{(aq)}$ is titrated, the Brønsted–Lowry net reaction is

$$CH_3COOH_{(aq)} + OH^-{}_{(aq)} \rightarrow CH_3COO^-{}_{(aq)} + H_2O_{(l)}$$

The graph will start at a "lowish" pH and then rise with one equivalence point. The equivalence point pH ought to be above 7 since the $CH_3COO^-{}_{(aq)}$ produced is a weak base—this is clearly a description of graph 4.

When $HOOCCOOH_{(aq)}$ is titrated, the Brønsted–Lowry net reactions are

i) $HOOCCOOH_{(aq)} + OH^-{}_{(aq)} \rightarrow HOOCCOO^-{}_{(aq)} + H_2O_{(l)}$

ii) $HOOCCOO^-{}_{(aq)} + OH^-{}_{(aq)} \rightarrow OOCCOO^{2-}{}_{(aq)} + H_2O_{(l)}$

The graph of this titration will start at a lowish pH and rise through two equivalence points. The first equivalence point will have a pH below 7 (the conjugate is the acidic amphiprotic, $HOOCCOO^-_{(aq)}$).

The second equivalence point will have a pH above 7 (the conjugate is the weak base $OOCCOO^{2-}_{(aq)}$). This corresponds to graph 1.

By default, the titration curve for $Na_2S_{(aq)}$ (really $S^{2-}_{(aq)}$, a weak base) must be 3. It is the only graph that starts high and then drops. (Note: Amphiprotics tend to form acidic solutions in water if they lie above $HCO_3^-{}_{(aq)}$ in the Relative Strengths of Acids and Bases Table and basic solutions in water if they lie below $HCO_3^-{}_{(aq)}$ in the table. $HCO_3^-{}_{(aq)}$ itself forms basic aqueous solutions.)

40. A

Dynamic equilibrium occurs when, in a closed system, a reversible reaction proceeds constantly in the forward and reverse directions such that the system's macroscopic properties are constant. A closed system cannot exchange matter with its surroundings. Thus, methane combustion in a Bunsen flame is not an equilibrium. (Note: No catalyst is present, the temperature is probably constant, and the state of the reactants and products is irrelevant).

41. D

This question really asks which equilibrium has the highest K value.

$1.1\times10^{-8} > 2.1\times10^{-9} > 5.5\times10^{-10} > 2.0\times10^{-10}$.

The higher the K value, the greater the amount of reactants converted into products. Consequently, the higher K value, for similar equilibria, the greater the percentage reaction at equilibrium.

42. D

For $aA + bB$ ° $cC + dD$

$$K = \frac{[C]^c [D]^d}{[A]^a [B]^b}$$

The terms for pure solids and pure liquids (one liquid only) are omitted from equilibrium constant expressions because the concentrations of these entities are themselves constant. For the acid equilibrium given, the expression is given by alternative D. (This equilibrium illustrates aqueous metal ion hydrolysis.)

43. D

Since for the acid given, the ratio of [acid] to K_a is much greater than 1 000, an approximation may be used to calculate $[H_3O^+{}_{(aq)}]$ as follows.

$$Al(H_2O)_6{}^{3+}{}_{(aq)} + H_2O_{(l)} \text{ ° } Al(OH)(H_2O)_5{}^{2+}{}_{(aq)} + H_3O^+{}_{(aq)}$$

Initially	0.585 mol/L	–	–	–
Change	$-x$	–	$+x$	$+x$
Equilibrium	$0.585 - x$		x	x

$K_a = \frac{x^2}{0.585 - x}$ where $x = [H_3O^+{}_{(aq)}]$

becomes $K_a = \frac{x^2}{0.585}$ since x is rather small/negligible

Thus $x = \sqrt{0.585\text{ mol/L} \times 1.4\times10^{-5}\text{ mol/L}}$

$= 2.9 \times 10^{-3}$ mol/L

(The quadratic solution is only different by about 0.2%).

If MC 42 was A, then MC 43 is A assuming $(-H_3O^+{}_{(aq)}) = [Al(H_2O)_5(OH)^{2+}{}_{(aq)}]$.

If MC 42 was B, then MC 43 is not calculable.*
If MC 42 was C, then MC 43 is not calculable. (assuming $[H_2O_{(l)}]$ Ñ 55.5 mol/L)

Not for Reproduction

NR12. 2.54

The pH of a 0.585 mol/L $Al(H_2O)_6{}^{3+}{}_{(aq)}$ solution must be calculated using an equilibrium calculation (using the quadratic or an approximation method) since $Al(H_2O)_6{}^{3+}{}_{(aq)}$ is a weak Brønsted–Lowry ($K_a = 1.4 \times 10^{-5}$) acid. Here is the calculation:

$$AAl(H_2O)_6{}^{3+}{}_{(aq)} + H_2O_{(l)}$$
$$\circ\ Al(OH)(H_2O)_5^{2+}{}_{(aq)} + H_3O^+{}_{(aq)}$$

Initially	0.585 mol/L	–	–	–
Equilibrium	0.585–x	–	x	x

$$K_a = \frac{x^2}{0.585 - x} \cong \frac{x^2}{0.585} \text{ since}$$

$[Al(H_2O)_6{}^{3+}{}_{(aq)}] > 1000K_a$

Thus, $x = [H_3O^+{}_{(aq)}] = 2.9 \times 10^{-3}$ mol/L

and $pH = -\log(2.9 \times 10^{-3} \text{ mol/L})$

$= 2.54$

The pH is the same whether a quadratic or approximate $[H_3O^+{}_{(aq)}]$ is used. If the rounded off or precise value of $[H_3O^+{}_{(aq)}]$ is used to calculate pH, the answer is unaffected.

For an aqueous solution, $pH = -\log[H_3O^+{}_{(aq)}]$, where $[H_3O^+{}_{(aq)}]$ is in units of mol/L. If MC 43 was D, (correct answer): $pH = -\log(2.9 \times 10^{-3} \text{mol/L}) = 2.54$.

If MC 43 is A, $(8.2 \times 10^{-6}$ mol/L), pH is 5.09.
If MC 43 is B, $(2.4 \times 10^{-5}$ mol/L), pH is 4.62.
If MC 43 is C, $(4.9 \times 10^{-5}$ mol/L), pH is 4.31.

44. C

Le Châtelier's Principle states that if an equilibrium is stressed, it will readjust in whatever way necessary to counteract / minimize the effect of the stress.

Decreased $[CO_{2(g)}]$ would shift the third equilibrium, and by implication the second equilibrium, to the right and decrease, not increase, the $[H^+{}_{(aq)}]$.

Decreasing $[O_{2(g)}]$ would pull the first equilibrium to the left and cause a decrease in $[H^+{}_{(aq)}]$.

Decreased $[H_2CO_{3(aq)}]$ would shift the second equilibrium to the right and lead to decreased $[H^+{}_{(aq)}]$.

A decreased $[HCO_3{}^-{}_{(aq)}]$ would result in less neutralization of $H^+{}_{(aq)}$ as the second equilibrium shifted toward the reactants. Obviously, increased $[H^+{}_{(aq)}]$ would result from this stress.

Copyright Protected

Written Response

1.

(a)

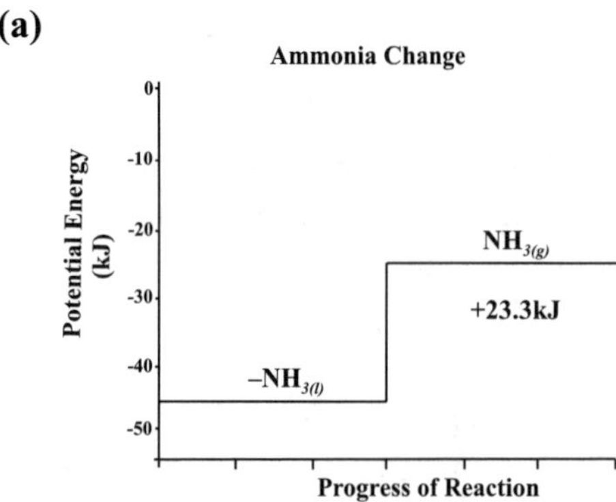

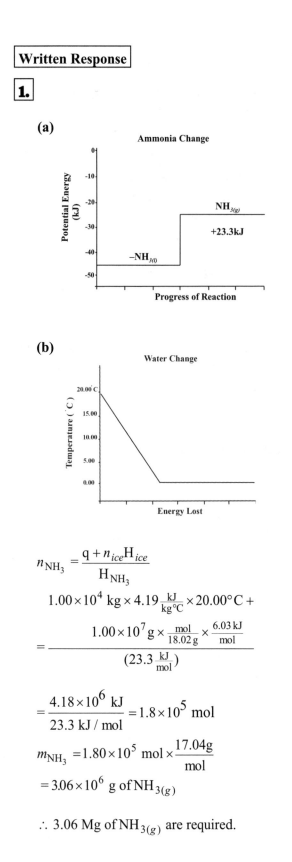

(b)

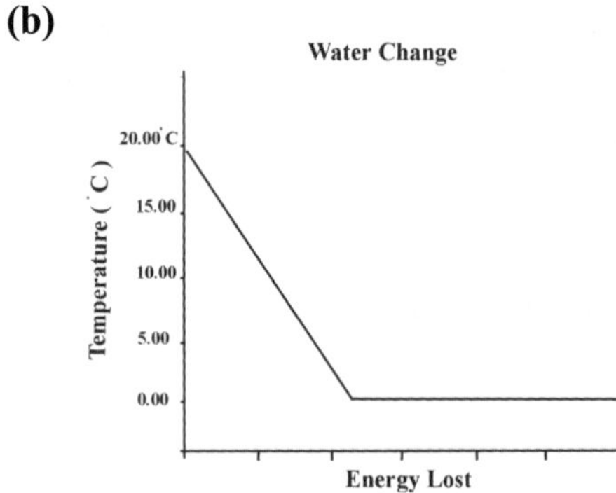

$$n_{NH_3} = \frac{q + n_{ice}H_{ice}}{H_{NH_3}}$$

$$= \frac{1.00\times10^4 \text{ kg}\times 4.19\frac{\text{kJ}}{\text{kg°C}}\times 20.00\text{°C} + 1.00\times10^7 \text{ g}\times\frac{\text{mol}}{18.02\text{ g}}\times\frac{6.03\text{ kJ}}{\text{mol}}}{(23.3\frac{\text{kJ}}{\text{mol}})}$$

$$= \frac{4.18\times10^6 \text{ kJ}}{23.3 \text{ kJ / mol}} = 1.8\times10^5 \text{ mol}$$

$$m_{NH_3} = 1.80\times10^5 \text{ mol}\times\frac{17.04\text{g}}{\text{mol}}$$

$$= 3.06\times10^6 \text{ g of } NH_{3(g)}$$

$\therefore$ 3.06 Mg of $NH_{3(g)}$ are required.

2.

$$N_{2(g)} + O_{2(g)} \circ 2\,NO_{(g)} \quad K = 1.0\times10^{-17}$$

$$\Delta H^\circ_{net} = \left(2\text{ mol}\times(\frac{+90.2\text{ kJ}}{\text{mol}})\right) - (0\text{ kJ})$$

$= +\ 180.4$ kJ

So, $N_{2(g)} + O_{2(g)} + 180.4\text{ kJ} \circ 2\,NO_{(g)}$

Since the equilibrium is endothermic, an increase in temperature will cause a shift toward the products. Thus, more of the pollutant gas $NO_{(g)}$ will be produced.

Since more products are present at the higher temperature (and by implication, fewer reactants) the value of *K* will increase. ($[NO_{(g)}]$)/P_{NO} is a numeration of the *K* expression).

Car manufacturers could design engines that burn at lower temperatures because this will shift the equilibrium to the left and decrease $[NO_{(g)}]$ /P_{NO}

Catalytic converters could be included to encourage the reaction:

$$2\,NO_{(g)} + 2\,CO_{(g)} \rightarrow N_{2(g)} + 2\,CO_{2(g)}$$

to remove $NO_{(g)}$

Data Booklet

z

a

b

x

c

y

Copyright Protected

1	2	3	4	5	6	7	8	9

Table of Common Polyatomic Ions

acetate (ethanoate)	CH_3COO^-	chromate	CrO_4^{2-}	phosphate	PO_4^{3-}
ammonium	NH_4^+	dichromate	$Cr_2O_7^{2-}$	hydrogen phosphate	HPO_4^{2-}
benzoate	$C_6H_5COO^-$	cyanide	CN^-	dihydrogen phosphate	$H_2PO_4^-$
borate	BO_3^{3-}	hydroxide	OH^-	silicate	SiO_3^{2-}
carbide	C_2^{2-}	iodate	IO_3^-	sulfate	SO_4^{2-}
carbonate	CO_3^{2-}	nitrate	NO_3^-	hydrogen sulfate	HSO_4^-
hydrogen carbonate (bicarbonate)	HCO_3^-	nitrite	NO_2^-	sulfite	SO_3^{2-}
		oxalate	$OOCCOO^{2-}$	hydrogen sulfite	HSO_3^-
perchlorate	ClO_4^-	hydrogen oxalate	$HOOCCOO^-$	hydrogen sulfide	HS^-
chlorate	ClO_3^-	permanganate	MnO_4^-	thiocyanate	SCN^-
chlorite	ClO_2^-	peroxide	O_2^{2-}	thiosulfate	$S_2O_3^{2-}$
hypochlorite	ClO^- or OCl^-	persulfide	S_2^{2-}		

1	2	3	4	5	6	7	8	9
1 1.01 1+,1− 2.2 −253 −259 H hydrogen								
3 6.94 1+ 1.0 1342 181 Li lithium	4 9.01 2+ 1.6 2467 1287 Be beryllium							
11 22.99 1+ 0.9 883 98 Na sodium	12 24.31 2+ 1.3 1090 650 Mg magnesium							
19 39.10 1+ 0.8 759 64 K potassium	20 40.08 2+ 1.0 1484 842 Ca calcium	21 44.96 3+ 1.4 2836 1541 Sc scandium	22 47.87 4+, 3+ 1.5 3287 1668 Ti titanium	23 50.94 5+, 4+ 1.6 3407 1910 V vanadium	24 52.00 3+, 2+ 1.7 2671 1907 Cr chromium	25 54.94 2+, 4+ 1.6 2061 1246 Mn manganese	26 55.85 3+, 2+ 1.8 2861 1538 Fe iron	27 58.93 2+, 3+ 1.9 2927 1495 Co cobalt
37 85.47 1+ 0.8 688 39 Rb rubidium	38 87.62 2+ 1.0 1382 777 Sr strontium	39 88.91 3+ 1.2 3345 1522 Y yttrium	40 91.22 4+ 1.3 4409 1855 Zr zirconium	41 92.91 5+, 3+ 1.6 4744 2477 Nb niobium	42 95.94 6+ 2.2 4639 2623 Mo molybdenum	43 (98) 7+ 2.1 4265 2157 Tc technetium	44 101.07 3+, 4+ 2.2 4150 2334 Ru ruthenium	45 102.91 3+ 2.3 3695 1964 Rh rhodium
55 132.91 1+ 0.8 671 29 Cs cesium	56 137.33 2+ 0.9 1897 727 Ba barium	57-71	72 178.49 4+ 1.3 4603 2233 Hf hafnium	73 180.95 5+ 1.5 5458 3017 Ta tantalum	74 183.84 6+ 1.7 5555 3422 W tungsten	75 186.21 7+ 1.9 5596 3186 Re rhenium	76 190.23 4+ 2.2 5012 3033 Os osmium	77 192.22 4+ 2.2 4428 2446 Ir iridium
87 (223) 1+ 0.7 — 27 Fr francium	88 (226) 2+ 0.9 1737 700 Ra radium	89-103	104 (261) Rf rutherfordium	105 (262) Db dubnium	106 (266) Sg seaborgium	107 (264) Bh bohrium	108 (277) Hs hassium	109 (268) Mt meitnerium

57 138.91 3+ 1.1 3464 918 La lanthanum	58 140.12 3+ 1.1 3443 798 Ce cerium	59 140.91 3+ 1.1 3520 931 Pr praseodymium	60 144.24 3+ 1.1 3074 1021 Nd neodymium	61 (145) 3+ — 3000 1042 Pm promethium	62 150.36 3+, 2+ 1.2 1794 1074 Sm samarium
89 (227) 3+ 1.1 3198 1051 Ac actinium	90 232.04 4+ 1.3 4788 1750 Th thorium	91 231.04 5+, 4+ 1.5 — 1572 Pa protactinium	92 238.03 6+, 4+ 1.7 4131 1135 U uranium	93 (237) 5+ 1.3 — 644 Np neptunium	94 (244) 4+, 6+ 1.3 3228 640 Pu plutonium

References

Lide, D.R. 2001. *CRC Handbook of Chemistry and Physics.* 82nd ed. Boca Raton: CRC Press.

Dean, John A. 1999. *Lange's Handbook of Chemistry.* 15th ed. New York: McGraw-Hill, Inc.

IUPAC *commision on atomic weights and isotopic abundances.* 2002. http://www.chem.qmw.ac.uk/iupac/AtWt/index.html.

Not for Reproduction

Legend for Elements

Solid	*Liquid*	Gas
Natural	Synthetic	

Note: The legend denotes the physical state of the elements at exactly 101.325 kPa and 298.15 K.

Key

26 55.85 3+, 2+ 1.8 2861 1538 Fe iron

- Atomic number → 26
- Atomic molar mass (g/mol)* → 55.85
- Common ion charges (most common first) → 3+, 2+
- Electronegativity → 1.8
- Boiling point (°C) → 2861
- Melting point (°C) †(measured at a non-standard pressure) → 1538
- Symbol → Fe
- Name → iron

* Based on $^{12}_{6}C$
( ) Indicates mass of the most stable isotope

10	11	12	13	14	15	16	17	18
								2 4.00 — — –269 –272† He helium
			5 10.81 — 2.0 4000 2075 B boron	6 12.01 — 2.6 — 4489 C carbon	7 14.01 3– 3.0 –196 –210 N nitrogen	8 16.00 2– 3.4 –183 –219 O oxygen	9 19.00 1– 4.0 –188 –220 F fluorine	10 20.18 — — –246 –249 Ne neon
			13 26.98 3+ 1.6 2519 660 Al aluminium	14 28.09 — 1.9 3265 1414 Si silicon	15 30.97 3– 2.2 281 44 P phosphorus	16 32.07 2– 2.6 445 115 S sulfur	17 35.45 1– 3.2 –34 –101 Cl chlorine	18 39.95 — — –186 –189 Ar argon
28 58.69 2+, 3+ 1.9 2913 1455 Ni nickel	29 63.55 2+, 1+ 1.9 2562 1085 Cu copper	30 65.39 2+ 1.7 907 420 Zn zinc	31 69.72 3+ 1.8 2204 30 Ga gallium	32 72.64 4+ 2.0 2833 938 Ge germanium	33 74.92 3– 2.2 — 817 As arsenic	34 78.96 2– 2.6 685 221 Se selenium	35 79.90 1– 3.0 59 –7 *Br* bromine	36 83.80 — — –153 –157† Kr krypton
46 106.42 2+, 4+ 2.2 2963 1555 Pd palladium	47 107.87 1+ 1.9 2162 962 Ag silver	48 112.41 2+ 1.7 767 321 Cd cadmium	49 114.82 3+ 1.8 2072 157 In indium	50 118.71 4+, 2+ 2.0 2602 232 Sn tin	51 121.76 3+, 5+ 2.1 1587 631 Sb antimony	52 127.60 2– 2.1 988 450 Te tellurium	53 126.90 1– 2.7 184 114 I iodine	54 131.29 — 2.6 –108 –112† Xe xenon
78 195.08 4+, 2+ 2.2 3825 1768 Pt platinum	79 196.97 3+, 1+ 2.4 2856 1064 Au gold	80 200.59 2+, 1+ 1.9 357 –39 *Hg* mercury	81 204.38 1+, 3+ 1.8 1473 304 Tl thallium	82 207.21 2+, 4+ 1.8 1749 327 Pb lead	83 208.98 3+, 5+ 1.9 1564 271 Bi bismuth	84 (209) 2+, 4+ 2.0 962 254 Po polonium	85 (210) 1– 2.2 — 302 At astatine	86 (222) — — –62 –71 Rn radon
110 (281) Uun ununnilium	111 (272) Uuu unununium	112 (285) Uub ununbium		114 (289) Uuq ununquadium				

63 151.96 3+, 2+ — 1529 822 Eu europium	64 157.25 3+ 1.2 3273 1313 Gd gadolinium	65 158.93 3+ — 3230 1356 Tb terbium	66 162.50 3+ 1.2 2567 1412 Dy dysprosium	67 164.93 3+ 1.2 2700 1474 Ho holmium	68 167.26 3+ 1.2 2868 1529 Er erbium	69 168.93 3+ 1.3 1950 1545 Tm thulium	70 173.04 3+, 2+ — 1196 819 Yb ytterbium	71 174.97 2+ 1.0 3402 1663 Lu lutetium
95 (243) 3+, 4+ — 2011 1176 Am americium	96 (247) 3+ — 3100 1345 Cm curium	97 (247) 3+, 4+ — — 1050 Bk berkelium	98 (251) 3+ — — 900 Cf californium	99 (252) 3+ — — 860 Es einsteinium	100 (257) 3+ — — 1527 Fm fermium	101 (258) 2+, 3+ — — 827 Md mendelevium	102 (259) 2+, 3+ — — 827 No nobelium	103 (262) 3+ — — 1627 Lr lawrencium

Copyright Protected

Chemistry Notation

Symbol	Term	Unit(s)
c	specific heat capacity	J/(g • °C) or J/(g • K)
C	heat capacity	J/°C or J/K
c	speed of light	m/s
E	electrical potential	V or J/C
E_k	kinetic energy	kJ
E_p	potential energy	kJ
ΔH	enthalpy (heat)	kJ
ΔH_f°	standard molar enthalpy of formation	kJ/mol
I	current	A or C/s
K_{eq}	equilibrium constant	—
K_a	acid ionization (dissociation) constant	—
K_b	base ionization (dissociation) constant	—
M	molar mass	g/mol
m	mass	g
n	amount	mol
P	pressure	kPa
Q	charge	C
T	temperature (absolute)	K
t	temperature (Celsius)	°C
t	time	s
V	volume	L

Symbol	Term
Δ	delta (change in)
°	standard
[ ]	concentration

Not for Reproduction

Miscellaneous

25°C..	equivalent to 298.15 K
Specific heat capacity.................. (at 298.15 K and 100.000 kPa)	c_{air} = 1.01 J/(g • °C) c_{wood} = 1.26 J/(g • °C) c_{glass} = 0.84 J/(g • °C) $c_{Styrofoam}$ = 0.30 J/(g • °C)
Mass of 1.00 mol of dry air..........	$m_{air} = 29.18$ g
Avogadro constant........................	$N_A = 6.02 \times 10^{23}$ particles/mol
Water autoionization constant...... (Dissociation constant)	$K_w = 1.00 \times 10^{-14}$ at 298.15 K (for ion concentrations in mol/L)
Faraday constant...........................	$F = 9.65 \times 10^4$ C/mol
Quadratic formula	$x = \dfrac{-b \pm \sqrt{b^2 - 4ac}}{2a}$
Gas constant	$R = 8.314$ (L • kPa)/(K • mol) or $R = 8.314$ J/(K • mol)
Ideal gas law................................	$PV = nRT$
Commonly accepted standards.....	STP = 273.15 K and 101.325 kPa (1 atm) SATP = 298.15 K and 100.000 kPa

Selected SI Prefixes

Prefix	Exponential Symbol	Value
tera	T	10^{12}
giga	G	10^{9}
mega	M	10^{6}
kilo	k	10^{3}
milli	m	10^{-3}
micro	μ	10^{-6}
nano	n	10^{-9}
pico	p	10^{-12}

Copyright Protected

Thermodynamic Properties of Selected Elements

Name	Formula	ΔH_{fusion}* (kJ/mol)	$\Delta H_{vaporization}$* (kJ/mol)	Specific Heat Capacity† (J/(g • °C))
aluminum	Al	10.79	294	0.897
argon	Ar	1.18	6.43	0.520
beryllium	Be	7.90	297	1.825
boron	B	50.2	480	1.026
bromine	Br_2	10.57	29.96	0.474
carbon (graphite)	C	117	—	0.709
chlorine	Cl_2	6.40	20.41	0.479
chromium	Cr	21.0	339.5	0.449
cobalt	Co	16.06	377	0.421
copper	Cu	12.93	300.4	0.385
fluorine	F_2	0.51	6.62	0.824
gallium	Ga	5.58	254	0.371
germanium	Ge	36.94	334	0.320
gold	Au	12.72	324	0.129
helium	He	0.014	0.08	5.193
hydrogen	H_2	0.12	0.90	14.304
iodine	I_2	15.52	41.57	0.214
iron	Fe	13.81	340	0.449
krypton	Kr	1.64	9.08	0.248
lead	Pb	4.78	179.5	0.129
magnesium	Mg	8.48	128	1.023
manganese	Mn	12.91	221	0.479
mercury	Hg	2.29	59.1	0.140
neon	Ne	0.33	1.71	1.030
nickel	Ni	17.04	377.5	0.444
nitrogen	N_2	0.71	5.57	1.040
oxygen	O_2	0.44	6.82	0.918
phosphorus	P_4	0.66	12.4	0.769
platinum	Pt	22.17	469	0.133
radon	Rn	3.25	18.10	0.094
scandium	Sc	14.1	332.7	0.568
selenium	Se	6.69	95.48	0.321
silicon	Si	50.21	359	0.705
silver	Ag	11.28	258	0.235
sulfur	S_8	1.72	45	0.710
tin	Sn	7.17	296.1	0.228
titanium	Ti	14.15	425	0.523
tungsten	W	52.31	806.7	0.132
uranium	U	9.14	417.1	0.116
vanadium	V	21.5	459	0.489
xenon	Xe	2.27	12.57	0.158
zinc	Zn	7.07	123.6	0.388

* at 101.325 kPa

† for the standard state of the element at 298.15 K

Thermodynamic Properties of Selected Compounds

Name	Formula	ΔH_{fusion}* (kJ/mol)	$\Delta H_{vaporization}$* (kJ/mol)	Specific Heat Capacity† (J/(g•°C))
ice	$H_2O_{(s)}$	6.01	—	2.00
water	$H_2O_{(l)}$	—	40.65	4.19
steam	$H_2O_{(g)}$	—	—	2.02
ammonia	$NH_{3(g)}$	5.66	23.33	2.06
methanol	$CH_3OH_{(l)}$	3.22	35.21	2.53
ethanol	$C_2H_5OH_{(l)}$	4.93	38.56	2.44
dichlorodifluoromethane (Freon-12)	$CCl_2F_{2(g)}$	4.14	20.1	0.60

* at 101.325 kPa

† at 101.325 kPa for the phase stated in the formula column

Calculated Molar Enthalpies of Combustion of Selected Organic Compounds at 298.15 K*

Compound	Formula	ΔH°_c (kJ/mol)
methane	$CH_{4(g)}$	−890.5
ethane	$C_2H_{6(g)}$	−1 560.4
propane	$C_3H_{8(g)}$	−2 219.9
butane	$C_4H_{10(g)}$	−2 877.3
pentane	$C_5H_{12(l)}$	−3 508.8
hexane	$C_6H_{14(l)}$	−4 162.9
heptane	$C_7H_{16(l)}$	−4 816.7
octane	$C_8H_{18(l)}$	−5 470.1
nonane	$C_9H_{20(l)}$	−6 124.8
decane	$C_{10}H_{22(l)}$	−6 777.9
benzoic acid	$C_6H_5COOH_{(s)}$	−3 226.7
methanol	$CH_3OH_{(l)}$	−725.9
ethanol	$C_2H_5OH_{(l)}$	−1 366.8

* products are $H_2O_{(l)}$ and $CO_{2(g)}$

Standard Molar Enthalpies of Formation at 298.15 K

Name	Formula	ΔH_f° (kJ/mol)
aluminum oxide	$Al_2O_{3(s)}$	–1 675.7
ammonia	$NH_{3(g)}$	–45.9
ammonium chloride	$NH_4Cl_{(s)}$	–314.4
ammonium nitrate	$NH_4NO_{3(s)}$	–365.6
barium carbonate	$BaCO_{3(s)}$	–1 213.0
barium chloride	$BaCl_{2(s)}$	–855.0
barium hydroxide	$Ba(OH)_{2(s)}$	–944.7
barium oxide	$BaO_{(s)}$	–548.0
barium sulfate	$BaSO_{4(s)}$	–1 473.2
benzene	$C_6H_{6(l)}$	+49.1
butane	$C_4H_{10(g)}$	–125.7
calcium carbonate	$CaCO_{3(s)}$	–1 207.6
calcium chloride	$CaCl_{2(s)}$	–795.4
calcium hydroxide	$Ca(OH)_{2(s)}$	–985.2
calcium oxide	$CaO_{(s)}$	–634.9
calcium sulfate	$CaSO_{4(s)}$	–1 434.5
carbon dioxide	$CO_{2(g)}$	–393.5
carbon monoxide	$CO_{(g)}$	–110.5
chromium(III) oxide	$Cr_2O_{3(s)}$	–1 139.7
copper(I) oxide	$Cu_2O_{(s)}$	–168.6
copper(II) oxide	$CuO_{(s)}$	–157.3
copper(II) sulfate	$CuSO_{4(s)}$	–771.4
copper(I) sulfide	$Cu_2S_{(s)}$	–79.5
copper(II) sulfide	$CuS_{(s)}$	–53.1
dinitrogen tetroxide	$N_2O_{4(g)}$	+11.1
ethane	$C_2H_{6(g)}$	–84.0
ethanoic acid (acetic acid)	$CH_3COOH_{(l)}$	–484.3
ethanol	$C_2H_5OH_{(l)}$	–277.6
ethene (ethylene)	$C_2H_{4(g)}$	+52.4
ethyne (acetylene)	$C_2H_{2(g)}$	+227.4
glucose	$C_6H_{12}O_{6(s)}$	–1 273.3
hydrogen bromide	$HBr_{(g)}$	–36.3
hydrogen chloride	$HCl_{(g)}$	–92.3
hydrogen fluoride	$HF_{(g)}$	–273.3
hydrogen iodide	$HI_{(g)}$	+26.5
hydrogen perchlorate	$HClO_{4(l)}$	–40.6
hydrogen peroxide	$H_2O_{2(l)}$	–187.8
hydrogen sulfide	$H_2S_{(g)}$	–20.6
iron(II) oxide	$FeO_{(s)}$	–272.0
iron(III) oxide	$Fe_2O_{3(s)}$	–824.2
iron(II,III) oxide (magnetite)	$Fe_3O_{4(s)}$	–1 118.4
lead(II) bromide	$PbBr_{2(s)}$	–278.7
lead(II) chloride	$PbCl_{2(s)}$	–359.4
lead(II) oxide (red)	$PbO_{(s)}$	–219.0
lead(IV) oxide	$PbO_{2(s)}$	–277.4
magnesium carbonate	$MgCO_{3(s)}$	–1 095.8
magnesium chloride	$MgCl_{2(s)}$	–641.3

Standard Molar Enthalpies of Formation at 298.15 K, con't.

Name	Formula	ΔH_f° (kJ/mol)
magnesium hydroxide	$Mg(OH)_{2(s)}$	–924.5
magnesium oxide	$MgO_{(s)}$	–601.6
magnesium sulfate	$MgSO_{4(s)}$	–1 284.9
manganese(II) oxide	$MnO_{(s)}$	–385.2
manganese(IV) oxide	$MnO_{2(s)}$	–520.0
mercury(II) oxide (red)	$HgO_{(s)}$	–90.8
mercury(II) sulfide (red)	$HgS_{(s)}$	–58.2
methanal (formaldehyde)	$CH_2O_{(g)}$	–108.6
methane	$CH_{4(g)}$	–74.6
methanoic acid (formic acid)	$HCOOH_{(l)}$	– 425.0
methanol	$CH_3OH_{(l)}$	–239.2
nickel(II) oxide	$NiO_{(s)}$	–240.6
nitric acid	$HNO_{3(l)}$	–174.1
nitrogen dioxide	$NO_{2(g)}$	+33.2
nitrogen monoxide	$NO_{(g)}$	+91.3
octane	$C_8H_{18(l)}$	–250.1
pentane	$C_5H_{12(l)}$	–173.5
phosphorus pentachloride	$PCl_{5(s)}$	– 443.5
phosphorus trichloride (liquid)	$PCl_{3(l)}$	–319.7
phosphorus trichloride (vapour)	$PCl_{3(g)}$	–287.0
potassium bromide	$KBr_{(s)}$	–393.8
potassium chlorate	$KClO_{3(s)}$	–397.7
potassium chloride	$KCl_{(s)}$	– 436.5
potassium hydroxide	$KOH_{(s)}$	– 424.6
propane	$C_3H_{8(g)}$	–103.8
silicon dioxide (α-quartz)	$SiO_{2(s)}$	–910.7
silver bromide	$AgBr_{(s)}$	–100.4
silver chloride	$AgCl_{(s)}$	–127.0
silver iodide	$AgI_{(s)}$	–61.8
sodium bromide	$NaBr_{(s)}$	–361.1
sodium chloride	$NaCl_{(s)}$	– 411.2
sodium hydroxide	$NaOH_{(s)}$	– 425.6
sodium iodide	$NaI_{(s)}$	–287.8
sucrose	$C_{12}H_{22}O_{11(s)}$	–2 226.1
sulfur dioxide	$SO_{2(g)}$	–296.8
sulfuric acid	$H_2SO_{4(l)}$	–814.0
sulfur trioxide (liquid)	$SO_{3(l)}$	– 441.0
sulfur trioxide (vapour)	$SO_{3(g)}$	–395.7
tin(II) chloride	$SnCl_{2(s)}$	–325.1
tin(IV) chloride	$SnCl_{4(l)}$	–511.3
tin(II) oxide	$SnO_{(s)}$	–280.7
tin(IV) oxide	$SnO_{2(s)}$	–577.6
water (liquid)	$H_2O_{(l)}$	–285.8
water (vapour)	$H_2O_{(g)}$	–241.8
zinc oxide	$ZnO_{(s)}$	–350.5
zinc sulfide (sphalerite)	$ZnS_{(s)}$	–206.0

Solubility of Some Common Ionic Compounds in Water at 298.15 K

Ion	Group 1 NH_4^+ H_3O^+ (H^+)	ClO_3^- NO_3^- ClO_4^-	CH_3COO^-	Cl^- Br^- I^-	SO_4^{2-}	S^{2-}	OH^-	PO_4^{3-} SO_3^{2-} CO_3^{2-}
Solubility greater than or equal to 0.1 mol/L (very soluble)	all	all	most	most	most	Group 1 Group 2 NH_4^+	Group 1 NH_4^+ Sr^{2+} Ba^{2+} Tl^+	Group 1 NH_4^+
Solubility less than 0.1 mol/L (slightly soluble)	none	none	Ag^+ Hg^+	Ag^+ Pb^{2+} Hg^+ Cu^+ Tl^+	Ca^{2+} Sr^{2+} Ba^{2+} Ra^{2+} Pb^{2+} Ag^+	most	most	most

Flame Colours of Elements

Element	Symbol	Colour
lithium	Li	red
sodium	Na	yellow
potassium	K	violet
rubidium	Rb	violet
cesium	Cs	violet
calcium	Ca	red
strontium	Sr	red
barium	Ba	yellow-green
copper	Cu	blue-green
boron	B	green
lead	Pb	blue-white

Table of Selected Standard Electrode Potentials*

Reduction Half-Reaction	Electrical Potential (V) $E°$
$F_{2(g)} + 2e^- \rightleftharpoons 2F^-_{(aq)}$	+2.87
$PbO_{2(s)} + SO_4{}^{2-}{}_{(aq)} + 4H^+_{(aq)} + 2e^- \rightleftharpoons PbSO_{4(s)} + 2H_2O_{(l)}$	+1.69
$MnO_4{}^-{}_{(aq)} + 8H^+_{(aq)} + 5e^- \rightleftharpoons Mn^{2+}_{(aq)} + 4H_2O_{(l)}$	+1.51
$Au^{3+}_{(aq)} + 3e^- \rightleftharpoons Au_{(s)}$	+1.50
$ClO_4{}^-{}_{(aq)} + 8H^+_{(aq)} + 8e^- \rightleftharpoons Cl^-_{(aq)} + 4H_2O_{(l)}$	+1.39
$Cl_{2(g)} + 2e^- \rightleftharpoons 2Cl^-_{(aq)}$	+1.36
$2HNO_{2(aq)} + 4H^+_{(aq)} + 4e^- \rightleftharpoons N_2O_{(g)} + 3H_2O_{(l)}$	+1.30
$Cr_2O_7{}^{2-}{}_{(aq)} + 14H^+_{(aq)} + 6e^- \rightleftharpoons 2Cr^{3+}_{(aq)} + 7H_2O_{(l)}$	+1.23
$O_{2(g)} + 4H^+_{(aq)} + 4e^- \rightleftharpoons 2H_2O_{(l)}$	+1.23
$MnO_{2(s)} + 4H^+_{(aq)} + 2e^- \rightleftharpoons Mn^{2+}_{(aq)} + 2H_2O_{(l)}$	+1.22
$Br_{2(l)} + 2e^- \rightleftharpoons 2Br^-_{(aq)}$	+1.07
$Hg^{2+}_{(aq)} + 2e^- \rightleftharpoons Hg_{(l)}$	+0.85
$OCl^-_{(aq)} + H_2O_{(l)} + 2e^- \rightleftharpoons Cl^-_{(aq)} + 2OH^-_{(aq)}$	+0.84
$2NO_3{}^-{}_{(aq)} + 4H^+_{(aq)} + 2e^- \rightleftharpoons N_2O_{4(g)} + 2H_2O_{(l)}$	+0.80
$Ag^+_{(aq)} + e^- \rightleftharpoons Ag_{(s)}$	+0.80
$Fe^{3+}_{(aq)} + e^- \rightleftharpoons Fe^{2+}_{(aq)}$	+0.77
$O_{2(g)} + 2H^+_{(aq)} + 2e^- \rightleftharpoons H_2O_{2(l)}$	+0.70
$I_{2(s)} + 2e^- \rightleftharpoons 2I^-_{(aq)}$	+0.54
$O_{2(g)} + 2H_2O_{(l)} + 4e^- \rightleftharpoons 4OH^-_{(aq)}$	+0.40
$Cu^{2+}_{(aq)} + 2e^- \rightleftharpoons Cu_{(s)}$	+0.34
$SO_4{}^{2-}{}_{(aq)} + 4H^+_{(aq)} + 2e^- \rightleftharpoons H_2SO_{3(aq)} + H_2O_{(l)}$	+0.17
$Sn^{4+}_{(aq)} + 2e^- \rightleftharpoons Sn^{2+}_{(aq)}$	+0.15
$S_{(s)} + 2H^+_{(aq)} + 2e^- \rightleftharpoons H_2S_{(aq)}$	+0.14
$AgBr_{(s)} + e^- \rightleftharpoons Ag_{(s)} + Br^-_{(aq)}$	+0.07
$2H^+_{(aq)} + 2e^- \rightleftharpoons H_{2(g)}$	0.00
$Pb^{2+}_{(aq)} + 2e^- \rightleftharpoons Pb_{(s)}$	−0.13
$Sn^{2+}_{(aq)} + 2e^- \rightleftharpoons Sn_{(s)}$	−0.14
$AgI_{(s)} + e^- \rightleftharpoons Ag_{(s)} + I^-_{(aq)}$	−0.15
$Ni^{2+}_{(aq)} + 2e^- \rightleftharpoons Ni_{(s)}$	−0.26
$Co^{2+}_{(aq)} + 2e^- \rightleftharpoons Co_{(s)}$	−0.28
$PbSO_{4(s)} + 2e^- \rightleftharpoons Pb_{(s)} + SO_4{}^{2-}{}_{(aq)}$	−0.36
$Se_{(s)} + 2H^+_{(aq)} + 2e^- \rightleftharpoons H_2Se_{(aq)}$	−0.40
$Cd^{2+}_{(aq)} + 2e^- \rightleftharpoons Cd_{(s)}$	−0.40
$Cr^{3+}_{(aq)} + e^- \rightleftharpoons Cr^{2+}_{(aq)}$	−0.41
$Fe^{2+}_{(aq)} + 2e^- \rightleftharpoons Fe_{(s)}$	−0.45
$NO_2{}^-{}_{(aq)} + H_2O_{(l)} + e^- \rightleftharpoons NO_{(g)} + 2OH^-_{(aq)}$	−0.46
$Ag_2S_{(s)} + 2e^- \rightleftharpoons 2Ag_{(s)} + S^{2-}_{(aq)}$	−0.69
$Zn^{2+}_{(aq)} + 2e^- \rightleftharpoons Zn_{(s)}$	−0.76
$2H_2O_{(l)} + 2e^- \rightleftharpoons H_{2(g)} + 2OH^-_{(aq)}$	−0.83
$Cr^{2+}_{(aq)} + 2e^- \rightleftharpoons Cr_{(s)}$	−0.91
$Se_{(s)} + 2e^- \rightleftharpoons Se^{2-}_{(aq)}$	−0.92
$SO_4{}^{2-}{}_{(aq)} + H_2O_{(l)} + 2e^- \rightleftharpoons SO_3{}^{2-}{}_{(aq)} + 2OH^-_{(aq)}$	−0.93
$Al^{3+}_{(aq)} + 3e^- \rightleftharpoons Al_{(s)}$	−1.66
$Mg^{2+}_{(aq)} + 2e^- \rightleftharpoons Mg_{(s)}$	−2.37
$Na^+_{(aq)} + e^- \rightleftharpoons Na_{(s)}$	−2.71
$Ca^{2+}_{(aq)} + 2e^- \rightleftharpoons Ca_{(s)}$	−2.87
$Ba^{2+}_{(aq)} + 2e^- \rightleftharpoons Ba_{(s)}$	−2.91
$K^+_{(aq)} + e^- \rightleftharpoons K_{(s)}$	−2.93
$Li^+_{(aq)} + e^- \rightleftharpoons Li_{(s)}$	−3.04

*For 1.0 mol/L solutions at 298.15 K (25°C) and a pressure of 101.325 kPa

Acid–Base Indicators at 298.15 K

Indicator	Suggested Abbreviation(s)	pH Range	Colour Change As pH Increases	K_a
methyl violet	$HMv_{(aq)}$ / $Mv^-_{(aq)}$	0.0–1.6	yellow to blue	~ 10^{-1}
cresol red	$H_2Cr_{(aq)}$ / $HCr^-_{(aq)}$	0.0–1.0	red to yellow	~ 10^{-1}
	$HCr^-_{(aq)}$ / $Cr^{2-}_{(aq)}$	7.0–8.8	yellow to red	3.5×10^{-9}
thymol blue	$H_2Tb_{(aq)}$ / $HTb^-_{(aq)}$	1.2–2.8	red to yellow	2.2×10^{-2}
	$HTb^-_{(aq)}$ / $Tb^{2-}_{(aq)}$	8.0–9.6	yellow to blue	6.3×10^{-10}
orange IV	$HOr_{(aq)}$ / $Or^-_{(aq)}$	1.4–2.8	red to yellow	~ 10^{-2}
methyl orange	$HMo_{(aq)}$ / $Mo^-_{(aq)}$	3.2–4.4	red to yellow	3.5×10^{-4}
bromocresol green	$HBg_{(aq)}$ / $Bg^-_{(aq)}$	3.8–5.4	yellow to blue	1.3×10^{-5}
methyl red	$HMr_{(aq)}$ / $Mr^-_{(aq)}$	4.8–6.0	red to yellow	1.0×10^{-5}
chlorophenol red	$HCh_{(aq)}$ / $Ch^-_{(aq)}$	5.2–6.8	yellow to red	5.6×10^{-7}
bromothymol blue	$HBb_{(aq)}$ / $Bb^-_{(aq)}$	6.0–7.6	yellow to blue	5.0×10^{-8}
phenol red	$HPr_{(aq)}$ / $Pr^-_{(aq)}$	6.6–8.0	yellow to red	1.0×10^{-8}
phenolphthalein	$HPh_{(aq)}$ / $Ph^-_{(aq)}$	8.2–10.0	colourless to pink	3.2×10^{-10}
thymolphthalein	$HTh_{(aq)}$ / $Th^-_{(aq)}$	9.4–10.6	colourless to blue	1.0×10^{-10}
alizarin yellow R	$HAy_{(aq)}$ / $Ay^-_{(aq)}$	10.1–12.0	yellow to red	6.9×10^{-12}
indigo carmine	$HIc_{(aq)}$ / $Ic^-_{(aq)}$	11.4–13.0	blue to yellow	~ 10^{-12}
1,3,5–trinitrobenzene	$HNb_{(aq)}$ / $Nb^-_{(aq)}$	12.0–14.0	colourless to orange	~ 10^{-13}

Relative Strengths of Acids And Bases at 298.15 K

Acid Name	Acid Formula	Conjugate Base Formula	K_a
perchloric acid	$HClO_{4(aq)}$	$ClO_4^-{}_{(aq)}$	very large
hydroiodic acid	$HI_{(aq)}$	$I^-{}_{(aq)}$	very large
hydrobromic acid	$HBr_{(aq)}$	$Br^-{}_{(aq)}$	very large
hydrochloric acid	$HCl_{(aq)}$	$Cl^-{}_{(aq)}$	very large
sulfuric acid	$H_2SO_{4(aq)}$	$HSO_4^-{}_{(aq)}$	very large
nitric acid	$HNO_{3(aq)}$	$NO_3^-{}_{(aq)}$	very large
hydronium ion	$H_3O^+{}_{(aq)}$	$H_2O_{(l)}$	1
oxalic acid	$HOOCCOOH_{(aq)}$	$HOOCCOO^-{}_{(aq)}$	5.6×10^{-2}
sulfurous acid ($SO_2 + H_2O$)	$H_2SO_{3(aq)}$	$HSO_3^-{}_{(aq)}$	1.4×10^{-2}
hydrogen sulfate ion	$HSO_4^-{}_{(aq)}$	$SO_4^{2-}{}_{(aq)}$	1.0×10^{-2}
phosphoric acid	$H_3PO_{4(aq)}$	$H_2PO_4^-{}_{(aq)}$	6.9×10^{-3}
nitrous acid	$HNO_{2(aq)}$	$NO_2^-{}_{(aq)}$	5.6×10^{-3}
citric acid	$H_3C_6H_5O_{7(aq)}$	$H_2C_6H_5O_7^-{}_{(aq)}$	7.4×10^{-4}
hydrofluoric acid	$HF_{(aq)}$	$F^-{}_{(aq)}$	6.3×10^{-4}
methanoic acid	$HCOOH_{(aq)}$	$HCOO^-{}_{(aq)}$	1.8×10^{-4}
hydrogen oxalate ion	$HOOCCOO^-{}_{(aq)}$	$OOCCOO^{2-}{}_{(aq)}$	1.5×10^{-4}
ascorbic acid	$H_2C_6H_6O_{6(aq)}$	$HC_6H_6O_6^-{}_{(aq)}$	9.1×10^{-5}
benzoic acid	$C_6H_5COOH_{(aq)}$	$C_6H_5COO^-{}_{(aq)}$	6.3×10^{-5}
ethanoic (acetic) acid	$CH_3COOH_{(aq)}$	$CH_3COO^-{}_{(aq)}$	1.8×10^{-5}
dihydrogen citrate ion	$H_2C_6H_5O_7^-{}_{(aq)}$	$HC_6H_5O_7^{2-}{}_{(aq)}$	1.7×10^{-5}
carbonic acid ($CO_2 + H_2O$)	$H_2CO_{3(aq)}$	$HCO_3^-{}_{(aq)}$	4.5×10^{-7}
hydrogen citrate ion	$HC_6H_5O_7^{2-}{}_{(aq)}$	$C_6H_5O_7^{3-}{}_{(aq)}$	4.0×10^{-7}
hydrosulfuric acid	$H_2S_{(aq)}$	$HS^-{}_{(aq)}$	8.9×10^{-8}
hydrogen sulfite ion	$HSO_3^-{}_{(aq)}$	$SO_3^{2-}{}_{(aq)}$	6.3×10^{-8}
dihydrogen phosphate ion	$H_2PO_4^-{}_{(aq)}$	$HPO_4^{2-}{}_{(aq)}$	6.2×10^{-8}
hypochlorous acid	$HOCl_{(aq)}$	$OCl^-{}_{(aq)}$	4.0×10^{-8}
hydrocyanic acid	$HCN_{(aq)}$	$CN^-{}_{(aq)}$	6.2×10^{-10}
ammonium ion	$NH_4^+{}_{(aq)}$	$NH_{3(aq)}$	5.6×10^{-10}
hydrogen carbonate ion	$HCO_3^-{}_{(aq)}$	$CO_3^{2-}{}_{(aq)}$	4.7×10^{-11}
hydrogen ascorbate ion	$HC_6H_6O_6^-{}_{(aq)}$	$C_6H_6O_6^{2-}{}_{(aq)}$	2.0×10^{-12}
hydrogen phosphate ion	$HPO_4^{2-}{}_{(aq)}$	$PO_4^{3-}{}_{(aq)}$	4.8×10^{-13}
water (55.5 mol/L)	$H_2O_{(l)}$	$OH^-{}_{(aq)}$	1.0×10^{-14}

Note: An approximation may be used when the concentration of the acid is 1000 times greater than the K_a.

Colours of Common Aqueous Ions

Ionic Species	Solution Concentration	
	1.0 mol/L	0.010 mol/L
chromate	yellow	pale yellow
chromium(III)	blue-green	green
chromium(II)	dark blue	pale blue
cobalt(II)	red	pink
copper(I)	blue-green	pale blue-green
copper(II)	blue	pale blue
dichromate	orange	pale orange
iron(II)	lime green	colourless
iron(III)	orange-yellow	pale yellow
manganese(II)	pale pink	colourless
nickel(II)	blue-green	pale blue-green
permanganate	deep purple	purple-pink

Not for Reproduction

MATHEMATICS AND SCIENCE DIRECTING WORDS

Discuss	The word "discuss" **will not** be used as a directing word on math and science diploma examinations because it is not used consistently to mean a single activity.
	The following words are specific in meaning.
Algebraically	Using mathematical procedures that involve letters or symbols to represent numbers
Analyze	To make a mathematical, chemical, or methodical examination of parts to determine the nature, proportion, function, interrelationship, etc. of the whole
Compare	Examine the character or qualities of two things by providing characteristics of both that point out their *similarities* and *differences*
Conclude	State a logical end based on reasoning and/or evidence
Contrast/Distinguish	Point out the *differences* between two things that have similar or comparable natures
Criticize	Point out the *demerits* of an item or issue
Define	Provide the essential qualities or meaning of a word or concept; make distinct and clear by marking out the limits
Describe	Give a written account or represent the characteristics of something by a figure, model, or picture
Design/Plan	Construct a plan; i.e, a detailed sequence of actions for a specific purpose
Determine	Find a solution, to a specified degree of accuracy, to a problem by showing appropriate formulas, procedures, and calculations
Enumerate	Specify one by one or list in concise form and according to some order
Evaluate	Give the significance or worth of something by identifying the good and bad points or the advantages and disadvantages
Explain	Make clear what is not immediately obvious or entirely known; give the cause of or reason for; make known in detail
Graphically	Using a drawing that is produced electronically or by hand and that shows a relation between certain sets of numbers
How	Show in what manner or way, with what meaning
Hypothesize	Form a tentative proposition intended as a possible explanation for an observed phenomenon; i.e., a possible cause for a specific effect. The proposition should be testable logically and/or empirically
Identify	Recognize and select as having the characteristics of something
Illustrate	Make clear by giving an example. The form of the example must be specified in the question; i.e., word description, sketch, or diagram

Copyright Protected

Infer Form a generalization from sample data; arrive at a conclusion by reasoning from evidence

Interpret Tell the meaning of something; present information in a new form that adds meaning to the original data

Justify/Show How Show reasons for or give facts that support a position

Model Find a model (in mathematics, a model of a situation is a pattern that is supposed to represent or set a standard for a real situation) that does a good job of representing a situation

Outline Give, in an organized fashion, the essential parts of something. The form of the outline must be specified in the question; i.e., list, flow chart, concept map

Predict Tell in advance on the basis of empirical evidence and/or logic

Prove Establish the truth or validity of a statement for the general case by giving factual evidence or logical argument

Relate Show logical or causal connection between things

Sketch Provide a drawing that represents the key features of an object or graph

Solve Give a solution for a problem; i.e., explanation in words and/or numbers

Summarize Give a brief account of the main points

Trace Give a step-by-step description of the development

Verify Establish, by substitution for a particular case or by geometric comparison, the truth of a statement

Why Show the cause, reason, or purpose

ORDERING INFORMATION

All School Orders

School Authorities are eligible to purchase these resources by applying the Learning Resource Credit Allocation (LRCA – 25% school discount) on their purchase through the Learning Resources Centre (LRC). Call LRC for details.

THE KEY *Study Guides* are specifically designed to assist students in preparing for unit tests, final exams, and provincial examinations.

KEY *Study Guides* – $29.95 each plus G.S.T.

SENIOR HIGH		JUNIOR HIGH	ELEMENTARY
Biology 30 Chemistry 30 English 30-1 English 30-2 Math 30 (Pure) Math 30 (Applied) Physics 30 Social Studies 30 Social Studies 33	Biology 20 Chemistry 20 English 20-1 Math 20 (Pure) Physics 20 Social Studies 20 English 10-1 Math 10 (Pure) Science 10 Social Studies 10	Language Arts 9 Math 9 Science 9 Social Studies 9 Math 8 Math 7	Language Arts 6 Math 6 Science 6 Social Studies 6 Math 4 Language Arts 3 Math 3

Student Notes and Problems (SNAP) Workbooks contain complete explanations of curriculum concepts, examples, and exercise questions.

SNAP Workbooks – $29.95 each plus G.S.T.

SENIOR HIGH		JUNIOR HIGH	ELEMENTARY
Chemistry 30 Math 30 Pure Math 30 Applied Math 31 Physics 30	Chemistry 20 Math 20 Pure Math 20 Applied Physics 20 Math 10 Pure Math 10 Applied Science 10	Math 9 Science 9 Math 8 Math 7	Math 6 Math 5 Math 4 Math 3

Visit our website for a "tour" of resource content and features at

www.castlerockresearch.com

#2340, 10180 – 101 Street
Edmonton, AB Canada T5J 3S4
e-mail: learn@castlerockresearch.com

Phone: 780.448.9619
Toll-free: 1.800.840.6224
Fax: 780.426.3917

2006 (3)

SCHOOL ORDER FORM

THE KEY	QUANTITY
Biology 30	
Chemistry 30	
English 30-1	
English 30-2	
Math30 (Pure)	
Math 30 (Applied)	
Physics 30	
Social Studies 30	
Social Studies 33	
Biology 20	
Chemistry 20	
English 20-1	
Math 20 (Pure)	
Physics 20	
Social Studies 20	
English 10-1	
Math 10 (Pure)	
Science 10	
Social Studies 10	
Language Arts 9	
Math 9	
Science 9	
Social Studies 9	
Math 8	
Math 7	
Language Arts 6	
Math 6	
Science 6	
Social Studies 6	
Math 4	
Math 3	
Language Arts 3	

SNAP WORKBOOKS Notes and Problems/ Student Notes and Problems	QUANTITY Workbooks	 Solutions Manuals
Chemistry 30		
Chemistry 20		
Physics 30		
Physics 20		
Math 30 Pure		
Math 30 Applied		
Math 31		
Math 20 Pure		
Math 20 Applied		
Math 10 Pure		
Math 10 Applied		
Science 10		
Science 9		
Math 9		
Math 8		
Math 7		
Math 6		
Math 5		
Math 4		
Math 3		

TOTALS	
KEYS	
WORKBOOKS	
SOLUTION MANUALS	

Learning Resources Centre

Castle Rock Research is pleased to announce an exclusive distribution arrangement with the Learning Resources Centre (LRC). Under this agreement, schools can now place all their orders with LRC for order fulfillment. As well, these resources are eligible for applying the Learning Resource Credit Allocation (LRCA) which gives schools a 25% discount off LRC's selling price. Call LRC for details.

Orders may be placed with LRC by
telephone: (780) 427-5775,
fax: (780) 422-9750,
internet: www.lrc.learning.gov.ab.ca
or mail: 12360 - 142 Street NW
Edmonton, AB T5L 4X9.

PAYMENT AND SHIPPING INFORMATION

Name: ______

School Telephone: ______

SHIP TO
School: ______
Address: ______
City: ______ Postal Code: ______

PAYMENT
☐ by credit card
VISA/MC Number: ______ Expiry Date: ______
Name on Card: ______
☐ enclosed cheque
☐ invoice school P.O. number: ______

#2340, 10180 – 101 Street, Edmonton, AB T5J 3S4 Tel: 780.448.9619 Fax: 780.426.3917
email: learn@castlerockresearch.com Toll-free: 1.800.840.6224
www.castlerockresearch.com

2006 (3)